D1880037

LIBRARIES
AND
FOUNDERS OF LIBRARIES

LIBRARIES AND FOUNDERS OF LIBRARIES

by

EDWARD EDWARDS

GYAN

Published by

GYAN

Gyan Publishing House
5, Ansari Road
Daryaganj, New Delhi-110002
Phone: 011-47034999, 9811692060
E-mail: books@gyanbooks.com

Distribution Network
gyanbooks.com
India, USA, Canada, UK, Australia, France

© Publisher

All rights reserved. No part of this work may be reproduced, stored, adapted, or transmitted in any form or by any means, electronic, mechanical, photocopying, micro-filming, recording or otherwise, or translated in any language, without the prior written permission of the copyright owner and the publisher.

ISBN : 978-81-212-6008-4 (PB)
First Published, 1864

2nd Impression 2021

Printed at: Gyan Press, Delhi.

The book is sold subject to the condition that it shall not, by way of trade or otherwise, be lent, resold, hired out, or otherwise circulated without the prior publisher's written consent.

Libraries and Founders of Libraries
Author: Edward Edwards

LIBRARIES

AND

FOUNDERS OF LIBRARIES.

BY

EDWARD EDWARDS.

NEW YORK:
G. P. PHILES AND CO., 64, NASSAU STREET.

1865.

PREFACE.

With the obliging assent of Messrs. Adam and Charles Black, about thirty pages of this Volume, chiefly in the Introductory Chapters, have been reprinted (with needful alterations) from the article Libraries, *in the last edition of the* Encyclopædia Britannica.

Those thirty pages excepted, the contents of the present Volume are now published for the first time, and have been, in large measure, based upon documents heretofore unused, and upon personal examination of the principal Collections which are described.

It follows that the present Volume—the Introductory Chapters *excepted—occupies ground which was but touched on in* Memoirs of Libraries (1859). *It is at once a new and independent work, and a continuation of the preceding work on the same subject. Should it be favourably received, it will be quickly followed by another new volume specially devoted to* The Founders of the British Museum, *based on original researches, and much of which is already prepared.*

LONDON, 5*th November*, 1864.

CONTENTS.

CHAPTER I.

INTRODUCTORY. — THE ANCIENT LIBRARIES OF EGYPT, OF JUDÆA, OF GREECE, AND OF THE ROMAN EMPIRE:—

CHAPTER II.

INTRODUCTORY. — MEDIÆVAL AND MODERN LIBRARIES. — ANTICIPATORY SURVEY OF THE SUBJECT, IN GENERAL:—

CHAPTER III.

OF SOME LIBRARIES OF MONASTERIES ABROAD:—

CHAPTER IV.

OF SOME LIBRARIES OF MONASTERIES AT HOME:—

CHAPTER V.

CONCERNING THE LIBRARIES OF SOME FAMOUS AUTHORS, OF VARIOUS PERIODS:—

CHAPTER VI.

CONCERNING THE LIBRARIES OF SOME CELEBRATED MONARCHS AND ROYAL PERSONAGES, OF VARIOUS PERIODS:—

CHAPTER VII.

HISTORY OF THE OLD ROYAL LIBRARY OF THE KINGS OF ENGLAND :—

CHAPTER VIII.

HISTORY OF THE STATE PAPER OFFICE:—

CHAPTER IX.

SECTION FIRST.

HISTORY OF THE PUBLIC RECORDS OF THE REALM, IN THEIR EARLY PERIOD OF GROWTH AND SEPARATE CUSTODY:—

CHAPTER IX.

SECTION SECOND.

HISTORY OF THE PUBLIC RECORDS, IN THEIR PERIOD OF INCREASED SEPARATION AND OF GROSS NEGLECT:—

CHAPTER IX.

SECTION THIRD.

HISTORY OF THE PUBLIC RECORDS, IN THEIR PERIOD OF PARTIAL AGGREGATION AND PREMATURE PUBLICATION:—

CHAPTER IX.

SECTION FOURTH.

HISTORY OF THE PUBLIC RECORDS, IN THEIR FINAL PERIOD OF THOROUGH AGGREGATION AND ARRANGEMENT:—

CHAPTER X.

THE LIFE OF THOMAS PARKER, EARL OF MACCLESFIELD.—THE LIFE OF NICHOLAS JOSEPH FOUCAULT. — HISTORY AND DESCRIPTION OF THE LIBRARY AT SHIRBURN CASTLE IN OXFORDSHIRE:—

CHAPTER XI.

THE LIFE OF CHARLES SPENCER, THIRD EARL OF SUNDERLAND. — HISTORY AND DESCRIPTION OF THE LIBRARY AT BLENHEIM PALACE :—

CHAPTER XII.

THE PUBLIC LIFE OF GEORGE JOHN, SECOND EARL SPENCER.—HISTORY AND DESCRIPTION OF THE SPENCER LIBRARY AT ALTHORP:—

APPENDIX A.

APPENDIX B.

NOTE ON THE LIBRARY OF KING EDWARD THE SIXTH :—

APPENDIX C.

SUMMARY CLASSIFICATION AND SYNOPTICAL VIEW OF THE PUBLIC RECORDS OF THE REALM :—

LIBRARIES, AND THE FOUNDERS OF LIBRARIES.

CHAPTER I.

INTRODUCTORY.—THE ANCIENT LIBRARIES OF EGYPT, OF JUDÆA, OF GREECE, AND OF THE ROMAN EMPIRE.

"Inde tenore pari, gradibus sublimia celsis
  Ducor ad intonsi candida templa Dei.
Signa peregrinis ubi sunt alterna columnis
  Belides, et stricto barbarus ense pater:
Quæque viri docto veteres cepere novique
  Pectore, lecturis inspicienda patent......
Quærentem frustra custos me, sedibus illis
  Præpositus, sancto jussit abire loco......
Nec me, quæ doctis patuerunt prima libellis,
  Atria Libertas tangere passa sua est.
In genus auctoris miseri fortuna redundat;
  Et patimur nati, quam tulit ipse, fugam."

Tristia, iii, 1.

General characteristics of the Evidence on Ancient Libraries.

Of the Libraries of the Ancients, the accounts that have descended to us are meagre and unsatisfactory. Some of the authors, to whom we owe such knowledge as we have, are either Encyclopædists, or geographers, or poets, intent on higher or on wider themes, and therefore treating of Libraries in a fashion merely incidental. Others of them derived their own knowledge at second-hand. Living, it may be, in the second or third centuries, and in Italy, we find them more communicative about the Libraries of the Ptolemies and of the Attali, than about the collections which lay almost at their own doors. The usual authorities, in a word, are but rarely bending their main attention to this particular subject. Still more rarely are they eye-witnesses of the facts for which they are made to vouch.

What can now be stated on this opening part of our theme,—and it must needs be stated briefly,—will, therefore, wear a fragmentary and hypothetical aspect. Too frequently, I fear, it will be but the abridgement of an oft-told tale. I begin by noticing the Libraries of Egypt. Part of this branch of the story rests on the authority of an historian, Diodorus of Sicily, and of a miscellany-compiler, Athenæus of Naucratis, but it has the advantage of supplementary testimony from the researches of modern Egyptologists.

The Libraries of Egypt.

Osymandyas, a king of Egypt, some fourteen centuries B.C., is said to have established a Library on the door or entablature of which was an inscription, that may be translated "*The Soul's Dispensary*,"* and on the walls of which were sculptures representing a judge, with the image of Truth suspended from his neck, and many books lying before him. So speaks Diodorus,† who had seen the building, but tells us nothing of its contents. Its books, whatever they were, are supposed to have perished during the Persian invasion under Cambyses.

Both Wilkinson‡ and Champollion§ identify with the building thus referred to by Diodorus the well-known monument,—usually designated the "Memnonium," but preferably the "Ramesium,"—on the door-jambs of one of

* Diodorus translated it by the Greek words ψυχῆς ἰατρεῖον (*Medicatorium animæ*).

† Diod. Siculus, lib. i, c. 2, § 49. (Bipont reprint of Wesseling, I, 149.)

‡ Wilkinson, *Manners and Customs of the Ancient Egyptians*, i, 111–116. See also Osburn, *Monumental History of Egypt*, ii, 459.

§ *Lettres écrites d'Egypte. . . .* en 1828 and 1829, 285.

the inner halls of which may still be seen representations of Thoth, the inventor of letters, and the goddess Saf, his companion, with the titles "Lady of Letters," and "Presidentess of the Hall of Books." This monument is familiar to thousands of persons who have never visited Egypt, as from it was obtained that "Head of the young Memnon," which has long been so conspicuous an object in the Egyptian Gallery of the British Museum.

There was also, according to Eustathius and other ancient writers, a library at Memphis, deposited in that temple of Phtha, from which Homer was absurdly accused of having stolen both the Iliad and the Odyssey.

But the most superb library of Egypt, perhaps of the ancient world, was that founded by Ptolemy Soter, at Alexandria, and enriched by many successive kings. About the year B.C. 290, there was wont to assemble, at the 'Museum' of Alexandria, a society of learned men, for whose use the first Ptolemy, as we are told, formed a collection of books, the extent of which has been very variously computed. Josephus* puts an official speech into the mouth of Demetrius Phalereus, as addressed to Ptolemy, in which he says, that there were about 200,000 volumes in the library, and "that in a little time there would be 500,000;" but the entire story—like that as to the origin of the Septuagint—is a fable, having no sort of authority. There is no evidence of the truth of Josephus' assertion that Demetrius Phalereus was librarian of the Alexandrian Library, better than that which exists for the seventy-two apocryphal books; the seventy-two interpreters; the six and thirty boats; and the six and thirty cells, each with a skylight.

* Josephi *Antiquitatum Judaicarum*, liber xii, c. 2 (Ed. Dindorf, 1845 i, 439).

Alexandrian Library.

Ptolemy Philadelphus, an equally liberal and enlightened prince, collected books in the Temple of Serapis, in addition to those accumulated by his father, and at his death left in it, according to the statement of Eusebius, about 100,000 volumes. He had agents in every part of Asia and of Greece, commissioned to search out and purchase the rarest and most valuable writings; and amongst those which he procured were the works of Aristotle, purchased of Neleus.* The measures adopted by Ptolemy Philadelphus, for augmenting the Alexandrian Library, seem to have been pursued by his successor Ptolemy Euergetes, with unscrupulous vigour. He caused, it has been said, all books imported into Egypt by foreigners to be seized and sent to the Academy or Museum, where they were transcribed by persons employed for the purpose; upon which the copies were delivered to the proprietors, and the originals deposited in the library. He borrowed of the Athenians—so runs the story—the works of Sophocles, Euripides, and Æschylus; caused them to be transcribed in the most elegant manner; retained the originals for his own library; and returned to the Athenians the copies which had been made of them, with fifteen talents† for the exchange. As the Museum, in which the library was originally founded, stood near the royal palace, in the quarter of the city called Brucheium, the books, it is supposed, were at first deposited there; but when this building had been completely occupied with books, to the number of 400,000 volumes, a supplemental library was erected within the Serapeum, or Temple of Serapis; and the books there placed gradually increased—if we are to follow the usual authorities—to the amount of 300,000 volumes; thus making, in both libraries, a grand

* Athenæus, lib. i, c. 4, ed. Schweighäuser.

† Computed to be equal to more than £3,000 sterling.

total of 700,000 volumes,—but "volumes" in a very different sense to that in which we now use the word, vague as that modern use too commonly is.

The difficulties arising from the *translation* into another language of such words as βίβλος, βιβλίον, τομος; *codex, liber, libellus, volumen, tomus, scapus; book, pamphlet, tract, volume,* and the multitude of like words in other tongues—like, but probably no two of the whole number precisely and absolutely equipollent—are quite enough to account for very wide discrepancies in library statistics, whether ancient or modern; but, as respects ancient libraries, more particularly, another large opening was made for error by that oscitancy of transcribers, as Addison calls it, which led them to use figures instead of words.

The Alexandrian Library continued in all its splendour until the first Alexandrian war, when, during the plunder of the city, the Brucheium portion of the collection was accidentally destroyed by fire, owing to the recklessness of the soldiers. But the library in the Serapeum still remained, and was augmented by subsequent donations, particularly by that of the Pergamean Library, amounting, according to Plutarch, to 200,000 volumes, presented by Mark Antony to Cleopatra; so that it soon surpassed the former both in the number and in the value of its contents. Seneca affirms that the Alexandrian Library was rather to be considered a pompous spectacle, than a place for the studies of the learned.* At length, after various revolutions under the Roman emperors, during which the collection was sometimes plundered and sometimes re-established, it was utterly destroyed by

* *De Tranquillitate Animi,* cap. 9.—"Non fuit elegantia illud, aut cura [He is referring to a passage in one of the lost books of Livy, in which those words occurred,] sed studiosa luxuria: immo ne studiosa quidem, quoniam non in studium sed in spectaculum comparaverunt;" &c.

the Saracens, under the orders of the Caliph Omar, when they acquired possession of Alexandria, A.D. 638. Amrou, the victorious general, was himself inclined to spare this inestimable treasury of ancient science and learning; but the ignorant and fanatical caliph, to whom he applied for instructions, ordered it—according to the well-known story—to be destroyed. "If," said he, "these writings of the Greeks agree with the Koran, or book of Allah, they are useless, and need not be preserved; if they disagree, they are pernicious, and ought to be destroyed." The sentence of destruction was executed with blind obedience. The volumes of parchment, or papyrus, were distributed to the four thousand baths of the city; and such was their incredible number, that six months, we are told, were scarcely sufficient for their combustion.*

This, at all events, is the received account of a memorable event, and, although often questioned, it has never been satisfactorily refuted. But it should be borne in mind, that the identification of the library destroyed by Omar, with the library which had been established, and *perhaps* restored in the Serapeum, is wholly conjectural. The Temple of Serapis had itself been demolished two hundred and fifty years before, by Theophilus, Archbishop of Alexandria, and it is certain that the library was then pillaged if not destroyed. Orosius has recorded the feelings of indignation aroused, towards the close of the fourth century, by the sight of the still empty shelves. (. . . *Nos vidimus armaria librorum, quibus direptis, exinanita ea a nostris hominibus,*

* Gibbon (*Decline and Fall of the Roman Empire*, vol. ix, p. 440) has endeavoured to disprove the positive account given by Abulfaragius, by means of negative arguments. But it may probably be thought that the direct and positive statement of an historian of such unquestionable credit as Abulfaragius, cannot be set aside by arguments of a negative and hypothetical character.

*nostris temporibus memorent.**) Besides the two great libraries which have been already described, Alexandria possessed a third in the Sebasteum, or Temple of Augustus, and a fourth of much later date than the others, attached to its famous "School." If the last-named collection was the object of Omar's fanaticism, the loss to learning must have been less severe than has usually been imagined.

The Holy Book which, in mediæval catalogues, we so often meet with under the designation 'Bibliotheca,' was, in fact, the first Library of the Hebrews, and in it their Synagogues possessed the seed not alone of the purest Theology, but of the truest History, the most pregnant Philosophy, and the loftiest Poetry, which the world has seen. In small compass, they had there the substance of the many thousands of volumes into which, in subsequent ages, the Holy Scriptures have been, by turns, illustrated or obscured, explained or merely diluted. To bring before the mind a vivid conception of the marvellous way in which that small collection of the early Synagogues has literally *grown* into a vast library, the traveller need but enter the Royal Library of the Kings of Wirtemberg, where he will find a series of nearly nine thousand several editions of the Bible, yet will learn that it exists in many forms and many tongues which are not there represented. But it needs not that a man should travel to Stuttgard to gain such a conception. He can put before his mind the assured fact that whilst that vast number of editions is but a proportion of the total number of editions and translations which have been printed, the entire aggregate itself, could it possibly be brought together, would look small in

The Libraries of the Hebrews.

* Orosius, ed. Havercamp, lib. vi, c. xv, 421.

comparison with a like collection of the Biblical apparatus. And if he be a man of few books, and but one tongue, he may be happy in the thought that, like the Hebrew of the early Synagogue, he can hold in his hand the pith and essence of all that vast accumulation, together with a supplement immeasurably more important.

Their archives.

The Hebrews had, too, at a very early period, their public archives. Those which Herod caused to be burned, for the purpose of destroying the muniments of the ancient families, so that his own obscurity of origin might no longer be made conspicuous by contrast, are said, by Eusebius,* to have reached almost as far back as to the origin of the Hebrew nation. But though he consigned the public records to the flames, those of individuals seem to have been beyond his power, and to have served, long afterwards, towards the re-establishment of the history of the subjugated people. There are, too, in early Jewish history some traces of Libraries, more strictly so called. But they are traces only, till we come to the era of the Maccabees. And, even then, we can only infer from an incidental passage or two, and from such an expression as "the multitude of books," that their collections had expanded beyond the sacred Scriptures and the ritualistic lore, and that their historical works had become numerous enough to induce the compilation of abridgements.

Libraries of the Persians and Assyrians.

Holy Scripture also mentions a library of the kings of

* "Porro autem, cum familiæ non Hebræorum solum, verumetiam eorum qui usque ad Proselytos genus suum referebant, ... ad illud tempus scriptis proditæ, in tabulariis reservarentur; Herodes . . . . annales illos de generum et familiarum antiquitate incendit: arbitratus se nobilem visum iri, cum nemo suum genus ex publicis illis monumentis depromptum, ad Patriarchas, vel ad Proselytos, vel ad eos qui Γειῶραι (*i. e.*, terræ incolæ qui cum Israelitis permiscebantur,) vocati sunt, omnino posset reducere."—Eusebius, *Historia Ecclesiastica*, lib. i, c. 7 (Edit. Christophorson, 1570, 15).

Persia, which some suppose to have consisted of the historians of that nation, and of memoirs on the affairs of State, but which appears rather to have been a depository of the laws, charters, and ordinances of the Persian kings. In the Book of Ezra it is stated that a search was made "in the house of the *rolls*, where the *treasures* were laid up in Babylon," for a decree issued by Cyrus ordaining a temple to be built at Jerusalem; the ordinance sought for, however, was found, not in Babylon, but at Acmetha, in Media.*

During the recent excavations in the palace at Nineveh, a vast collection of clay tablets, inscribed with cuneiform inscriptions was found, which may have formed, it is thought, a sort of royal library. The progress made in deciphering the inscriptions, in this cuneiform character, was long since brought before the yearly meetings of the British Association held at Glasgow and at Cheltenham, by Colonel Sir Henry Rawlinson, in two most interesting lectures. This system of cuneiform writing was found to be closely allied to the hieroglyphic system; and, although many of the rock inscriptions of Persia were trilingual, each of the languages, the Chaldee, Assyrian, and Babylonian, being unknown, it seemed at first to defy all attempts at translation; yet this has been accomplished, to a great extent, by a remarkable combination of learning and ingenuity. More than 20,000 of these tablets, more or less injured by fire, are now in the British Museum; and there can be no doubt that the extensive series, when fully deciphered, will be the means of furnishing most important additions to our knowledge of the ancient world. Of a portion of these cuneiform inscriptions, lithographic fac-

Clay Libraries of Assyria.

* Ezra, ch. v, ver. 17; and vi, 1, 2.

similes have been published by the Trustees of the British Museum.*

More recently, M. Jules Oppert (to whom was entrusted, by the French government, the mission of examining and reporting on the acquisitions for which the British public are mainly indebted to the research and energy of Mr. Layard) has copied a considerable series of these inscribed tablets, and has expressed his conviction that there is a large class of them to which, in a special and unique sense, the designation of a "Public Library in Clay" is applicable. These he believes to have been prepared by command of Sardanapalus V. (about B.C. 650), expressly for purposes of public instruction; and he quotes a remarkable inscription to this effect: "Palace of Sardanapalus, king of the world, king of Assyria, to whom the god Nebo and the goddess Ourmit have given ears to hear and eyes to see what is the foundation of government. They have revealed to the kings my predecessors this cuneiform writing. The manifestation of the god Nebo . . . of the god of supreme intellect,—I have written it upon tablets,—I have signed it,—I have put it in order,—*I have placed it in the midst of my palace for the instruction of my subjects.*"†

Amongst the Greeks, as amongst other nations, the first libraries consisted merely of archives, deposited, for better preservation, in the temples of the gods. It has been often said that Pisistratus the tyrant was the first who established a public library in Athens; but the statement rests mainly on the testimony of Aulus Gellius, who

Libraries of the Greeks.

* *A Selection from the Historical Inscriptions of Chaldæa, Assyria, and Babylonia.* Edited by Sir H. Rawlinson and E. Norris. 1861, &c.

† *Rapport à M. le Ministre de l'Instruction Publique,* printed in the *Archives des Missions Scientifiques,* Mai, 1856, v, 179.

wrote about seven hundred years after the time of Pisistratus. In this alleged library, the founder is said to have deposited the works of Homer, which he had collected with great difficulty, and at a very considerable expense; and the Athenians themselves were at great pains to increase the collection. The reputed fortunes of this library were various and singular,—if true. It was transported to Persia by Xerxes; brought back by Seleucus Nicanor; plundered by Sylla; and at last restored by the Emperor Hadrian. The entire story, however, is a conjectural one. That Pisistratus was a promoter of learning, and that he rendered eminent service by his Homeric researches, is incontestible. But that he formed anything which even remotely resembled a library, in the ordinary meaning of the term, is an assertion unsupported by adequate evidence; and just as little foundation is there for the romantic vicissitudes which complete the tale. Nor is there much better authority for the statement, that when, on the invasion of the Roman empire by the Goths (A.D. 260), Greece was ravaged, and in the sack of Athens they had collected all the libraries, and were upon the point of setting fire to this funeral pile of ancient learning, one of their chiefs interposing, dissuaded them from the design, observing at the same time, that as long as the Greeks were addicted to the study of books, they would never apply themselves to that of arms.

Strabo's account of the Library of Aristotle.

Strabo has stated that Aristotle was the first known collector of a library, and that to him was also due the honour of having suggested to the Ptolemies the formation of that great collection above mentioned, which was scarcely more a wonder of antiquity than it has been a conundrum of modern scholarship. Aristotle bequeathed his library, with many of his own writings, to Theophrastus, who appears to have made considerable additions to it, and who, in his turn, bequeathed it to Neleus. The latter, according to Strabo, carried the collection to Scepsis in the Troad, where it subsequently fell into disorder, and was at length concealed in a cave, that it might escape the eager researches of the kings of Pergamus. "At length," continues Strabo, "but not before the books had been injured by damp and worms, they were sold to Apellicon of Teos,—rather a collector than a philosopher (φιλόβιβλος μᾶλλον ἢ φιλόσοφος),—who, by unskilful attempts at the restoration of defective and mutilated passages in the writings of Aristotle, increased the injury by corrupting the text."* On the capture of Athens by Sylla, the Library of Apellicon—not that of Pisistratus—was seized by the conqueror and carried to Rome.

But Strabo's account of the matter—on which mainly was founded the absurd story so long current as to the loss for several generations of the Aristotelian writings—is entirely at variance with that given by the epitomist of Athenæus, according to whom the Library of Neleus had long before been bought by Ptolemy Philadelphus and transferred to Alexandria, "with all those which he had collected at Athens and at Rhodes."† This statement accords better with the known existence and publicity of Aristotle's works, but has its own difficulties. It is, however, at least matter of reasonable probability that, from whatever cause, part of the collection went to Alexandria, and part remained at Scepsis. From the rivalry of the Attalic kings with the Ptolemies, it may well have resulted that the fame of the acquisition for Alexandria of part of the library of Aristotle, may have given a keener edge to their covetousness of what remained.

* Strabo, lib. xiii, pp. 608, 609.

† Athenæus, *Deipnosophistæ*, lib. i, 4.

Next to the Alexandrian Library, that of Pergamus was the most conspicuous, and, according to Plutarch, contained 200,000 volumes. It was founded and successively enriched by the kings of Pergamus, all of whom were zealous promoters of the arts, and one of whom is said to have been the inventor of parchment (*Charta Pergamena*). Attalus seems to have surpassed his predecessors in magnificence, and after their example to have devoted no small part of his treasures to the augmentation of the Library he had inherited. As I have noticed already, the Pergamean Library was presented by Antony to Cleopatra, in order to form the foundation of a new library at Alexandria.

Library of Pergamus.

Scanty as these details are, they may suffice to show that the Libraries of ancient Greece were neither few nor unimportant, notwithstanding the obscurity of their history.

Of the Libraries of Rome, of which we possess accounts more or less authenticated, the earliest seems to have been that which was established by Æmilius Paulus, about the year B.C. 168. Having subdued Perses, king of Macedonia, he brought the Library of the vanquished monarch to Rome. Sylla having visited Athens, on his return from the first campaign against Mithridates, acquired the Library of Apellicon, and added it, as it appears, to the Library of Æmilius Paulus. Lucullus, another successful soldier, had a similar taste for books, and doubtless profited by his opportunities. His collection was both large and choice. But the use which he made of his collection was still more honourable to that princely Roman, than the acquisition or possession of it. His Library is said to have been open to all comers; and the Greeks who visited Rome resorted to the galleries and porticos of Lucullus as to the retreat of the Muses, where they spent whole days in conversation on literary

Ancient Libraries of Rome.

subjects. But although both Sylla and Lucullus liberally gave public access to their literary treasures, still their Libraries can, in strictness, be considered as only *private* collections. Amongst the various projects which Julius Cæsar had formed for the embellishment of Rome was that of a *public* Library, which should contain the largest possible collection of Greek and Latin works; and he had assigned to Varro the duty of selecting and arranging them; but it has been supposed that this design was frustrated by the assassination of the dictator; and that the establishment of public Libraries did not take place until the reign of Augustus.

The Libraries of Rome.

The honour of the first foundation of an institution so useful to literature is ascribed by the elder Pliny* to Asinius Pollio, who erected a public Library in the atrium of the temple of Liberty, on the Aventine Hill. This Library, it is added, was formed *ex manubiis*, and in it was placed a bust of Varro. It would seem probable, from the latter circumstance, that Varro after all may have carried out the plan entrusted to him by Cæsar, and that Pollio may have merely enlarged the Library thus begun. The exploits that were most likely to have yielded him the spoils of war, were of a date long subsequent to that of Cæsar's commission to Varro.†

Augustus, amongst other embellishments which he bestowed upon Rome, erected two public Libraries, viz., the Octavian and the Palatine. The Octavian Library, which was thus denominated in honour of the Emperor's sister, stood in the portico of Octavia; and the charge of it was

* "Qui primus *bibliothecam dicando*, ingenia hominum rem publicam fecit." (Plinius, *Historia Naturalis*, lib. xxxv, c. 2.)

† Comp. Merivale, *History of the Romans under the Empire*, ii, 426.

committed to Melissus, who had been manumitted by Augustus. The Palatine Library was added by Augustus to the Temple of Apollo, which he had erected on the site of that part of the Palatine House which had been struck by lightning. There were deposited the corrected books of the Sibyls; and, from two ancient inscriptions quoted by Lipsius and Pitiscus, it would seem that it consisted of two distinct collections, one Greek and the other Latin.* This Library, having survived the various revolutions of the Roman empire, existed until the time of Gregory the Great, whose mistaken zeal led him to order the writings of the ancients to be destroyed. The successors of Augustus, though they did not equally encourage learning, were not altogether neglectful of its interests. Suetonius and other authors inform us that Tiberius enlarged the Libraries founded by Augustus, placing therein, and in the other Libraries of Rome, copies of the works, as well as the statues, of his favourite poets, Euphorion, Rhianus, and Parthenius. It may be gathered also, from some incidental notices, that he instituted another collection in his own house, called the Tiberian Library. Vespasian, following the example of his predecessors, established a Library in the Temple of Peace, which he erected after the burning of the city by order of Nero; and even Domitian, in the commencement of his reign, restored at great expense the Libraries which had been destroyed by the conflagration, collecting copies of books from every quarter, and sending writers to Alexandria to transcribe volumes in that celebrated collection, or to correct copies which had been made elsewhere. Various writers have asserted that there was a Library attached to

Libraries of Augustus.

And of Vespasian.

* Plutarch, *in Marcello*, 30; Suetonius, *de Illustribus Grammaticis*, c. 21; Idem, *in Augusto*, c. 29, 31; Lipsius *de Bibliothecis*, c. 7; Pitiscus, *Lexicon*, i, 276. The statement as to Gregory is of doubtful authenticity.

the Temple of the Capitol; but they have not informed us by whom it was founded. Lipsius ascribes it to Domitian; whilst Donatus refers it to the Emperor Hadrian, by whom it was at least enlarged, if not founded, and who probably erected the Tiburtine Library, at Tibur, in the vicinity of Rome.*

The Ulpian Library.

But the most magnificent of all the Libraries founded by the sovereigns of imperial Rome was that of the Emperor Ulpius Trajanus, from whom it was denominated the Ulpian Library. It was erected in Trajan's Forum, but afterwards removed to the Viminal Hill, to ornament the baths of Diocletian. In this Library were deposited the "elephantine books," written upon tablets of ivory, wherein were recorded the transactions of the Emperors, the proceedings of the Senate and Roman magistrates, and the affairs of the provinces. It has been conjectured that the Ulpian Library consisted both of Greek and Latin works; and some authors affirm that Trajan commanded all the books which could be found in the cities he had conquered to be immediately conveyed to Rome, in order to increase his collection. The Library of Domitian having been consumed by lightning, in the reign of Commodus, was not restored until the time of Gordian, who rebuilt the edifice, and founded a new Library, adding thereto the collection of books bequeathed to him by Quintus Serenus Sammonicus, the physician, amounting, it is said,† to no less

* Suetonius, *in Tiberio*, c. 70, and *in Vespasiano*, c. 9; Aulus Gellius, lib. xvi, c. 8; Comp. Lipsius *de Bibliothecis*, c. 20; Suetonius, *in Domitiano*, c. 20.

† "...Sereno Sammonico, qui patri ejus amicissimus, sibi autem præceptor fuit, nimis acceptus, et carus usque adeo, ut omnes libros S. Sammonici patris sui, qui censebantur ad LXII millia, Gordiano minori moriens ille relinqueret: quod eum ad cœlum tulit, &c." Capitolinus, *in Vit. Gordiani Junioris*, c. 18.

than 62,000 volumes. Donatus conjectures that this Library was deposited in the palace of Pompey.*

In addition to the imperial Libraries, there were others to which the public had access in the principal cities and colonies of the empire. Pliny mentions a public Library which he had founded for the use of his countrymen; and Vopiscus informs us that the Emperor Tacitus caused the historical writings of his illustrious namesake, as well as those of some other historians, to be deposited in the Libraries. But the irruptions of the barbarians who overran and desolated the western empire proved more destructive to the interests of literature than either volcanoes or earthquakes, and soon caused the disappearance of those Libraries which, during several centuries, had been multiplied in Italy.

Libraries in the Roman provinces.

When Constantine the Great (A.D. 330) made Byzantium the seat of his empire, decorated that city with splendid edifices, and called it after his own name, desirous to make reparation to the Christians for the injuries they had suffered during the reign of his predecessor, he commanded the most diligent search to be made for those books which Diocletian had doomed to destruction. He caused transcripts to be made of such as had escaped the fury of the Pagan persecutor; and, having collected others from various quarters, he formed the whole into a Library at Constantinople. On the death of Constantine, however, the number of books in the Imperial Library is said to have been only 6900; but it was successively enlarged by the Emperors Julian and Theodosius the younger, who augmented it to 120,000 volumes. Of these, more than half

Libraries of Constantinople.

* Donatus, *Roma Vetus*, lib. iii, c. 8, p. 296. (Edit. of 1665.)

Libraries of Constantinople.

were burned, in the seventh century, by the command of the Emperor Leo III., who thus sought to destroy all the monuments that might impede his opposition to the worship of images. In this Library was deposited the only authentic copy of the proceedings of the Council of Nice; and it is also said to have contained the poems of Homer, written in golden letters, together with a magnificent copy of the Four Gospels, bound in plates of gold, enriched with precious stones; all of which were consumed in the conflagration. The convulsions which distracted the lower empire cannot have been favourable to the interests of literature. In the eleventh century, learning flourished for a short time during the reign of Constantine Porphyrogenitus; and this emperor is said to have employed many learned Greeks in collecting books, and forming a Library, the arrangement of which he himself superintended. But the final subversion of the Eastern Empire, and the capture of Constantinople in 1453, dispersed the learned men of Greece over Western Europe, and placed the literary remains of that capital at the mercy of the conqueror. The Imperial Library, however, was preserved by the express command of Mohammed, and continued, it is said, to be kept in some apartments of the Seraglio; but, whether it was sacrificed in a fit of devotion by Amurath IV., as is commonly supposed, or whether it was suffered to fall into decay from ignorance and neglect, it has been repeatedly asserted that the Library of the Sultan now contains only Turkish and Arabic writings, and not one Greek or Latin manuscript of any importance. The opinions of competent scholars continue, nevertheless, to be divided on this point. Even in Germany, where the expectation of important accessions from this quarter has confessedly declined, we find an authority so eminent on such questions as that of

Tischendorff still on the side of the old belief. He thinks it probable, he says (writing in 1845), "that the Seraglio of the Sultan conceals ancient and valuable MSS., though complete obscurity prevails as to their contents;" and he proceeds to ask who in our day would have credited the existence of "walled-up" Libraries, yet a walled-up Library was very lately one of the mysteries of Cairo.*

Upon the whole, it appears that books were abundant, both at Rome and at Constantinople, and that learned men in those cities had at their command greater resources than might at first be supposed. Some idea of the quantity of books accessible to persons of study and research may be formed from the great number of references and citations to be found in the works of some ancient authors; in those of Strabo and Pliny, for example. It must always be borne in mind, for reasons which have been glanced at already, that a very erroneous impression would be made were the alleged contents of ancient Libraries to be reckoned according to modern computation. The numbers would necessarily be greatly increased, when the several "books" of Homer, of Livy, or of Pliny, were each reckoned as a distinct roll or volume. Balbi has plausibly carried this suggestion a step further by the idea that, in many cases, these rolls of the ancients might be regarded as equivalent to little more than our modern "parts" of books, or "numbers" of periodicals. According to this view, the largest Libraries in ancient times might be represented by the contents of a modern collection containing from 50,000 to 80,000 volumes.

* Tischendorff, *Travels in the East* (1847), 273. Of Mr. Coxe's recent researches the reader will find an account in the Chapter entitled, "The existing Libraries of the Levant."

CHAPTER II.

INTRODUCTORY.—MEDIÆVAL AND MODERN LIBRARIES.—ANTICIPATORY SURVEY OF THE SUBJECT, IN GENERAL.

> Wings have we,—and as far as we can go
> We may find pleasure.........
> Books, we know,
> Are a substantial world, both pure and good;
> Round these, with tendrils strong as flesh and blood,
> Our Pastime and our Happiness will grow.
> There find I personal themes, a plenteous store;
> Matter wherein right voluble I am;—
> To which I listen, with a ready ear;—
> Some shall be named,—pre-eminently dear......
>
> *Personal Talk*, iii.

To the youthful student of the History of Modern Literature, I can scarcely imagine a greater puzzle,—at the outset of his studies,—than the problem that rises before him, when he turns from the earlier pages of that admirable manual of his special subject, which he owes to the judicial temperament, the wide researches, and the ripe scholarship, of Mr. Hallam, and betakes himself, as he surely ought to do, to the perusal of such works as the "*Mores Catholici, or Ages of Faith*" of Mr. Kenelm Digby, or "*The Dark Ages*" of Dr. S. R. Maitland. To the markedly critical and judicial intellect of Mr. Hallam, all lovers of letters are quite as deeply indebted, as to the stores of information which a life mainly devoted to literature had untiringly amassed. Yet, to many readers, it cannot but be per-

The "Dark Ages" and the "Ages of Faith."

plexing to find so moderate and so accomplished a critic constantly representing Monks as the bitter enemies of learning; mediæval Universities as the abodes of "indigent vagabonds, withdrawn from useful labour;" * bookselling as a trade the existence of which, "in what we properly call the dark ages," is "very improbable;" † and mediæval Libraries as places in which the choice treasures of ancient learning were habitually suffered to moulder into ruin.‡ When, towards the close of his gloomy survey of the monkish ages, Mr. Hallam comes, at length, upon a writer whom he can cordially praise, as having displayed sagacity in reasoning upon human character, and as having shown his power of generalizing what he had seen, "by comparison and reflection," he gives point to his eulogies by the remark:—"*Nothing of this could have been found in the Cloister.*"

The pages of Digby and of Maitland—as of many writers both earlier and later, on like subjects,—display, on the other hand, the vivid portraits of a multitude of mediæval worthies (almost every man of whom wore a monkish garb), who, in the midst of many difficulties, were life-long, though not exclusive, lovers of learning, and zealous labourers in preserving, increasing, and transmitting it. Those pages abound in references to evidence which cannot, I think, be gainsaid. Whence then this disparity between the views of writers,—all of them scholars; all of them able and truthful men?

Relative value of Classics and of Christianity.

One leading cause of that diversity, I venture to think, lies in the almost constant disregard by Mr. Hallam—so far as his dealings with Monks are concerned,—of the *relative* interests of humanity, in literature, strictly so

* *Introduction to the Literature of Europe*, I, 185.
† Ibid. ‡ Ibid. I, passim.

called, and in matters of even graver import than literature. And it may not, perhaps, be altogether fanciful to suggest that there is, possibly, some slight connection between that too obvious disregard, and a certain provoking fondness for the use of the ambiguous and greatly abused word "Nature," as a personality. Whatever reason there may, unhappily, arise hereafter to regret, in our future historians, some among the many admirable qualities of Hallam, there will be, we may hope, on the other hand, some reason for thankfulness that the writers to come will becomingly and reverently put the word "God," for the word "Nature," whenever they may have to deal with the question "Why, at such and such an age in the world's history, were there so few great men?" * But, be this as it may, even book-loving monks were most decided in their opinion that the transmission of Christianity was, on the whole, a more important thing for the world than even the transmission of Classics. Whilst many of those worthy "Restorers of Learning," in the fifteenth century, who have been pre-eminently singled out by Mr. Hallam, and by many other writers, for grateful laudation (well merited in its right degree), were of the directly opposite opinion,—and made no secret of the fact.

There is, however, abundant proof that, during the whole of the long period which intervenes between the reign of Justinian, when Greek and Roman literature yet "lay open to the light of common day," and the fall of Constantinople, when misbelievers at once wreaked their vengeance—if tradition may be trusted—on some of the noblest monuments of that literature, and disseminated its study, by sending its cultivators, as exiles, throughout Europe, the works and the influence of classic authors were never lost.

* See Hallam, *Introduction to the Literature of Europe*, ut supra.

In every century, from the fifth to the fifteenth, we may discover (if we look for them) mediæval writers whose extant works evince some measure of acquaintance with the great authors of Classic Antiquity.

When the Empire of the West sank under the overwhelming pressure of barbarian invasion, those institutions which had been founded and nurtured in the midst of civilization, were, no doubt, swept away by the torrent which desolated Italy, and spread its ravages over all parts of the Empire. But Learning, though stripped of her ancient glories and expelled from her favourite haunts, found an occasional asylum in the Monasteries, which, amidst all the violence and anarchy that reigned without, were sometimes permitted to remain in undisturbed tranquillity, respected even by the barbarians who had overthrown an Empire.

Learning protected in Monasteries.

It is doubtless true that comparatively little is recorded of the libraries of those ages which intervened between the fall of the Roman empire and the revival of letters in the fifteenth century. But, every age produced learned and inquisitive men, by whom books were highly prized, and industriously collected. Tonantius Ferreolus formed in the fifth century a remarkable collection in his 'Castle of Prusiana,' between Nismes and Clermont. Publius Consentius formed another collection, at his villa near Narbonne,—of which, Sidonius Apollinaris tells us, the books were both choice and numerous. Cassiodorus, minister of Theodore, King of the Goths, retired to a monastery which he had built, and there founded a library for the use of the monks, about the middle of the sixth century. At a later period, Charlemagne, so distinguished as a patron of learning, instituted, near Lyons, a library, which, according to the statements of historians, contained many books bound in a manner which spoke, very audibly, of the estimation in which they were held by their owner. Everard, Count of Friuli, formed (in the ninth century) a considerable collection, rich in Fathers of the Church and in some of the curiosities of History, although quite devoid, as it seems, of classic authors. His contemporary, Charles the Bald, King of France, formed a library of choice and precious books, some of which now adorn the British Museum. Pope Sylvester II was an ardent collector of Classics as well as of Theologians. But the Monks, after all, were the great collectors of the middle ages.

That on the general merits of the Monastic Institute the most conflicting opinions should still extensively prevail, cannot be matter of legitimate surprise, if we call to mind that Monasticism played a great part in the world for a thousand years; and that during that long period the most incongruous views as to what a monk ought rightly to be, and to do, were current, even within the walls of monastic communities. But this diversity of opinion extends also to that more limited phase of cloister life which has relation to literature. Whilst some writers contend that but for monks ancient learning would have wholly perished, others—as we have had occasion to see already—have gone the length of asserting that in monks literature has always had its worst enemies.

To arrive at any useful or adequate conclusion on such a question, it must be remembered that at no time and in no country was literature in any of its forms the main object of monastic life. In the earlier ages, when the embers of Paganism were still smouldering, the preservation of Pagan poetry would have seemed a strange employment for the Confessors and Missionaries of Christianity. The labours of the Scriptorium originated not so much in the love of letters as in the love of souls. As the monk became less of a mere ascetic, and aspired to become a civilizer, he necessarily began to be a collector of books, and then their author or their transcriber. But, for a long time, the books that he gathered, and those that he composed, were in the main either theological or ethical. Here and there, however, individual minds of special energy grew large enough to perceive classical beauty, without relaxing their grasp of such Christian truth as they had, and became the venerated masters of numerous disciples. If monastic literature reflects but too much of the corruption of mediæval Christianity, it remains still undeniable that from Bibles transcribed by monkish hands, and from the best productions of the Fathers of the Church, *preserved in monkish libraries*, the men who successively wrestled with that corruption, and were the instruments by which Christianity was kept alive, drew their inspiration and their solace. And that very corruption, in some of its results, as, for example, in the religious use of a dead language, contributed to the preservation of ancient learning.

At almost all periods of its history, the Order of St. Benedict stands foremost amongst the cultivators of learning and of the arts. Yet whilst the rule of the Founder contains much about visiting the sick, relieving the poor, and keeping the body in subjection, it contains very little indeed about books. Nor is there much more about them in the various constitutions of the successive "Reformers" of the Order. But no Order was so fortunate in the possession of a long line of men remarkable for mental vigour and force of character. If the early Benedictines are less conspicuous at periods of comparative enlightenment than at periods when all around them was gloomy, they were unquestionably

The Rule of Saint Benedict.

the first pioneers and builders up of European civilization, and they laid its foundations broad and deep enough to resist the attacks of their own unworthy successors. They never sank so low as did most other Orders of Monks; and at a long subsequent period, in producing the illustrious Congregation of St. Maur, a service was rendered to learning —in the special sense of that term—which neither has, nor is likely to have, any parallel in monastic history, or many parallels elsewhere.

Of some few Benedictine Libraries, and also of some collections formed by monks of other Orders, I submit to the reader a few brief notices in the next two chapters; the first of which treats of Monastic Libraries abroad; the second, of such collections amongst ourselves.

Revival of learning in the Fourteenth Century.

The revival of learning is, as I have said, usually reckoned to have commenced in the fifteenth century; but even in the fourteenth a decided advancement is discernible. This has been well put in a little-known but very able book:—"Gross and degrading ignorance was wearing away from the bulk of the community in several parts of Europe; the educated classes were acquiring a better taste and more expanded views; and a general awakening of the energies of the human mind was perceptible. This scarcely needs other evidence than is afforded by the works of Dante, Petrarch, Boccaccio, Chaucer, and Gower, and by the fact that those works were not merely produced in that age, but were extensively read and admired." But those inestimable treasures of ancient literature which the religious houses had saved from the ravages of revolution, anarchy, and barbarism, now began to be drawn forth and studied. The continuance of the Eastern Empire till the middle of the fifteenth century, afforded an uninterrupted protection to Greek learning during those periods when Western Europe was laid waste by the Gothic nations; and hence, on the revival of letters, the study of the Greek authors first engaged the attention of those persons whom an awakening impulse now directed to the cultivation of learning. But the study of the kindred authors of Rome soon followed; and the monuments of ancient wisdom and genius which had been preserved in so many of the Monasteries, furnished ample materials for laying the foundations of a new, a more extensive, and a more durable edifice of civilization. For, with the Classics, monasteries had handed down to us that, without which even Classics would have been worthless.

"More than half a century before the taking of Constantinople by the Turks, the learned men of the imperial city, apprehending the approaching ruin of the Empire, began to emigrate into Italy, where they opened schools, and became the preceptors of princes, as well as the guides of the public taste, which they directed towards the study of the classical writers of Greece and Rome. The fall of Constantinople, in 1453, filled the Italian cities with these learned strangers. At this period the Italians required only to receive, as it were, an impulse, and to be provided with the means of study. They had for some time been placed in those peculiar circumstances which have repeatedly proved favourable to the advancement of the human mind. A number of independent States were crowded upon a narrow space of territory, throughout which the same language, diversified by dialects, prevailed, exhibiting, in a sort of secondary form, that of ancient Italy; whilst the formation of new Libraries, suggested or favoured by the importation of manuscripts from Constantinople, proved the means not

First formation of modern libraries.

only of making more widely known the works of the Greek authors (which had never really fallen into oblivion), but of prompting those researches which issued in the recovery of the Latin writers, many of whom had long been forgotten. The appetite for books being thus revived and quickened, neither labour nor expense was spared in accumulating them; learned men were despatched in all directions throughout Europe, Western Asia, and Africa, to collect manuscripts; and, in the course of a few years, most of the authors now known were brought together in the libraries of Rome, Naples, Venice, Florence, Vienna, and Paris. Aided by the munificence of princes and popes, the scholars of the fifteenth century applied themselves to the discovery, restoration, and publication, of the remains of Greek and Roman literature;" and, in the course of some eighty years, a large proportion of the existing treasures of antiquity was committed to the press. Since that time additional discoveries have been made; but the principal improvements of a subsequent date have consisted in the emendation of the texts of ancient authors, partly by a more extensive collation of manuscripts than the first editors possessed the means of making, and partly also by the lights and aids of a cautious and judicious criticism.*

Thanks to the labours of Panzer, the pre-eminence of Italy in this noble task is capable of being shown, at a glance, in the easy form of tabulated figures. Yet Germany has the honour of having printed the first edition of the first

* Isaac Taylor, *History of the Transmission of Ancient Books*, p. 106. "This restoration," continues Mr. Taylor, who has treated this branch of the subject in careful detail, and with eminent ability, "of the remains of ancient works to their pristine integrity, has not been effected like that of a dilapidated building or mutilated statue, by the addition of new material in an imagined conformity with the plan and taste of the original work, but by the industrious collection and replacement of the very particles of which it at first consisted."

classic author who was given to the world by means of the new art. That first edition of the "Offices" of Cicero (Mentz, 1465), being also, possibly,—for in this claim it has a rival—the first book in which Greek type was used. Between 1465 and 1500, two hundred and ninety partial editions of CICERO appeared—taking the various seats of printing in their aggregate—and one collective edition. Of VIRGIL, Panzer registers seventy collective and twenty-five partial editions; of HORACE, forty-six partial, and eleven collective editions. During this period, Venice was the Capital of the printing-press, and it issued, before the close of the century, 2835 books, the first of which was also a Cicero—printed, however, by a German printer, John of Spire, in 1469. No other city—save one—approached a third of this number of impressions, and the exception is Rome, where, up to 1500, 925 books had been printed. Paris had produced 751 books; Cologne 530. In Mentz, the cradle of printing, 134 works only had appeared prior to the close of 1500.* Fourteen years before that date, Archbishop Berthold had put the Mentz printers under censorship.

Comparative view of the progress of the printing press in the chief countries of Europe, up to the year 1500.

During the same period, England had produced but a hundred and forty-one printed books, of which London and Westminster claim 130; Oxford, seven; St. Alban's, four. No real classic came from an English press until 1497, when Pynson printed Terence. No Greek characters are met with in an English book of earlier date than Linacre's Latin version of *Galen De Temperamentis*, printed at Cambridge in 1521.

The invention of printing, by virtually exempting books from the operation of the law which subjects all human things to decay, has also greatly promoted the process of

* All these computations rest on the authority of Panzer, but I avail myself of the tabulated summaries given by Mr. Hallam.

Diffusion of Literature in the Fifteenth Century.

their renovation. "By giving to the issue of an edition of a standard work a degree of importance several hundred times greater than that which belonged to the transcription of a single copy, it has called forth a proportionally larger amount of learning, diligence, and care, in the work of revision; and, by enabling each successive editor to avail himself of the labours of his predecessors, all the advantages resulting from the concentration of many minds upon the same subject have further been secured. Since the fifteenth century, therefore, the lapse of time, instead of gradually impairing and corrupting the literary remains of antiquity, has incessantly contributed to their renovation."* What was then unknown or doubtful, imperfect or corrupted, has been ascertained, restored, and completed; and the learning and industry of the four centuries which have since elapsed, having been constantly directed towards the same objects, although they can scarcely be said to have left few questions of literary antiquity open to controversy, yet they have undoubtedly broadened the firm territory which the scholar has fairly won, and have greatly narrowed that debatable land which he has yet to struggle for, among the mists and marshes of mere conjecture.

Several of the great libraries of Europe date their first beginnings during the hundred years between 1365, when Charles V of France had already won renown as a collector of choice manuscripts, and 1465, when the art of printing had established itself, without having as yet materially interrupted the labours of the copyists. Within this period are included the foundation of the Imperial Libraries of Paris and of Vienna, of the Laurentian Library at Florence, and of the Library of the Vatican; and the liberal gifts of

* Taylor, ubi supra.

books which were made by Sir Richard Whittington to the Franciscans of London; by Humphrey, Duke of Gloucester, to the University of Oxford; by King Henry VI to All Souls College; and by Niccolo Niccoli to his fellow-citizens of Florence. It also witnessed the commencement of those splendid collections of Frederick, Duke of Urbino, and of Matthias Corvinus, King of Hungary, which eclipsed all preceding libraries, and were counted amongst the marvels of the age. But, unfortunately, whilst the Urbino Library has escaped the almost total destruction which befel that of Corvinus, it has lost much of its value by division. Its manuscripts are still conspicuous amongst the treasures of the Vatican, but they are less accessible to students than they were in the romantic seat of the old dukes; and the printed books are scattered, some being at Castel Durante, others in the Library of the "Sapienza" at Rome, and others, again, still remaining at Urbino.*

Within the same period, too, is comprised the foundation of the oldest of those town libraries in which Germany has become rich. As early as 1413, Andreas von Slommow established a library at Dantzic, in connection with the church of St. Mary.† His example was followed by Conrad von Hildesheim, at Ratisbon in 1430; ‡ by Heinrich Neidhart, at Ulm in 1440; § and by Conrad Kühnhofer, at Nuremberg in 1445.|| Nor was France far behind in a similar foundation, although in that country the first step was not followed up with equal vigour. There is an account of the purchase of books for a public library by the Common

* Dennistoun, *Memoirs of the Dukes of Urbino*, vol. iii, pp. 228—232.

† Petzholdt, *Handbuch deutscher Bibliotheken* (Halle, 1853, 12mo), pp. 78, 79.

‡ Ibid., p. 314.

§ *Serapeum* (Leipsic, 1844, 8vo), vol. v, pp. 193—202.

|| Petzholdt, *ut sup.*, p. 280.

Council of Aix, in the year 1419.* For any such record, or for any entry at all respecting such an institution, in the proceedings of an English municipality, it will, I fear, be necessary to descend almost two centuries. The striking contrast which for many generations existed between Great Britain and some of the Continental States, as respects the possession of Libraries publicly accessible, was none the less, but rather the more, deplorable for the fact that in earlier days it had been, as there is good hope that in future days it will yet be, quite otherwise. In that first revival of letters for which the Europe of the middle ages was so greatly indebted to the genius and energy of Charlemagne, we find Alcuin writing to his imperial patron, that nothing so wrought within him a longing to return to England as the memory of the books which there had abounded, and of which in France there were so few. He repeatedly urges the Emperor to send messengers to England for manuscripts. So highly were those prized which he had himself brought with him to the court, that they became the foundation of a special school of scribes and illuminators in the country round Aix-la-Chapelle, which for many ages, it is said, remained faithful to Saxon traditions.

More than five centuries later, we find the patron saint of British book-lovers, Richard Aungerville, Bishop of Durham, in the midst of his lamentations at the degeneracy of morals, and at the supremacy of the lust of power and gain over the old love of knowledge, bursting into a cry of triumph at the apparent dawn of a brighter day. He quaintly recalls, indeed, the almost tumultuous pleasure with which, in his youth, he used frequently to visit "Paris, the paradise of the world! . . . where are delightful Libra-

* Rouard, *Notice sur la Bibliothèque d'Aix* (Aix, 1831, 8vo), p. 40. See also Pitton, *Histoire d'Aix*, p. 591.

ries in cells redolent of aromatics, . . . flourishing green-houses filled with all sorts of volumes, . . ." but thinks there are already indications, that as "the admirable Minerva once deserted Athens, and then retired from Rome, she has, in like manner, given the slip to the Parisians, and has at last happily reached Britain, the most renowned of islands."*

The good bishop practised what he taught. He is the first recorded donor of books to the University of Oxford. Richard of Bury. His example was followed by several other prelates and eminent personages; but all these benefactions were destroyed in the stormy days of the Reformation. Perhaps of all the incidental losses that were swallowed up, if we may so speak, in that great gain, there was none more deserving of regret than the loss of a precious opportunity for adding literary to religious reform. Many of those who most hated monkish corruptions have borne striking testimony to the worth of monastic Libraries, even after long years of neglect and injury. Poggio Bracciolini, indeed, who visited England about 1420—and who never lost an opportunity of throwing dirt at monks, careless whether it fell on a gown yet spotless, or on one which was already hopelessly bemired,—says that he had seen many English monasteries, all filled with the books of modern doctors, whom a learned Italian would not think worthy of a moment's attention. They have, he adds, few works of the ancients, "and these are already our's, in better shape."† But Erasmus (who liked a bad monk as little as did Poggio, yet remembered that he had once known and had loved a few good monks), when he travelled over the same ground, some seventy years later, wrote thus: "It is marvellous

* *Philobiblon* (Inglis' version), pp. 53—66.

† Poggii *Epistolæ*.

what a treasure of old books is to be found here, far and wide."* And that stern opponent of the Roman Church, our own Bishop Bale, keenly laments that in "turning over the superstitious Monasteries, so little respect was had to the Libraries, for the safeguard of those noble and precious monuments. . . . Avarice was the . . . . dispatcher which made an end both of our Libraries and books, unto the no small decay of the Commonwealth." And then he adds, in glowing words, that expression of deep regret that so favourable an occasion had not been seized for the establishment of *County Libraries* throughout England, to which I have elsewhere adverted, and concludes thus:—"But to destroy all, without consideration, is, and will be, unto England for ever, a most horrible infamy among the grave seniors of other nations."†

It was not until the reign of James I that Great Britain could boast even a "Royal Library," worthy of the name. In 1570, Sir Humphrey Gilbert had vainly pressed on the attention of Queen Elizabeth the superior advantages which men of letters enjoyed in other countries, and the national glory which would result from the establishment of a Royal Academy and Library, upon an adequate scale. But what the monarch failed to do, was in process of time undertaken by some private persons. In 1580, Clement Littill laid the corner-stone of the Library of the University of Edinburgh. In or about 1588, Sir Robert Cotton commenced that noble collection of manuscripts which long afterwards was to become not the least fruitful germ of our National Museum. In 1597, Sir Thomas Bodley resolved (to use his own words) "to take his full farewell of all State

* Erasmi Epistolæ, xiv (*Mirum est dictu, quam hic passim, quam dense veterum librorum seges efflorescat.*")

† Bale's preface to John Leland's *New Year's Gift to K. Henry VIII.*

employments, . . . and to set up his staff at the Library door in Oxon."* And, in 1601, a most worthy, though most unusual, memorial of the gratitude of an army, laid the foundation of the fine Library of Trinity College, Dublin.

Yet poor as (in the retrospect) we are apt to think our insular condition, at the beginning of the seventeenth century,—as respects Libraries and the other appliances of literary study,—that condition had enough of promise and of seminal vitality in it to bring upon us, within one generation, something of envy from the most intellectual of neighbouring nations. Gabriel Naudé,—as we shall see more fully hereafter,—in the course of those eager and almost world-wide researches for books, which enabled him at length (as the trusted agent and librarian of Mazarin) to raise "a cry of invitation never yet heard in the Republic of Letters," partly prepared the way for his loved enterprise by frequently pointing to the superior facilities enjoyed by the writers and students, not alone of Italy but of England. When longing to endow Paris with a greater and finer Library than even that of the King, he was wont to sound the praises of Oxford, as well as those of Rome and Milan. The Libraries of all those cities were, he said, liberally accessible, but he desired to be more liberal still. And it is probably true that, by his instrumentality, the honour of founding the first absolutely FREE LIBRARY † of the world

British Libraries formerly the object of foreign envy.

* *Vita Thomæ Bodlei*, Cotton MS., Titus, C. vii, fol. 171, verso.

† I say "absolutely Free," because—as will be seen more fully in a subsequent chapter—the claim to this distinction hinges entirely on a question of degree. More than twenty years earlier, Archbishop Williams had founded a public library in Westminster Abbey, and had made it freely accessible "to all professors of learning." Mazarin and Naudé were not content to stop there. The Cardinal, indeed, when he wrote to Famiano, to consult him as to an inscription to be placed above the Library door, says simply, that he had founded it "*per servitio del*

fell, at length, to a Cardinal of the Roman Church and statesman of France.

Growth of Royal Library at Paris under Lewis XIV.

Under Lewis XIV, the chief Library of Paris grew from little more than 5000 volumes to 70,000. But it did not become really public until 1737. And its progress in the half century which followed the death of Lewis XIV was not, relatively speaking, equal to that which it had made in the like period before that event. At Lewis' death it was undoubtedly chief among Libraries. At the outbreak of that Revolution, one of the thousand results of which was to endow it with vast heaps of books, without endowing it with the means and appliances which make books useful, it held, numerically, but the fourth, or perhaps even the fifth rank, among the great collections of Europe. The first place in point of extent—certainly not the first place in point of worth, although its intrinsic value was, and is, very great—had been gained, almost in a single lifetime, by the conjoined collections of two accomplished and liberal-minded Polish Bishops, the brothers Count Joseph and Count Andrew Zaluski. This noble Library was counted in 1795, and then contained, according to the official statement, more than 262,000 volumes. Four years earlier it could, under the known circumstances, scarcely have contained fewer volumes, and there are some reasons for thinking that it may even have contained a larger number. It had been made public by Count Joseph Zaluski, Bishop of Kief, as early as 1747. The smaller collection of Count Andrew, Bishop of Cracow, came to its

publico," (*Lettere del Card. Mazzarino*, 11 Sept. 1648.—MS. in the Library of the Duke of Aumale). But Naudé is more explicit: "It shall be open to all the world, without excluding a living soul." Such are his words in the curious *Dialogue entre Mascarat et Saintange*, which was published, without a date, under the general title of *Jugement de tout ce qui a esté imprimé contre le Cardinal Mazarin* (1659?).

augmentation ten years later. In its endowment both brothers co-operated. Very memorable is its subsequent history [see, hereafter, the chapter on Russian Libraries], and very literally true is the strange-looking remark of the Russian official writer of 1861, that in that unpretending series of facts about a mere collection of books, is exhibited, by detachments as it were, "*the history of a whole century of European civilisation.*"*

The Zaluski Library at Warsaw.

Whilst the Zaluski Library was still in its rightful abode, and before its books had undergone any Procrustean mutilations, in order to make them fit the Russian packing-cases, it was, as I have said, the largest Library in the world. Next to it (in the view of the statistician Adrien Balbi, who had taken far greater pains with Library-figures than any other writer of his date) came the Imperial Library of Vienna, with nearly 200,000 volumes; followed, at some distance, by the Libraries of Berlin and of Göttingen, which Balbi puts, in a bracket, at 160,000 each. The Royal Library of France, by the actual counting of Von Praet, in 1791, is known to have contained but 152,868 volumes.†

When Balbi wrote (1834-5), the official authorities of the Bodleian Library, like those of the British Museum, did not really know what was the number of the volumes under their charge, respectively. Balbi conjectured, upon the best evidence he could get, that "Bodley" might probably contain 135,000 volumes, at about the date when the Paris Library contained 152,000. Of the Museum Library he makes no mention at all. It is now well known that the number so assigned to Oxford exceeded the truth; and

* *Catalogue des Publications de la Bibliothèque Impériale Publique de St. Petersburg*, 1861.

† Van Praet, *Catalogue des livres sur Vélin*, preface.

that the British Museum, at a period thirty years later, contained but about 115,000 volumes. When the present Principal Librarian, Mr. Panizzi, became (in 1837) Keeper of Printed Books, he found, indeed, the 115,000 volumes, or thereabouts, of 1820 more than doubled—mainly by the splendid addition of the Library of King George the Third. But, on his promotion in 1856, he left the Library of Printed Books stored with nearly 560,000 volumes; and much less remarkable for its growth, than for the care, judgment, and far-spreading research with which its deficiencies had been (in a great degree) filled up; for the admirable way in which books gathered from all parts of the world had been organized and catalogued; and for the liberal and thoughtful appliances by which the implements of study had been made thoroughly serviceable to students. The History of Libraries affords—so far as my knowledge extends—no record of equal achievement. Of the details, and also of the helpers, of the work, something will be told in the fitting place.

Growth and Improvement of the Printed Library at British Museum, under Mr. Panizzi.

"Bodley" has not grown in the same extraordinary manner, but it has grown considerably, and its usefulness has increased even more largely than its number of volumes. We continue to be without an exact official statement of its yearly increment. But Dr. Bandinel, in 1849, returned the number of printed volumes—to an order of the House of Commons—at 220,000, and there is ground for the conclusion that in 1864 it is rapidly approaching to 300,000 volumes, exclusive of MSS.

It is apparent, therefore, that much has been done to remove an old reproach from the British name, as respects the provision of those great Libraries which are the storehouses of learning, and the magazines of authorship. For to the old renown of Britain, in that particular, had succeeded a reproach which was sufficiently just, and sufficiently long-lived, to become old in its turn. Alcuin, in the eighth century; Richard of Bury, in the fourteenth century; Erasmus, on the verge of the sixteenth; even Gabriel Naudé, in the middle of the seventeenth, had held up Britain as an example to foreign countries. From the middle of the seventeenth century downwards, the tables are turned, and the contrast, when drawn at all, is drawn the other way. Men of unquestionable claim to speak on such matters were wont to shame English indifference by pointing to foreign zeal, in the liberal amassing and the wise ordering of Libraries. John Dury, in his *Reformed Library-Keeper;* John Evelyn, in his Correspondence; Richard Bentley, in the *Dissertation on Phalaris;* Michael Maittaire, in his *Annales Typographici;* Thomas Carte, in his *History of England;* Edward Gibbon, in the *Decline and Fall;* William von Schlegel, in the Preface to the *Ramayana*, are at one in their testimony on this head. Happily the testimony, both of authors and of readers, has now good reason to return once again to its more ancient channel.

Comparative decline of British Libraries in 17th Century.

But, besides the Libraries for the learned, and for those who aspire to become learned, other collections are needed for readers of a class to whom such an ambition is unknown. And, in this path, Englishmen may fairly boast that they have rather set an example than waited to follow one. The task was not easy, but those who worked at it—with many shortcomings—had the one merit which often repairs defect, and ekes out small means,—they persevered, in spite of obstacles.

Libraries for the People.

As early as the reign of Anne, there had been a first step in legislating for Libraries, by the passing of the Act entitled *An Act for the better preservation of Parochial Libraries* in England, but its sole object was to keep up, by a corporate succession, such *clerical* Libraries as might be given to or founded by the Incumbent of a Parish, for his own use and the use of his successors. It gave neither means of maintenance nor facilities of access. It simply pointed to a way of preserving parsonic heir-looms, so to speak, and it soon became null. A somewhat truer and livelier germ of popular Libraries had been put into the ground many generations earlier, when the Bishops of the English Church enjoined on their Clergy that they should place English Bibles, "of the largest volume, where your Parishioners may most commodiously resort to the same, ... the charges of which *shall be rateably borne* between you the Parson, and the Parishioners aforesaid." But the Marian persecutions intervened, and the germ was killed.

It was not, in fact, until 1850 that a practical measure—based on evidence which had been gathered by a Parliamentary Committee in 1849—for founding, maintaining, and administering FREE LIBRARIES for the British people, by a permanent rate, equably levied and responsibly expended, passed the Legislature. That it did then so pass is due, in the main, to the untiring exertions, within the House of Commons, of WILLIAM EWART.

Within the first ten or eleven years of its operation that measure secured for public use, and for continuous, permanent renovation from time to time, some 260,000 volumes of books, and made them so thoroughly accessible to readers that each volume of the 260,000 is, on an average, actually used ten times within each year, and is renewed when worn out.

The Libraries so formed are unconnected with any sort

of sectarian influence, or of class distinction. There is nothing of almsgiving in their establishment;—nothing of clap-trap oratory, or of money-seeking expedients, in their means of continued support;—nothing of restriction or exaction in their terms of accessibility. They are not the Libraries of working-people; or of poor people; or of trades-people; but the Libraries of THE CITY, THE TOWN, or THE PARISH, in which they are placed. They are not only FREE, but PERMANENT. They will never become "schools of political agitation" (as one of the opponents of the first "Libraries Bill" asserted, in the House of Commons, that they would become), but, if they can be said to have any conceivable political tendency at all, it must needs be a "Conservative" one, since they plainly widen that public domain in which all classes have a common interest. Whilst essentially independent of gifts, they have been liberally, even munificently, promoted by liberal men. And they are, as yet, but at the threshold of their public usefulness.

CHAPTER III.

OF THE LIBRARIES OF MONASTERIES, ABROAD.

> "*Here Man more purely lives, less oft doth fall,*
> *More promptly rises, walks with stricter heed,*
> *More safely rests, dies happier, is freed*
> *Earlier from cleansing fires, and gains withal*
> *A brighter crown.*" On yon Cistertian wall
> *That* confident assurance may be read... ......
> .... The potent call
> Doubtless shall cheat full oft the heart's desires;
> Yet, while the rugged age on pliant knee
> Vows to rapt Fancy humble fealty,
> A gentler life spreads round the holy spires;
> Where'er they rise, the sylvan waste retires,
> And aëry harvests crown the fertile lea.
>
> *Ecclesiastical Sonnets*, II, 3.

MONTE CASSINO has been called the Sinai of the Middle Ages. It was certainly the cradle of a great series of Monastic Communities whence issued an illustrious band of the Missionaries, both of Religion and of Civilisation, whose labours were destined to bear rich fruit over all Europe. The Monks of Monte Cassino had become famous as early as the eleventh century for their transcriptions, not only of theological books, but of Virgil, Horace, Terence; of the *Idyls* of Theocritus; of the *Fasti* of Ovid; and of not a few of the Historians both of Greece and Rome. They not only formed a good library for themselves, but they disseminated the products of their Scriptorium far and wide.

Activity of the Scriptorium of Monte Cassino.

At Monte Cassino, indeed, as elsewhere, the learned and laborious monks of one generation were followed by but too many of the ignorant and idle monks of another. When, in the fourteenth century, Boccaccio visited them, and respectfully requested to see their famous library, a monk, he tells us, answered him gruffly:—"Go up; it is open." And truly, he continues, it was so open, that grass was growing in it. The books were covered with dust; many were without covers; others were torn and mutilated. With all allowance for the vein of exaggeration so clearly traceable in this anecdote (handed down, probably from Boccaccio's own lips, by his disciple, Benvenuto da Imola,)* there is no doubt that the famous Monastery had fallen from its first love. But, at a later day, we have, again, better accounts of it. Monte Cassino was always a cynosure to poets and scholars. Tasso, indeed, when he spent there his last Christmas on earth, was intent on higher themes than those of literature, and has left no record of his visit to the then recently restored Library. But, three centuries after the visit of Boccaccio, we have the experiences of the illustrious Maurist Mabillon, of Dom Michel Germain—the gossip of the Benedictines—and of the companions of their tour. A little later come those of Montfaucon. And, almost five centuries afterwards, we have the elaborate explorations of M. Renan and of M. Daremberg; and also those of Mr. Robert Curzon.

The visit of Boccaccio.

Mabillon and Germain found the Library to have been again newly renovated. They were not struck with much admiration for the printed books, but found about five hundred MSS., whence they extracted into their note books "some good things." The Muniment Room, too, they tell us, contained "some fine MSS., which are kept there for fear

The visit of Mabillon.

* In his Commentary on Dante, *Paradiso*, xii, 74.

the Seculars should ask for them over-pressingly."* Montfaucon speaks of a noble series of Longobardic charters and of Papal Bulls.† Renan found the eight days which he spent in the Library of Monte Cassino, "the most fruitful days" of his long literary tour.‡ Mr. Curzon tells us (after all the vicissitudes of twelve centuries, and their inevitable intercalation of brutish monks amongst the intelligent and pious ones,) that Monte Cassino yet contains 800 volumes of MSS., chiefly of the eleventh and twelfth centuries, and also a wonderful collection of Charters and Records.†

and that of M. Renan.

and of Mr. R. Curzon.

The Library of Fleury.

The Library of Fleury on the Loire was another famous Benedictine collection. Abbot Macarius, in 1146, levied a graduated library rate for its maintenance and enlargement, and that rate is said to have continued in force during four centuries. The beauty and variety of the Fleury MSS. became very celebrated. The devastating but perhaps inevitable "wars of Religion" ruined the Library. Such of the fine books as were not destroyed fell into the hands,—partially or successively,—of Pierre Daniel, of Jacques de Bongars, of Paul Petau (Petavius), of Jacques Gravisset, and of Queen Christina of Sweden. Gifts, and the chances of successive centuries, have now scattered them amongst five or six several libraries, in almost as many different countries. Some are in the Public Library of Berne; others in the Town Library of Geneva; others in the Town Library of Orleans; others, again, in the Imperial Library at Paris, and in the Vatican Library at Rome. Could the individual books

* *Correspondance inédite de Mabillon et de Montfaucon avec l'Italie*, i, 169—172.

† *Diarium Italicum*, c. 22.

‡ *Archives des Missions Scientifiques*, i, 384—387.

§ *Notices of Italian Libraries* (privately printed, 1855).

speak, as audibly as do their written pages, they could doubtless tell of many "moving accidents, by flood and field."

Clugni, in Burgundy, is more famous still. Berno founded the Abbey, but a certain Odo, son of Abbo, a citizen of Tours, was the virtual creator of its library, and upon the groundwork he had laid, Abbot Maiolus, and many of his successors, liberally built. Maiolus had, in his day, to make a good many journeys on horseback,—an elevation which has often been perilous to scholars,—and was fond of reading, as he rode along. Sometimes, he chose his author so unwisely, as to fall asleep, and to fall off; and more than twice or thrice his life had nearly been the penalty. Under Peter the Venerable, the library grew largely,* and many interesting particulars about it may be seen in that clever and lively volume which Dr. S. R. Maitland has devoted to the elucidation of *The Dark Ages*.

The Library of Clugni.

Most famous, perhaps, of all Monasteries, in a bibliothecal sense, was the Abbey of Corbie in Picardy. It has been said that as early as the eleventh century an express conventual regulation made it incumbent on every novice, on the day of his "profession," to give to the infant Library of Corbie some book, but I doubt the sufficiency of the evidence on which the statement rests. Be that as it may, we possess an unquestionable catalogue of this celebrated library, as it stood in the twelfth century,—in a MS. which passed successively from the hands of De Thou, of Puteanus, and of Meerman, into those (1824) of Sir Thomas Phillipps, of Middle Hill, by whom it was shown to the present writer in 1856. The collection of Corbie was already, at the date of that catalogue, of notable extent. Under "AUGUSTINUS"

The Library of Corbie.

* See Vogel, *Fernere Nachrichten über einige Klosterbibliotheken, &c.* (*Serapeum*, v, 123—144.)

thirty-nine entries appear; under "BEDA," thirteen; under "BOETIUS," fifteen; under "HIERONYMUS," sixteen; under "PRISCIANUS," four; under "VIRGILIUS," seven; under "CICERO," five; under "LUCANUS," four. Juvenal, Persius, Martial, Ovid, Statius, Terence, all occur,—as single entries,—together with Livy, Pliny, and Seneca. There is also a considerable number of such works of History as were then attainable.*

Fragments of a still earlier Catalogue—but only fragments—were discovered by Cardinal Mai, in a Queen Christina MS., preserved, amongst the literary collections of that Queen, in the Library of the Vatican, and were published by him in 1841. A third Catalogue was also found in the same Christina MS., but this was attributed by Mai, not to Corbie in Picardy, but to Corvey in Westphalia—an opinion opposed by German archæologists immediately on its enunciation, and since then amply controverted, on independent grounds, by M. Leopold Delisle, of the Institute, in an able paper which he published, in 1860, in the *Bibliotheque de l'Ecole des Chartes*.

Corbie was founded, as early as in the seventh century, by Queen Bathilda, and was probably peopled by a colony of monks from Luxeuil. It soon became eminent for the activity of its Scriptorium, in behalf of which certain grants

* *Catalogus liborum in Bibliotheca Corbeiensi insitus, &c.* (MS. at Middle Hill, No. 1825). Amongst the works of History, or bearing upon History, mentioned in this document are "Gai Cæsaris Historia," "Tiberii Cæsaris Pragmaticum," "Victoris Chronica." Following in the train of much better scholars, I had attributed (in *Memoirs of Libraries*, 1859, vol. i, p. 239) this Middle Hill MS. to the other Corbic, or Corvey, in Westphalia (*Corbeia Nova*), but it clearly belongs to the French Corbie. Just as clearly, the famous Tacitus MS. there spoken of, belonged to the German Monastery, not the French one, although French writers seem reluctant to admit the cogency of the claim.

for the more effectual purveyance of vellum were conferred on the monks. And a sort of rate was levied; partly towards a salary for the librarian, and partly towards the cost of bookbinding, in the very simple fashion of the time. This rate had the special sanction of Pope Alexander III (1159-81).* Some of the Italian monasteries,—and notably those of Monte Cassino and of Rome,—contributed to the enrichment of the Library of Corbie, which, in its turn, contributed, sometimes by gift but more frequently by loan, to the literary wants of other communities. Usually, when books were borrowed, other volumes were deposited in pledge. On one such occasion, the book pledged was regarded by the worthy monk who had the care of the library as so heretical, that he proposed to the community that it should be formally burnt. In some cases, the deposited books remained in the Corbie Library, until its dispersion; and, having survived, can still be identified as the property, originally, of other monasteries.

The Scriptorium of Corbie and its peculiar privileges.

The literary zeal of the Corbie community, like that of monastic communities elsewhere, slackened in the fourteenth century. But, as the tonsured scribes became idler, the professional scribes of Paris became more diligent, and were largely employed by various benefactors of Corbie, for the enrichment of its library. Eminent for liberality of this kind was a certain Etienne de Conti, who long administered the affairs of the Abbey, and was nominated as Abbot, but set aside by the Pope. He died in 1413, and is memorable as one of the continuators of the Martinian Chronicle. Some of the fine books given by him to Corbie may still be seen, both at Paris and at Amiens. For one such volume he

The gifts of Etienne de Conti to the Library of Corbie.

* Ziegelbauer, *Historia rei literariæ Ordinis S. Benedicti*, i, 471; Delisle, *Recherches sur l'ancienne Bibliothèque de Corbie* (Bibl. de l'Ecole des Chartes, 5e sér., tom. i, pp. 393—439, and 498—515).

paid to the transcriber a sum equal, perhaps, to some £33 of present English money. But the decline of learning in the convents was not effectually arrested, until the date of the Maurist reform. Sometimes, the monks gave away the books they had ceased to value; at others, their laxity permitted them to be stolen. When, long afterwards, they roused themselves from their slumbers, they evinced their new-born zeal by scattering, broadcast, accusations of plunder. Pithou, Brisson, Sirmond, and André Du Chesne, are among the later scholars whom they charge with purloining their books.

Decline of monkish zeal for literature.

A similar accusation was brought against a far more illustrious name, and the circumstances are curious. The President de Thou has himself recorded—in his Memoirs—his visit to Corbie during the civil wars, in the discharge of his official duties;—his regret at observing the gross neglect into which the library had fallen;—and his selection from its remains of some fine books which, he says, he "put aside," as worthy of being printed, in better and more quiet days. The monks on the other hand go the length of asserting—and it is assertion merely—that De Thou caused a magazine of corn to be established in the Monastery for the service of the royal troops, and then took occasion to fill the empty hogsheads in which the corn had been brought, with the choicest manuscripts he could lay his hands on. Certain it is that in De Thou's collection, as in many other collections, there were books—still elsewhere identifiable—on which one can yet read the inscription "*Liber S. Petri Corbeie*," which explains the charge, without proving it.

De Thou's visit to Corbie.

Whatever its losses, a Catalogue, dated in 1621—now preserved amongst the MSS. of the Imperial Library—shows that the collection was still a fine one. When, in 1636, the Spaniards made their memorable inroad, Corbie

The fate of the Library in the "Year of Corbie," and afterwards.

fell into their power. After the recapture, the Library was sealed up by the Bishop of Chartres. The monks petitioned Richelieu, but in vain, for its continuance with them intact. They laid great stress on the free access which the learned had long enjoyed to the treasures of monastic libraries. The great minister, nevertheless, empowered one of the Maurist Benedictines,—Jerome Anselme Le Michel,—to select the choicest MSS. for the Library of Saint-Germain-des-Prés, and accordingly about four hundred volumes were removed thither, in 1638. Forty years later, these accessions appear among the other MSS. of the Abbey of St. Germain, catalogued precisely like those of its original collection. Until 1791, the four hundred volumes from Corbie seem to have been preserved entire.

In that year, twenty-five choice volumes were stolen. These were seen, soon afterwards, in the collection of Dubrowski. They are among the many and splendid "acquisitions" of the now magnificent Library of St. Petersburgh. In 1794, the Library of St. Germains suffered greatly from fire, but the remaining Corbie MSS. escaped. They were removed, about a year afterwards, to the National Library of Paris, which they still adorn.

Fate of the MSS. which had remained at Corbie, until the Revolution.

About three hundred MSS. had been left at Corbie in 1638, when the finest books were transferred to the metropolis. In 1662, they were inventoried, along with the printed books. At an early stage of the Revolution—probably in 1791—these were carried to Amiens. In 1793, it was officially certified that all the MSS. entered in the Inventory of 1662 were duly present, with the exception of seven volumes. Seventy-five of the more valuable MSS. were transferred to Paris (to rejoin the other Corbie MSS.) during the Consulate of Napoleon, in 1803.

What then remained, and still remains, at Amiens, was put into good order in 1828, but it was then ascertained that the seven volumes originally missing had been increased by other losses, which had occurred in the interval. Since that date, the Amiens MSS. have been admirably catalogued by M. Garnier. The survivors, therefore, of the famous collection of Corbie must now be sought in the great repositories of Paris and St. Petersburgh, and in the Town Library of Amiens. A few scattered volumes occur amongst private collections.

CHAPTER IV.

OF THE LIBRARIES OF MONASTERIES, AT HOME.

Here, then, I cannot choose but bitterly exclaime
Against those fools that all Antiquity defame,
Because they have found out some credulous ages laid
Some fictions with the truth, whilst Truth or Rumour staid;
And that one forward time (perceiving the neglect
A former of her had), to purchase her Respect,
With toys so trimm'd her up, the drowsy world t'allure
And lent her what it thought might appetite procure
To man, whose mind doth still variety pursue;
And therefore to those things whose *grounds* were very true,
Though naked yet and bare (not having to content
The wayward curious ear), gave fictive ornament:
And fitter thought, the truth they should in question call,
Than coldly sparing that, the truth should go and all.

Poly-olbion.

THE traveller who looks at the few and slight fragments of monastic architecture yet to be seen at Canterbury, has before him—as is well known, nowadays, to almost every traveller—the little that is left of the earliest seat of Christianity in England, about which our information is distinctly historical, and plainly separable from mere tradition. Such travellers, too, as care about the history of collections of books, will have some pleasure in the thought that they are also looking upon the site of England's first known Library.

The Library of Christ Church Monastery at Canterbury.

That infant and tiny collection of the Holy Scriptures and of two or three books of Theology, came from St. Gregory, and with St. Augustine. Towards the close of the seventh century, Theodore of Tarsus, it is recorded, added a large number of books to the small foundation of Augustine. Archbishop Parker was fully persuaded that he possessed some fine MSS. which had belonged to his remote predecessor Theodore, and about the year 1570 showed them to the antiquary Lambarde.

Archbishop Ælfric was another great benefactor to the Library of Christ Church Monastery, but within five years after his death came the devastating sack of Canterbury by the Danes. The Library was gradually restored by the successive exertions of Lanfranc, of Anselm, and of Walter. Before the close of the thirteenth century, Prior Henry de Estria was able to compile a catalogue containing nearly three thousand entries. That curious document I had the satisfaction of making generally accessible to students of mediæval antiquities, by printing it,* for the first time,—from the Cottonian MS. *Galba, E. iv,*—in *Memoirs of Libraries* (1859).

And that of St. Augustine's Monastery.

Of the companion Canterbury Library—that of the Monastery of St. Augustine—Sir Frederick Madden has given some account, in an interesting communication to *Notes and Queries.*† A fifteenth-century catalogue of it is

* But with much hesitation, on account of its great length, and the consequent interruption of an already too much broken and too fragmentary narrative. By several scholars, however, that small contribution to the wider knowledge of our early collections was generously welcomed. By one who was an eminent and life-long student of such subjects, the late lamented Beriah Botfield, M.P., for Ludlow, it was so much prized that, at the time of his death, he was about to have reprinted it in full, at his own cost, with other documents of like character. A portion of his collections will appear under the editorship of Mr. Bradshaw.

† *Notes and Queries*, 2nd series, i, 485.

amongst the MSS. of Trinity College, Dublin.* Apart from its riches in Theology, the collection was conspicuous for its English chroniclers, and for its numerous works in the amusing and manners-painting field of French Romance.

Libraries of Northern Monasteries.

But, ere long, the Monastic Libraries of our northern counties began to vie with the primitive Libraries of Kent. Archbishop Egbert founded a Library at York, to which Alcuin was wont to look back with fond regret, when mourning over the penury of books at Tours. Wearmouth owed a fine collection of books to the repeated Italian journies of Bennet Biscop, its first Abbot, and the dearly loved tutor of Beda. The Abbey of Whitby, after its restoration by William de Percy, gained a Library of considerable value. Of this collection there is extant a twelfth-century catalogue in which occur the names—and it may fairly be hoped that, with all allowance for the curious blundering of that age in the ascription of works to famous names, there was something to warrant them—of Homer, Plato, Cicero, and Juvenal; together with a large number of works on Theology, Ethics, and the History of the Church. At a later period, the Benedictine Abbey of Durham possessed a noble Library, including many copies of the Holy Scriptures, in the Vulgate version; the precious *Evangeliary* ascribed to the venerable hand of Beda; many ecclesiastical historians; a long array of the garrulous, credulous, and imitative—but most laborious and most useful—old chroniclers of the Monasteries; and a formidable body of the tough Divinity of the Schoolmen. Very famous is one priceless book, which then was the chief literary treasure of the Monastery of Durham, as it is now one of the most conspicuous among the thousand literary treasures of the British Museum, the *Gospels of Saint Cuthbert*, of the

The Library of Durham Abbey.

* D. i, 19.

perilous adventures of which, in its transit from Lindisfarne, old Simeon of Durham has given so curious an account.

But of the Library of Durham Abbey, Theology and Church History was not the exclusive furniture. There were also to be seen the Metaphysics and the Ethics of Aristotle; the Orations and the Rhetoric of Cicero; the Institutes and the Declamations of Quintilian; the poetical works of Virgil, Horace, Ovid, Terence, Juvenal, Claudian, Lucan, and Statius; the Histories and historical works of Sallust, Suetonius, Valerius Maximus, Quintus Curtius, and Eutropius. There also was a large and most curious collection of the versifiers of the Middle Ages,—of small account, indeed, as poets, but invaluable as exponents and illustrators of the manners and customs, the studies and the modes of thought, of that seedtime of the modern world.

The Library of Peterborough

The catalogue of another remarkable Benedictine Library has been printed by Gunton, the historian of Peterborough. In that collection, nearly 1700 separate works had been brought together, and bound, as it seems, in 344 volumes. Poetry, and especially French poetry, is unusually conspicuous. Church history, too, abounds. Among the Classic authors appear Aristotle, Cicero, Virgil, Persius, Statius, Sallust, Seneca, and Dares Phrygius. Deprived, by their profession, of the civilising influences of female society, the good monks of Peterborough seem to have solaced themselves by a special devotion to the classic poet of Love. The number of entries under "Ovid" is a larger one than is to be found under the name of any other Roman author.

Libraries of the Mendicant Orders.

The stern rule and the grim vow of poverty . . .

"Del padre corse, a cui, com' alla morte,
La porta del piacer nessun disserra,"......

seemed to bode small encouragement to letters at the hands of the Mendicant Orders, yet as early as in 1350 we find an English prelate making grave complaint to the Pope that secular priests met with serious difficulty in furnishing themselves with needful books, for the prosecution of their studies, whether in Divinity or in Arts, because "all books are bought up by Friars, so that in every convent of Friars there is a large and noble Library."* To like effect, but in a different tone, is the testimony of Richard of Bury:—"When I happened to turn aside to the towns and places where the Mendicants had their convents, I was not slack in visiting their Libraries. There, amidst the deepest poverty, I found the most precious riches treasured up. . . I must especially extol the Preaching Friars . . . as overflowing with an almost divine liberality; as being, not selfish hoarders, but worthy professors of true knowledge."†

Among the London Franciscans, those who were established on the site of the present Christ Hospital,—and for whom Sir Richard Whittington built a noble Library in 1421-22,‡ at a cost equal perhaps to £3000 of our present money,—are very notable for the number of books they had amassed. The Franciscans of Oxford were also conspicuous in this direction, and to them that eminent prelate and eminent statesman, Robert Greathead, Bishop of Lincoln, bequeathed his collection, at his death in 1253. Anthony Wood echoes the old and silly cry that the diligence of the Franciscans in stocking their Libraries was "looked upon by wise men as an injury to laymen," who by this means "found it difficult to get books."§ And he

* Richard Fitzralph, *Defensorium Curatorum adversus eos qui privilegiatos se dicunt*; sign. c. iii, recto. I quote from an undated edition, probably printed about 1480.

† *Philobiblon*, c. 8.

‡ *Monasticon*, vi, 1520.

§ Wood, MS. Collections, quoted in *Monasticon*, vi, 1527-8.

bears testimony to their liberal comprehensiveness in study, when he adds: "I have found by many ancient manuscripts that these Friars bought many Hebrew books of the Jews, when they were disturbed in England."* The poor "disturbed" Jews, doubtless, in bargains made under such circumstances, met with more than their match, but there can be no better evidence of the culture and insight of the Mendicants of that age.

Much might be said of the Monastic Libraries of Evesham, of Exeter, of Glastonbury, of Ramsey, of Rievaux, of Saint Albans, of Salisbury, of Westminster, and of Winchester. But I content myself with referring the reader, who may be desirous of pursuing this branch of the subject, to a list (which he will find in the Appendix) of the known Catalogues—whether printed or as yet unprinted—of those collections, severally. A collective edition of the Monastic Catalogues, such as the late Mr. Botfield would have liberally provided, had his life been spared, would be of eminent service to inquirers into the history of mediæval literature, and I trust it may yet be hoped for, although its completion may have to come from another quarter.

* Wood, MS. Collections, quoted in *Monasticon*, vi, 1527-8.

CHAPTER V.

CONCERNING THE LIBRARIES OF SOME FAMOUS AUTHORS, OF VARIOUS PERIODS.

Blessings be with them,—and eternal praise,—
Who gave us nobler loves, and nobler cares,—
The POETS, who on earth have made us heirs
Of Truth, and pure delight, by heavenly lays!

Personal Talk, iv.

[To POETS] we have owed another gift,
Of aspect more sublime; that blessed mood
In which the burthen of the mystery,—
In which the heavy and the weary weight
Of all this unintelligible world,—
Is lightened;—that serene and blessed mood,
In which the affections gently lead us on,—
. . . .
While, with an eye made quiet by the power
Of Harmony, and the deep power of Joy,
We see into the life of things.

Lines on revisiting the Wye.

IT needs no research to establish the fact that some of the greatest Poets that have ever lived owed very little to books, of any kind. The works and teachings of God, in the visible universe without; the intuitions and the faculties implanted by God, in the individual soul within, have repeatedly shown themselves more than sufficient for the equipment of the Poet towards his high calling. But it would need great research to show, in any adequate manner, how world-wide, in many other instances, is the elaborate book-knowledge which has been made to subserve the loftiest work of the creative Imagination. Whilst some poets seem, in the most literal and exclusive sense, to have looked into their hearts, and written; others have amassed books very discursively, and have studied them very laboriously, before committing themselves to the working out of their long-pondered themes.

Diversities of Poets in respect to the use and treatment of books.

And even among those of the poets who have really been ripe scholars, and very Nimrods in the book-field, there have obtained the most curious diversities in their treatment of books. Some have been accomplished bibliographers, accurate in the technicalities of the science; curious in paper, in margins, and in bindings. Others have cared only for the knowledge within, and have been as regardless of the material qualities of the printed paper and the tanned skin, as people are wont to be of the peel of an orange when they have sucked its juice. Some have stored up their books with as keen an eye to the future, as the miser has when he hoards his money. Others have been content to beg or to borrow a multitude of volumes, as need occurred and opportunity offered, and have made their notes even more freely and more copiously in the books of their friends, than in the few which they could call their own. Some poets have made books their inseparable companions; have used them as pillows in their ordinary sleep; and have even laid their heads upon them in the agonies of death. Others have left behind them the books which they had used familiarly, in almost every house and every lodging which they ceased to occupy, so as to supply to those who came after them a sort of mute itinerary of their journey of life.

But, after all, the cardinal diversity in the treatment of

books is that which poets have, only in common with meaner men. Petrarch has expressed it pithily, in his now little-read but pregnant treatise *De Remediis utriusque Fortunæ:* "Books have brought some men to knowledge, and some to madness. As fulness sometimes hurteth the stomach more than hunger, so fareth it with wits; and, as of meats, so likewise of books, the use ought to be limited according to the quality of him that useth them."*

Petrarch himself is an eminent example of the book-loving poet, with powers of digestion and of assimilation quite on a par with his appetencies. The earliest anecdote that has come down of him tells of a boy's Library, eagerly stored up; enjoyed with that special zest which belongs to stolen pleasures; then suddenly pounced upon by an angry father, and committed to the flames, from which the youthful student was scarcely able to rescue, at the risk of his fingers, the half-consumed but still precious pages of his Cicero and his Virgil. In after-life, Petrarch met at Rome with the Coryphæus of the book-collectors of the fourteenth century, Richard d'Aungerville of Bury, and had much talk with him on themes of literature and antiquarianism, and about "the abundant supply" † of fine books which the Englishman had already gathered. At Paris, he visited King John, the first founder of the magnificent Library of the kings of France, and the father of the three most eminent book-lovers of the succeeding generation. Doubtless, such communications strengthened the tastes which had evinced themselves so markedly in youth.

Petrarch's Conversations with Richard of Bury.

Petrarch was not merely a collector for his own gratification. He aspired to become the founder of a permanent

* I quote the Elizabethan and racy translation of old Thos. Twyne (1579, f. 62).

† *De Remediis*, ut supra.

His gift to the Church of St. Mark at Venice.

Library for Venice. "*Francesco Petrarca desidera de haver herede il B. Marco Evangelista, si così piacera a Christo ed a lui, di non so quanti libretti i quali egli possiede al presente, o che forse possedera in futuro,*" &c. Such are the characteristic words in which his love of literature, and his devotion to Saint Mark, were expressed, in the year 1532.

But the poet's gift did not prosper, as he had hoped. In spite of his careful subjoinder to the words already quoted, of the pointed warning that his gift was made on condition that the books should not be sold, or in any way misused; but be preserved in a fitting place, safe from fire and from damp; to the honour of the Saint; as a memorial of the donor; and for the perpetual use and comfort of students;* the collection was allowed to fall into entire neglect. When Cardinal Bessarion, a century afterwards, became the real founder of the *Marciana,* no attention seems to have been turned to the previous gift of the illustrious poet. Nor was it until one of his many biographers,—Tomasini, Bishop of Citta-Nuova,—visited Venice towards the middle of the seventeenth century, and made elaborate researches for them, that the scanty remains of the precious volumes were at length found in a long-deserted chamber. Some, he tells us, had crumbled into dust; others had petrified into fossils.† A few were rescued, and may yet be seen.

Tomasini's researches after Petrarch's Library.

* "*Con questo che i libri non sieno venduti, ne per qual si voglia modo mal trattati, ma sieno conservati in alcun luogo da esser deputato a questo effetto, il qual sia sicuro dal fuoco, et dalle pioggie, a honor di esso Santo, ed a memoria di esso, Francesco ed per consolazione, ed commodo perpetuo degli ingegnosi, ed nobili di questa citta, che si diletteranno di cose tali.*" Tomasini, *Petrarcha Redivivus*, (1635), 84.

† "Adeo quicquid hic erat partem in pulverem inter manes pene collapsum, partim (dictu mirum) in saxa mutatum." Ib. 85.

Boccaccio's collection had nearly shared the same fate. A little before the date of Petrarch's donation to St. Mark's, the jovial author of the *Decameron* had been alarmed by a prediction that the remainder of his term on earth was short. He wrote to Petrarch to apprise him of his fears, and of his resolution entirely to change his mode of life, and to put his worldly concerns in order. He told the dearly loved friend that several persons were desirous to purchase his Library, but that he would rather see it acquired by Petrarch himself, on his own terms. After some remonstrances on a change so sudden, and so sweeping, the poet replied that if Boccaccio was really determined to part with his collection, he was grateful for the preference; and would see that the books should not be scattered, or fall into unfit hands. "But," he continued, "though we live apart, we are of one mind. Since I lost the successor of my studies, the heir of my labours, it has been my purpose to bestow my library on some religious community who will preserve our memory. But I can put no price on your books. . . *That* you must needs do yourself. I lay one condition only on the bargain: If you will spend with me the brief time that remains to us (as I have always wished, and you have often promised), you shall enjoy at once your own books and mine." It was not so determined. Petrarch lived till July, 1374; Boccaccio little more than one year longer. His books were bequeathed to the Augustinians of Florence, but doubtless they had been weeded before his death. Otherwise, by his own account of them,* they were certainly but a questionable addition to a monkish library. They, or some of them, are still shown to visitors in the Laurentian Library.

The Library of Boccaccio.

Its gift to the Augustinians.

* See it quoted in the Abbé de Sade's *Mémoires pour la Vie de Pétrarque, III.*

From the Poets of love and heralds of the Revival, we leap across the chasm of nearly two centuries, to reach the keen anatomist of human character, the deep thinker, and (in several respects) the great prototype of modern Essayists, Michael de Montaigne. Born in 1533, in the thick of the greatest fermentation of mind which the world has seen, and endowed with faculties fitted alike for the sharp conflict of man with man, and for the self-concentration of the scholarly recluse, he was destined to leave us an immortal book, in which a marvellous candour is combined with a scarcely less marvellous prudence.

Montaigne, and his Library in Perigord.

Montaigne's inscriptions or mottoes.

But it is not only in his *Essays* that Montaigne is self-depicted for all time to come. Many men have drawn life-like, though usually very evanescent, portraits of their own minds, by the mere choice of the books they have gathered around them for their familiar use. Montaigne's Library was eminently of that sort. But the present tourist in the valley of the Dordogne at first sees only bare walls, where the reader of the famous chapter *Des Livres*, in the second book of the *Essays*, sees a room full of the best company. But closer examination will show him that the room is less denuded than it looks to be. Besides its books, Montaigne filled it with inscriptions, some of which were the seeds and others the summaries of famous papers in the *Essays*, And he did this, as he did so many other things, after a fashion of his own. His education, from the very cradle, was according to a new model, framed by a crotchetty father. And so well did his mind take the ply that we constantly find him contriving an uncommon way of doing even common things. It is, therefore, no matter for surprise that when he conceived the fancy of decorating his library with mottoes, he chose to have branding irons made, and then, climbing a ladder, *burnt in* his inscriptions, letter by letter with his own hands, on the beams and rafters, with infinite pains and perseverance.

The Inscriptions in Montaigne's Library.

Most characteristic are these mottos. Solomon, Homer, Horace, Persius, Lucretius, Terence, are all laid under contribution. But no writer, except Lucretius, is so often quoted in them as Saint Paul, *e.g.*, "*For if a man think himself to be something, when he is nothing, he deceiveth himself.*"* "*And if any man think that he knoweth anything, he knoweth nothing, yet, as he ought to know.*"† "*I say .... to every man that is among you, not to think of himself more highly than he ought to think, but to think soberly.*"‡ The citations from Ecclesiastes, and those from the Latin poets, are to very like purpose. The "*Quantum est in rebus inane,*" and the "*O miseras hominum mentes*" of Lucretius; even the

...“*Quid æternis minorem*
Consiliis animum fatigas?”

of Horace, are but variations on the sad theme of The Preacher: "*Vanity of Vanities, all is vanity.*"§ Whilst the "*Seest thou a man wise in his own conceit? There is more hope of a fool than of him,*"‖ of Proverbs, only repeats the warning of St. Paul, from another point of view. The inscriptions which adorned the other rafters are chiefly in Greek, sometimes with an admixture of Latin words in the same sentence; and seem, for the most part, to be of Montaigne's own compilation or adaptation. "*Amidst the see-saws of the intellect nothing is absolutely firm.*" "*I do*

* Gal. vi, 3.

† 1 Cor. viii, 2.

‡ Rom. xii, 3. Usually, Montaigne quotes the Vulgate, but here he abridges and slightly alters it; "*Ne plus sapite quam oportet, sed sapite ad sobrietatem,* instead of "*Non plus sapere,*" &c.

§ Eccles. i, 2.

‖ Prov. xxvi, 12.

not comprehend;—I pause;—I examine;—following the lead of custom and good sense."* "*No one ever possessed absolute certainty; no one ever will possess it.*" A third may be rendered by the words of our own homely proverb, "*Much may be said on both sides.*" Another goes deeper: "*Who knows but that what we call dying is beginning to live; and that what we term life is really death.*" Among the remaining inscriptions, the most notable are the passage from Lucretius—

> "[Quum tamen] *Omnia cum cœlo, terraque, marique,*
> *Nihil sint ad summam summai totius* [omnem];"†

the *Homo sum, humani a me nihil alienum puto,*" of Terence; the "*Dust and ashes, what have you to be proud of?* borrowed from Ecclesiasticus; and the apophthegm, in Greek again,—"It is not so much things that torment man, as the opinions which he forms of things."‡

Montaigne's country-seat is in Perigord, not far—some three miles, perhaps—from Castillon, memorable as the place where fell

> The Frenchmen's only scourge,
> Their kingdom's terror, and black Nemesis;

Description of Montaigne's Tower. part of it is now a ruin, but the "Tour de Montaigne" is yet religiously preserved. The first floor of this circular tower formed his occasional bedroom, and a smaller square chamber adjoining it, his dressing room. The corresponding

* This sentence Montaigne expressed partly in Greek, partly in Latin—written thus on the main beam, in capital letters:—"ΟΥ ΚΑΤΑΛΑΜΒΑΝΩ—ΕΠΕΧΩ—ΣΚΕΠΤΟΜΑΙ, MORE DUCE ET SENSU."

† *De Rerum Natura,* vi, 678, 679. The words within brackets are omitted.

‡ Payen, Nouveaux Documents sur Montaigne (1850), 56—60; Bigorie de Laschamps, *Michel de Montaigne* (1860), 485—493.

rooms on the second floor were his library and study. Hence, as from a watch-tower, when tired of books and pen, and disinclined for any more active exercise or for company, he could overlook a large portion of his house and domain. But to describe his tower and its contents in other words than his own would be impertinent:—"I see beneath me my garden, my court-yard, my base court, and most parts of my house. Now, I turn over the leaves of one book; now, of another. Sometimes I fall into a reverie; sometimes I dictate my dreams—as you see—whilst walking up and down. . . . . . . Here I pass most of the days of my life, and most hours of the day. Close to it is a cabinet where, in winter, I can have a fire. . . . . From my writing table I can see all my books, ranged on five tiers of shelves, all round the room. . . . . . . Here, I am really lord; and I strive to keep my domain intact, that this one corner may be free from invasion, whether conjugal or filial, or neighbourly. Elsewhere, my rule is but nominal. Miserable, to my mind, is the man who has no retreat, where he can be really by himself; where he can be his own courtier; where he can hide himself. Ambition well rewards her votaries by keeping them always in evidence, like a statue on a market-place. Truly, a great fortune is a great servitude; * and the most secret retiring-place of such people is no retirement at all. . . . . . For my part, I should find it much more tolerable to be alone always, than never to be alone."†

Montaigne's choice of his books was quite as characteristic as his mode of using them: "I but rarely read modern books," he says, "because I think those of the

Montaigne's choice of authors.

* Seneca: "Magna servitus est magna fortuna." *Ad Polybium Consolatio*, c. 26.

† *Des trois Commerces.* (*Essais*, B. iii, c. 3.)

ancients fuller and nobler. I seldom use Greek books, since I am but an imperfect master of the language." Plutarch, in his French garb, became a prime favourite. So were Virgil and Lucretius; Catullus and Horace—such is his own order of enumeration—Lucan, Terence, and Seneca. Cicero he read copiously, but was much more prone to criticise him than to praise. And the authors towards whom we have that feeling are often, it may be added, the authors from whom readers get most profit. Of all Roman poetry, the *Georgics* seemed to him the flower. "I think it," he says, "the most finished work of Poetry. It enables one to put the finger on passages in the *Æneid*, which the author would certainly have brushed up a little,* had he had the time." Of "the good Terence," he says that howsoever often he read him, some new grace and beauty was sure to come in view. After alluding to comparisons which had been made between Virgil and Lucretius, "I think," he adds, "the comparison is an unequal one, but I have need to re-fortify myself in that opinion, every time that I find myself under the charm of a noble passage in Lucretius."† Without the delay of counting the quotations contained in the *Essais*, it can scarcely, I think, be unsafe to estimate the classic authors there severally cited, as amounting to more than a hundred. And the various works of all these, at the least, must have adorned his tower.

Montaigne's Books of Modern Literature.

In modern literature his range seems a narrow one, as we now look back upon it, along the vista of three hundred years, and call to mind the masterpieces which occupy our own shelves, and which date their birth within that period. But in History, with a multitude of minor note, he had

* Ausquels l'aucteur eust donné encore quelque tours de pigne."—*Des livres*, b. II, c. 10.

† Ib.

Eginhard, Joinville, Commines, Du Bellay, Froissart, Macchiavelli, and Guicciardini. If with the modern Poetry we group that allied section of literature which Montaigne himself calls "*les livres simplement plaisants*," he had in that pregnant department, Rabelais, Boccaccio, Petrarch, Ariosto, Tasso, and Dante, without mentioning one name—not even that of Ronsard—in the long list of those second-rate poets, of which only at that date France itself could boast; and of some of whom it may safely be said that their fame would not have sunk quite so low, had not their contemporaries lifted it so much too high. Our Father Chaucer, I suppose, and all his followers, would have been useless to Montaigne. And the whole tribe of the Chivalric Romances were the object of his unqualified disdain.—"As to the *Amadis* and the books of that sort they were not able to charm me, even in my childhood. I will say too," he adds, "whether it be said boldly or rashly, that this scrutinizing old soul of mine has ceased to warm, not only to Ariosto, but even to Ovid. His fluency and his inventiveness, which were formerly a joy, are now scarcely an amusement. I give my opinion freely on all subjects (as you see), those included which lie, perhaps, beyond my competence, and over which I claim no kind of jurisdiction. What I say, exhibits the measure of my own insight, not the measure of the things themselves."*

The modern books in Montaigne's Library.

Directness, vigour, and simplicity, are the qualities which Montaigne prized next to fullness of matter. For mere rhetoricians, and for the weavers of ingenious and subtle speculations and "argumentations," he had an infinite contempt: "I seek books which make their first onset into the thick of the fight. . . . . I know what 'Death' means, and what 'Pleasure' is. There is no need to waste time in

* *Essais*, b. ii, c. 10.

Qualities in writers prized by Montaigne.

anatomizing them for me. That sort of thing may do for the school, the bar, and the pulpit, where we have ample leisure to go to sleep; certain that if we wake up in a quarter of an hour or so, we shall be in good time to recover the thread of the argument."* The only class of writers in whom, as it seems, he could tolerate something of long-windedness, were those who were describing what they had themselves done or seen. But, he adds, "I would rather know what Brutus said to one of his private friends in his tent on the eve of the battle, than hear his speech to his army on the morrow." Finally, it must suffice to say that he had a special fondness for collections of letters. Of the thousand volumes, or thereabout, which as he tells us he had on his shelves, one hundred were epistolographers.

Montaigne's opinions of books.

Montaigne had inherited the books of La Boëtie, but these he has nowhere particularised. Nor do we know accurately the date of the dispersion of Montaigne's Library. Mainly by the zealous exertions of his devoted admirer, Dr. J. F. Payen, of Paris, about forty volumes have been recovered or identified. Those which Dr. Payen has himself succeeded in obtaining will, it is to be hoped, never again be scattered. Many of these have that precious peculiarity of an appended critical summary or estimate, in Montaigne's own hand, the motive and purpose of which he has described in these characteristic words: "To compensate a little for the treacherousness of my memory, —a fault so excessive that more than once it has happened that I have taken up, as new and unknown to me, books which I had carefully read some years before, and had even scrawled over with my notes,—I have, for some time past" [He is writing in 1580], "formed the habit of adding, at

* *Essais*, b. ii, c. 10.

the end of every book, . . . the time when I finished reading it, and the judgment to which, on the whole, my perusal has led me." Three of these critical opinions he has quoted in his essay *Des Livres,* those namely which he wrote on Commines, on Guicciardini, and on the *Mémoires* of Du Bellay. All his notes are in French. "Whatever tongue my books may speak, I speak to them," he says, "in mine." Amongst the most copiously annotated of his books which are now known to exist, are the *Commentaries* of Cæsar; the *Odyssey;* and, most precious of all, a copy of the 1588 edition of his own *Essais,* covered with notes and variations in his autograph, which copy was given to the Feuillants of Bordeaux, by his widow, and is now preserved in the Public Library of that city.* A copy of the *Histoire des Rois et Princes de Poloigne,* "printed at Paris, in 1573, has but a single line of comment in Montaigne's hand, but bears on its title page this note in the hand of a subsequent possessor: "*Achepté a Bordeaux de la bibliothèque de feu Michel de Montaigne, autheur des Essais, le* 3 *Juin* 1633." Montaigne died on the 13 September, 1592. So that within forty-one years, at all events, his library had been either dispersed or sold in the lump.

Collectors seek as eagerly for the books of another illustrious Frenchman of the sixteenth century, as for those of Montaigne, but for different reasons, and with better success. Both Montaigne and Thuanus knew how to use books, with profit to the world as well as to themselves. But the one cared little for the garb, if the wearer was to his mind; the other delighted to clothe his favourites in the

* The accomplished bibliographer M. Gustave Brunet published the "various readings" of this copy in 1844. They had been previously used by Naigeon for his Edition of 1802.

richest coverings, and was almost as anxious about the spotless purity of their "condition," as about the weight and worth of their contents.

The life and character of De Thou.

James Augustus de Thou was born in the house of his ancestors at Paris, on the 8th of October, 1553. He is one of the very many famous men who had an infancy so fragile that it was thought doubtful if they would reach manhood. But, as often chances, the weakness which checked the growth of De Thou's body fostered the growth of his mind. Having a natural aptitude of hand, he learnt to write before he knew how to read. Dionysius Lambinus, Francis Hotman, James Cujas, were among his instructors. Joseph Scaliger was one of his earliest friends. The first public event which deeply impressed him was the day of St. Bartholomew. The sights which met his eyes as he went to church, on the morning of that awful Sunday, without daring (as he tells us) to shed a tear, were burnt in alike on his memory and his heart. For some days he shut himself up, young as he was, in the house, rather than run the risk of having to gaze on the like again.*

Long years afterwards, when the youth of promise had become the man of mature age and of European fame, those horrors would rise intrusively before his view, but "now," he would say, "I can weep at them."†

The years 1573, 1574, and 1575, were spent by De Thou chiefly in Italy. He visited eagerly the libraries of Florence, of Venice, and of Rome. It was at Venice that he made his first considerable acquisitions for the noble library which he had begun to form before he left home,‡ and he

* *Commentariorum de Vita Sua*, liber i. (Buckley's Edit., p. 11).

† Ib., lib. iii.

‡ Ib., lib. i, (Buckley's Ed., p. 23)......"bibliothecam *jam inchoatam* multum locupletavit."

added largely to them at Lyons on his return. Four subsequent years were devoted to reading and to intercourse with men eminent in letters and in law. He then resumed his travels by visiting the Netherlands, but was disappointed in the plan he had formed for crossing into England. He did not fail, however, to visit Antwerp and Plantinus. Notwithstanding the miseries of the time, he found seventeen presses still at work.*

De Thou's public career.

It was not until 1578 that De Thou entered the Parliament. Even at twenty-five the charm of retirement, and the attractions of study, made him regard the magistracy as lying wide apart from his proper sphere in life,† and he prayed God with great earnestness, he tells us, that the councillor, whose place he was to fill, might recover from the malady, the fatal issue of which had been anticipated by the virtual choice of a successor. But it was the destiny of De Thou to have greatness repeatedly thrust upon him. His present dignity did not preclude his enjoyment of a long tour in Germany in 1579. In subsequent years he had several occasions to travel, often on public business, in various parts of France, and he everywhere profited by the opportunities of becoming acquainted with eminent men, and of laying up stores of information for that *History of his Own Times*, the plan of which had been conceived at least as early as 1581.‡ At Bourdeaux, he became acquainted with Montaigne, then Mayor of that city, whom he characterises as a man of open disposition, an enemy of all constraint, clear from all participation in political intrigues, and thoroughly conversant with affairs, especially with those of Guienne.§ This friendship was formed in

De Thou's intercourse with learned men.

* *Commentariorum de Vita Sua*, lib. i. (Buckley's Edit., p. 27).

† Ib., p. 27.

‡ Ib., lib. ii.

§ Ibid.

1582. He had much learned intercourse, about the same time, with Pierre Pithou, and with Vinet de Barbezieux; and he records a trivial incident which has still its interest. Vinet showed him a letter from George Buchanan, in which that illustrious scholar described the feelings with which he entered on extreme old age, regarding himself as a man already dead to the world around him. "Those words," says De Thou in his Autobiography, "I never forgot."

Until he had entered his thirty-fourth year, De Thou continued to be an ecclesiastic, having taken the "minor orders" at an early age. When he became a President of Parliament he was divested of his orders, and soon married Mary de Barbançon de Cany. In 1589, he made another tour through Italy and Switzerland, visiting the Libraries, and everywhere courting the conversation of men of letters, of statesmen, and of diplomatists. To this wide intercourse and to his own active participation in affairs, his History owes no small part of its merits, as certainly as to his learning, his judicial intellect, and his diligence in the labours of the study.

De Thou served Henry IV throughout his reign as one of his ablest diplomatists, and most trusted councillors. His functions were as various as were his talents. In 1593, as we shall see hereafter, he was made Superintendent (literally "Grand Master") of the Royal Library. A few years later he became—somewhat against his will—one of the triumvirate who replaced Sully in the direction of the Finances of France. But he seems always to have found time for some measure of progress in his great work, the first eighteen books of which he published in 1604. These were followed in 1607-9 by sixty-two more books. The remainder (comprising Books 81-138) did not appear until three years after his death. De Thou's History had the honour of figuring in the Roman prohibitory Index, side by side with the Decree in which the Parliament of Paris condemned the assassin of Henry IV.* De Thou's History of his own Times.

It is to the honour of England that by far the finest and most complete edition of the *Historia sui temporis* came from an English publisher (1733). Few, if any, of our own historians have appeared with even an approach to like splendour, in combination with critical skill, and a copious apparatus. Thomas Carte and Dr. Mead share with Buckley, the publisher, the credit of this beautiful edition. Had the book been written in almost any tongue save Latin, Buckley's edition would probably have been now among the costly rarities of literature.

De Thou's History has been translated into French, but not into English. Johnson once contemplated the task, and Carte actually commenced it, but Mead purchased his MS. and other materials, and preferred to give liberal encouragement to the sumptuous reprint of the original.†

Modest, laborious, and disinterested in every stage of his diversified career, De Thou's immortal work bears in every chapter the impress of the virtues of the man, as legibly as it bears those of the genius and insight of the writer. Eminently impartial and tolerant, although produced in an age of furious hatreds and of sanguinary persecutions, it owes nothing of its impartiality or of its tolerance to that sceptical and mocking spirit which has often been so serious a drawback from the splendid merits of French literature. De Thou's candour is not greater than his earnestness. Nor would it be easy to find, in such brief compass, such expressive testimony to the merits of an author as lies in the simple statement that the work which Bossuet quotes

* Duplessis, art. *De Thou*, in *Biographie Universelle*, xlv, 504, note.
† Nichols, *Literary Anecdotes*, ii, 25.

repeatedly as "a faithful history,"* is the same which Bayle characterises as a "master-piece."†

The Library of De Thou.

The Library which, as we have seen, De Thou began before he was of age, continued to be the object of his solicitude almost to the day of his death (7 May, 1617). No cost and no pains were spared to obtain books at once in their best editions, and most sumptuous form. In the case of important new books, copies peculiarly choice were sometimes printed expressly for this collection.‡ Theology; Greek and Latin Classics; Modern History; the best Literature, not only of France, but of all the great nations of the Continent of Europe, were here assembled, with such careful *selection* that, after the lapse of nearly half a century, and after large expenditure, the number of printed volumes was still but 8000; that of MSS. nearly 1000. "The preservation of this Library," said De Thou, in his last Will, "is for the advantage as well of literature as of my family. I forbid that it should be sold, scattered, or divided."§ The custody of it he confided to Pierre Dupuy, with instructions that the collection should be made liberally serviceable to students, under proper restrictions. But his precautions were vain. The noble Library of which it had been said, "He who has not seen it, has not seen Paris" (*Lutetiam non vidisse censetur, qui* Bibliothecam Thuanam *non vidit*), was

Provisions respecting it in his Will.

* *e. g., Défense de l'Histoire des Variations*, Disc. 1. (*Œuvres*, 1836, vi, 334.)

† *Dictionnaire*, § Ronsard, Note B (Ed. 1820, xii, 568).

‡ D'Argonne, *Mélanges*, I, 26 [published under the pseudonym of Vigneul-Marville].

§ *Bibliothecam meam......quam integram conservari non solum familiæ meæ, sed etiam rei literariæ interest, dividi, vendi ac dissipari veto, eamque communem cum numismatis aureis, argenteis et æreis antiquis inter filios, qui literis operam navabunt, facio, ita ut etiam exteris aliisque philologis ad usum publicum pateat, etc.* Thuani *Testamentum*, (*Sylloge Scriptorum varii argumenti*, forming the 7th vol. of the *Historia*, in Buckley's Ed., c. vii, p. 2).

kept entire for little more than sixty years after its founder's death. The historian's descendants suffered many misfortunes, but for so long they preserved and augmented his Library.* It was not the greatest of their calamities that in the second generation, the discharge of diplomatic functions under "the great" monarch, entailed debts which necessitated the alienation of the most precious of heirlooms. In 1679, a public auction of the printed books began, but, at a very early stage of the sale, the President de Menars intervened; purchased the whole Library—the volumes which had been already dispersed, of course, excepted—in bulk; and during subsequent years, largely augmented it. At his death it passed, successively, to Armand Gaston, Cardinal de Rohan, and to his heirs, the Cardinal de Soubise and the Prince de Soubise, who also made considerable additions. At the Prince's death, in 1787, it had grown to nearly 50,000 volumes. His heirs endeavoured in 1788 to find a purchaser for the whole at the price of £12,000, but obtained an offer of £8000 only. Disappointed in this effort, they offered the Library to public sale early in the following year. Partly by means of an arrangement with a prominent bookseller, and partly by the effect of English competition, the sale produced about £10,400.† It is supposed that if the same books were now sold in the same way they would certainly bring three times that sum, and perhaps much more. The sale, which began in January, 1789, lasted till May. Of those who crossed the Channel to attend it, probably not one had the smallest anticipation that they were then on the birthplace, and at the very eve, of a Revolution, so mighty in results as to make the May of 1789 for ever memorable.

Sale of the conjoined De Thou and Soubise Libraries in 1789.

* Quesnel, *Catalogus bibliothecæ Thuanæ* (1679), *præfatio*.

† Brunet, *Manuel*, v, 842 (Edit. of 1863).

De Thou's Manuscripts had been purchased by Colbert; and passed, in 1730, into the Royal Library. Bishop Huet tells us* that he made great exertion to obtain the purchase for that Library of all De Thou's Collections intact, but vainly; the king refusing his sanction.†

The Library of Grotius.

Many men have owed their chief enjoyment of life to books. Grotius owed, literally, to the love of books his life and liberty. But, beyond the famous incident at Louvestein,‡ and the facts that he began early to collect books; was wont to spend over them the hours that others allotted to sleep; and, as all the world knows, turned them to very noble account, little is recorded about his Library. He enjoyed the correspondence and friendship of De Thou, although there was almost half a century of difference in their ages. Born at Rostock, April 10, 1583, he is said to have disputed publicly on mathematics, jurisprudence, and philosophy in the University of Leyden in 1597, and there-

* Huetii *Commentarius de rebus ad eum pertinentibus*, 65, seqq.

† Collectors have often been puzzled by the variety of the armorial bearings which occur on Thuanus volumes. To indicate them minutely would involve long heraldic descriptions, occupying too much space for a note. But it may be useful to state, briefly, that at least five sorts of armorial decorations occur on legitimate De Thou books, viz.: (1. 1574—1587). *De Thou*, simply, with his name under the shield. (2. 1587—1601.) *De Thou* and *De Barbançon*, with the monogram J.A.M.and Θ. (3. 1603—1616.) *De Thou* and *De La Chastre*, Quarterly, with the monograms J. A. G. Θ. (4. 1642—1659?) *De Thou*, as borne by J. A. de Thou, Baron de Mesley, with *La Chastre*, *Picardet*, and *Le Prévost*. (5. 1660?—1663.) The same, with additional quarterings, surmounted by a *Count's* coronet, and with the motto *Mane nobiscum, Domine*. Engravings of all will be found in M. Briquet's *Notes sur . . . les Armoiries de J. A. De Thou*, in the *Bull. du Bibliophile*, xiv, 896-903.

‡. Hæc ea, quæ Domini solita portare libellos,
Grotiadæ fuerat pondere facta gravis;
Mutatum neque sensit onus: quod enim illa ferebat,
Id quoque, sed spirans, bibliotheca fuit.

fore when he was but fourteen years of age. In the following year he was presented to Henry IV. Such precocities but seldom support in manhood their early promise. Grotius, however, outstripped all expectation. Before the year 1600 had expired, he had given to the world editions of Martianus Capella, and of Aratus, with notes of sterling value, and had translated into Latin an elaborate work on Navigation. In the following year he published poems which placed him, at a leap, in the first rank of modern Latin poets. In 1609, he published *Mare Liberum*.

The library incident which gives Grotius a place in these pages occurred in 1620. During the fierce conflicts of Remonstrants and Contra-Remonstrants which induced so many disorders in the United Provinces, Olden-Barneveldt and Grotius were tried for treason. Barneveldt was sentenced to death; Grotius to imprisonment for life and the confiscation of his property. He was strictly confined in the Castle of Louvestein, near Gorcum, but was allowed to receive from time to time a supply of books—partly his own, partly borrowed from his friends—which were carried to and fro in a large chest. At first, that chest was rigidly examined, but the functionaries, who had always found it filled with books, at last shirked the trouble of a search which had so often been fruitless. On this negligence becoming habitual, the wife of Grotius formed a plan for freeing him, after twenty weary months of confinement. Having obtained the usual permission to exchange the books, she contrived to get the workman into the chest instead of the tools; remaining herself in his chamber, and entrusting the chest with its precious contents to the care of a faithful and sharp-witted maid-servant. When borne away, as had been usual, by two soldiers, it was thought by one of them to be even heavier than it was wont to be, and he asked jestingly

The escape of Grotius from Louvestein.

—"Have we got the Arminian himself here?" The good wife had nerve enough to answer, with a smile: "You have, perhaps, some Arminian books." The chest reached Gorcum safely, whence, by the help of friends, its half-stifled tenant speedily escaped to Brabant,* to resume the career which has given lustre to his name.

The Library of Swift.

The special interest which attaches to the Library of Jonathan Swift arises from his habit of lavishly annotating his books. Like Montaigne, he often marked on them the date of perusal, and wrote on the fly-leaves a summary of the opinion he had formed of the Author. Very outspoken are these reviewals, but, unlike those of Montaigne, they usually bear the stamp of having been written in hot haste, and with that wonderful flux of vehement objurgation in which Swift, I suppose, has never been surpassed. In addition, too, to his summaries, he often loads the pages with marginal notes containing minute criticisms on his author's particular statements and opinions. The range of these annotations is a wide one. And many have been preserved, although the books that contain them were dispersed, soon after his death, in 1745.

The books annotated by Swift.

Among the Greek books known to have been thus commentated are works of Plato, Xenophon, Herodotus, Strabo, Philostratus, Dio Cassius, Suidas, Stobæus, Isocrates, Procopius, and Polybius, together with the *Anthology*, and the *Antiquæ Musicæ Auctores*. Among the Latin classics, Virgil, Horace, Terence, Tacitus, Eutropius, Justin, Livy, Valerius Maximus, and the *Historiæ Augustæ Scriptores*. In French literature, Rabelais, Boileau, and La Bruyere. In English History, Clarendon, Herbert of Cherbury,

* Luden, *Hugo Grotius nach seinen Schicksalen und Schriften dargestellt*, 165—168. Comp. Grotii *Epistolæ*, Ep. 142.

Burnet, and Ludlow's *Memoirs*. In General and Foreign History, Comines, De Thou, Baronius, Davila, and Morrei. In English poetry, the works of Pope and Garth. In Philosophy and Polygraphy, the works of Bacon, Hobbes, Bodin, and Machiavelli. The only modern poet—not English or French—whom I notice in the long catalogue, as occurring among the annotated authors, is Tasso, whose *Jerusalem* Swift possessed only in the translation of Fairfax. Among the minor and miscellaneous books, occur the *Discourse on Trade* of Sir Josiah Child, the *Commonwealth of Oceana* of Harrington, the *Satyre Menippée*, the *History of the Common Law* of Sir Matthew Hale, the *Prophecies* of Nostradamus, the *Travels* of Bernier, the *Rehearsal transposed* of Marvel, and Thomas Burnet's *Theory of the Earth*. So that it may fairly be inferred that there is but little hyperbole in calling Swift's studies encyclopædical. But they had whimsically characteristic exceptions. He possessed no Shakespeare, nor will any allusion be found to Shakespeare throughout the nineteen volumes of his works and letters.* And of the three dramatic authors who do occur in the Catalogue of his Library—Ben Jonson, Wycherley, and Rowe—two were gifts.

Swift's character as a writer.

Swift, indeed, although he had a truly creative genius, was not in the best sense a poet, and had no love for poetry. With all his marvellous endowments, he could never raise himself above his own personality. In his most enchaining fictions, the passions and hatreds of the party pamphleteer are continually peeping from the curtain. In *Gulliver* he has created a world of his own, peopled with beings of most unquestionable originality, yet in describing Lilliput and the Lilliputians, he has an eye constantly introverted upon

* Scott has noticed this characteristic fact (*Memoirs of Swift*, 2nd ed., 466).

England and the English. His directness, his strength, and felicity of expression, no less than his pungent wit, his cutting satire, and his wonderful power of vivid description, are more than enough to keep him in that conspicuous place amongst great yet secondary writers, which has so long been assigned to him, but his lack of those nobler qualities which belong rather to the soul than to the intellect will ever prevent him from rising higher. In the first rank of authors there are no cynics. And Swift was something more than cynical; in the consummate writer, even when at his best, there was always a strong dash of the Mohock.

Swift's elaborately annotated copy of Clarendon is preserved in Archbishop Marsh's Library at Dublin. Scott caused the notes to be transcribed into his own copy at Abbotsford, and has printed them in his edition of Swift, together with the notes on Burnet's *History of his own Times*, on Addison's *Freeholder*, and on Tindal's *Rights of the Christian Church*. The Clarendon, with the Works of Plato, and "My best Bible," were specially bequeathed to Dr. Francis Wilson, who seems to have died before Swift. There is no other mention of the Library in the Dean's will.

Goethe's Libraries at Frankfort and at Weimar.

In that charming picture of life at Frankfort, as it was a hundred years ago, which we have in the early chapters of the *Aus meinem Leben: Dichtung und Wahrheit*, Goethe has himself told us what sort of library it was which formed his first literary tastes and led to his earliest acquisitions. "My father," he says, "possessed the beautiful Dutch editions of the Latin classics which, for uniformity's sake, he sought to complete in quartos. In Roman antiquities, and in the choicer works of Jurisprudence, he was well provided. There was no lack of the great Italian poets, and for Tasso he had a special love. He had, too, the best and most recent works of travel, and took delight in correcting and extending, by their help, his own copies of the older travellers, Keysler and Nemeitz. Nor had he failed to collect around him the most useful works of reference, such as Dictionaries and Encyclopædias of all sorts."* This part of the Library, in bindings of suitable gravity, lined the walls of the study or office. The rest of it had a room apart—a sort of entresol—and was, for the most part, neatly bound in vellum, with elegantly written lettering-pieces. Of more miscellaneous contents, it was doubtless greatly more attractive. The German poets of the day,—such as they were,—gave Goethe a rage for versifying; and in comparing notes with other boys, having a like fancy for rhyming, he owns that his own productions seemed to him already to have outstripped their competitors.† The paternal library.

Canitz, Hagedorn, Drollinger, Gellert, Kreutz, Haller, stood on a row in this part of the Library in handsome half-bindings. Klopstock, the good father would by no means admit to the like distinction. Poetry without rhyme was to him no poetry at all. But the *Messiah* was smuggled in, by an old friend of the family, and was not merely read, but learnt almost by heart.‡

The numerous plates with which Merian had adorned certain well-known editions of the Bible, and of the *Historische Chronik* of Gottfried, in weighty folio, led the admiring childish eyes from the illustrations to the text. And to the medley of images and impressions of fact and fable which thus began to people that capacious brain, were

* *Aus meinem Leben*, B. i, (Par., 1836, iii, 323).
† Ib. (325).
‡ Ib. (339).

speedily added another large store from the *Metamorphoses* of Ovid, the *Telemachus* of Fenelon (in Neukirch's translation), and the *Crusoe* of De Foe. But, whatever the charms of wanderings like these, along "the shores of old Romance," the boy-poet was not so engrossed by them as to be incapable of deriving great delight from Anson's *Voyage round the World*, and from following, with his fingers on a globe, the circumnavigator's course. All these materials for mind and memory seem to have been derived from the paternal Library. The first slender foundation of that collection of his own which the traveller now visits with so much interest in the 'Frauenplan' at Weimar, was laid by a series of boyish purchases, for a few kreutzers, at the stall of a dealer in chap-books. *Eulenspiegel, The Four Sons of Aymon, The Emperor Octavian, The Fair Melusina, Fortunatus with his Purse*, and the rest of that numerous tribe, down to *The Wandering Jew*, had, of course, to compete with the attractions of tarts and sweetmeats, but they were often victors.* Very blurred was the type, and very fragile the paper, but a couple of the smallest coins happily sufficed to replace a damaged copy.

The foundation of Goethe's youthful Library.

Goethe's first acquaintance with Homer was made in the course of a visit to an uncle, the Pastor Stark, in whose Library he found a sort of abridged prose translation of the *Iliad*, entitled *Homer's Narrative of the Conquest of the Kingdom of Troy*. This, he tells us, at first gave him inexpressible pleasure,† but he was disgusted at the absence of any account of the fall of the city.

Family Readings at Frankfort.

In the family circle at Frankfort, which Goethe has so vividly photographed for us, the excellent practice of reading some chosen book aloud was in full vogue. But it was

* *Aus meinem Leben*, B. i (Par., 1836, iii, 326).

† Ib. (p. 328).

of grave importance to make no mistake in the choice, for the worthy head was utterly intolerant of vacillation and incompleteness. Whatever book was begun must needs be finished, even if it should prove as long a business as the siege of Troy itself. Thus Bower's *History of the Popes*, incautiously commenced on a certain winter's evening, led to a dreary time. I doubt if Goethe was ever of Clarendon's paradoxical opinion that there is profit even in reading bad books, because though they fail to serve the author's end, they will always serve some other, yet he has certainly borne this testimony in favour of poor Bower, that his reluctantly won knowledge of the *History of the Popes* stood him in some stead in after times.* The very repulsiveness of the book so read may have helped to impress it on the memory, by another operation of that mysterious law which brings to the minds of most of us, on revisiting a scene we have been parted from, the vivid recollection of what was formerly felt or suffered there.

The youthful Goethe was not deterred by the bulk or the dryness of Gesner's *Isagoge*, or of Morhof's *Polyhistor*, from plunging into their depths. Still more acceptable were the multifarious tomes of Bayle's *Dictionary*, with their perversely but amusingly discursive ramblings into all the bypaths, and only too often into the ditches, of history and of social life. He owns that for a time he got more of confusion than of knowledge into his head from this labyrinth of reading.

An auto-da-fé of books at Frankfort.

Another book-incident of that early period dwelt long in the poet's mind. He witnessed in the market-place of Frankfort the public burning of a French romance of ill fame; and could not rest until he had hunted np a copy. That copy, he adds, was to his own knowledge very far

* *Aus meinem Leben*, B. i (Par., 1836, iii, 328).

indeed from being the only copy which owed both its acquisition and its circulation, to the anxious care of the magistrates.

His book acquisitions at Leipsic.

When he had passed from the paternal home to his student life at Leipsic, he records his exchange, with a friend, of a set of German books for a set of classics, but the classics did not keep a really durable hold upon Goethe. His recent able biographer, Mr. Lewes, says truly that to him the ancient artists were far more fruitful than the ancient writers. Yet he was continually returning to them. At a later period he notes that he never really enjoyed Homer till he read him at Palermo. In this early time, his transitions are very rapid. In 1770 he writes to Herder, "I read only the Greeks."* Next year, Shakespeare engrosses him: "The first page of his that I read," he says, "made me his for life; and when I had finished a single play, I stood like one born blind, on whom a miraculous hand bestows sight in a moment."† His Strasburgh notebooks indicate much reading in German, as well as in the newly acquired English.‡ He has admiration to spare for Ossian and for Pope. But as we get further into the "Storm and Stress" period, the influence on his mind of French literature, and especially of the French drama, theretofore considerable, quickly declines. Still more notable is the emphatic acknowledgment: "I loved the Bible and treasured it. . . . . To it I owed my moral culture. Its narratives, its doctrines, and its imagery, were deeply impressed on my mind."§ In

Goethe's youthful studies.

* "Die Griechen sind mein einzig Studium."—*Briefe an Herder.*

† *Oration on Shakespeare*, as translated by Lewes, *Life of Goethe*, 2nd edit., 91.

‡ They also contain, at this date, many extracts and analyses from Mendelssohn, Fabricius, Giordano Bruno, and the *Imitation.*

§ *Aus meinem Leben*, ut supra.

maturer days he made vast strides in all literatures, save only *that*.

Description of the House and Library.

The house and the Library have been described by Mr. Lewes in words which may well, without apology, be quoted at some length:—"The passer-by sees through the windows the busts of the Olympian Gods, which stand there as symbols of calmness and *completeness* [?] On entering the hall, the eye rests upon . . . . the plan of Rome which decorates the wall, and on Meyer's *Aurora* which colours the ceiling. The group of Ildefonso stands near the door; and on the threshold welcome speaks in the word '*Salve.*'" After describing the rooms devoted to reception, and to the art-collections, Mr. Lewes proceeds: "Compared with the Weimar standard of the day, those rooms were of palatial magnificence; but compared even with the Weimar standard, the rooms into which we now enter are of a more than bourgeois simplicity. Passing through an ante-chamber, where in cupboards stand his mineralogical collections, we enter the study, ... furnished with a simplicity quite touching to behold. In the centre stands a plain oval table of unpolished oak. No arm-chair is to be seen, no sofa, nothing which speaks of ease. A plain hard chair has beside it the basket in which he used to place his handkerchief. Against the wall, on the right, is a long pear-tree table, with book-shelves on which stand lexicons and manuals. Here hangs a pincushion, venerable in dust, with the visiting cards and other trifles which death has made sacred. Here, also, a medallion of Napoleon, with this circumscription: '*Scilicet immenso superest ex nomine multum.*' On the side wall, again, a book-case with some works of poets. On the wall to the left is a long desk of soft wood, at which he was wont to write. On it lie the original MSS. of *Götz*, and the *Elegies*,

The Study.

and a bust of Napoleon, in milk-white glass which in the light shimmers with blue and flame-colour: hence prized as an illustration of the *Farbenlehre*. A sheet of paper with notes of contemporary history is fastened near the door, and behind this door schematic tables of music and geology. The same door leads into his bedroom. From the other side of the study, we enter the library . . . . Rough deal shelves hold the books with paper labels on which are written '*Philosophy*,' '*History*,' '*Poetry*,' &c., to indicate the classification. It was very interesting to look over this collection, and the English reader will imagine the feelings with which I took down a volume of Taylor's *Historic Survey of German Poetry*, sent by Carlyle, and found in the piece of paper used as a book-mark, a bit of Carlyle's own handwriting."*

Plutarch, among the ancients; Niebuhr, Carlyle, Béranger, Victor Hugo, Delavigne, Salvandy, and Scott, among his own contemporaries, were the authors whom Goethe is recorded to have read or listened to,—"with the eagerness of youth,"—in the latest years and months of his life. The final book, of all, which occupied him—it was in his hands on the day immediately preceding the day of his death (22 March, 1832)—was Salvandy's *Seize Mois, ou la Révolution et les Révolutionnaires*.† In this instance, it was doubtless the author's subject, not his powers, that gained for a now forgotten book so memorable a distinction. The last audible words which Goethe uttered were these,—"*More light!*" Those pregnant words were swiftly answered.

Death of Goethe.

Among the many famous men who listened with deep emotion to the words "*Goethe is dead*," Scott will often rise

* Lewes, *Life of Goethe*, 376-378.

† Ib., 558.

to the memory, as the tale of that death is told. He was about to gratify a long cherished wish by turning much out of his way, in coming home from Italy, to pay Goethe a visit at Weimar. The news reached him at Naples. "Alas for Goethe!" he said, "but he, at least, has died at home. Let us to Abbotsford." In talking with Mr. Cheney, a day or two afterwards, he returned to the subject. His interlocutor told him that, in the previous year, he had seen Goethe, despite his great age, in full possession of all his faculties. "It is better," said Scott, "to die than to survive them." . . . . "The worst of all," he added thoughtfully, "would have been to have survived their partial loss, and yet to be conscious of his state." And then he adverted, with deep feeling, to certain works of Goethe which their illustrious author might well, in his latter moments, have wished to recall.* It is evident that Scott spoke under some such presentiment as that which haunted Swift when he said, in his country walk, "I, too, shall die from the top, like that tree."

Scott's remarks on the Death of Goethe.

To pass from Swift to Goethe, and to Scott, is to pass from a region of thick gloom, where even the light is as darkness, into the broad sunshine. Scott's career, indeed, was for a while obscured by some dark clouds, of a sort which Goethe never knew, but they made the sunset more glorious. Still happier was it that Scott could call to mind his own long array of immortal creations, without any reason to wish any one of them cancelled, on graver grounds than that of youthful immaturity. To Abbotsford, as to Weimar, many a grateful pilgrimage will be made for ages to come, and there is some reason to hope that at both the pilgrim may long be able to look on the workshop, just as the great

* Lockhart, *Life of Scott* (1845), 749.

workman left it. So curious is the infelicity which has usually attended the homes of poets, that the hope must needs be mingled with fear; but as yet, at all events, the library and study at Abbotsford, like the library and study in the *Frauenplan* at Weimar, remain as they were in their day of power. The same year saw both tenantless.

The beginnings of the Library of Scott.

Scott, as a boyish collector of books, began just as Goethe did. The visitor at Abbotsford may still see several volumes of ballads and chap-books, to one of which he has prefixed this MS. note:—"This little collection of stall tracts and ballads was formed by me, when a boy, from the baskets of the travelling pedlars. Until put into its present decent binding, it had such charms for the servants, that it was repeatedly, and with difficulty recovered from their clutches. It contains most of the pieces that were popular about thirty years since [*i.e.* about 1780], and I dare say many that could not now be procured for any price." This note was written in 1810.

Principal contents of the Abbotsford Library.

In Scottish History, and especially in two prominent sections of that history,—the Ecclesiastical, and that which relates to the Jacobite insurrections,—the Library at Abbotsford is, of course, richly stocked both in MSS. and printed books. Equally well provided is it in the departments of early Poetry and early Romantic Prose Fiction, both British and Foreign. Of the works of Scott's contemporaries there is, as may well be imagined, a goodly array in the shape sometimes of presentation copies of the printed editions; sometimes of MSS. in the autograph of the writers. Among special curiosities of another kind may be mentioned a copy of the first edition of Burns' *Poems*, in which Scott, with a stroke of grave satire on the Government of that day, has inserted an Excise Report, in the poet's autograph; and a copy of Byron's *Private*

Correspondence, in the suppressed edition, partially printed in 1824. Among Scott's own MSS. preserved at Abbotsford, are three folio volumes of Notes of Law Lectures, penned in 1791, and autographs of several of the Poems.

But there is nothing more distinctively characteristic of this famous Library than its wonderful assemblage of works on Demonology and Witchcraft, and the curious themes allied therewith. Probably no other such collection was ever formed. With so many striking features, a Catalogue of the Abbotsford Library might have been made a book at once most amusing and instructive—a really valuable contribution to the History of Literature, as well as a delightful appendage to Lockhart's Life. Few Catalogues have been printed so sumptuously,* and none ever deserved fine printing less. It omits to indicate those presentation copies of books which are so characteristic of this Library. It professes to be classified, and it enters under the heading "ENGLISH HISTORY, TOPOGRAPHY, AND ANTIQUITIES,"—to take a random sample, at a glance—the four following books: Camus' *Triumphs of Love;* Lord Manchester's *Al Mondo, a Contemplation of Death and Immortality;* Burton's *Nine Worthies of the World;* and Swift's *Tale of a Tub;* while under the heading "AMERICAN HISTORY AND LITERATURE, AND WORKS ON THE COLONIES," appear Paterson's *National Character of the Athenians*, and Auldjo's *Narrative of an Ascent of Mont Blanc.* It professes to illustrate the use Scott made of his Library, but instead of briefly citing the characteristic and pithy passages,—which would, at once, have turned a mere catalogue into a book of high literary interest,—it tells the reader to see such and such pages, throughout the entire range of the hundred volumes of his works.

* For the Maitland Club. (Glasg. 1838, 4to.)

Description of the Library and Study at Abbotsford.

The general aspect of the Library and Study was excellently described, many years ago, in a paper written for Allan Cunningham's *Anniversary;* and the picture continues in substance to be a truthful one:—"The Library," wrote the anonymous author in 1829, "is an oblong of some fifty feet by thirty, with a projection in the centre opposite the fire-place terminating in a grand bow-window, also filled up with books, and, in fact, constituting a sort of chapel to the church. The roof, . . . and the book-cases are of richly carved oak; the cases reaching high up the walls all round. The collection in this room amounts to some fifteen or twenty thousand volumes; . . . British History and Antiquities filling the whole of the chief wall; English Poetry and Drama, Classics and Miscellanies, one end; Foreign Literature, chiefly French and German, the other. The cases on the side opposite the fire are wired and locked, as containing articles very precious and very portable. One consists entirely of books and MSS. relating to the Insurrections of 1715 and 1745; . . . and another of treatises *De re magica*, both of these being . . . collections of the rarest curiosity. My cicerone pointed out, in one corner, a magnificent set of Montfaucon, fifteen volumes folio, bound in the richest manner in scarlet, and stamped with the royal arms,—the gift of King George IV. There are few living authors of whose works presentation copies are not to be found here. My friend showed me inscriptions of that sort in, I believe, every European dialect extant. The books are all in prime condition, and in bindings that would satisfy Dr. Dibdin. . . . . . . Connected with this fine room . . . is a smaller Library, the *sanctum* of the author. This room . . . contains, of what is properly called furniture, nothing but a small writing table in the centre, a plain arm-chair covered with black

Scott's Sanctum.

leather, and a single chair besides. . . . On either side of the fireplace there are shelves filled with books of reference, chiefly, of course, folios. . . . A light gallery runs round three sides of the room, and is reached by a hanging stair of carved oak in one corner. There are only two portraits —an original of the beautiful and melancholy head of Claverhouse, and a small full length of Rob Roy."* A few years later another visitor to Abbotsford remarked that so many of the volumes were enriched with comments or anecdotes in Scott's own hand, that to look over his books was in some degree to converse with him.†

One darling ambition of the founder of Abbotsford has not, in the providential course of events, been realized in accordance with his hopes. The misfortunes which overclouded his later years threatened, for a time, to defeat another long-cherished wish by stripping Abbotsford of its most precious heirlooms. But this latter failure was averted, and so averted as to shed new lustre on house and founder. The Library of Abbotsford, with the entire contents of the house, were, in 1830, restored to Scott by his trustees and creditors, "as the best means the creditors have of expressing their very high sense of his most honourable conduct, and in grateful acknowledgment of the unparalleled and most successful exertions he has made, and continues to make for them."‡ Visits to Abbotsford are now paid to the abode not alone of a famous author, but of a man who chose the sacrifice of health and life as preferable to failure in an obligation, the fulfilment of which most even among honourable and sanguine men would have deemed an impossibility. The life was sacrificed, but the task was achieved.

* Reprinted by Lockhart, (its author,) *Life of Scott*, 554.

† J. L. Adolphus, MS. journal, printed ut sup. 664.

‡ Ib. 714.

Southey and his abode at Keswick.

By Robert Southey was collected a Library greater, I suppose, in intrinsic value, and certainly much more numerous, than ever before had been brought together by a man whose whole estate and means lay, as he once said of himself, in his inkstand. More than fourteen thousand volumes, skilfully chosen, and still more skilfully used, were collected in that unpretending abode at Keswick, which, beside Abbotsford, or beside the house in the *Frauenplan*, would look like a hut. But, both within that hut and around it, was some of God's noblest handiwork.

In a merely literary point of view, Southey doubtless filled a larger space in the eyes of his contemporaries than he fills now, or is likely to fill hereafter. In this he is unlike Scott. Nor did he share Scott's ambition to found a family, for which opportunity was not wanting. But he conferred nobility on the profession of letters by the spirit in which he followed it. His example is a bracing and invigorating one. Some of his works will endure as long as good literature is valued in Britain. And of him it may be said, as it has been already said of Sir Walter Scott, in all truthful sobriety, that (whatever his share in those temporary mistakes and exaggerations which belong to humanity, and above all to humanity in times of political conflict) "his services, direct and indirect, towards repressing [not the justly reforming, but] the *revolutionary* propensities of his age, were vast—far beyond the comprehension of vulgar politicians."* In common with his greater contemporaries, Scott and Goethe, Southey was well assured that the improvements most urgent and most pregnant are precisely those with which Parliaments and Parties have nothing to do.

The first book Southey possessed—some of the tiny stories of "Newberry's gilt regiment" only excepted—was

* Lockhart, *Life of Scott*, 759.

Hoole's translation (a "translation" in Bottom's sense) of the *Gerusalemme Liberata*. But he had already perused it. As a very small boy he had been attracted to the *Gerusalemme* by the story of the Enchanted Forest, which Mrs. Rowe had versified; but he had whimsically imagined that a book about Jerusalem must needs be in Hebrew—hoping, however, to learn Hebrew, that he might read it "when he grew to be a man." His father's Library consisted of the *Spectator;* of three or four volumes of the *Oxford Magazine*, one volume of the *Freeholder's Magazine*, and one of the *Town and Country Magazine;* of Pomfret's *Poems;* of the *Death of Abel;* of nine plays (including *Julius Cæsar*, *The Indian Queen*, and a translation of *Merope*), and a pamphlet. This was the entire collection of a prosperous and well-connected Bristol tradesman eighty years ago. But a neighbouring Circulating Library early widened the field of the incipient poet, by introducing him to Spenser. A chance acquaintance gave him a *Paradise Lost;* but Milton, as may be supposed, attracted him much less than Spenser, whom he idolized. To these he soon added Pope's Homer, Hoole's Ariosto, Mickle's *Lusiad*, Josephus,—in threescore sixpenny numbers, which he preserved to the end of his days,—and poor Chatterton's *Poems of Rowley*, which came to him, of course, with all the power of local association. To this stock, before he was thirteen, he had added some acquaintance with Virgil, Horace, and Ovid, and considerable familiarity with Shakespeare, Beaumont and Fletcher, and Sidney's *Arcadia*. On this foundation, he began to write Epics.

Southey's first books and early readings.

Library of Southey's father.

Of Southey's reading, either at Westminster or at Balliol, there is little record. At Westminster, some of his dearest and most lasting friendships were formed. But on his life at Oxford he could never look back with any pleasure, although his ultimate views about public education contrast so strikingly with the rash assertion of 1793,—"No son of mine shall go to a public school or University." Before he left Balliol, he estimated that he had written at least 35,000 verses, of which three fourths were good for nothing.*

Southey's peninsular journey.

The pursuit of poetry was soon interrupted by a journey into Spain and Portugal,—with his uncle and benefactor, Herbert Hill,—where a new literature and a new field for labour opened to him. To that journey, we owe the *History of Brazil*, one of his best books, and to it we should have owed other and probably greater books, on subjects for which he had a pre-eminent faculty, had it not been for the life-long necessity of making the labour of the day supply the wants of the day, which forced him to work in fields that other and smaller men could have tilled equally well. A letter written by Coleridge in 1801, from Greta Hall, fixed Southey's abode at Keswick, not immediately, indeed, but for life:—"Our house," said Coleridge, "stands on a low hill, the front of which . . . is an enormous garden. Behind the house is an orchard, and a small wood on a steep slope, at the foot of which flows the river Greta, which winds round and catches the evening lights in front of the house. In front, we have . . an encamped army of tent-like mountains which, by an inverted arch, gives a view of another vale. On our right, the lovely vale and the wedge-shaped lake of Bassenthwaite; on our left, Derwentwater and Lodore full in view, and the fantastic mountains of Borrowdale. Behind us, the massy Skiddaw, smooth, green, high, with two chasms, and a tent-like ridge in the larger."† This is the scene, as it was mirrored in

Coleridge's description of Greta Hall, in 1801.

* *Life and Correspondence*, I, 197.

† Coleridge to Southey, 13 April, 1801.

the eyes of a poet. But a single view of it, even by eyes in which dwell no poetic insight, is sufficient to people the memory with images of beauty for ever. Southey, as he lifted his eyes from his writing table, could command its best points, and his grave now lies within view of the study-window.

Southey settled at Greta Hall in 1803. Within four years Thomas de Quincey saw there a collection of books which was even then, in all senses, he says, a good one; embracing the cardinal classics, English, Spanish, and Portuguese; and decorated externally with a reasonable elegance.* Many rare MSS., chiefly in Spanish or Portuguese, were already gathered, and these it was Southey's habit to lay, on their sides, on ornamental brackets. The collection thus commenced grew rapidly. It comprised eventually a noble series of books on Church History and on the History of Literature, a fine assemblage of the works of early English poets, and not a few modern books, precious for the autographs and notes with which they were enriched. Coleridge, especially, had the habit of writing copious commentaries alike on the very few books which he bought, and the very many which he borrowed. When the Greta Hall Library came to be sold (1844) many volumes fetched, on this score, twenty times their ordinary price, whilst, on the other hand, the mere "rarities" of bibliographers and bibliomaniacs sold sometimes for the half, sometimes for less than the fourth, of the prices which, at some former sales, they had attained.†

Extent and character of Southey's Library.

* De Quincey, *Autobiographic Sketches*, ii, 343.

† *Sale Catalogue of Southey's Library*, with prices, *MS.*, passim. Coleridge's notes, for example, raised the price of Burnet's *Life of Bedell* to seven pounds, and that of the little book of Rimius on the Moravians —usually sold for three or four shillings—to five guineas. His own *Lay Sermon*, annotated, sold for two pounds five shillings. Sir William

In other books, too, there were curious instances of the capricious "accidents" of an auction. A copy of the *Acta Sanctorum*—of course a very fine copy of the whole fifty-three volumes—sold for a hundred and fifteen pounds. Thirty-five volumes of French tracts, uniformly bound, passed (to M. Van de Weyer) for fifteen shillings. Among the MSS. of the poet's own works which were included in this sale were *Espriella's Letters* (£9 : 9 : 0); *History of Brazil* (£12 : 10 : 0); *Madoc*, in its first form (£15 : 10 : 0), and also in its revised form (£16); and *The Curse of Kehama* (£31 : 10 : 0). The total produce of the sale was a little less than three thousand pounds.

A Book collector of an original pattern.

I close this already long chapter with a few words—some of them better words than mine—about a good and famous man who collected books (as indeed he used and wrote them) after a fashion entirely his own. "Not for him," says one who knew him well, "were the common enjoyments and excitements of the pursuit. He cared not to add volume unto volume, and heap up the relics of the printing-press. All the external niceties about pet editions, peculiarities of binding or of printing, rarity itself, were no more to him than to the Arab or the Hottentot. . . . He seeks but to appease the hunger of the moment. . . . If his intellectual appetite were craving after some passage in the *Œdipus*, or in the *Medea*, or in Plato's *Republic*, he would be quite contented with the most tattered and valueless fragment of the volume, if it contained what he

Denny's curious tract entitled *Pelecanicidium* (occasioned, I suppose, by the publication of Donne's *Biathanatos*), brought £6 : 15 : 0, but at Bindley's sale it had brought £13. The most curious instance, perhaps, of fluctuation of price is the sale of Luis de Escobar's *Las quatrocientas respuestas*, for six pounds, fifteen shillings. At the White Knights' sale that small volume had produced seventy-five pounds.

wanted; but, on the other hand, he would not hesitate to seize upon your tall copy in russia, gilt and tooled. Nor would the usual exemption of an Editio Princeps from sordid every-day work restrain his sacrilegious hands. . . . The learned world may very fairly be divided into those who return the books borrowed by them, and those who do not. Papaverius belonged decidedly to the latter order. . . . . . Some legend there is of a book-creditor having forced his way into the Cacus den, and having there seen a sort of rubble-work inner wall of volumes with their edges outwards, while others, bound and unbound, the plebeian sheepskin and the aristocratic russian, were squeezed into certain tubs, drawn from the washing establishment of a confiding landlady. . . . . . What became of all his waifs and strays, it might be well not to inquire too curiously. If he ran short of legitimate *tabula rasa* to write on, do you think he would hesitate to tear out the most convenient leaves of any broad-margined book, whether belonging to himself or another? It is said he once gave in 'copy' written on the edges of a tall octavo *Somnium Scipionis*, and as he did not obliterate the original matter, the printer . . . made a funny jumble between the letter-press Latin and the manuscript English. All these things were the types of an intellectual vitality which despised and thrust aside all that was gross and material in that wherewith it came in contact."*

That richly-stored intellect, that warm and tender heart, have passed to their rest. There remains no one book which will worthily represent to the readers of a future generation the outcome of the powers, attainments, and life-discipline of Thomas De Quincey. The *Confessions*, indeed, will long rank among the best specimens of classic

* Burton, *The Book-Hunter*, 42-44.

English prose; but that enchaining book is only a splendid fragment. Happily, the fugitive papers, in which so much of his mind found its only expression, have long been safe from the hazards of entombment in old,—often in obscure, periodicals. And, for a long time to come, other relics will now and then rise unexpectedly to light, by the appearance in sale-rooms and in booksellers' shops of some of the many volumes which the "English Opium Eater," like his friend Coleridge, delighted to annotate, as they came to his hand, regardless alike of their ownership and of their fate.

CHAPTER VI.

CONCERNING THE LIBRARIES OF SOME CELEBRATED MONARCHS AND ROYAL PERSONAGES, OF VARIOUS PERIODS.

Nor stony tower, nor walls of beaten brass,
Nor airless dungeon, nor strong links of iron,
Can be [obstructive] to the strength of spirit.

Julius Cæsar, I, 3.

........................Let me not live,
After my flame lacks oil, to be the snuff
Of younger spirits, whose apprehensive senses
All but new things disdain; whose judgments are
Mere fathers of their garments; whose constancies
Expire before their fashions..................

All's Well that ends Well, I, 3.

In this chapter I group together some collections remarkable in their day, but more from the character and fortunes of their owners than from their actual contents. Many adventitious circumstances serve to heighten our interest in particular books; none, I suppose, more prominently, or more naturally, than their known influence over famous men in their formative period; or their known value in solacing the dark days of those who have fallen from power, or from a lofty station, into the depths of adversity. It can never, I imagine, be other than matter of enduring interest to know the books that have charmed—whether in youth or in maturity, in the flood or in the ebb of fortune—the men who, for a season, have seemed to "bestride the narrow world, like a Colossus." One memorable instance conjoins both kinds of attraction. But, first of all, we will glance at some instances of a minor order.

Isabel of Bavaria, a collector of the 14th century.

Among the royal personages of France, Charles V, his son Charles VI (prior to the time of his mental aberration), and the Consort of that prince, Isabel of Bavaria, seem to be the earliest who took delight in gathering books. The collection formed and augmented by those two princes became the nucleus of the Imperial Library, the history of which will receive notice hereafter. The small but curious collection of Queen Isabel (mother of the "fair Katherine and most fair," of our fifth Henry,) deserves some special mention on its own merits. Isabel's personal history is a melancholy one, standing very much in need of such small gleams of light, as it may be capable of deriving from that love of books, which prompted her to make them her companions, not alone in her abodes at Tours, Paris, or Vincennes, but during her many journies in that stormy time.

Her library and its curiosities.

Isabel's Library was in two sections—called "*Livres*" and "*Romans*."* The former term seems to have denoted books of learning and devotion; the latter everything that was written in the vulgar tongue.† Psalters and Books of Hours are especially notable in her Inventory, both for their number and their rich illumination and decorations. Copious are the entries in the royal accounts on this score. Occasionally the Queen caused books of this kind to be compiled expressly for her use. Amongst the French MSS. of the Imperial Library is still preserved ‡ (*Fonds du*

* *Registre des Comptes royaux*, MS. in Paris Archives, as quoted by Vallet de Viriville (*Bulletin du Bibliophile*, XIII, 665).

† Vallet de Viriville, ubi supra.

‡ Ib.

Roi, 7296) "A Book of Devotions, in which is contained the Passion of our Lord," which opens thus:—"To the honour of God, of the sovran Virgin, and of all Saints, and at the command of the most excellent and dread Lady, and puissant Princess, Isabel of Bavaria, by the grace of God, Queen of France, I have translated this Passion of Our Saviour Jesus from Latin into French, without adding to it moralities, histories, examples, or figures, in this year 1398." This MS. seems to be a copy of the original as compiled for Isabel, written forty years later for Mary of Cleves, Duchess of Orleans. The same collection contains an illuminated *Book of Hours,* which belonged to Isabel herself, and is bound in the rich embroidery of the period.

But the circumstance which chiefly makes Isabel's collection a notable one, is the series which it included of the productions of Christina de Pisan, in the original MSS. dedicated and presented by the poetess to her royal and liberal patroness. One of these lies before me as I write, and is a superb volume on vellum, in folio, of 796 pages, richly and copiously illuminated, and of beautiful scription.* The first miniature occupies half the recto of the second folio, and represents Queen Isabel, amidst the ladies of her court, receiving the authoress, who, on her knees, presents her book. The dedicatory preface begins thus:—

Dedication Copies of the Poetical productions of Christina de Pisan.

"Tres excellent de grant haultesse,
Couronnée poissant princesse,
Très noble Royne de France,
Le corps enclin vers vous m'adresce,
En saluant par grant humblece."

* * * * *

* "*Poesies de Christine de Pisan.*" Harleian MS., 4431. A miniature on folio 3 represents Christine in her study. This portrait is repeated many times in the long series of beautiful vignettes. Among the auto-

Another curious and apparently inedited collection of mediæval poetry by Otho de Grandison,* a knight of Burgundy, now in the Imperial Library, was bought by the Queen in Paris in January, 1399, for fourteen livres and eight sous, parisis.† It is entitled *Livre des Cent Ballades*. Finally, a significant entry in the accounts of 1398 indicates that the poor king, in some paroxysm of his terrible malady, had injured a volume of the *Chroniques de France*, lent to Isabel by that noted lover of fine books, Philip the Bold.

Catherine of Medicis, and her Library at St. Maur.

Another Queen Consort of France, whose celebrity is of a much darker hue than Isabel's, supplies one of the many examples which show that high accomplishments and fine tastes may most easily coexist, not merely with great criminality—*that* is a truth which the runner may read—but coexist at once with gross vices, and with a narrow intellect. Nor can it excite reasonable surprise that even in her taste for books, Catherine de Medicis found the temptation to a new crime, and the means of committing it. Garrulous old Brantome tells the story thus: "Strozzi"—he is speaking of the famous Marshal who was killed at the siege of Thionville, in 1558—"had a very choice Library. It could not be said of him, as Lewis XI said of one of his prelates, who had a noble collection of books which he never read, 'He is like a hunchback, who possesses

graphs and mottos on the fly-leaf of this magnificent volume are the following: "*plus che en vous de Gruthuse.*" "M. Nulle la vault. Ɍivieres." "Henry Duke of Newcastle, his booke, 1676."

* Or, according to M. Vallet de Viriville, and M. Paulin Paris (*Manuscrits François*, v, 165), Otho de Granson.

† The entry of purchase is in the royal accounts of that year. There is no express identification of the volume, now numbered 7999 (*Fonds du Roi*), yet sufficient implied proof, as I infer from M. Vallet de Viriville's able notice in the *Bulletin du Bibliophile*, already referred to.

a fine large hunch, but never looks at it.' The Marshal often visited, examined, and read his books. They had come to him from Cardinal Ridolfi, a connexion of the Medicis, by purchase, after the Cardinal's death. The Ridolfi Collection had been estimated as worth more than 15,000 crowns, so choice were the books. But when Strozzi was killed, the Queen-Mother laid hands on the Library, promising to pay the son for it 'some day.' But he never got a penny. I well remember his telling me, in former days, how sore he felt about it."* The Strozzi MSS. in Greek and Latin alone, numbered about eight hundred, chiefly of great antiquity. The Marshal's military life had given him opportunities of collecting, so that we may hope his inheritance was not quite so much diminished by the spoliations of Catherine as might at first appear.

Fate of Catherine's Library at her death.

The Queen considerably augmented her "collection," and at her death it was estimated to contain about four thousand five hundred volumes, many of which comprised several distinct works. She died in debt, and her creditors were clamorous that her precious books, pictures, drawings, and jewels, should be sold for their benefit. The civil commotions impeded an immediate decision, and the Queen's librarian remained watchfully at his post. At length, De Thou intervened, and obtained Letters Patent from Henry IV for the amalgamation of the Library with that of the Kings of France. Francis Pithou and others had previously been directed to inspect and value the collection. It is worthy, they reported, to be preserved in France "for posterity, for the maintenance of good literature, and honour of the kingdom;" and because, they add, "it would be impossible to obtain or collect such

* *Vies des Capitaines étrangers* (Œuvres, i, 434.)

a Library, in these days, at any price, or in any country."*

Nor does this high eulogy seem overstrained. Besides Classical MSS., of the choicest sort, Strozzi had formed and Catherine had augmented a noble series of the first printed editions of ancient authors. Very naturally, the great classics of modern Italy were there in their best shapes. The series of French chroniclers and of minor works illustrative of French history is such as, of itself, to give fame to the collection. In the department of French poetry, too, this Library, says M. Le Roux de Lincy, contains "inestimable treasures."† Some of them are thought to be unique. In another and little-trodden path, Catherine, as a collector, had anticipated to some extent Walter Scott. She had formed a remarkable series of books on judicial astrology, a pseudo-science for which her infatuation is as well known, as is the bigotry which she could don or doff at her will.

Her fine bindings.

Her love for magnificent bindings has been sung by Ronsard. Its indulgence was checked by the conflicts and disasters of the time. Many of the most valuable MSS. remained unbound until their acquisition by Henry IV. But several fine examples remain. Characteristically enough one of these is the *Histoire des Prouessess et Vaillantises de noble Seigneur messire Simon, Comte de Montfort, faites par luy pour la foy Catholique et l'Eglise de Dieu, contre les Albigeois hérétiques*. This manuscript is bound in calf, richly ornamented, and bears Catherine's arms and her usual medallion, with the motto, *Ardorem extincta testantur vivere flamma.*‡ This volume is not with the bulk of the St.

* *Inventaire, &c.*, MS., as quoted by Le Roux de Lincy, in his *Notice sur la bibliothèque de Catherine de Medicis* (*Bulletin*, XIII, p. 918).

† Le Roux de Lincy, ut supra.

‡ *MS. Sainte-Geneviève*, H. F. 10.

Maur collection in the Imperial Library, but is found in that of Saint Genevieve. Not a few other volumes which bear the arms and devices of Catherine are met with in other collections, both public and private. Henry, when he found how much money needed to be expended upon the appropriate binding of the Library he had acquired, set apart to that purpose, the revenues of the Jesuits whom he had been compelled to exile.*

The convulsions which grew so naturally out of the rule on the Continent of the Valois and the Medicis, gave unusual opportunities for bringing to England treasures of art and literature, which Stuart government was, in its turn, again to scatter. Charles I had more inclination to pictures than to books. But he was a reading man, and a discriminating critic of the books to which his tastes inclined him. Like most men who really love books, he could not always resist the temptation to scribble in them. Sometimes he would write, from Martial,—

Charles I, of England, as a collector and virtuoso.

Rebus in angustis facile est contemnere mortem;
Fortiter ille facit qui miser esse potest;†

or, from Claudian,—

Fallitur egregio quisquis sub principe credit
Servitium. Nunquam libertas gratior extat
Quam sub rege pio;—

* Le Roux de Lincy, ut supra, 915—941. In this able article, M. Le Roux has printed copious and most interesting extracts from the Inventory itself.

† We owe this fact to Sir Philip Warwick, who makes Charles vary the quotation thus: "Rebus in *adversis* facile est contemnere *vitam*," &c., *Memoires* (1827), 281.

and this favourite quotation* marks the rock that was fatal to him. Sometimes, as in the famous copy of Shakespeare (1632) which is now one of the treasures of the Queen's Library at Windsor, *Dum Spiro, Spero*.

Charles the First's Shakespeare.

In his appreciation of Shakespeare, Charles was greatly in advance of his age. He loved him, and could quote him felicitously on occasions. From Shakespeare he derived his latest consolations—as far as merely secular literature is concerned—and the copy which had been so constantly in his hands was his dying gift to Sir Thomas Herbert. This "closet companion of his solitudes"† bears numerous tokens of the assiduity with which it was studied.

His remarkable fondness for dramatic literature in general, is widely known. Lord Orrery has recorded his disputation with the King about writing plays in rhyme, and its result. It is said that both Massinger and Shirley would submit to him their plays in manuscript, and sometimes accept an emendation or a hint. But this love for the literature of leisure was compatible with a keen enjoyment of less flowery paths.

Men familiar with musty records have characterised Charles as "a great antiquary." Harvey has narrated the evidences he had himself received of the king's intelligent interest in physiology. Musicians tell us of his acquirements in music; painters of his quick insight into the vital qualities of pictures. These are not the testimonies of flatterers. And if they were, we have the witness of a political assailant that Charles so excelled in arts as that he might, if need were, "have got a livelihood by them"; and the testimony to his knowledge and skill, both in polemical

* Both Herbert and James Harrington noticed, in their conversations, Charles' fondness for these lines.

† This is Milton's expression, either in the *Iconoclastes*, or the *Defensio*.

and in historical literature, of Clarendon. Unhappily for himself, the two things he wanted were precisely the two which he could not do without,—truthfulness and statesmanship. He had courage, self-command, and fortitude. He had many of the attractive qualities which turn friends into devotees. But he never had that most essential of all gifts, the power of choosing, with his whole heart, one course out of two courses, instead of choosing *both*. He is an exhaustive illustration of Bacon's saying,—"Prosperity doth best discover vice, but Adversity doth best discover Virtue." And long as is the catalogue of unhappy monarchs, there is none, perhaps, in the list who experienced in sadder fashion, that— The tastes and character of Charles I.

> "A crown,
> Golden in show, is but a wreath of thorns;
> Brings dangers, troubles, cares, and sleepless nights,
> To him who wears the regal diadem."

What is known of the external history, so to speak, of Charles' personal Library, is obscure, but curious. He bought many books in his youth, and received from his mother the gift of a splendid series of volumes bound in crimson and purple velvet. These, with other choice books on antiquities, on numismatics, on painting, on architecture, and on emblems, he was wont to keep in his "Cabinet Room," first at St. James', then at Whitehall. Of these books, there is in the Harleian MS., 4718, what purports to be an Inventory, but it is usually without titles, so that one cannot even learn from it who were the authors chosen for Charles by Anne of Denmark. This "Inventory" is a curiosity in its way, and may merit an extract. The first entries read literally thus:— Vander Doort's Inventory of Charles' Cabinet Books at Whitehall.

> "Im'pris 19 books in Crimson velvet, whereof 18 are bound 4to and
> "ye 19th in folio, which book in folio adorn'd with some silver
> "guilt plate, and ye 2 claspes wanting."
> "*Given to ye King by Queen Ann of famous memory.*"

"Item more 15 books 13 thereof being in long 4to and ye 2 lesser "cover'd over also with purple velvet.

"*Given also to ye King by ye said Queen Ann*"...........

The twelfth entry reads thus:—

"Item a book in fol. of wood Prince of Alberdure" [*i.e.* Wood Prints of Albert Durer] "being ye inscription in high Dutch "of ye proportions of Men."*

"*Given to ye King when he was prince by his Servt. Vanderdoort.*"†

Vanderdoort seems to have been the author of this catalogue, the bulk of which is devoted to Charles' pictures. His stupidity elicited many objurgations from Horace Walpole.

Disposal of Charles' books after his Execution.

The numerous Commonwealth papers preserved in the State Paper Office (now a department of the General Record Office), which relate to the disposal of Charles' property, and the settlement with his creditors, afford no particulars of interest about his books. But there is a paper of subsequent date (*Domestic, Charles II*, B. 26), containing an enumeration, not a Catalogue, of books formerly belonging to Charles I, which is of especial curiosity, when compared with the inscription on the fly-leaf of a Bible, given to the Church of Broomfield, in Essex, in the year 1723. This paper is endorsed "*Mr. Rosse. King's bookes.*" It enumerates (by language and size only) a hundred and fifteen volumes, then "at Mr. John Atwode's, at Bromfield, near Chemsford," and recites that Christopher Glascocke, of Felsted, made a catalogue of them, on which he spent four days; and that £400 had been offered for the books. After a long search, I have not been able to find any other paper in the Record Office throwing light on the fate of these books. Thomas

Discovery of books in Essex, which had belonged to Charles I.

* "*Vier Bücher von Menschlicher Proportion,*" Nuremberg, 1528, fol.

† *An Inventory*, &c., Harl. MS., 4718, pp. 20—23.

Ross was appointed keeper of the Royal Library in 1660.* Probably, therefore, this paper was drawn up shortly after that date.

The inscription on the Broomfield Bible reads thus:— "*This Bible was King Charles the First's, afterwards it was my grandfathers, Patrick Young's, Esq., who was Library-Keeper to His Majesty; now given to the Church at Broomfield, by me,* Sarah Attwood, *August 4th,* 1723."

The Library of Lewis II of Bourbon, Prince of Condé.

Germain Brice, the historian of Paris, briefly describes the library of an illustrious contemporary of Charles I, in these words:—"At the Hotel de Condé . . . . . is a very large library, containing books and maps very curious and rare".† The great Condé shared Charles' love for the arts and for the splendid decoration of his houses, but seems to have cared even more for books than for pictures. He liberally encouraged the labours of many of the great authors of his day, and with some of them he lived on terms of friendly intercourse. It appears by a note to the *History of Paris*, by Sauval, that his library comprised nearly ten thousand volumes; and by some verses of the accomplished antiquary, but very wretched poet, Michael de Marolles, that Isaac de La Peyrère, author of the once famous book *Præadamitæ*, was his librarian. The Great Condé had inherited from his father Henry, third Prince of Condé, a considerable library, which he had formed in his house at Bourges, "with great care and large expenditure," according to Lewis Jacob, the Carmelite (whose descriptions, however, are usually somewhat too emphatic), who described it in 1644,‡ two years before Henry's death.

* Entry Book, XXII (Chas. II) MS., S.P.O., pp. 178, 179.

† *Description nouvelle de............la Ville de Paris*, II, 162.

‡ *Traicté des plus belles Bibliothèques*, 624, 625.

MS. of the Condé Library.

But the special interest of the Condé collection arises from the circumstance that although the Library has been partially dispersed, a Catalogue of some of its choice manuscripts has survived.* This list is provokingly concise, and inaccurate, but it shows that the great warrior had gathered a rich assemblage of national Chronicles, of Romances of Chivalry, and other mediæval works; and of Poetry in various languages. Three youthful essays of Condé himself are thus designated :—

> "17. Discours de Sallustius Crispus de la Guerre de Catalina; escrit de la main de S. A. S.
> "51. Livre d'Arithmetique et de Géométrie; de la main de S. A. S.
> "52. Usage du Compas de Proportion; de la main de S. A. S."

Twenty-two other MSS. relate either to his own history or to the history of the Bourbon family. Some of these are of great curiosity, and are not otherwise known.

In 1791, the Library of the Condé family—both at Paris and at Chantilly—was confiscated, with those of other emigrants. In 1815, its restoration was of course claimed. The Count de Pradel, then Minister of the Royal Household, instructed Anthony Barbier, the eminent bibliographer, and Librarian of Napoleon (then holding the office of "Administrator of the Libraries of the Crown"), to report to him on the subject, and especially as to the books of which had been composed—partly from the Palace Library, partly from other confiscated collections—the fine Library of the Town of Versailles. In his reply, Barbier informs the Minister of the course taken during the Revolution with the confiscated books, enumerates the new public collections which had been formed, describes the

Confiscation of the Condé Library;

* It is preserved in the Imperial Library at Paris (*Fonds de Fontette*, Part LXI, *a*), and has been printed by M. Le Roux de Lincy, in the *Bulletin du Bibliophile*, XIV, 1169—1364.

exchanges which had been made with booksellers for newer books, in certain cases; and then adds:—"These details will prove only too completely, how impossible it is to return to the emigrants the Libraries they claim. But there are some libraries, of which the bulk has been kept together. The books of the princes of the Royal family bear the arms of France, and these can be identified."* But he strongly urges on the Minister that to claim their restitution from the Versailles Library (to which most of the royal books, it seems, had been given), would only increase the importunity of the emigrants generally, whilst the royal example in munificently confirming the gift to the Municipality, as regarded the King's own books and those of the Princes of the Blood, would show the impossibility of admitting claims to other Libraries "dispersed in every corner of France, and even in places which are now beyond the limits of France." Barbier's arguments, however, were overruled. Part of the Condé Library was restored; belongs now, by the Will of the last Duke of Bourbon, to H.R.H. the Duke of Aumale, and is preserved at Twickenham; but the statements of M. Barbier sufficiently explain the incompleteness of the restitution.

and its partial restoration.

The unfortunate king who had to bear the punishment of the misdoings of so many men utterly unlike himself, as well as the inevitable penalties of his own weakness, seems to have taken but a lukewarm interest in books until the

* *Correspondance d'A. A. Barbier* (*Bulletin du Bibliophile*, xiii, 490-493). The worthy librarian proceeds to suggest that the King might bestow, instead, on the claimants, some of the many magnificent books printed for the Government, "and thus give them a touching proof of royal sympathy in their misfortunes; when they would naturally cease to claim things which the Revolution had devoured, or to which a useful destination had been given."

gloomy days of the *Temple*. The Utopia of Lewis XVI, must have lain, one is inclined to think, in a life mainly divided between hunting and lockmaking; diversified, however, by acts of real kindness and goodwill to the people about him. After the fatal 10th of August, books and the exercises of devotion occupied most of his time.

Readings of Lewis XVI, during his confinement in the Temple

In the "little tower" of the Temple there was already a small library, which appears to have belonged to Barthélemy, keeper of the Archives of the Order of Malta. Into this library, in the early days of his imprisonment, the King would go after dinner, and take down the *Etudes de la Nature*, of Bernardin de Saint Pierre, or some volumes of the *Mercure François*.* On one evening, it was remembered, he tried to amuse the sad family circle, by giving out enigmas from the *Mercure* for solution. On other occasions, the Queen or Madame Elizabeth would read aloud some book of history, or the *Cecilia* of "little Burney;" and then the Dauphin would be set to read a play of Racine or of Corneille. When Manuel came to strip Lewis of his "Orders," he was found reading Tacitus.

When removed to the great tower, he devoted many hours daily to the perusal of Latin authors, and occasionally to Montesquieu, or Buffon, to Pluche's *Spectacle de la Nature*, to Hume's History in the original; and to Tasso, also in the original.† Some portion of the day was invariably given to the *Imitation*. Contemporary Newspapers he sometimes, yet rarely, asked for; and sometimes refused, when offered, as, indeed, he had good reason for doing. Many of the journals, even of 1792, already show the depths of vileness into which journalism could sink. These the "municipals" eagerly put in the king's

* Hanet Cléry, *Journal du Temple*, 63, seqq.

† Ib., 93.

way.* But he would sometimes read the diatribes of his assailants with composure.†

Much of Lewis' time was devoted to the education of his son. The small Library of the Temple was slenderly provided with the needful books; so that in November the King drew up a list of books to be supplied from his own library at the Tuileries by the Town Council. This list included the works of Virgil, Horace, Ovid, and Terence; of Tacitus, Livy, Cæsar, Aurelius Victor, Eutropius, Cornelius Nepos, Florus, Justin, Quintus Curtius, Sallust, Suetonius, and Velleius Paterculus; the *Vies des Saints*, the *Fables* of La Fontaine, *Télèmaque*, and Rollin's *Traité des Etudes*.‡ Most of these he obtained, and used assiduously, during the short interval of life which remained to him. Geography he seems to have known well enough to teach, almost without the aid of books.

The Library of the Temple augmented.

Not long before his death, Lewis met with an enigma or "logogriph," whilst reading the *Mercure*. Cléry could not interpret it; on which the king said, "Do you not see that the word is '*sacrifice?*' and then abruptly added, "Such books as these are not fit for me now. Bring me that volume of the *History of England* which contains the Death of Charles I." He read it intently on that and on the following days.§ It was then that Cléry learnt that since the tenth of August the king had read, in the Temple, nearly two hundred and fifty volumes.

Lewis reads the History of Charles I.

On his way to the scaffold, he conversed very calmly, not only on the solemn themes appropriate to his position, but on the merits and style of the Latin historians. He criticised

* Hanet Cléry, *Journal du Temple*, 99.

† Conversations of M. de Malesherbes, reported by Hué, *Dernières Années de Louis XVI.* (Edit. of 1860,) 433.

‡ Dubois de Beauchesne, *Louis XVII*, 519.

§ Hanet Cléry, ut sup. 155.

with point and felicity, it is said,* the "long speeches" which Livy puts in the mouths of his generals in the field, and showed the utmost firmness and self-possession. His very last words were, "I wish that my blood could cement the happiness of Frenchmen."

We have now to glance at—in his literary aspect—another soldier, far greater than Condé in the field, who combined with that supremacy, eminent statesmanship, and some measure of literary distinction. But the literary character of Frederick, like the rest of his career and life, was coloured by the calamities of his youth. They taught him audacity, patience, and fortitude, but they seem to have given a cynical twist, both to his intellect and to all his sympathies. And that ply, once taken, became inerasible. No one has borne stronger testimony than has Frederick himself, to the laboriousness, the economy—self-denying in all things save one,—and the other good points, of his eccentric father. But the contrast between father and son is none the less salient. The one is passionately German; the other, almost ludicrously French. The one carries religious orthodoxy to the verge of slavishness; the other (at one time, at least), carries religious scepticism almost to the verge of blasphemy.

The early calamities of Frederick the Great.

We know more about the education, and especially about the self-education, of Frederick, than is usually known even of the training of princes. Frederick's candour concerning himself is one of his strong points. He was a copious letter-writer. And he had almost always around him men given to diarizing. The first book that laid firm hold of him, when he had reached manhood, and could choose for himself,

* By one who accompanied him, and whose report is cited in *Histoire du dernier règne*, i, 262.

seems to have been Bayle's *Dictionary*. Denina tells us that he was so constantly talking about it at Rheinsberg, that he set all the ladies of that small court agog to read it, and he adds, maliciously, that only one lady took the very reasonable precaution of consulting her "pasteur," as to the portions which it might be desirable for a woman to skip.* Frederick retained his affection for Bayle, and long afterwards completed that Abridgement of the Dictionary which was published by his secretary, Thiébault.† "That precious monument of our age,"‡ is the King's matured expression for the work which had delighted him in youth. "Bayle is first among the dialecticians of Europe," he wrote in 1780.§

The favourite authors of Frederick.

Among the modern authors who shared with Bayle (and with Voltaire, Frederick's passionate admiration for whom needs not to be particularised) the studies of this Rheinsberg period (1736-40) were John Baptist Rousseau, Rollin, Fleury, Malebranche, and Locke. Even Bossuet and Massillon seem to have captivated him by the charms of diction and style, whatever may have been his relish for their solemn themes. Yet it is fair to bear in mind that, according to Denina (who knew him well) he had read the Bible very assiduously. And he wrote sermons and funeral orations, sometimes in avowed imitation, sometimes in mocking irony, of those great divines.

Frederick as a poet.

Of the origin of his love for poetry, he gave Voltaire this account:—"In the flower of my youth an amiable person

* Denina, *Essai sur la vie . . de Frédéric II*, 25. It was the singular fortune of this writer to publish a book, which at one time induced Frederick the Great to invite him to the Court of Berlin; and at another, induced Napoleon, as we shall see hereafter, to invite him to the Tuileries.

† Thiebault, *Mes Souvenirs de vingt ans*, i, 119.

‡ *Œuvres*, vii, 126.

§ Ib., 106.

inspired me with two passions at once. You will readily guess that one was love. The other was poetry. The little miracle of nature, along with every possible grace, possessed taste and sensibility, and was anxious to communicate them to me. I succeeded tolerably in love, but only poorly in poetry. Thenceforward I have been amorous pretty frequently, and always poetical (*toujours poëte*)."* Frederick's first publication, the *Anti-Machiavel*,† exhibits considerable knowledge of history; and his subsequent historical writings possess conspicuous and original merit. In that field he might well have won distinction, had he been a private man; but as a poet he would certainly have stood but a very poor chance of winning either laurels or bread.

Frederick's appreciations of the Classic writers.

Of the ancient historians, Tacitus and Suetonius were Frederick's favourites, if we judge by the frequency of his readings, and the testimony of those who talked with him. Yet, in the preface to the *Histoire de mon temps* (1775), we find him, after praising the *Commentaries*, proceed sweepingly to condemn all the historians of antiquity after Cæsar, as producing nothing but "panegyrics or satires."‡ Of the old poets, he seems to have preferred Virgil, Horace, Tibullus, and Propertius. But all the ancients were known to him mainly by French translations.§ Of Homer he seems to have known very little, in any way, or at any time of life. In the work just mentioned (which he revised and

* *Correspondance avec le Roi de Prusse* (Edit. of 1836), 35.

† The *Anti-Machiavel* was written in 1739, but not published until the autumn of 1740. But Friedrich's first literary production, an essay *De la Politique actuelle de la Prusse*, dates from February, 1731, when he had just completed his nineteenth year. His literary labours—spread over fifty years—seem to have closed with an imitation of a passage in *Athalie*, in 1780 or 1781.

‡ *Œuvres* (1846-58), ii, xxii.

§ *Œuvres*, passim. Comp. Aug. Boeckh, *Ueber . . Friedrichs . . Classische Studien*, pp. 6, 9, seqq.

remodelled at the age of sixty-three) he says:—"An unprejudiced man will prefer the *Henriade* to the poems of Homer. The *Iliad* depicts to us the manners of Canadian savages."* And he then adds: "Boileau need not shrink from comparison with Juvenal or Horace. Racine outstrips all his ancient rivals."

Nor did he rate the great philosophers of antiquity much higher. In his youth he wrote to Von Suhm:—"In less enlightened times than ours the Socrates, the Platos, and the Aristotles, were the luminaries of the world; and the human race was perverse, and gave itself up with avidity to its passions. Our age can boast the Des Cartes, the Leibnitzes, the Newtons, and the Wolffs—as much in advance of the others as mature age is of infancy—and yet there is no reason to apprehend that their philosophy will ever induce us to prefer spiritual things to sensual."† In later days he would probably have modified the terms, without substantially altering the sense.

Frederick's estimate of German literature.

German literature, during Frederick's youth, already gave some indications of its splendid maturity; but for these he had no eyes. Its many faults and deficiencies he could, at all periods of his life, see as with a lynx's beam. Only five or six years before his death he writes elaborately of his painful researches "to disinter our native Homers, our Virgils, our Anacreons, our Horaces, . . . our Thucydides, our Livys." "I find nothing. My labour is all in vain. Let us be sincere, and confess in good faith, that, so far, Literature has not prospered on our soil. Germany has had philosophers who bear comparison with the ancients,

* Un homme sans passion préférera la *Henriade* aux poëmes d'Homère . . . . . L'*Iliade* nous peint les mœurs des Canadiens.—*Histoire de mon temps.* (Ib., 37.)

† *Correspondance avec M. de Suhm* (*Œuvres*, xvi, 281, 282).

and who, in more departments than one, have surpassed them. But as to Literature, let us admit our poverty. . . In the petty class of Fables, indeed, we have had Gellert, who ranks besides Phædrus and Æsop. The poems of Canitz are tolerable. . . . If I review the historians, I find only the *History of Germany* of Mascou, which I can but cite as least defective."* . . . . At length he reaches Goethe—the Goethe, of course, of 1780—"And now," says Frederick, "we have *Goetz von Berlichingen* on the stage,—a detestable imitation of those wretched English plays. The pit applauds, and calls enthusiastically for the repetition of these disgusting platitudes."†

The allusion in this characteristic passage to the English drama leads me to glance, for a moment, at Frederick's notions about our own literature. Several of Shakespeare's plays—Hamlet amongst them—had been performed at Berlin in the year immediately preceding the King's composition of his treatise *De la Littérature Allemande.* "Go," he says, "to our theatres; there you will see the wretched plays (*les abominable pièces*) of Shakespeare, and the audience ready to faint away with delight at farces worthy of Canadian savages. I call them so, because they sin against every law of the drama. . . . . There we have porters and grave-diggers, who make their entrance and hold conversations, in character with their calling (*dignes d'eux*)! and then come kings and queens! How can such an absurd medley of vileness and grandeur, of tragedy and buffoonery, captivate us?"† Milton escapes somewhat more easily. The *Paradise Lost*, he says, condescendingly,

Frederick's opinion on English authors.

* *De la Littérature Allemande* (*Œuvres*, vii, 93, 94).

† Ib., 109.

‡ Ib.

is "a little better" than—the *Behemoth* of Hobbes!* Milton was "a man of strong imagination, who had borrowed the subject of his poem from one of those religious farces which, in his day, were still represented in Italy; *and it is to be especially observed that at that time England was peaceable and wealthy.*" This last pièce of information is not thrown in quite so gratuitously as may appear, in the absence of the context. It was a favourite thesis of Frederick, that only times of peace were favourable to the growth of a national literature.

Of course, in criticising the great authors of France, Frederick stood on more familiar ground. But he is not always happy, even there. Of the *Lettres Persanes* he has said, truly enough, that they belong to a class of literature unknown to antiquity, but sure to reach a very remote posterity.† Fontenelle he compliments as an honour to France, and as a writer who had learned how to "divest astronomy of its pedantic repulsiveness."‡ The *Petit Carême* of Massillon is filled, he says, with "passages of the sublimest eloquence." He is less fortunate when, in criticising the French historians, he brackets together Gregory of Tours, Joinville, and Pierre de L'Estoile, as "feeble compilers, who wrote what they had learned by chance."§ Comines and De Thou he praises highly.‖

* "Ainsi le *Béhémoth* ne peut se regarder que comme un libelle de parti. Le *Paradis* de Milton *vaut mieux* sans doute." (Ib., p. 119.) A king, as Voltaire once said, is the master of his favours. Frederick is pleased to confer the *Leviathan* on John Toland. And in the same treatise he makes Horace a little present.—"*Tot verba, tot pondera*, as Horace says in the *Poetica*." (Ib., p. 104.) The ranks of the Latin writers he similarly strengthens by assigning to them Epictetus and the Emperor Marcus Aurelius.

† *Œuvres*, ii, 37.

‡ Ib., xvi, 281.

§ Ib., ii, xxiii.

‖ Ib.

The Libraries of Frederick the Great at Potsdam, Sans Souci, &c.

Frederick's characteristic love of order and exactness were eminently shown in the arrangements of his libraries. Of these he had several separate collections placed at his various residences, and mainly composed of the same books, bound usually in red morocco, with gilt leaves; and distinguished by an initial letter on the back, indicative of the particular collection to which the book belonged; as "V." for Vignes (which was Frederick's name for the original villa at Sans-Souci); "S." for the new villa at Sans-Souci; "P." for Potsdam; "B." for Berlin, and so on. The books were arranged broadly, in classes, but without regard to size. Frederick, like Napoleon, preferred small-sized books, even for his Palace libraries; but when he was forced to put up with folios, he would have them placed on the same shelves with the octavos and duodecimos, if the subjects were the same, without any care for appearances. Thick books, of any size, he would cause to be rebound in sections, for more convenient use. Whenever a book was taken from its shelf, he would order a ticket to be put in its place, as if the library had been public. When presentation copies of German works came to him, they would be quickly dispatched to Berlin. French authors who were in special favour with him he would sometimes cause to be reprinted in compact editions to his taste.*

There are here, as in what has been already said of his choice of books, many small peculiarities which bring to one's mind the habits and fancies of Napoleon. But it is less frequently—as will be seen more plainly by-and-by —by resemblance than by contrast. They were alike in the disadvantage of knowing the great authors of antiquity almost entirely by translations. They were alike in pos-

* Dantal, *Mittheilungen über Friedrich den Grossen*, passim.

sessing a taste for plays as well as for works of history. They were alike in preferring little books to big. In most other particulars of book-craft they were very unlike. Frederick delighted in metaphysical speculations—and very foggy many of them were—which to Napoleon were simply detestable. Napoleon loved poets too well to have tolerance for poetasters, and would as lief have imitated Lewis XVI, by spending his time in making second-rate locks, as have imitated Frederick, by spending it in writing fourth-rate verses. Most cardinal of all was their difference in the relative regard for form and substance in books. Frederick would find pleasure, by the hour, in the veriest trash, if it did but wear a graceful garb. Napoleon tore away all literary wrappings and semblances, to get at the pith of a book, just as impetuously as he swept away the mere obstructions of a hostile army, to get at its heart.

Comparison of Frederick with Napoleon as lovers of books.

The last books read to Frederick were Voltaire's *Essai sur les mœurs et l'esprit des Nations;* his *Siècle de Louis XIV;* and his *Siècle de Louis XV,*—breaking off (30th July, 1786) at the account of Damien's attempt on that king's life.* The last books that Frederick read, by himself, were the *Vie d'Henry IV,* and La Harpe's translation of Suetonius.† A little earlier, Dantal had read to him some of the best pieces of the French Drama. Its later works he disliked. When *Figaro* had been read to him, long before, he exclaimed, "What a gulf between the Harlequin Beaumarchais, and a Molière! He gives us nothing but tricks and surprises, fit only for the playhouse of a suburb."‡ The same comedy was read to

Frederick's last readings.

* Dantal, *Mittheilungen*, 32.

† Preuss, *Lebensgeschichte des grossen Königs Friedrich*, ii, 339.

‡ Thiébault, *Mes Souvenirs*, i, 133.

Napoleon at St. Helena. "We have there," said the Emperor, "the whole of the Revolution, in its germ."

Frederick as a writer.

A writer (whose place among the enduring glories of Literature is too well assured by a series of noble books, written in bygone days, to be now imperilled by any amount of grotesque paradox, or by any number of excursions into the region of unknown tongues,) has lately said that Frederick would have stood higher had he never written a line. Had Mr. Carlyle been pleased to add the words "of verse," his assertion would be scarcely questionable. But his own book owes enough to Frederick's writings of another kind to afford, of itself, an ample answer. Strange, indeed, would it have been, had a man largely endowed with some of God's choicest gifts, been capable of writing thirty volumes, of the whole of which any such assertion could be true. In his youth, Frederick had said, "Books make up no small part of true happiness." In his old age, he said, "My latest passion will be for literature."* The man who could truly—whatever his limitations—say this, at *both* extremes of life, and yet, in its prime, be an utter fool in the choice of his pursuits, and in the self-estimate of his powers, is a phenomenon we have yet to make acquaintance with in human story. That a man so endowed as Frederick was should, at the close of a long life, know of no better "comfort under affliction" than—the third book of Lucretius, is sad, but not at all surprising. His latest biographer tells us, inimitably, that "Frederick recognised honestly the *uses* of Religion; took a good deal of pains with his preaching clergy; . . . and expected to be obeyed by them, as by his sergeants and

* *Œuvres posthumes*, xi, 271.

corporals."* Literature gave Frederick many surprises, as well as many enjoyments, in his life-time. But I doubt if he ever got so much of the first-named emotion out of any book, as he would get, could he once again revisit the glimpses of the moon, out of his own "Life," as told by the most eminent and most brilliant of his biographers. As to the "Prussian Dryasdusts," Frederick would simply regard *them* as racy of the soil.

Frederick bequeathed his Library, with nearly the whole of his other possessions of every kind, to his successor. His Will† contains no stipulations as to the maintenance of the Libraries, but that which he most familiarly used is kept up, I am told, like the rest of the palace of Sans-Souci, in its old condition, and appears to be freely shown —I have not myself seen it—to visitors. Two especial curiosities are usually pointed out, with becoming reverence,—the autograph manuscript of Frederick's *Eloge du Sieur La Mettrie*, and a portrait, by his hand, of Voltaire.

Present state of Frederick's Library at Sans Souci.

Of the youthful literary tastes and studies of NAPOLEON very little is recorded in those early chapters of Fauvelet de Bourienne, which seem really to be his, and to be far more trustworthy than the rest of the bulky compilation from notes and diaries, which M. de Villemarest was good enough to publish under the name of the Schoolfellow and Secretary of Napoleon. But the early papers of Napoleon himself have been curiously preserved, and they contain not a few

The early studies and books of Napoleon.

* Carlyle's *Friedrich*, iii, 598.

† Printed by Preuss, *Lebensgeschichte*, ii, 350—354. "Willingly, and without regret, I resign this breath of life which animates me, *to that beneficent Nature*, by whom it was lent; and my body to the elements of which it is composed."—Such is the first of the thirty-three clauses of Frederick's will. As "a philosopher," he goes on to say, "I have lived; as such, I wish to be buried."

indications of his favourite books, and of the ways in which he first turned his reading to account. Of these papers M. Libri, if he was not the discoverer, was at least the first imparter to the public. Most of them, however, remain still substantially unpublished.

Bourienne tells us—and he had good access to know—that the authors who chiefly attracted Napoleon in his school-days, were Polybius, Plutarch, and Arrian. All of these he read for recreation, and in French. In mathematics, as everybody knows, his progress was great. "He has always distinguished himself for his application to mathematics," are the words of the School Inspector in 1784. And to these are added, "He knows History and Geography respectably; Latin, and the usual accomplishments, very poorly."* The papers epitomized by Libri tell us much more than this. They contain, with a great mass of other matter, a series of notes, extracts, and criticisms, on a multitude of writers of various ages, made, as it seems, between 1785 and 1793.

The subjects of these studies are as diversified as can well be conceived. Amongst the ancients, Herodotus, Strabo, Pausanias, Diodorus Siculus, Cæsar, Tacitus; amongst the moderns, Tasso, Ariosto, Bossuet, Vertot, Denina, Buffon, Filangieri, Mably, Necker, Adam Smith, are conspicuous. Of Rousseau, also, he read a good deal, and criticised him keenly. There are, for example, copious extracts from the *Discours sur l'origine et les fondemens de l'inégalité de l'Homme*, in which the famous passages about a "state of nature" are vigorously and incisively refuted at

* "Il sait très passablement son histoire et sa geographie. Il est assez faible pour les exercises d'agrément et pour le latin, où il n'a fait que sa quatrième."—Kéralio, *Compte rendu*, quoted by Bourienne, i, 21.

The Note-books and other MSS. preserved by Cardinal Fesch.

great length. Elsewhere, Napoleon contents himself with writing at the end of various paragraphs—copied out, nevertheless, in full—"*I do not believe that,*"—"*I believe nothing of all that;*" and so on. The notes of his historical reading embrace the History of France, of England, of Germany, of the Arabs, of China, and of the Indies.* On the liberties of the Gallican Church, on the Bull *Unigenitus*, and on the history of the Sorbonne, his extracts and notes are abundant.† On other and more miscellaneous questions of policy, Napoleon's lucubrations, at this period, are also numerous, but these seem usually to take the form of original essays, or of materials obviously prepared for essays.‡ The papers bear throughout the impress of frankness and earnestness, and have a strong dash of that imaginative sort of "republicanism," which alone, in these latter days, seems to be compatible with deep-thinking and strong volition, and therefore differs very essentially from the sort then dominant in France.

These seven years of study, fruitful as they were, were

* These details (little known in England) will not, I hope, be deemed too minute. Scott had taken some pains to inform himself on the early literary tastes and habits of Napoleon, but with such small success, that we find him saying: "Napoleon read very extensively, but .. with little discrimination, and more to amuse himself than for the purpose of instruction." Elsewhere he conjectures that Napoleon "was a slow composer, and fastidious in the choice of his language."

† "I have been reading the history of the Sorbonne and what has been written about the quarrels between Rome and the Gallican Church. I might have offered myself for a degree in theology. Religious questions have always had much attraction for me." (1789.)

‡ Libri, *Souvenirs de la jeunesse de Napoléon.* (*Revue des deux Mondes*, Quatrième Série, xxix, 784—809.) These papers were preserved, it seems, by Cardinal Fesch, but were unused and unexamined until they passed into the hands of M. Libri. Even the brothers of Napoleon had believed them lost. They were for two days in the hands of the venerable General Pelet, who has vouched for their authenticity.

continually varied by travel. At their outset (1785) we find Napoleon at Valence with his regiment; then at Lyons and Douai. Next year, he is in Corsica; then in Paris; then in garrison at Auxonne (1788); then at Besancon, at Seurre, at Dole; and again in Corsica, on leave of absence (1790); in the following year he is again in garrison at Valence, where, by the way, he subscribes to a Circulating Library; then again in Paris, and after another brief period of duty at Valence, in Corsica for the third time.* But with all this rapid change of place, the studies seem to be unbroken; and the eye of the student watches every passing event as intently as if he had nothing else to do. Nor is any opportunity of putting himself in evidence, suffered to pass unimproved.

The early pamphlets of Napoleon.

The *Lettre à Matteo Buttafuoco* — Napoleon's first pamphlet—treats of Corsican politics, and was written in Corsica, but printed at Dôle (early in 1791), when he was living in barracks at Auxonne, whence he would go, it was long remembered, at a very early hour, to correct the press; returning, after a walk of some twenty-four miles, in time for his share of garrison duty. Two years later, he published his *Souper de Beaucaire,* a brief and vigorous dialogue on the politics of the hour, written in the spirit of the hour. This pamphlet shows notable progress in style and diction, and doubtless by its political timeliness and caution assisted in paving the way for that rapid promotion which transformed the Captain, of 1793, into the General of Brigade, of 1794. Thenceforward, we must be content to trace the reader and the student in the still extant and interesting records of the libraries, which at various periods he caused to be collected, or to be planned, for his personal use.

* Nasica, *Mémoires sur la jeunesse de Napoleon,* passim.

But a few words must first be said of other and eminently characteristic productions, of this same youthful period, which were not given to the press, and which, until recently, were supposed, even, as I have said, by Napoleon's brothers, to have perished. As early as 1789, Napoleon had written a *Memoir on Corsica*, intended for the perusal of Necker. This he submitted to a worthy monk who had been, in his own time, second master at Brienne. Father Dupuy (then living in retirement at Laon) read the MS., and when he returned it, criticised it freely. The substance, he said, was good, but he found many repetitions, many ill-chosen words, many superfluous reflections. Worst of all, he found much plain-speaking which he thought "too bold, under a monarchy." It is only the truth, rejoined the author, and "the very women are beginning to utter it." But he seems to have suppressed the Memoir. Next year, he wrote a brief "*History of Corsica*," remarkable for the union of rhetoric and passion, with an elaborate examination of sources and authorities, both printed and manuscript.*

Before writing either of these papers on Corsica, Napoleon had sketched the plan of a '*Dissertation on regal authority*.' The work was to begin with a general view of the origin and growth of the kingly functions. It was to show how *a military government favoured the aggrandizement of kingly power*; and then to review, in detail, the gradual "usurpations of kings" in the chief monarchies of Europe. "*There have not been many kings who have not deserved dethronement*." These are Napoleon's words, and they were written six months before the meeting of the States General at Versailles.†

* Libri, ut supra, 794—798.

† Thanks to Mr. Carlyle, we are all familiar with Sigismundus "*super*

His Library in Egypt.

Shortly before he left France for Egypt, Napoleon drew up, with his own hand, the scheme of a travelling library, the charge of collecting which was given to John Baptist Say, the Economist. It comprised about three hundred and twenty volumes, more than half of which are historical, and nearly all, as it seems, in French. The ancient historians comprised in the list are Thucydides, Plutarch, Polybius, Arrian, Tacitus, Livy, and Justin. The poets are Homer, Virgil, Tasso, Ariosto, the *Télémaque* of Fenelon, the *Henriade* of Voltaire, with Ossian, and La Fontaine. Among the works of Prose Fiction are the "English Novelists in forty volumes," of course in translations, and the indispensable *Sorrows of Werter* (which, as he himself told Goethe, Napoleon had read through seven times, prior to October, 1808). In this list the Bible, together with the *Koran*, and the *Vedas*, are whimsically, but significantly, entered under the heading, "Politics and Ethics" (*Politique et Morale*).*

Disposal of the Library of the Directory after 18 Brumaire.

Soon after the victory of Brumaire (9 Nov. 1799), the Consuls decreed that a selection of books for the personal use of each of themselves should be made from the Library of the Directory, and that the remainder should form a library for the newly created Council of State. Lebrun and Sièyes chose an assortment of books, chiefly in the faculties of Politics and Polite Literature, to the number of about eighteen hundred volumes each. Napoleon took a long series of works on the Military Arts and on History. Ripault, who had been made private librarian to the First Consul, had previously reported that

Grammaticam." Napoleon seems already to have asserted a like prerogative. But he not only bends grammar to his will; he invents new words;—amongst them the verb *regrader* and the verb *usager*.

* *Correspondance de Napoleon Ier.* iv, 37, 38.

after examining 800,000 volumes of books in the public stores (*depôts*), he was of opinion that not more than a hundred volumes out of that vast accumulation would be suitable for the First Consul's use,* and had requested that the Library of the emigrant Prince of Monaco might be placed at his disposal. This suggestion was not approved, but Napoleon ordered that the Catalogue of the Library of the Directory should be submitted to him, in order that he might make his own choice from that.†

One of those Brienne School reports which have been preserved from oblivion on account of their mention of Napoleon, indicates "gratitude" as one of the notable points of his character. It continued to be so, during his life, and was sometimes shown in unusual ways. The *History of the Revolution of Italy* by Charles Denina was one of the books he had read with satisfaction in his studious days. The historian had obtained, through the fame of that first book, a professorship at Turin, which he afterwards lost by some conflict with the censors of the press. He had then, as we have seen, been attached to the service of Frederick II, but with Frederick he was not permanently a favourite. In Denina's old age—he was then seventy-three—Napoleon met with him at Mentz, remembered his early obligation to the book, and made the author his librarian, jointly with Ripault. In 1807, Ripault was succeeded by the eminent bibliographer, Anthony Augustus Barbier, on whom the brunt of the duties of the librarianship naturally devolved.

Denina, the historian, made assistant Librarian to Napoleon.

The librarian of Napoleon had certainly no sinecure. The Emperor would often summon him, at all hours;

Barbier's experience as Librarian to Napoleon.

* Barbier, *Rapport sur la formation de la Bibliothèque du Conseil d'Etat*, § 2.

† *Correspondance de Napoleon Ier,* vi, 533.

sometimes to read to him; sometimes to report on new books; sometimes to indicate the sources of information on particular subjects. When absent from Paris with the army, or on a tour, Napoleon would have a frequent supply of books, with analytical notices of their contents. At other times, he would require his librarian to make literary reports on themes which had attracted his thoughts. Amongst the papers thus called for, were an abstract of the Life and Campaigns of Marlborough; a detailed narrative, historical and geographical, of the Campaigns on the Euphrates, including those of Antony, Trajan, and Julian; an account of the sources of French History; a list of Greek and Latin works yet untranslated into French; a report on the extant MSS. relating to the suppression of the Templars; another on the original documents illustrative of the treatment of Galileo, by the Roman Inquisition. At a subsequent period, it may be added, those very Galileo documents were removed from Rome by Napoleon's command, and entrusted to Barbier, for publication, but the events of 1814 occasioned the abandonment of the work.*

Napoleon seems to have been dissatisfied with all the Camp Libraries that had been formed for his use, on the score of the bulk of the best editions of books, and the meagreness of the small editions. When at Bayonne in July 1808, on the eve of the momentous events in the Peninsula, he dictated to Meneval the scheme of a Library, to be printed expressly for the purpose, in duodecimo volumes, without margins; and to extend to a thousand volumes, bound in thin covers and with loose backs. In this new plan, "Religion" took its place as the first class. The Bible was to be there, in its best translation, with a selection of the most important works of the Fathers of the

Napoleon's scheme for a new Camp Library.

* *Vie de Barbier*, passim.

Church, and a series of the best dissertations on those leading religious sects—their doctrines and their history—which have powerfully influenced the world. This section was limited to forty volumes. The *Koran* was to be included, together with a good book or two on Mythology. One hundred and forty volumes were allotted to Poetry. The Epics were to embrace Homer, Lucan, Tasso, *Telemachus*, and the *Henriade*. In the Dramatic portion, Corneille and Racine were, of course, to be included, but of Corneille, said Napoleon, you shall print for me "only what is vital" (*ce qui est resté*), and from Racine you shall omit "*Les Frères ennemis*, the *Alexandre*, and *Les Plaideurs*." Of Crébillon, he would have only *Rhadamiste* and *Atrée et Thyeste*.* Voltaire was to be subject to the same limitation as Corneille.

Napoleon's preferences in the French Drama.

The class of History was to comprise the best books on Chronology, the chief classic texts, and such sufficient number of French works as would supply a detailed history of France; also Machiavelli on Livy, Montesquieu, and the best historical works of Voltaire. In Prose *Fiction*, Napoleon indicates the *Nouvelle Héloise*, and Rousseau's *Confessions*. "There is no need," he adds, "to specify the masterpieces of Fielding, Richardson, and Le Sage; they, of course, will have a place; and also Voltaire's tales. Then follows, by way of postscript, this note: "Neither the *Emilius*, nor the *Dissertations*, nor the *Correspondence* of Rousseau, is desired. And the same remark holds good of Voltaire."

The Emperor further directed that M. Barbier should furnish him with a methodised and annotated catalogue;

* Afterwards, at Longwood, Crébillon was wholly condemned. The Emperor read *Atrée* aloud, but could not get on with it. We all agreed, says Las Cases (*Vie privée*, iii, 52), that it was "not at all tragic, but simply horrible and disgusting."

with detailed estimates for printing and binding; and with particulars of the weight of the books, and the number, dimensions, and cubical contents, of the necessary cases.

Enlarged scheme of a Camp Library, in 1809.

Unless I greatly mistake, this plan is none the less interesting because of its only partial execution. It is thoroughly characteristic of the man; and, in the June of the following year, it recurred to his thoughts. He had brought in his train, from the Tuileries, a considerable travelling collection, arranged in a series of massive mahogany boxes (exchanged afterwards for leather ones, as being more durable), instantly convertible into book-cases, but, on reaching Schoenbrunn, he expressed great dissatisfaction at the absence of certain books which, as it seems, had been omitted, on account of their bulk. "The Emperor," he then wrote to Barbier, "daily feels the want of an historical travelling Library. It should be in five or six divisions, as—I, Chronology and Universal History; II, Ancient History (§ 1, by Ancient Writers; § 2, by Modern Writers); III, History of the Lower Empire (in like subdivisions); IV, History, both General and Particular ("such as Voltaire's Essays"); V, the Modern History of the different States of Europe. The collection must include Strabo, the *Ancient Atlas* of Danville, the Bible, and some History of the Church. A certain number of men of letters—"and of taste"—must be entrusted with the revision and correction of these editions, and "*with the suppression of everything that is useless, such as editorial notes, and the Greek or Latin texts,*" preserving only the French translation. "A few Italian works," adds Napoleon, —"of which there are no translations—may be retained in Italian. When these three thousand volumes of History are finished, a like number, in Natural History, Travels, and Literature, may follow; but these, for the most part,

Napoleon and his Libraries.

will present little difficulty. A large proportion of them exists already in the 18mo. size."*

In compliance with the Emperor's orders, Barbier drew up a detailed list of such a Library. He calculated that by employing a hundred and twenty compositors and twenty-five editors, the three thousand volumes could be produced, in satisfactory shape, and within six years, at a total cost of £163,200, supposing fifty copies of each book to be printed.† But in six years Napoleon was at St. Helena.

The printing was begun, but was soon broken off. Meanwhile, the Library which Napoleon had in actual use was improved and enlarged from time to time, and gave rise to not a little correspondence. "When our head-quarters are in villages," wrote Meneval, "there are many hours of the day which His Majesty would employ in reading," but the books he asks for are often wanting. On the other hand, we have many which in his eyes are worthless. Such are the works of Parny and of Bertin, the *Vie des Marins célèbres*, and the *Théâtre des auteurs du second ordre*. These and several others he has turned out. The *Æneid* and the Milton are in verse; His Majesty prefers to have translations in prose. He desires, too, to have Tacitus and Gibbon in French; Tasso, both in Italian and in French; and a Gil Blas. "Eleven volumes of Mme. de Sévigné take up too much room; send us a selection. The new romances you have lately sent are detestable. It would be much better to send old ones." The Emperor

Authors and books rejected by Napoleon.

* *Souvenirs sur le Bibliothècaire de l'Empereur*, ut infra.

† Barbier added that if, instead of printing fifty copies, three hundred copies were printed, and two thirds of the impression disposed of to the trade, almost four fifths of the cost might be recovered. *Souvenirs sur le Bibliothècaire de l'Empereur.* (*Bulletin du Bibliophile*, v, 273.)

Napoleon's love of choice printing and binding.

finds much fault, too, both with the printing and the binding. "I will have fine editions and handsome bindings. *I am rich enough for that.*" Such, writes Meneval, are his own words. The poor librarian, who was prohibited from sending books of a larger size than duodecimo, and yet must send choice ones, was almost in despair.*

Literary anecdote of Napoleon at Elba.

The most curious anecdote of a literary kind which has been told of Napoleon, in connection with his residence in the Island of Elba, wears, on its face, a very apocryphal aspect, and, in point of authority, has no better voucher than a MS. note on the fly-leaf of a copy of Symmons' *Life of Milton*, signed by a totally unknown "J. Brown." Mr. Brown's intelligence and historical knowledge are sufficiently indicated, under his own hand, in the statements that Napoleon was in custody at Elba, and that Sir Colin Campbell was his keeper. Yet the story is worth quoting. This almost anonymous annotator asserts that in 1815 he heard Colonel Stanhope state, at the table of the late Duke (then Marquis) of Buckingham, at Stowe, that Colonel Campbell had just told him of some remarkable words spoken by Napoleon at Elba, during one of the many conversations which he, Colonel Campbell, had held with the Emperor in the previous year. Speaking, on one occasion, of the battle of Austerlitz, Napoleon said that a particular disposition of his artillery, which, in its results, had a decisive effect in winning the battle, was suggested to his mind by the recollection of four lines in Milton. The lines occur in the sixth book, and are descriptive of Satan's artifice during the war in Heaven :—

* *Souvenirs sur le Bibliothècaire, &c.* (*Bulletin du Bibliophile*, v, 933—944).

> . . . . "In hollow cube
> Training his devilish engin'ry, impal'd
> On every side *with shadowing squadrons deep*
> *To hide the fraud.*"

The indubitable fact that these lines have a certain appositeness to an important manœuvre at Austerlitz, give an independent interest to the story; but it is highly imaginative to ascribe the victory to that manœuvre. And for the other pretensions of the tale, it is unfortunate that Napoleon had learnt a good deal about war, long before he had learnt anything about Milton.

At St. Helena, the Emperor began with a collection, small indeed, but larger and more varied than his campaigning Library had ever been. This first collection he brought with him in the *Northumberland*. At Plymouth, it had been increased by considerable purchases of English books; and it was on board ship that Napoleon's brief study of our language began. But the mass of the Longwood Library came afterwards (in June, 1816); and Las Cases has given a graphic account of the eagerness with which the illustrious prisoner helped to unpack the cases with his own hands, and of his entire absorption in the books on Egypt, to read which he sat up all night, keeping Marchand with him, and dictating notes on his readings, from time to time. On another day, but on the same occasion,—it seems to have taken three days to bring this Library up to Longwood,—he buried himself in a long series of the *Moniteur*, and kept at it—a short interval for dinner, I suppose, is to be excepted—for twenty-four hours at a stretch; "and he seemed," says Las Cases, "to find as much amusement in it as others find in a novel."*

The Library at the Briars; and at Longwood.

* *Vie privée de Napoleon*, &c., ii, 297. The Orderly Officer at Long-

Books of travel in Africa—especially those of Mungo Park—were eagerly pounced upon.

The even-ing readings at Longwood.

The long evenings at St. Helena were usually devoted to reading aloud, Napoleon himself being often the reader. His love for books of history continued with him to the last. Dramatic literature, too, of almost all countries, had for him an immense and enduring charm. It follows, very naturally, that his own reading was remarkably effective. Not less so were his incidental remarks and ejaculations. One one occasion he interrupted the reading for an instant, to exclaim, "To Corneille, France owes some of her great deeds. Had he lived in my time, I would have made him a prince." Years before, and in a very different scene—it was in the Council of State, on perhaps the only occasion that Napoleon was seen, *there*, with tears in his eyes*—he had said: "They know little of human nature who blame Corneille [on the score, he meant, of false antithesis] for putting in the mouth of the Elder Horace the famous passage,

"Qu'il mourut; *ou qu'un beau désespoir alors le secourût.*"

Les Horaces is not specifically mentioned among the Longwood readings, but that line must have come sometimes into Napoleon's mind, during the long years of hopeless exile.

Napoleon on Voltaire.

For the "bombast and tinsel" of Voltaire, the dramatist, which Frederick thought so admirable, Napoleon had great disrelish. *Œdipe* is the only dramatic production of that author which he liked to read or to listen to. *Mahomet* (a special favourite with Frederick) he could not tolerate.

wood reports "Napoleon's great delight" with these books of 1816.—*Lowe Papers*; Addl. MSS. in Brit. Mus., 20208.

* It was immediately after Dupont's surrender at Baylen, and it was to Dupont that the Emperor applied the quotation.

"He turns a great man into a scoundrel who deserves the gallows," was Napoleon's remark, to which he added, in his incisive way—his criticisms were often like vigorous sword-thrusts—"Voltaire delights in ascribing to petty intrigues the conquests of Opinion." He had criticised Mahomet just as vehemently in his memorable conversation with Goethe in October, 1808, winding up his diatribe with a recommendation to the poet to write a tragedy on the *Death of Cæsar*, for the purpose of showing what great benefits to the human race might have been looked for from such a man, "*had time been given him to develope his vast designs.*"* Once or twice he ventured to criticise English poets, as he knew them by translation. Thus, seeing an Englishman reading *Paradise Lost*, on board the *Northumberland*,—"Your British Homer," he said, "lacks taste, harmony, warmth, naturalness."† Singularly infelicitous as a criticism on Milton; one is not so sure of its injustice to the *Paradis Perdu* of Delille. Curious it is to find the autocrat of six and forty just as fond, not only of Homer, but of *Ossian*, as had been the youth of twenty. At Longwood, as at Valence, Homer, in French, would keep Napoleon out of his bed until long after midnight. The praises of Ossian he never wearied of sounding.‡

Among the legion of minor books read first in exile, and reviewed as they were read, was his brother Lucien's *Charlemagne*:—"What ability; what time and labour; thrown away! Twenty thousand verses—some few of them good verses—but the whole colourless, aimless, and resultless." Once, having read some book of which he

Napoleon's criticisms.

* Lewes, *Life of Goethe* (1863), 499.

† *Bonaparte à Sainte-Hélène* (1816), 96.

‡ "Read again"—such was his advice to the Englishman of the *Northumberland*—"the poet of Achilles. Devour Ossian. Those are the poets who lift up the soul, and give to man a colossal greatness." Ib.

himself was the subject, he commented thus:—"I find things positively affirmed about me and my motives, as to which it would severely task all my faculties to form, *to myself*, any clear and decided conviction of the truth. . . . The exact and literal truths are things difficult, indeed, for History to seize upon. Happily, they are, in very many cases, matters rather of curiosity than of real importance."* These readings were further diversified,—at one time, by Napoleon's studies in English under Las Cases;† at another, by his teaching Mathematics to young Bertrand. The book he used in this last pursuit—the *Cours de Mathématique* of Bézout—lies before me. It has his pencil marks and notes in its margins. Sometimes he has indicated the date of the lessons.‡

Those poor rooms within which the reorganizer of France, the Conqueror and the Legislator of a Continent, whilst struggling with mortal disease, by turns criticised the great writers on the Art of War, and taught a boy the Elements of Trigonometry; the rooms which witnessed the long readings,

* Las Cases, ut sup. iv, 237, 238.

† These English studies were the less successful, from Napoleon's undue expectation of quick progress. A note written to his preceptor has been printed in the weekly paper, called "*Notes and Queries.*" It runs thus: "Count Las Cases, Since six week I learn the English, and I do [make] not any progress. Six week do [make] fourty and two day. If I might have learn fivty word for day, I could know two thousand two hunderd. It is in the Dictionary more of fourty thousand. . . . After this you shall agree that to study one tongue is a great labour."

‡ This memorial of a season which we Englishmen, generally, are now coming to look back upon with something of the feelings of shame and mortification, with which, as we have good evidence, Statesmen and Poets regarded it long years ago, is worthily preserved among the "Additional MSS." in the British Museum, whither it came from the library of Bishop Butler.

the rapid dictations, and the keen arguments on Herodotus and Æschylus, on Tasso and Cervantes, of a man who will be the theme of the historians and the poets for many generations to come, were quickly turned into stables and haylofts; but the words spoken and written there retain all their power. And he must needs be a keen-witted man who could fairly calculate what Napoleon III owes to the Bathursts and the Hudson Lowes; who could deduce the full working on French minds and French imaginations, of the memories—and of the legends—of Longwood.

At this date, the Bathursts and the Lowes are not, reasonably, the objects of anger, but of pity. They but did what it was in their nature to do, and they had the tacit, though temporary, approval of the majority of their countrymen. They had, also, whatever of sanction may be wrung out of the fact, that the object of their petty persecutions had sometimes permitted much worse things to be done under his own rule. Yet very few men will, I think, turn over the original* documents (now publicly accessible), which tell the story of St. Helena, from our own English point of view, without a strong sensation of disgust.

Among those youthful papers of Napoleon which I mentioned at the outset, are numerous rough and boyish notes

* It has been, I see, quite recently denied that Sir H. Lowe tried to turn British officers into spies. I have had occasion to learn something about that, from the lips of those who were concerned. But there is no need to travel out of Sir H. Lowe's own papers for conclusive evidence. His conversations at Plantation House were recorded, under his own eye, by his military secretary. Thence we learn that on a certain occasion "The Governor said [to O'Meara] . . . that, for his part, *he did not understand how any subject of conversation* [with Napoleon] *could be introduced, which there was any necessity of keeping from his knowledge as Governor of this island.*" *Notes of Conversation*, . . . 25 Nov. 1817, Additional MSS. in Brit. Mus. 20146, f. 28, verso.

on Geography, which close with these words: "*Sainte-Hélène—petite île.*" The island, then so obscure, is now for ever famous, and its fame casts upon England "a shadow, not to pass away"—

> "Because it was not well, it was not well,
> Nor tuneful with our lofty chanted part
> Among the Oceanides,—that Heart
> To bind, and bare, and vex with vulture fell.
> I would, my noble England! men might seek
> All crimson stains upon thy breast,—not cheek!"

CHAPTER VII.

HISTORY OF THE OLD ROYAL LIBRARY OF THE KINGS OF ENGLAND.

O Ceremony, show me but thy worth?
What is thy Soul of Adoration?
* * * * *
'Tis not the balm, the sceptre, and the ball,
The sword, the mace, the crown imperial,
The inter-tissued robe of gold and pearl,
The farced title running fore the King,
The throne he sits on, nor the tide of pomp
That beats upon the high shore of this world.
* * * * * *Henry V*, iv, 1.

I CONNECT, in this and the two following chapters, an outline of the History of the Royal Library, with some notices of that of our chief Repositories of Records, because, as will appear hereafter, there are many points of substantial and close union between the two themes. Part of the early history of the Royal Library itself has to be sought in the annals of "the Treasury of the King's Exchequer at Westminster." The State Paper Office (which has so recently been combined with the main Record Repository in the new Rolls House) is, historically, "the King's Library for matters of State and Council." They are all, in fact, branches of one subject.

Be the cause what it may, it is unquestionable that, on the whole, the Kings of England cannot be praised for any distinctive love of literature; for any conspicuous zeal in its encouragement, or its extension. There are, indeed, exceptional instances, but they are few. In this respect, the English nobility, at almost all periods, contrasts very advantageously with the English monarchs, and need not shun comparison with the aristocracy of any, the most favoured country. But among the sovereigns,—as if by some special fatality,—even the two men who stand out of the common line, as possessing at once a considerable tincture of learning, and a more than average share of natural capacity, were mere egotists. Henry the Eighth's egotism was that of a voluptuary. James the First's egotism was that of a pedant. Neither achieved for literature anything that merits record, although both enjoyed noble opportunities. Henry permitted the princely revenues of the monasteries to be squandered amongst courtiers and parasites. James laboriously accumulated those acts of tyranny and persecution, which, in the next age, had for their inevitable result the ruin of a better king than himself, and the exile and destitution of the most illustrious divines and scholars in the Church of England. He lavished wealth and honours on a Carr, and sent a Raleigh to the scaffold. Both Henry VI and Charles I would doubtless have been more salient exceptions to the rule, but for their civil wars.

Earliest beginnings of a Royal Library.

This being so, it is not surprising that for several generations of our kings we have to search out the faint traces of such a collection, chiefly amongst Wardrobe Books, and Inventories of Household Furniture. The earliest entries of that kind which have, as yet, come under my own eye (during long searchings, both at the Rolls House, and at the old Paper Office), belong to the reigns of Edward I and Edward II. As late as Henry VIII, the lists of books are mixed up with lists of beds and tables. And even in the reign of Elizabeth, the office of "Keeper of the Books" is conjoined with that of "Distiller of Oderiferous Herbs;" —the worthy pluralist having, it may be noted, a better salary as a perfumer, than as a Librarian.

In the Close Rolls, indeed, there occurs an incidental mention of a Keeper of the King's Books (*Custos librorum Regis*) as early as 1252, but it is only in a precept directing him to deliver colours to a certain painter.* Two years earlier, there is mention of a French book, which seems to have been the King's, although it was then in the custody of the Master of the Knights Templars, who is ordered to deliver it to an Officer of the Wardrobe,† apparently that the King's painters might copy from it, when employed in painting a room called "the Antioch Chamber." But there are in these casual entries no distinct indications whatever of the actual contents of the "Royal Library."

Among the books incidentally described in the Wardrobe Accounts of 28th Edward I (A.D. 1299-1300) are these:— "A book which is called *Textus*, in a case of leather, on which the magnates are wont to be sworn; a book which begins *Prologus in Cronica;* a book of Romance, [*i.e.*, a book not in Latin, *unus liber de* Romauntz], which begins *Cristiens sevoet entremettre;* a book which begins *Paladi Rutili* [doubtless Palladius Rutilius, *De re Rustica*]; a book which begins *Ut de mundo sit utilis;* a book which begins *Sanctissimo . . in Christo Patri;* a book which is called *Summa*

Wardrobe accounts of the Plantagenets.

* "Mandatum est Radulpho de Dungun, *Custodi librorum Regis*, quod magistro Willielmo pictori regis habere faciat colores," &c.—*Rot. Claus.* 36 Hen. III, m. 22.

† "Mandatum est . . R. de Manford, ... quod faciat habere Henr. de Warderoba . . . quendam librum magnum, et Regum in quo continentur, *Gesta Antiochæ*," &c.—*Rot. Claus.*, 34 Hen. III, m. 12.

Tancredi," and so on; most of the others being either Service books or Household books.* Other books belonging to the Royal Library at this period were kept in the Treasury of the Exchequer. Thus, in Stapeldon's Exchequer Inventory, of the following reign, appear, "a book, bound in red leather, *De regimine Regum;*" also, "a small book on the Rule of the Knights Templars (*De regula Templariorum*);" a "stitched book *De vita Sancti Patricii;*" and "a stitched book, in a tongue unknown to the English, which begins thus, *Edmygaw douit duyrmyd dinas.*" Again, other "various stitched books and rolls, in the Welsh language," are mentioned, without further description, but with the apologetic remark that they are "very foreign" to the English tongue.† Sir Francis Palgrave has conjectured that the first-named treatise in Welsh, is, probably, a collection of the Bardic prophecies.‡ The list closes with the *Chronica* of Roderick de Ximenez, Archbishop of Toledo, "bound in green leather."

The Library of the Treasury.

In another volume of unlike nature to Stapledon's Inventory, (known as "Memoranda of the Treasury, from 39 Edw. III to 35 Hen. VIII," and printed, by the late Sir F. Palgrave, with other documents, in 1836), is an entry of the delivery into the King's Treasury, in 1419, of five volumes, namely, a *Bible;* a copy of the Book of *Chronicles;* a Treatise on the Conception of the Virgin Mary (*De Conceptione Beatæ Mariæ;* a *Compendium of Theology;* and a book entitled *Libellus de emendatione vitæ.*§ But these books were trans-

* *Liber quotidianus Contrarotulatoris Garderobæ*, anno Reg. Edw. I. 28vo. MS. in the Library of Society of Antiquaries. [Printed as an Appendix to the *Archæologia.*]

† *Kalendarium de Bullis*, &c. [By Walter Stapledon, Bishop of Exeter, 1323] (MS. Rolls House,) pp. 180, 203.

‡ *Ancient Kalendars and Inventories of the Exchequer*, I, lxxxiii.

§ *Memoranda*, &c. (MS. Rolls House), f. 49, verso.

ferred, in the following year, to the Monastery of Sheen. In 1426, a "book called Egesippus," and "another book called *Liber de Observantia Papæ*," were delivered out of the library in the Treasury to the secretary of Cardinal Beaufort, to be lent to the Cardinal for a limited period.* Hegesippus, *De Bello Judaico et urbis Hierosolymorum Excidio*, in a MS. ascribed by Casley to the eleventh century, is still among the Royal MSS. (14, C. VIII). There are also entries in the following year of the loan, by Ralph Lord Cromwell, Treasurer of England, of "various books on the civil law, and other books," to the Master of King's College, Cambridge, and of their subsequent gift to that house, with the assent of the Lords of the Council.†

Small encouragement of infant printing by the Kings of England.

The early history of printing in England contains, I think, no one fact distinctly indicative of any fostering of the infant art by the king. The only incident which conjoins the names of Caxton and of Edward IV is a record, on the Issue Roll of the Exchequer, of a payment of £20 to Caxton, in June, 1479, "for certain causes and matters performed by him for the said Lord the King."‡ Caxton's first dated book, it will be remembered, is of 1477, but the entry seems scarcely to accord with a mere purchase of books; whilst the payment would have been sure of grateful commemoration by the illustrious recipient, had it been made by way of encouragement for their production. Probably, therefore, it may have been but the payment of services rendered at Bruges, whilst Caxton was governor

* *Memoranda*, &c. (MS. Rolls House), f. 78. There are subsequent entries of the return and re-loan of the same volume to the same borrower.

† Ib., f. 79.

‡ *Issue Roll of the Exchequer*. (MS. Rolls Ho.) 15 June, 19 Edw. IV.

of the English Factory there, and in the service—in some sort—of Edward's sister, Margaret, Duchess of Burgundy.

But, in the Wardrobe Accounts of Edward IV—preserved in the Harleian MS. No. 4780—there are some entries, respecting the "coveryng and garnysshing of the Books of oure saide Souverain Lorde the Kinge," which indicate his possession, in 1480, of certain choice volumes, all of them, apparently, being manuscripts. Livy; Froissart; Josephus; *The Gouvernal of Kings and Princes;* a book *Of the Holy Trinite;* a *Bible Historiale;* another *Bible;* and a work entitled *La Forteresse de Foy*, are among the books which in that year were bound by Piers Bauduyn.* The price paid for "binding, gilding, and dressing" Froissart and the *Bible Historiale* was twenty shillings each; for several others, sixteen shillings each; for "three small bookes of Franche," six shillings and eight pence, together. Another entry at the same date shows that the king's books accompanied him from London to Eltham Palace; that some were put into "divers cofyns of fyrre," and others into "the king's carr."† Other entries show that the bindings were of figured cramoisy velvet, with rich laces and tassels, with buttons of silk and gold, and with clasps bearing the king's arms.‡ All the books named above, the "Gouvernal" excepted, are still to be seen among the Royal MSS.; but the identity of the copies is only conjectural. A fine *Bible Historiale*, now marked 19, D. 22, has an inscription recording its purchase for 100 marks, by William de Montacute, Earl of Salisbury, after the battle of Poitiers, where it had been captured among the baggage of the French king. The Earl (who died in 1397)

* Harl. MS., 4780, 21, verso. † Ib. ‡ Ib., 40, verso.

gave it to his Countess, who, in her Will, instructed her executors to sell it for "40 livres."* The only allusion to books which I find in King Edward the Fourth's Will relates merely to "boks apperteignyng to . . oure Chapell," which are left to the Queen, such books being excepted "as we shall herafter dispose to goo to oure said Collage of Wyndesore."†

Henry VII and his Library at Richmond.

In Henry VII, a taste for books had to struggle with an inordinate avarice of money. The superb series of the productions of the press of Anthony Verard, upon vellum, which adorned his library (and is now one of the innumerable attractions to curiosity-seekers at the British Museum), shows plainly that the love of fine books was strong enough to vanquish the love of broad pieces. The accounts of his Privy Purse tell—as I shall show in some detail presently—the same tale. This king's principal Library was lodged in his palace at Richmond, and seems to have been kept there intact for at least a century after his death. Quintin Paulet is the only Royal Librarian whose name I have yet met with in the records of this reign. His name occurs often between 1495 and 1504. Henry VIII appointed Giles Du Wes to be keeper of the Library "at Richemounte," with a salary of £10 a year, in the first year of his reign.‡ William Tillesley filled the same office, and had the same salary, in Queen Mary's time.§ In the reign of James I, the Library was shown to John Zinzerling—visiting Richmond as a literary tourist—and it still bore the designation of "the Library of Henry VII." The only

* Royal MS. 19, D. 22, at beg.

† Additional MSS. in Brit. Mus. (Transcripts by Rymer, for the *Fœdera.*) No. 4615.

‡ Privy Seal (Rolls House) 20 Sept. 1509.

§ *Household book of Mary*, MS., quoted by Lysons, i, 441.

book of which he makes specific mention is a "*Genealogia Regum Angliæ* ab Adamo." This is a MS. roll of the 15th century, and may yet be seen among the Royal MSS. in the British Museum.* Henry's inkstand was shown to Zinzerling, and also his bed-chamber, yet bearing the stains of his blood.† Charles I often lived here, and it was here that he collected many of his pictures. But in the Parliamentary survey of the palace, and its appurtenances, made in 1649, there is no mention of any library.‡ Most probably it had been removed by Charles to Whitehall. After the Restoration, I find the *Genealogia,* which Zinzerling had seen at Richmond about 1612, entered in a Catalogue of Charles the Second's MSS. at Whitehall, made in 1666.§

The Privy Purse Expenses of Henry VII contain a remarkable series of entries of payments for books, as well for the purchase of printed ones, as for copying manuscripts, and for binding. For instance: "To one Smerte for an English boke, 20*s*.;" "To Frances Mareyn, for divers bokes by bill, 65*s*.;" "To Master Peter, for certain bokes, opon a bille, £11 : 3 : 4;"¶ "To Hugh Dewes, for printed bokes, 13*s*. 4*d*.;"** "To a boke-bynder, 6*s*. 8*d*.;"†† "Delivered to Quintyn, for bokes, £20;"‡‡ "for 2 new bokes, bought of Ursyn, £2;"§§ and so on. Some of the payments indicate that the king's love of books was widely known.‖‖ On one occasion £23 appears to have been given for one book.¶¶

* 14, B. 8.

† Iodoci Sinceri [*i. e.*, Joannis Zinzerling] *Itinerarium* (1627), 309.

‡ MS. (Rolls House) [printed in *Monumenta Vetusta.*]

§ Royal MS., App. 71, f. 8. (*Catalogus librorum MSS. Bibliothecæ Regiæ*, 1666.)

‖ Additional MS., B. M., 7099, f. 22.

¶ Ib., 27.

** Ib., 31.

†† Ib., 34.

‡‡ Ib.

§§ Ib.

‖‖ "To a woman that brought a book, £2." Ib.

¶¶ Ib., 41.

An entry of the payment of two pounds to Clement Clerk for writing of *The Amity of Flanders* seems to indicate something more than mere transcription of a treaty.*

There occur throughout these accounts several items of "rewards" to poets. "To the blynde poet in reward, ten nobles;" "To my lady the Kinges Moder poet, ten nobles;" "To the Rymer of Scotland, in rewarde, twenty nobles."† The blind poet is Bernard Andreas, the biographer of Henry. The "King's Mother's poet" is probably, in Mr. Craven Ord's opinion, as appears by the MS. note he has affixed to the entry, no less a person than Erasmus, one of whose letters from London is dated two days later than the date of this payment (Dec. 3, 1497). The rhymer of Scotland is perhaps Dunbar. But, in monetary appreciation, the poets are, as usual, quite outshone by the dancers. "A little maid that danceth" gets twelve pounds. Another damsel, of the same graceful calling, thirty pounds. Interspersed with these entries of pastime are some which look as grim as a death's head at a banquet —"To Sir William Stanley, *upon his execution,*‡ ten pounds." "To Sir Robert Clifford, five hundred pounds." Clifford, it will be remembered, was Perkin Warbeck's counsellor and "friend."

Three book entries (it may finally be added) seem to relate to the productions of Verard's press already mentioned:—"To a Frensheman for certain bokes, fifty-six pounds, four shillings;"§ "to Antony Verard, for two bokes called *The Gardyn of Helthe* (1502) six pounds;"‖ "To a Frensheman for printed bokes (1505), ten pounds, fifteen

* Additional MS., B. M., 7099, f. 37. † Ib., 43.

‡ *Sic* in MS. § Ib., f. 62. ‖ Ib., 75.

shillings."* Richard Pynson's name occurs as receiving in 1503 a reward of twenty shillings. In the following year, Henry lends him ten pounds, "upon a prest for masse bokes to be printed."† In 1505, the king gives the monks of Richmond books, bought of Henry Jacob, to the value of forty-six pounds ten shillings.‡ Henry's expenditure for jewels was enormous, like his son's. In one entry appears a payment of £30,000 for precious stones and jewels "from beyond sea."§ He had, too, a similar love for gaming and wagers, but does not seem to have indulged it to equal lengths. The book contains many evidences of his large commercial speculations on the Continent, as well as many proofs that, whatever his essential avarice, he was more open-handed in the small matters of daily life than quite consists with the usual delineations of his character.

Henry's fondness for French literature has been repeatedly noticed, like his proneness to diarize. "He was," says Bacon, "a prince sad, serious, and full of thoughts and secret observations; and full of notes and memorials of his own hand. . . . . . He was rather studious than learned; reading most books that were of any worth in the French tongue. Yet he understood the Latin."‖

Westminster Library of King Henry VIII.

Neither of Henry VII nor of his more famous son has anything been recorded which shows distinctly any real interest in the nascent literature of England itself. We have a complete Catalogue of the Library of Henry VIII at Westminster (formerly preserved in the Augmentation

* Additional MS., B. M., 7099, f. 91. † Ib., f. 88.

‡ Ib., 93. At fol. 91, is an entry of a gift to the Church Library (as it seems) at Richmond.

§ Ib., 87.

‖ Bacon, *Life and Reign of Henry VII* (Kennet, i, 637).

Office, and now in the General Record Office), taken towards the close of his reign. It contains two entries under the name of Boccaccio, and two under that of Petrarch, but none under "Chaucer." The works of Chartier, of Coquillart, and of Marot, occur, with many other books in French, and amongst them the *Breviarium d'Amours*, the *Songe du Vergier*, and three copies of the *Roman de la Rose*. Dante appears thus:—"Danti's works in the Castilian tongue." The only English author of note is Gower. The only Greek authors are Thucydides, Herodianus, Plutarch, Galen, and Aristotle (*Ethica; Politica; Naturalia*). The principal Latin classics in the collection are Virgil, Horace, Ovid, Livy (both in Latin and in French), Pliny, Quintilian, and Quintus Curtius. Of Cicero, the *Orationes*, the *De Finibus*, and the *De Officiis*, also occur; with a French translation of the treatise *De Senectute*. Orosius appears twice. The chief Historians of England which appear in this catalogue are Henry of Huntingdon; St. Ives, Bishop of Chartres; a "*Cronica from K. Richard I to K. Henry V;*" a "*Cronicle of England, written;*" and Polydore Virgil; together with a series of chroniclers which are thus sweepingly described in a single entry:—"*Policronica.* Item, *Cronica Nich. Trivet.* Item, *Parva prophetia de Regibus Anglis.* Item, *Historia de gestis Britonum.* Cum plurimis aliis Cronicis et Opusculis." The chief foreign chroniclers are Comines, Froissart, Monstrelet, and the *Cronica Martiniana*, usually attributed—in part, at least—to John Philip de Lignamine. The only complete English Bible which I find entered in this catalogue (compiled, it is to be remembered, in 1542 or 1543) is thus entitled: "*Biblia, in lingua vernacula, cum antiqua translatione.*"

English Chronicles in Henry VIIIth's Library.

Its Theology, &c.

The works of the Fathers are so numerous as to form a capital feature in the collection. Works on the Civil Law also occur very frequently. Of Primers, the Library seems to have possessed more than sixty, which are thus concisely described:—"Primer in great volume; Primer in Latine *ad usum Sarum;* Primers printed in volume, gilted and covered with vellat, 20; Primers bound in lether and gorgeously gilted, 36; Primer written covered with cloth of gold; Primer printed; Primer written in volume unbound." "Processionals printed, 12; Processionals written, 2," also occur. Many of the entries are so brief and vague as to give no intelligible notion of the book intended. Thus "Portraiture" is an entry, without further explanation; and three books are catalogued under the word "*Volumen.*" Another entry reads thus:—"Bookes written in tholde Saxon tonge, two thome of the Pentituik and Sayncts lives. The other of Medecine." The catalogue is alphabetical and in two parts, to the second of which this heading is prefixed: "*Adhuc Index Librorum qui habentur in prænominata Bibliotheca, quorum quidam inculti, quidam ex antiqua impressione.*" After this, a new alphabet begins.

Greenwich Library of King Henry VIII.

Besides this Library at Westminster, and that at Richmond (collected by his father), Henry VIII had a Library at Greenwich, but of this no catalogue seems to have been preserved. There is, however, amongst the Harleian MSS., an inventory, taken after the King's death, which shows that this collection then contained three hundred and forty-one printed and MS. volumes (329 of which were kept in the Library proper, and twelve volumes elsewhere), besides numerous unbound MSS., scattered about the Palace; but it describes none of them save the following: "a greate booke called An Herballe; twoo great Bibles in Latten; one booke of Aristotle; a Mass-booke covered with black vellvet."* Again, "a lytle booke of parchment with Prayers, covered with crymson velvet";† "a New Testament, glozed, written, unbound;‡ a booke, wrytten in parchment, of the processe betwene King Henry th'eight and the Ladye Katherine, Dowager."§ The bulk of the books is entered in this fashion: "In one deske, xxxj bookes, covered with redde;" "in another desk, xxxvij bookes;" "under the table, cvij bookes;" and so on.

Henry had also a Library at Windsor, containing a hundred and nine volumes, none of which are particularised, otherwise than as comprising ninety-eight "boarded books," sixteen "pasted books," and three "paper books." The covering of one of the "boarded books" was of velvet, with silver clasps.‖ At Newhall (sometimes called Beaulieu), in Essex, he had a small Library, of about sixty volumes, including Livy, Cæsar, Cicero, and Sallust; the works of Saints John Chrysostom, Augustine, Jerome, Cyprian, Ambrose, Gregory, Bernard, and Thomas Aquinas; the *Cornucopia,* and several other Dictionaries; the Chronicle of Eusebius, the *Fasciculus Temporum,* and another Chronicle here called *Cronica Volatonii.*¶ At Beddington, in Surrey, he had a series of the beautiful editions of Historians, Chroniclers, and Romancists, printed by Anthony Verard, thus enumerated in the Inventory: *Lancelot,* Monstrelet, Froissart, Orosius in French, *Chroniques de France,* each being in two or more volumes; together with other copies of Froissart, apparently MSS.; *Le graunt Voiage de Jerusalem;* and, finally, "a greate booke of parchment, written and lymned

Other Libraries at Windsor, Newhall, and Beddington.

* Harl MS., 1419, A., f. 56, verso.
† Ib., f. 61.
‡ Ib., f. 62, verso.
§ Ib.
‖ Ib., f. 20.
¶ Ib., f. 66, and verso.

with gold of graver's worke, *De Confessione Amantis*."* This last is probably identical with the fine copy of Gower's poem now marked "18, C. 22," which has some beautifully "lymned" initial letters, although it is without miniatures. There is no absolutely precise means of identifying the printed volumes with the noble series of Verards on vellum, struck off for Henry the Seventh, yet they are probably the same.

The Verards now in the British Museum.

Henry's Books at St. James's.

In the Inventory of Furniture at St. James's the only literary entries are a "book of parchment containing divers patterns,"† and the foundation-book of Henry the Seventh's Chapel,‡ a beautiful copy of which has been recently acquired for the British Museum. Two or three other books appear in an appendix; *e. g.*, "a white book written on parchment;"§ "one book covered with green velvet, contained in a wooden case;" "a little book covered with crimson velvet;"‖ "a Description of the Holy Land, and a book covered with velvet, embroidered with the King's arms, declaring the same, in a case of black leather, with his Grace's arms."¶ "A booke of paternes for phiosionamyes" seems to have caught the special fancy of Edward VI, as on the margin of this entry is written, "taken by the King's Majesty himself."** Many of Henry's books accompanied him, occasionally, in his removals from one palace to another.††

It is evident, therefore, that Henry VIII had a marked

* Harl. MS., 1419, B., f. 85, verso. † Ib., 173.
‡ Ib., 214. § Ib., 215, verso. ‖ Ib., 216.
¶ Ib., 246, verso. ** Ib., 157.
†† *Privy Purse Expenses* [printed by Nicolas], passim. Entries of payments to boatmen for carrying books from Greenwich to York Place, and from York Place to Hampton or Richmond, are frequent, and there are several entries of payments for the carriage of books from monasteries.

taste for books. But there is no commensurate proportion between his very slender outlay in this direction and his enormous outlay on plate and jewels. The ponderous folios of the Inventory of 1547, which I have so freely quoted, are crowded with evidences of his lavish expenditure on articles of mere luxury and show. And the evidence of his Privy Purse books is to the same effect. Within three years only (1530-32) we find him disbursing £10,800 for jewels alone—exclusive of plate—and little more than £100 for books and binding. But his Library and his jewel-house tell exactly the same tale in another particular. They show conclusively that

His comparative expenditure on Books and Jewellery.

> "He was, to wit, a stout and sturdy thief,
> Wont to rob Churches of their ornaments."

Some of his finest jewels were plundered from monastic treasuries; some of his finest books were the spoils of monastic libraries. Among the "Royal MSS."—some of which are now before me—are books that were once shown to visitors with pride by the cowled librarians of Lincoln, of Bury St. Edmund's, of Ramsey, of Worcester, of Jervaux, and of Sempringham. The Latin Gospels of the eleventh century, marked 1, D. 3, was the gift of a certain Countess Goda to the monks of Rochester; the Evangeliary of the ninth century, marked 1, A. 18, was the gift of King Athelstan to Christ Church, Canterbury. Several choice MSS., historical and theological, were written by the hand of Matthew Paris, in the busy Scriptorium of St. Alban's. But the books thus casually preserved, by the care of better men than their royal acquirer, are insignificant, when compared with those which he caused to be scattered and destroyed.

Edward the Sixth had but little time to improve the

The Royal Libraries of England under Edward VI.

Libraries he had inherited, but was able to show his love for learning in a far more effectual way. Yet this minor means was not neglected. He made some addition of books, and gave the charge of the chief collection to Roger Ascham. When Martin Bucer died, Sir John Cheke wrote to Dr. Parker, one of Bucer's executors: "I pray you, let Mr. Bucer's books and scroles unwritten, be sent up and saved for the King's Majesty."* The arrangement ultimately made, as Strype records it—without, in this instance, citing his authority—was a somewhat strange one. The King had the Manuscripts; the Duchess of Somerset, the greater part of the printed books; and Cranmer, the remainder. The widow, it seems, expected to receive for this Library a hundred pounds, but in fact received only eighty.† Such is Strype's account of this curious partition. I have looked in vain among the State Papers of Edward's reign for the means of setting at rest the doubts that suggest themselves. They contain several letters which mention Bucer and his affairs, but none that clear up this point.

The Library of Bucer.

Many testimonies to the learning and varied attainments of the youthful king are widely known. None of them is more remarkable than Jerome Cardan's account of his conversation with Edward in 1552. After speaking of his great skill in languages, and of that gravity "which truly befitted the regal majesty," Cardan adds that he was bland and companionable, fond of music, laborious in affairs, and of a liberal mind. The tokens, he elsewhere says, of early death were already visible in Edward's face.‡ Yet, urged by the courtiers, he constructed for him a horoscope, in

Cardan's conversation with Edward VI.

* *Letters of Illustrious Men*, MSS. of Corpus Christi College, Cambridge, quoted in Strype's Cranmer, App. No. 51.

† Ib. *Memorials*, 357, 358. ‡ *Geniturarum Exemplar*, pp. 5-19.

which are predictions of what was to happen to the poor monarch *in his fifty-sixth year.* Cardan afterwards apologised* for missing the mark so widely, by citing, amongst other things, the fate of earlier astrologers who had too accurately foretold sad stories of the deaths of kings. He often recurred in after life to his talk with Edward, and would say that in him was the making of a philosopher, as well as of a king.

Almost the only conspicuous incident in relation to the Royal Library, during the reign of Mary,† is the submission of a memorial "for the recovery and preservation of ancient writers and monuments, and . . . . concerning the erecting of a Library, without any charge to the Queen's Majestie," in the year 1556. Its author was Dr. John Dee, afterwards Warden of Manchester, a man who combined eminent attainments in Mathematics, and a respectable tincture of Divinity, with Quixotic adventurousness and with marvellous feats as a "Discourser with Spirits." But his notions about a Royal Library belong rather to the Ghost-seer than to the man of science. His plan was a very simple one, and by no means new. Whether or not he had consciously borrowed it from Ptolemy Evergetes, the reader must judge. But true it is that he contents himself with the proposition that the Queen of England, in order to form a sumptuous Library, and to become an illustrious patron of literature, had nothing to do beyond the appointment of a Commission,

Dee's proposal to Queen Mary for the enlargement of the Royal Library.

* *Geniturarum Exemplar,* ut supra.

† Among the Royal MSS., two Latin Psalters are preserved, which were gifts to Mary. One of them (2, B. 7) is splendidly illuminated, with miniatures of the fourteenth century, and has that combination of the grotesque with the beautiful which is often seen in mediæval books, as in mediæval sculpture.

clothed with powers to demand, under penalty, from all owners of Manuscripts throughout the realm, their transmission to London, there to be copied, and then returned, provided a claim was made by the owner, and made in due form and at a proper time. In case of omission, or of informality, both book and copy were to remain in the Queen's collection. This proposal was, of course, resultless.*

Even under Elizabeth, with her varied accomplishments and more than respectable scholarship, the history of the Royal Library has still to do rather with project than performance. Several eminent men concurred in urging on the Queen the advantages which would accrue from the establishment of a great national collection of books, adequately endowed. Foremost among these were Archbishop Parker, Sir Humphrey Gilbert, and Sir Robert Cotton, who reminded the Queen of the pattern set us by "the more civilised nations, . . Germany, Italy, and France," countries in which pains had been taken "to encourage learning by Public Lectures, Libraries, and Academies." It was the wish of these eminent men, and of those who had aided them in the establishment of the original "Society of Antiquaries," to obtain a Charter of Incorporation, and a public building in which they might establish, for public use, "*The Library of Queen Elizabeth.*" But Her Majesty was still greatly under the influence of Cecil, and Cecil in

Proposals of Archbishop Parker and of Sir R. Cotton and others, for erecting a great Library.

* Several years afterwards, Dee wrote from Antwerp to Burghley, telling him, amongst other things, that he had bought a copy of the curious book of Trithemius, entitled *Steganonographia*, "meet and commodious for a Prince." He asserts that its rarity was so great that "1000 crowns had been offered in vain" for a copy. MSS. S. P. O. *Domestic*, Eliz., vol. xxvii, No. 63.

such matters was, I think, but a Gallio,* despite his chancellorship of Cambridge, and his own considerable attainments in literature. Elizabeth herself may have had some misgivings about the possible consequences of a too elaborate study of what her successor called the "arcana of government."

It does not appear that the petition actually presented to the Queen has been preserved, but in the rough draft of it, now amongst the Cottonian MSS., the promoters express their intention that the Library shall "be well furnished with divers ancient books and monuments, which otherwise may perish; and that, at the costs and charges of divers gentlemen who will be willing thereunto;" and they entreat Her Majesty "to bestow out of Her Grace's Library such and so many of her books concerning History and Antiquity, as it shall please her to grant, for the better furnishing of this Library."†

Hentzner's Account of Queen Elizabeth's Library.

When Paul Hentzner, the German tourist, visited England towards the close of Elizabeth's reign, he saw the Queen's Library at Westminster, and describes it as well stored with Greek, Latin, Italian, and French books, bound, for the most part, in velvet of various colours, but chiefly red; and some of them adorned with pearls and gems. Among the choice books which are now kept in the "Select Cases" of the British Museum, are several of those which

* That is, as far as the public was concerned. His own library was a considerable one. Camden, it may be remembered, calls it "*bibliotheca instructissima,*" and borrowed largely from it. Of Lord Burghley's pains in collecting books from the Continent there is evidence in his correspondence with Thos. Windebank.—MSS. S. P. O. *Dom.*, Eliz. vol. 20.

† *A Project touching a Petition to be exhibited unto her Majesty for the Erecting of Her Library, and an Academy.* Cotton MS. Faustina, E. V., ff. 67, 68. To this draft there is appended, in Camden's hand, the names of Cotton, Doddridge, and Ley (afterwards Earl of Marlborough).

thus excited Hentzner's admiration. Especially noticeable are the *Historia Ecclesiastica* of Sozomen and Evagrius (1569); the presentation copy of John Foxe's *Gospels, in Anglo-Saxon and English*, of 1571; the treatise *De Antiquitate Britannicæ Ecclesiæ*, by Archbishop Parker, of 1572 (said, but with doubtful accuracy, to have been the first book privately printed in England); and the *Fiore della Retorica*, of 1560.

Purchase of the Library of Lord Lumley, by Prince Henry.

In the reign of James I, the Royal Library received, at first, diminution, instead of enlargement; Sir Thomas Bodley having obtained from the King warrants permitting him to select books for his new Library at Oxford, as well as to receive timber from the royal forests.* But on the death of John, Lord Lumley, his fine collection was purchased for Prince Henry, and established in Saint James' Palace. There does not occur among the State Papers of this reign any account either of its precise extent, or of the sum paid for it. The Privy Purse Books of the Prince have perished (as it seems) by the neglect of bygone days, with a solitary exception, in the accounts for the year 1609-10. In that one surviving document occurs an entry about the Library of Lord Lumley, in the following words: "*To Mr. Holcock, for writing a Catalogue of the Library which His Highness hade of my Lord Lumley*, £8 : 13 : 0."† This payment was made at the end of the year 1609.

Lord Lumley had long been a liberal collector of books,

* MSS. S. P. O. James I, *Docquet Book*, 3 May, 1611.

† Ib., *Dom.*, James I, lvii, No. 87, p. 4. This valuable document illustrates both the tastes and the charities of Prince Henry very strikingly. He gives very long prices for great horses. His charges for tennis balls sometimes amount to twenty-five pounds (in the money of 1610) in a single quarter. But the entries which indicate his kindliness of nature are more numerous still.

and had inherited a valuable Library from his father-in-law, Henry Fitz-Alan, Earl of Arundel, who had gathered manuscripts in days when the treasures of the old monastic Libraries were scattered about at the mercy of chance, and who had obtained part of the Library of Cranmer. Most of Lord Arundel's books bear his title in close neighbourhood to that of his son-in-law. Edward Wright, the mathematician, was made Librarian of the Prince's Library, with a salary of thirty pounds a year, to the sore disappointment of the already eminently learned Patrick Young, who had sought the office, with the help of his constant patron, Bishop Montagu.*

Prince Henry survived his purchase only three years, but he added to it from time to time. In the book already quoted there are many entries of this kind:—"*To a Frenchman, who presented a book to His Highness*, £4 : 10 : 0,"—indicating small but frequent augmentations; and he is said to have acquired the entire collection of a certain learned but now forgotten Welshman, named Morice.†

Partial dispersion of the Prince's Library.

At Henry's death, a considerable portion of his Library was preserved, and ultimately combined (at St. James') with the old Royal Library, but part of it was dispersed. Several private collections can show books which bear the conjoined names—"*Tho. Cantuariensis. Arundel. Lumley.*" Meanwhile, Patrick Young's unwearied patron had procured him a commission to catalogue the Whitehall Library for the King, and had afterwards procured for him its keepership. He is the first "Royal Librarian" of whose persistent energy in the discharge of that office we have distinct proof. He obtained several important additions of books from the Continent. He exerted himself vigorously, on the death of Isaac Casaubon, to prevent the return to

* Smith, *Vita Patricii Junii*, 10. † Ib.

France of the books which it had cost that great scholar so much pains to get out of France. For Casaubon had left most of his books in De Thou's charge, and when he wrote for them, after his establishment in England, De Thou was —for a time, at least—prohibited by Queen Mary from sending more than a few of those most "essential to his [*i. e.* Casaubon's] studies," in the hope, as it appears, that if the Library should be detained, its owner must needs return.

Casaubon's conversations with James.

Casaubon's account of his literary intercourse with James is curious, but it tends as much to bring out his own turn for adulation as the King's inordinate vanity. The talk on the first interview ran upon the pamphlets of the French renegade Reboul, now utterly forgotten. Next day it turned on historians, and especially on Tacitus, Plutarch, and Comines, with all of whom it pleased James to find fault. Tacitus, he thought excessively overrated. Plutarch, he condemned for his "injustice towards Julius Cæsar." Comines, he convicted of levity of judgment, and of proneness to praise Englishmen ironically. The great critic's courtly expressions* of amazement at the King's utterances would seem very open to the reproach cast at Comines, but for their entire accordance with many passages in his Diary which cannot be taken otherwise than seriously.

James' literature, indeed, seems at no time of life to have lifted him above either his pedantry or his absolutism. Could he have had his full will, English and Scottish authors would have written under a censorship as severe as was ever established by any Spanish Inquisition in its palmiest days. When he read *The Fairy Queen*, he seems

* "Non sine stupore tantum regem de literis audivi pronuntiare."—Casauboni *Ephemerides*, 785, 786.

chiefly to have seen in it an allusion to his mother's trial, and strove hard to wreak his vengeance on Spenser at second-hand, by working on the hopes and fears of his expectant courtiers in England. How, in his later days, he treated Sir Robert Cotton, I shall have occasion to show, from his own papers, and from those of his victim, by and bye. In 1610, he is found meddling with literature both in France and in England. In his own kingdom, he directs the Stationers' Company "to suffer nothing to be imprinted concerning the death of the late French King, unless it be such things as shall have the signification of our Lord Treasurer's pleasure."* In France, at the very same moment, he employs one agent to seduce printers into a breach of French law by publishing surreptitiously a translation of his own book, the *Apologia pro Juramento Fidelitatis*,† and another agent to get from French printers, by some sort of fraud, treatises obnoxious to his policy.‡

James' dealings with literature.

In the Household Rolls of James no Librarian, other than the Librarian of Richmond, appears. In those of Charles (*e. g.* 1626 and 1633), the "keeper of the Library" is entered under the class "Artificers."§

As I have shown in the preceding chapter, Charles I seems to have done very little for the augmentation of the Library of his predecessors. In the Domestic Papers of

The Royal Library under Charles I.

* Sir Thomas Wilson to Waterson, 14 May, 1610, MS., S. P. O.; *Dom.*, James I, liv, 43.

† Tourval to Salisbury. Ib., lv, 7.

‡ In the same year, another agent writes to Salisbury, that he has "taken out of the hands of a printer at Bourdeaux," a treatise on the union of England and Scotland, because it is "of a dangerous lecture, in my opinion."—D. Home to Salisbury, 25 Oct., 1619. Ib., lvii, 104.

§ *Book of Fees, &c.*, James I and Charles I. Addit. MSS. in B. M., 12508.

that reign there is scarcely any mention of it. Patrick Young continued to be its keeper until 1648, and was then temporarily succeeded by Hugh Peters, who, fanatic as he may have been, protected the Library from spoliation at the hands of the tumultuous soldiers. Peters' examination on this subject by a royal commission in 1660 will be referred to hereafter. Of the fact that he had the custody of the Library for three or four months, there is no doubt, although no entry of his appointment appears on the Journals of the House of Commons, where in 1648 it may naturally be looked for.*

The gift of the Alexandrian MS. to King Charles I.

But to this otherwise vacant period in the annals of the Royal Library belongs the acquisition of the book which has long held the first place amongst its treasures. By the gift of Cyril Lucar, the ill-fated Patriarch of Constantinople, Charles received in 1628, at the hands of Sir Thomas Roe, his ambassador to the Porte, the venerable "Alexandrian Manuscript" of the Greek Bible. To Roe, the credit of the acquisition is fairly due. As early as 1624 he had obtained this Bible from the Patriarch, to be given to King James. Roe made no pretensions to critical skill in MSS., and therefore contents himself,—when writing to Lord Arundel the earliest account of it that came to England,—with telling Cyril's own story, without comment:—"He hath given me an autographal Bible intire, written by the hand of Tecla, the protomartyr of the Greeks, that lived in the time of St. Paul, and doth aver it to be true and authentical, of her own writing, and the greatest antiquity of the Greek Church." In 1626, he wrote of it to Arch-

* The probability is that he was appointed by a Select Committee long previously appointed to take charge of books "sequestrated," but I have searched the Record Office for the Minutes of that Committee without success.

bishop Laud, and then says it was "written by the virgin Tecla, ... who was persecuted in Asia, and to whom Gregory Nazianzen hath written many epistles. She died not long after the Council of Nice."*

Young's endeavour to print the Alexandrian MS.

Young made many endeavours to do for Biblical literature, in the seventeenth century, what was not fully done until the nineteenth, by publishing a fac-simile edition of this famous MS., with all needful supplementary aids. Having failed to induce the King to take the matter up, he prevailed on the Assembly of Divines, in 1644, to petition the House of Commons that "the said Bible may be printed for the benefit of the Church, the advancement of God's glory, and the honour of the kingdom." The House appointed a Committee to confer with Mr. Young, and to consider of the best course for printing it, adding to their resolution the words—"and the care hereof is especially recommended to Mr. Selden."† But the desired result was not attained. The times were little propitious for undertakings like these.

Charles's plan for promoting the publication of Greek MSS.

That nothing effective had been previously done by Charles is not, in the least degree, surprising. Before his main difficulties met him, he had given a significant example of his notion of "all possible encouragement" by a royal patron to works of learning. Writing to Laud, in January 1634,‡ he speaks of Young's edition of the Epistle of Clement, and of the intention of his librarian, with the aid of the Bishop of Peterborough, to bring out one or more Greek books yearly, from MSS. either in the King's Library, or in other collections. To this project His Majesty is inclined to give "all possible encouragement,"

* Roe, *Negotiations*, 335, 618.

† *Journals of the House of Commons*, iv, 9.

‡ MSS. S. P. O. *Dom.*, Chas. I, cclviii, 59.

and therefore directs the Archbishop, first, to appropriate to the purchase of Greek type certain fines inflicted by the High Commission Court upon the King's printers, "for base and corrupt printing;" and, secondly, to require the said printers to print one such volume yearly "*at their own cost of ink, paper, and workmanship.*" Laud accordingly sends the King's instructions to the printers, in January, 1634.*

The Library at St. James' placed in the charge of Bulstrode Whitelocke.

In July 1649, it was referred to the Council of State to consider of the means of preserving "the books and medals at St. James' from imbezzlement." The Council then asked Bulstrode Whitelocke, First Commissioner of the Great Seal, to take that charge upon him, as Library Keeper, and to appoint his own deputy. "I knew the greatness of the charge," says Whitelocke, "and considered the prejudice that might fall out by being responsible for those rich jewels, ... yet, being informed of a design in some to have them sold and transported beyond sea, ... and being willing to preserve them for public use, I did accept of the trouble of being Library Keeper, and therein was . . much persuaded by Mr. Selden, who swore that if I did not undertake the charge of them, . . . those choice books and manuscripts would be lost; and there were not the like to them, except only in the Vatican, in any other Library in Christendom."† On the express recommendation of the Council of State, Whitelocke appointed John Dury—the friend of Milton—to be Deputy-keeper, and directed an inventory of the collection to be made. By a subsequent entry in the Order Book of the Council of State (in March 1652), it would seem that George Wither, the poet, had

* MSS., S. P. O. *Dom.*, Chas. I, cclix, 12.

† Whitelocke, *Memorials* (1732), 415, 416.

been (in some way not now explicable) connected with the Library, which is there described as "the Public Library at Saint James'."* Whitelocke's embassies, and other public cares, must have made his librarianship little more than nominal. On the eve of the Restoration, the Council of State appointed a Committee to report "what books or other things are in the Library at James'; whether any of them have been imbezzled, and by whom; and how the same may for the future be preserved for public use."† But no report on the subject is now preserved.

Very soon after the return of Charles II, the keeping of the library was committed to Thomas Rosse, but it would appear from his petition to the King in 1661, that he had at first no formal appointment, and received neither "supply nor subsistence."‡ In August of that year a salary or "annuity" of £200 was granted to him.§ In June, 1665, he had a formal grant of the office for life, with reversion to Richard Pearson. Rosse was in the household of the Duke of Monmouth, and his second petition to the King, just before the date of the last-named grant, shows that the royal librarianship was in those days diversified by occasional service at sea:—"Your petitioner," he says, "is now in your Majesty's royal fleet, and very uncertaine of his returne, having contracted great debts,‖ . . . and hath no certaine subsistance to maintaine

Librarianship of Thos. Rosse.

* *Order Book of the Council of State*, MS., Interreg., S. P. O., v, 454.

† Ib., xxiv, 604, Sept. 1659.

‡ *Domestic Papers*, S. P. O. Chas. II, xi, 44.

§ *Docquet Book*, S. P. O. Chas. II, p. 132. *Entry Book*, Chas. II, xxii, 178, 179.

‖ This clause might suggest the idea that His Majesty's "Royal Fleet" was the Fleet Prison, but the context bears in another direction.

his wife and family, in case he should dy, but Your Majesty's sallary for the keeping of the said library, and his imployment under his very good master . . . . the Duke of Monmouth."* This plurality of incongruous offices having led, perhaps, to an intended new appointment for the keepership, a "Memorial for the Library at St. James', to preserve it," was addressed to the King, entreating his consideration of certain matters "before the Library be disposed of into any other hands." The points urged are these:—That the library contained all the monuments of learning which, time out of mind, had belonged to the King's predecessors; that it contained many *ancient records* of great concernment to the royal family; "that no library in England, and perhaps nowhere else, can compare with the magnificence of the binding of the books;" that all the medals and many MSS. had been taken away, some of which "may bee found;" that the books remaining there were then almost useless, first, because the room was too small, and secondly, because no complete catalogue had been made; and, finally, "that none but the present Library Keeper can give a true account of that which is wanting, and how it may be recovered." The anonymous Memorialist, therefore, prays the King to order an inspection of the library; the preparation of a "perfect Catalogue;" the setting apart of the Records and State Papers; the proper arrangement of the other books, "for common use;" and the placing in the Privy Council Chamber of a counterpart of the lists, both of State Papers and of books. It is further requested "that there be a Supervisor over the Library Keeper, by whose advice all things should be done concerning it, from time to time."†

Memorial to Charles II on the improvement of the Royal Library.

* *Dom. Pap.*, S. P. O. Chas. II, cxxii, 95.

† Ib. (Undated papers), Bund. 26.

If the statements in this Memorial be trustworthy, it cannot well have been written later than 1666, as a Catalogue of the Library bearing that date was drawn up, of which a portion is still preserved among the "Additional Manuscripts," in the British Museum. It is an extremely rough and perfunctory document, and its utter want of order may probably make it the more faithful a type of the collection itself. In another manuscript—now in the Lansdowne Collection—I find a numerical classification of this Catalogue of 1666, made almost a century later. It is there said that the books entered in the class "Theology" are 2350; those in "History and Law," 1423; and those in the other classes, 2429. All these were either in Greek, Latin, or English. In addition to these, there were 1370 French, 1333 Italian, and 377 Spanish, books; making a total of 9282.* In 1663, by the "Sedition Act," the Library had become entitled to a copy of every book printed in England.†

Acquisition of the Theyer MSS.

By the purchase of the Theyer MSS., in the year 1678, the Library obtained the only very important acquisition made by Charles II during his reign. It comprised a valuable series of manuscripts on History and Theology, and of mediæval works on the Natural and Mathematical Sciences, which had been previously purchased of John and Charles Theyer's representatives by Robert Scott, an eminent bookseller. The collection extended to about 336 volumes,‡ including not less than 700 several treatises, some of which were of the highest value. Many of them

* *Notes on the Library of Charles II*, Lansdowne MS. 701, f. 150.

† *Statutes at large*, 14 Charles II, c. 33.

‡ Of these 312 are catalogued in the *Catalogi Librorum Manuscriptorum* of 1697, without any mention of the fact that they were then in the Royal Library; perhaps, because of Bentley's opposition to the insertion in that work of any account of the Royal Library at all.

had been in the Library of the Priory of Lauthony, and had passed into the possession of the Theyers by the marriage, as it is said, of an ancestor with a Mrs. Hart, the sister of the last Prior. Amongst them were the autograph theological collections of Cranmer, (which had been repeatedly sought for without success), and a remarkable series of the works of Roger Bacon. Scott appraised his purchase for re-sale at £841. Drs. Jane and Beveridge valued them, for the King, at £560. In the choicer lots, they seem to have proceeded on the very simple principle of giving the bookseller the half of what he asked. Thus, the Cranmer volumes, for which Scott claimed £100, are reduced to £50. The Roger Bacon MSS., appraised at £80, are reduced to £40. It is stated, in a note to the original catalogue, that the number of Manuscripts "that never was in print" is 270.*

Charles II on posthumous fame.

Rosse is said by Aubrey to have revived the proposal for printing the Alexandrian Bible in fac-simile. He proposed to have it engraven on copper-plates, and told the King it would cost but £200. Mr. Rosse, writes Aubrey, also "said it would appear glorious in history, after your Majesty's death. 'Pish,' said the King, 'I care not what they say of me in History, when I am dead.'"† In better days, a magnificent fac-simile was produced at the public charge, admirably edited by Mr. Baber. But almost two centuries had to elapse before the task first contemplated by Patrick Young, was worthily and fully accomplished.

Pearson, Rosse's reversioner, died before him. At his own death, in 1675, he was succeeded by Frederick Thynne, with Henry Justel as Deputy. After Thynne,

* *Account of the Theyer MSS.*, in Royal MS., App. 70, *passim.*

† Aubrey, *Remaines of Gentilisme*, &c., Lansd. MS., No, 231, f. 169, verso.

came the most eminent man who has ever held the office, Richard Bentley. Edmund Gibson, afterwards Bishop of London, was his competitor. Bentley declined to accept it during pleasure,—so we are told by Casley,*—and had the patent drawn for life. The salary and allowances amounted at this time to £330. He entered on the office in 1693, but his patent was not sealed until April, 1694.

The librarianship of Richard Bentley.

In the preface to the famous *Dissertation on Phalaris*, we have Bentley's own account of his vigorous way of setting about his new duties. "I was informed," he says, speaking of the Copy-tax, that "the copies had not of late been brought into the Library, according to the Act. Upon this I made application to the Stationers' Company. . . . The effect whereof was that I procured near 1000 volumes, of one sort or other, which are now lodged in the Library."†

In the anonymous and undated *Proposal for Building a Royal Library, and establishing it by Act of Parliament,* which I believe to have been written by Bentley himself during the reign of William III,‡ these thousand volumes are stated to be still unbound, and therefore useless. "There has been," he says, "no supply of books from abroad for the space of sixty years past, nor any allowance for binding, so that many valuable manuscripts are spoiled

Bentley's Proposal for remodelling the Royal Library.

* In a MS. communication to Dr. Ward, preserved amongst Ward's "Gresham Collections" in B. M. Casley's account goes on to say, that Bishop Stillingfleet remarked sneeringly, after Bentley had solicited his aid: "These young men think themselves fit for anything." But the assertion is on its face improbable.

† *Dissertation on Phalaris*, preface.

‡ Evelyn wrote to Bentley on Christmas Day, 1697:—"...I found Sir Edward Seymour at his house...I told him I came not to petition the revival of an old title...but to fix and settle a public benefit...This, with your paper, he very kindly received."—*Diary and Correspondence*, iii, 369.

for want of covers." He repeats the complaint of Charles's memorialist, as to the smallness of the room, and proceeds to urge, "as a thing that will highly conduce to the public good, the glory of His Majesty's reign, and the honour of Parliament," (1) the building of a new Library in Saint James' Park; (2) the settling of a yearly revenue, by Act of Parliament, for the purchase of books; (3) that, upon due occasion, the Curators be empowered to "take up money at interest, upon this Parliamentary fund, so as to lay out two or three years' revenues to buy whole libraries at once;—as, at this very time, the incomparable collections of Thuanus, in France, and Marquardus Gudius, in Germany, might be purchased at a very low value." And he concluded his *Proposal* by a thought, afterwards repeated and amplified by Berkeley in his memorable and pregnant tract, *The Quærist*, on the sure return, even in the mere pecuniary sense, of public money laid out in the making a great metropolis to be also a great mart of learning.*

The Royal Library under Bentley.

Whether Bentley's first zeal enabled him in some degree to improve the condition of the Royal Library, according to the small means which alone were at his command, or whether the failure of that public support which was essential to the working out of his great plan for placing a library of 200,000 volumes within reach of English students at the beginning of the eighteenth century, discouraged him from any further exertion, there is now, I suppose, no means of telling. Whatever improvements he

* In this paper, too, Bentley uses a name which I had the satisfaction, almost a hundred and fifty years afterwards, of suggesting as that of the first institution raised under Ewart's Act, namely a "FREE LIBRARY." His words are these:—"'Tis easie to foresee how much this glory [that is, the glory of our nation], will be advanced by erecting a *Free Library*, of all sorts of books."

may have made, if any, were certainly ruined by the imbecility in higher places, which occasioned *four* removals of the royal collection within Bentley's lifetime, and indeed within nineteen years.* After the fire at Ashburnham House, in 1731, the books were allowed to remain, for a considerable time, without any arrangement whatever. The very sequence of the volumes of a set was neglected.†

Diversity of Bentley's pursuits.

But, in truth, Bentley's marvellous career as scholar leaves little room for speculating on the possibilities of his librarianship. Those—they will never be many—who are competent to survey his achievements in the field of classical criticism, find them enough to fill even so protracted a life as his, without taking into account the many abortive or uncompleted projects, on which he expended much labour. Those, again, who know, or can conceive, what is involved in a forty years' series of law suits,‡ in all sorts of courts, and in which the stakes were more than commensurate with the duration and bitterness of the struggle, will be apt to think that during some of those years, at all events, the man's whole vigour and vitality must have been diverted from literature to law.

His preferments in the Church.

And, besides all this, it is to be remembered that, in the fashion of that day, Bentley had a multiplicity of professional functions, which, had it also been the fashion of the day to perform them, would have left him but scanty leisure either for literature or for law. The Master of Trinity was not

* Namely, from St. James' to Cotton House, in 1712; from Cotton House to Essex House, in 1722; from Essex House to Ashburnham House, in 1730; and, after the fire, in 1731, to the Old Westminster Dormitory,—Casley, in Additional MSS., 6209, f. 240.

† Lansdowne MS., 701, ubi sup.

‡ The pith of so much of this famous contest as turned upon the *Statutes* of Trinity College may be seen, compactly, in a letter of Bishop Fleetwood to King George I.—MSS. S. P. O. *Dom.*, Geo. I, Bund. I.

only Royal Librarian, but he was Regius Professor of Divinity. He was also Rector of Haddingham, Rector of Wilburn, and Archdeacon of Ely. Bearing this in mind, it is suggestive to see Dr. Bentley (at a time when he already held all these preferments, except the Professorship,) proposing to undertake a complete edition of the classics, *in usum Principis Frederici*, on condition that he had a thousand a year, for life, for that service. Whilst the matter was under discussion, as well as long afterwards, Bentley was wont to speak, in his familiar conversations, of his famous project for a new edition of the Greek Testament, based entirely on manuscripts, the youngest of which should be nine hundred years old, as the one task by which his name was to go down to posterity.

There is small need, then, to wonder that although few men ever entered on a librarianship with grander ideas of the service to be done in that calling, than did Bentley, probably no man ever did less in it during so long a term of office. It is the name, not the labour, of the illustrious scholar which has reflected dignity on the post he held. But it is to his honour that he made a strong effort to secure for the Royal Library that fine collection of his patron Bishop Stillingfleet, from which he had himself learnt so much in his early manhood. His endeavours to prevent Stillingfleet's library from being exported to Dublin were as fruitless, as had been his earlier effort to prevent Vossius' library from being exported to Leyden.

Bentley's effort to obtain Stillingfleet's Library.

The Librarian's Apartment at St. James'.

Bentley's librarianship leaves at St. James' another memory, besides that of good intentions. The book-rooms there were in disorderly condition, and the disorder gave occasion to some of Swift's hardest hits at the librarian, in the *Battle of the Books*. There is yet cause for regret that Bentley permitted that same disorder to be a pretext for inducing Queen Mary to refuse Archbishop Sharp's request that a list of the Royal Manuscripts might be included in the *Catalogi Librorum Manuscriptorum Angliæ et Hiberniæ*, of 1697. But those unsightly rooms witnessed many a gathering of the immortals. Thither were wont to come, once or twice a week, Christopher Wren, John Locke, and Isaac Newton.

Bentley surrendered his patent as librarian on the 2nd February, 1724,* and had a regrant of it for his own life, and that of his son, by whom he was eventually succeeded. The new patent bore date on the 12th of March, following. David Casley, their deputy, was for a long period the only working librarian. In 1734, he rendered a real service by publishing his *Catalogue of the Manuscripts in the King's Library*, but by a special infelicity, what was then a considerable boon to scholars, has, in our day, proved (thus far,) a permanent misfortune to them. Casley's Catalogue—one of the worst, in point of arrangement, that was ever printed —has been allowed to continue the only catalogue of what, in certain points of view, is the finest portion of the vast library of the British Museum. In Bibliography, as in Literature at large, a bad book is much worse than no book at all. Casley, with great labour and under many difficulties, did what he could, but had he done nothing, we should long ere this have had an excellent catalogue of the Royal Manuscripts.

The younger Bentley resigned his office on the 28th October, 1745,† in favour of Claudius Amyand, who had letters patent in November. Finally, in 1757, King George II presented the Library of his predecessors, after

* Surrender Rolls (2 Feb., 11 Geo. I, 1724), No. 15, m. 15, 16.

† Ib., 19 Geo. II, No. 38. m. 35, 36.

its many vicissitudes, to the safe and efficient custody of the Trustees of the British Museum. At that date, the number of printed and probably of bound volumes appears to have been about 10,200; and that of Manuscripts, bound and unbound, nearly 2000. Some losses had probably been sustained in the fire of 1731. Among the unbound manuscripts and neglected "refuse" were many documents of much interest and value, which in quite recent years have first been made available, by the care of Sir Frederick Madden. All that is now to be desired is an adequate Catalogue.

Transfer of the Royal Library to the British Museum.

CHAPTER VIII.

HISTORY OF THE STATE PAPER OFFICE.

It is observed that the Science of Antiquities hath in this last age been cultivated in England with more industry and success than in several ages before. Of this, divers causes have been conjecturally assigned.........For my part, though I do not oppose any of those conjectures, yet I think another probable cause may be assigned; and that is, the Encouragement that hath been given to these Studies, by several persons of eminent learning, and of superior order in the Realm.

MADOX, *The History and Antiquities of the Exchequer*, iii.

THERE is an old tradition that King Henry VIII first caused a particular room in his Palace to be assigned for the preservation of State Papers, and himself fixed on that room over the ancient or "Holbein" gateway of Whitehall, in which part of the contents of the "Paper Office" continued to be kept, until the gateway was pulled down in the middle of the last century; the tradition, however, at present, lacks distinct and sufficient evidence.* But the official statement, hazarded (without any sort of reference)

* But I have little doubt that evidence will eventually be found, since there is, in the Office itself, a list, plainly of that reign, thus entitled: "*Baggs of boks, lettres, and other writings remayneing in the Study at Westminster, and in severall Tilles within the same.*" This Catalogue is intrinsically curious, and merits publication, although some of the papers it describes have long since disappeared. It includes documents relating to all kinds of business, domestic and foreign; and contains several entries about books which had been confiscated. Another entry indicates that "Attainders of Queens Consort" had come to be regarded almost as an established branch of public business:—"A bag of Confessions, &c., touching the Matyer of *the last* Queen attaynted."

in the preface to the first volume of the Collection of *State Papers of Henry VIII*, printed in 1830, that "in 1578, an Office for keeping papers and records concerning matters of State and Council was established,"* is directly in the teeth of evidence which is precise and irrefragable.

T. Wilson's account of early History of Paper Office.

Thomas Wilson, fourth in succession of the *recorded* Keepers of the Paper Office, was the nephew of the first Thomas Wilson, Master of Requests, Master of St. Katherine's Hospital, Keeper of the Papers, and ultimately Secretary of State to Queen Elizabeth, and Dean of Durham. He had been bred to the public service, under his uncle's eye, from his boyhood. In 1623, a chance expression of Secretary Sir George Calvert,—that the Paper Office was "an Office to little purpose"—excited Wilson's anger, and led him to tell Sir George what he knew of its history: "*Not to reach higher than my own knowledge,*" writes Wilson, "it is forty-five years since" (he is writing in 1623) "*I* knew it, an office then established under the great seal, and in the custody of Doctor Wilson, when he was but Master of Requests, . . . myselfe being then in his howse att Saint Katherine's, before my going to Cambridge, a boy of sixteen years old, whom he employed in wryting and bundeling of such papers as wer then and now are heer in this office. When he was made Secretary, Doctor James gat the office, and had a fee of forty pounds a year, by my Lord of Leycester's meanes; . . . . [then, at his death,] Sir Thomas Lake gatt it."†

* *State Papers*, &c., I, xiii, xiv. The mistake is repeated in the late Mr. Thomas's tract on the Paper Office, published in 1849; and may possibly have grown out of a hasty reading of the words "then established"—[*i. e.*, then existing] in the very letter I quote, although that letter is nowhere mentioned, by either writer.

† *Dom. Papers*, Jas. I, S. P. O. (Unbound).

When, in 1578, Wilson first employed his nephew in "bundling" the State Papers, he had been Keeper of them at least seventeen years.* Many years earlier, namely, in 1554, there occurs proof that the office was in working order under Mary.† Possibly, when first established by Henry—prior to the assignment of the gateway chamber—the papers generally may have been kept, for a time, in the Council chest, along with the documents proper to that repository. In the sixth year of that reign, Thomas Tamworth was appointed Clerk of the Council Chamber, and "Keeper of the Books and Records there."‡

Paper Office in Mary's reign.

By James I,—at the instance, as it seems, of the Lord Treasurer Salisbury,—directions were given for a re-arrangement of the contents of the Paper Office, "into a sett forme of Lybrarie." By his Letters Patent of the 15th March, 1610, he appointed Thomas (afterwards Sir Thomas) Wilson, and Levinus Muncke, to be "Keepers and Registrars of Papers and Records." Wilson alone was sworn to the due execution of the office.§ The fee was three shillings and fourpence a day. But Salisbury gave Wilson in addition a "Clerkship of Imposts," and also a salary of forty pounds a year as "transcriber of State Papers."‖ On Salisbury's death, a commission was issued to his successor, Lord Suffolk, and others, directing them to take possession of his papers in Salisbury House, and to deliver them to Wilson and Muncke. In an undated paper (written, probably, in 1614) Wilson describes the Papers as of two sorts, "those that have been kept at Whitehall of long time; and those that were brought from

James's re-organization of the office as a "sett Lybrarye."

* *Dom.*, Eliz. S. P. O. xvii, 36, 38, 40 (1561).

† *Dom.*, Mary, iv, 17. "*A Breviate of ... a packet remaining in the Office of State Papers, relative to the reception of the Prince of Spain.*"

‡ *Pat. Roll*, 6 Hen. VIII, Part 1, m. 18 (7 July, 1514).

§ *Dom.*, Various, Bundle 129.

‖ Ib. See next page.

Salisbury House by myself, which are far the greater in number;" and he adds:—"I have spent eight years in reducing them out of extreme confusion, . . . and have made registers; . . . . and [have] bound the most part of such books, according to their subjects, . . . and years. But now, these books must be all broken, and the papers that were thus divided must be made up of all in one, according to their heads and countries."* In this same year the patent was surrendered, and a new one issued to Thomas Wilson and Ambrose Randall.† Shortly afterwards, Wilson petitions the King to grant "to your painfull and diligent servant, some small diett of two dishes of meat a meale for himself and his servants, or ells . . some reasonable allowance for the same;" and to the Lord Treasurer Suffolk he addresses another earnest petition for a certain annuity of forty pounds, "that is allowed for such as the Lord Treasurer for the time being may assign, that take pains in searching and abstracting of Records for his Majestie's service," . . to be granted, he prays, "to me, an old crazy man, *like him that left it.*"‡ I have searched in vain for any particulars of that curious bequest, the proceeds of which Wilson seems to have possessed under Cecil. Suffolk, however, refused to continue it.§

An ancient bequest to the Treasury for transcription of Records.

In July, 1618, the Commissioners of the Treasury directed Wilson to endeavour to obtain for his Office, such treaties and other important documents as were wanting to it. This he was to do, either by the intervention of foreign ambassadors, or by other fit and lawful means. The room assigned to the Papers had become too small. Wilson petitioned the King to authorise an enlargement, and also

Wilson's proposals for the extension of the Paper Office.

* *Dom.*, Various, ut sup.

† He is called in the official documents sometimes "Randall," sometimes "Randolph."

‡ Ib.

§ *Dom.*, James I, civ, 92.

to enable him to form a Library of printed books of reference. "It pleased your Majesty," he wrote, "to tell me, the last time that I had the honour to speak with you about the Office of your Papers, that you would make it the rarest office of that quality in Christendom; and thereupon . . . to give me your warrant for recovery of all such things as were unjustly detained from thence, with which I am now in hand. There is one thing more which would add much to the perfection thereof, if your Majesty would . . cause to be provided . . all such books of the several Laws of Kingdoms and States, of History, Chronology, and Policy, as I have set down in a Catalogue;" . . . and he adds, "I have devised the way how it [*i.e.*, the additional room required] may be done without one penny cost to your Majesty . . . . There is a fair room, already, built of stone, near unto the Office, . . . which now serveth to no use." This, like many other applications of the most unwearied petitioner of a petitioning age, was fruitless, but he obtained an enlargement of his Office in another way, the story of which is curiously illustrative of the manners of the times.

And for a Printed Library of Reference.

There was a room, he says, "under the Office for the Papers, which was my Lord of Worcester's larder. I gave to Mr. Sadleir, my Lord's Secretary, to gett the graunt of it, . . a suite of satten, and satten lace unto it, which cost me twelve pounds. Item, after I had obtained it, I presented to My Lord himself divers bookes,—one of the Pictures of all the Princes and famous men of the world, cutt in brass and very fayrely bound and guilt; and the King's Works, bound in crimson velvett; and Hacklutt's . . . *Voyages*, in two volumes. Item, I gave to my Lord Chamberlaine, for obteyning his good will to assigne it unto me, divers rare Italian bookes, as *Paralelle Militare; Fatti di Armi famose*, . . in two volumes; Diodati his new

Wilson and the Lord Treasurer Worcester.

Italian Bible, bound in black velvett; and divers other bookes, very fayrely bound and guilt; whereupon his Lordship sent Mr. Maxwell to putt me into possession of the roome. . . . Item, I gave Mr. Martin, my Lorde of Worcester's cooke, for his good will not to oppose, twenty shillings, and promised to give him so much yearly. . . . So that I have payd out of my purse for itt, in all, twenty pounds, besydes bookes which I wold not have given for as much more."*

While the poor Keeper was making these exertions to improve his office, he had also to make repeated applications for arrears of his salary, and was at length, he says, forced to sell "of his poor estate, twenty pounds a year." He is continually sending in "Bills of Services," and complaining of his hard case. James employed him in many affairs, both domestic and foreign, and his name is mixed up with more than one of the scandals of a disgraceful reign. Thus, for example, in October, 1619, he sends the king a bill "for making for His Majesty a cathalogue of all Sir Walter Ralegh's bookes, being in number between six and seven hundred; and that by His Majestie's express commandement, and delivered to himself."† Again, when Sir Edward Coke's papers were first seized,—in January, 1622,—Wilson was employed in their manipulation.

Wilson employed to catalogue the Library of Raleigh.

By this laborious officer, the State Papers were classed under twelve heads. The first two of these comprise what is now the class "DOMESTIC PAPERS," and in Wilson's arrangement they are called *Britannia Australis*, and *Britannia Septentrionalis*, each of them containing these seven following subdivisions :—(1) *Regalia*; (2) *Legalia*; (3) *Ecclesiastica*; (4) *Militaria*; (5) *Politica*; (6) *Criminalia*; (7)

His classification of the State Papers in 1618-9.

* *Dom.*, Various, S. P. O. (Unbound Papers) 129-131, No. 58.

† Ib., No. 75.

Mecanica. Headings III to X, inclusive, are the names of foreign countries, beginning with *Gallia* and ending with *India.* These are now comprised in the class "FOREIGN CORRESPONDENCE." XI is called *Tractatus Principum;* and XII, *Mixta.*

A note, by another hand, explains this last-named class "*Mixta*" thus—Before Wilson's time, says the writer, "there was all the business which had been left by men employed in this State from 13th Henry VIII, 1522, untill 1590, with some elder things, from Edward the Third's tyme till Henry VIII. All which are digested under the title of '*Mixta,*' into twenty severall cupboards."* But, in truth, the documents originally kept in the Paper Office went back, in some instances, to an earlier date than that of Edward III. As late as under the keepership of Sir Joseph Williamson, there was one document, at least, of the 43rd Henry III (1258).†

Wilson's labours seem, at length, to have been in some degree rewarded by a pension of £100 a year; but of this he himself gives an incoherent account. In one paper he says it was given him "for rearing this poor and painful office out of a chaos." In another, he describes it as the reward of "service done in Spain."‡ But his complaints about arrears still continue, and the requests he makes of the King for compensation curiously confirm the accounts we have from other sources of the union in Charles, as in James, of habits of niggardliness and plain injustice with

* Yelverton MS., No. 8 (Transcript).

† *A Catalogue or Collection of the particular Instructions and Letters remaining in the Office of the King's Papers' Chamber, at Whitehall, Tempore H.* 3, *&c.* (Additional MSS. in Brit. Mus., No. 11595). This Catalogue was bought by Sir F. Madden, of Longman and Co., in 1839.

‡ *Dom.,* Var., S. P. O., Bund. 129, No. 136.

habits of capricious and reckless bounty. On one occasion, the Keeper of Papers asks to be empowered to keep also a "Register of Honour," in order to inflict a new tax on the unlucky men on whom knighthood was thrust. On another occasion, he entreats the king to give him "the nomination of an Irish Earl," promising that if that be granted, the petitioner "will never trouble your Majesty with any other suit," and will even "be content to take the money due to him *out of the Customs of Ireland, or out of such means as he shall find.** Three months later (14th July, 1629) death released him from his labours, his petitions, and his disappointments. In November, the office was regranted to the reversioner Randall, in conjunction with William, afterwards Sir William Boswell, and the fee was increased to eight shillings and ninepence three farthings† a day.

In December, 1634, Secretary Sir Francis Windebank issued his warrant to examine the books and papers of Sir Edward Coke, who had died in September, and to "seize all such as may concern his Majestie's service, or as may in any wise be behovefull or prejudiciall to the same." And many papers, including the MS. of Coke's most famous works, were seized accordingly, and deposited in the Paper Office.‡ This warrant seems to disprove the statement, which has constantly been repeated by Coke's successive biographers, to the effect that Sir Francis violated the sacredness of a death-bed, and personally made his seizure during the great lawyer's dying moments. The case is bad enough, without aggravation. Under parliamentary pressure, in 1641, Charles ordered the return of the books and papers,

* *Dom.*, ut supra, No. 160. I do not infer that either request was granted, but simply that the requests themselves (coming from Wilson) are fair evidence of practice.

† So in the MS. *Dom.*, Var., Bund. 129.

‡ Ib.

but the order was only partially complied with. Some of the documents seized in 1634 may, I think, still be seen at the Rolls House.

In the destructive fire at Whitehall in January, 1619, the contents of the Paper Office had escaped serious injury, owing, as poor Sir Thomas Wilson told the King, to "his Majestie's prophetical spirit," which, as it had formerly enabled him to save the country by a miraculous detection of the Gunpowder Plot, had now enabled him to save the State Papers by that marvellous forecast which had led the King to order a partial removal of the more important documents just before the occurrence of the fire. But both the removal and the hasty "tossing into blankets" of the papers which had been left, disturbed the old classification, which probably was never fully restored. Wilson's more immediate successors seem to have taken the post on its smoothest side. When, as in the case of Sir Henry Wotton, valuable bequests were made expressly to the Office, no pains were taken to profit by them. Wotton's bequest included the valuable negociations of Sir Nicholas Throckmorton. But the papers devised in 1637 did not reach the Office until two hundred and twenty years afterwards.* They came at length, in 1857, by a gift of the late Mr. Wilson Croker, made two days before his death.

Early in the Interregnum, Milton was the means of making an important addition to the papers.† And, much later, he had a warrant to make extracts in the Office, pro-

* This is really so, although in an elaborate report of T. Astle and others, made to the Committee on Public Records in 1800, they are said to be "in this office." (First Report, App., p. 68.)

† *Dom.*, Various, S. P. O., Bund. 129.

The Paper Office during the Commonwealth.

bably with a view to those historical plans of which after-events precluded the fulfilment. It has been often said that the Commonwealth men robbed the Paper Office. They lie open enough to censure on some points, but this charge is wholly without proof, and opposed to probability. All students who are familiar with these stores of historic material will be ready to admit that in all the points of relative completeness, of fulness and clearness of record, of systematic arrangement and indexing, and of legible scription,—the Commonwealth documents are models. The difference between a Cromwell and a Charles II was mirrored grandly—as we all know—in the foreign policy of the two periods. It was also mirrored humbly, but quite as characteristically, in Cromwell's order that his State Papers should be in English, and in plain writing; and in Charles's order that barbarous Latin and more barbarous Court-hand should resume their sway.

The Petitioning of 1660.

Both the correspondence and the petitions of the years immediately succeeding the Restoration eminently combine amusement with instruction. No request is too wild to be made by a courtier, and no charge too absurd to be made against a Roundhead. There are many papers in both sections of documents which illustrate this assertion, and relate directly to our subject, but I mention only one. A certain Nicholas Bowdon states in a petition to His Majesty that, in the evil days, "he had had a faire studdy of lawe books in the Inner Temple, taken away *by John Selden*," and, *therefore*, "your Petitioner having discovered some few lawe books . . . *of John Bradshawe's*, he prayes that the same may be seized upon, for your Petitioner's use, hee havinge been bred upp some parte of his tyme in the studdy of the law." To save the King trouble, he encloses the form of a comprehensive warrant empowering him to seize "books *supposed to be* the late goodes of Sarjeant Bradshawe." Amongst them were 122 folios, 54 quartos, and 95 octavos, besides sixty volumes of MSS.* But, by the side of other (and successful) petitions of that intoxicated time, Mr. Bowdon's request seems moderate and forbearing.

The Paper Office under Joseph Williamson.

From December 1661, to the beginning of 1702, the history of the Paper Office lies very much in the personal biography of Sir Joseph Williamson. The son of a poor vicar in Cumberland, he came to London at an early age and in very humble guise, in the train of a certain Mr. Richard Tolson, who sat for that county, as a supplementary member of the Long Parliament. By his master's favour he got admitted into Westminster School, and thence, partly by his own attainments and partly by the good report made of him by Busby, into Queen's College, Oxford, where Dr. Langbaine, then Provost, paid his expenses, and Dr. Thomas Smith was his tutor. His assiduity and other good qualities continued to win for him influential friends. At length, in December, 1661, Thomas Raymond having, upon due consideration, surrendered the office of "Clerk and Register of Papers,"† Sir Edward Nicholas granted it to Williamson, who seems to have laboured assiduously in its duties until his good parts and his natural ambition led to his employment in a great variety of business, both public and private, which drew away attention from the keepership of papers, although he

* *Dom.*, Chas. I, xx, 51.

† Raymond had obtained a reversionary grant of the office, July 20, 1641, with a fee of three shillings and fourpence a-day. He entered on it in July, 1649, with £80 a year, which was afterwards increased to £160.

retained the office until his death, and then made, by Will, its most important augmentation.

The fate of Secretary Nicholas' papers.

The Council books, the "Register of the Committee of Intelligence," the "Domestic Correspondence," and Williamson's own Note-books and Letter-books, abound with notices and minutes of lost, embezzled, and neglected papers, and with warrants for their recovery. Sir Edward Nicholas' papers had been specially unfortunate. Those of his first period of service, under Charles I, had been seized by the Parliament when he fled from London, before the outbreak of the Civil Wars. These seem to have been only partially preserved. A large portion of the subsequent and very interesting papers which had accumulated during his attendance on the King, up to the fall of Oxford, were burnt by Charles's order, lest they should experience the fate of the papers seized in the cabinet at Naseby. "Among them," said Nicholas himself, were "things of a very mysterious nature, but I looked not into one of them, to obey the King's command." But a portion of Sir Edward's correspondence of this period, having descended to John Evelyn, may still be seen at Wotton. Other accidents seem to have made inroads upon the papers even of his third and quieter secretaryship, under Charles II. And the case seems to have been much the same with the papers of his successors. Thus, at a meeting of the Cabinet, held at Windsor in 1680, at which the King and the principal ministers were present, I find the following minute recorded:—"His Majesty being this day informed that many of his Papers of State relating to business and negotiations, . . . since His Majestie's happy restauration, are wanting, to the great prejudice of his affaires, His Majesty was pleased to order in Councill that the Right Honourable the Lords of the Committee for Forraine Intelligence doe informe themselves of this matter, causing strict inquiry to be made,"* and so on, in the usual fashion,—and doubtless with no more than the usual result.

Among the diversified parts which Williamson played on the stage of life, were those of "Gazetteer," or Editor of the London Gazette (1666); Clerk of the Council (1667-74); Purveyor of News-Letters (1670); Plenipotentiary at Cologne (1674); Principal Secretary of State (1674); Member of Parliament for Thetford (1674, 1678, &c.) and for Rochester (1689-1700); President of the Royal Society (1678); Recorder of Thetford (1685). His employments as Gazetteer, and as Newsletter-writer, throw light on the times, and well deserve to be dwelt on for a moment;—the story will have at least the merit of novelty. Varied pursuits and employments of Williamson.

The *London Gazette* (as it has been entitled for very nearly two centuries) was first established soon after the Restoration, although it did not receive its present title or form until 1665. Roger L'Estrange had rendered great service, in a bad cause, by what was then termed, euphuistically, the "surveyorship" of the press. He was rewarded by being made Editor of the official Gazette. On the one hand, the Ministers obtained publicity for such matters as they wished the public to know or to believe. On the other hand, the Gazetteer took care *not* to let the public know what the Ministers might deem dangerous or undesirable information. The "surveyorship," one is pleased to learn, had not proved a very remunerative service. "The excessive charge of entertaining spies and instruments for The "London Gazette" of Charles the Second's day.

* *Minutes of the Lords of the 'Committee of Intelligence,'* 4 August, 1680 (Additional MSS. in B. M., 15643, fol. 38). See also, in the earlier years of this reign, *Entry Book*, vol. xvi, pp. 65, 87, &c. (MS., S. P. O.)

the reducing of the Press, cost me above £500, out of my pocket, the first year," complains L'Estrange to Lord Arlington, not for the first time. As to the Gazette, he says, "I found it £200 per annum [profit], I have brought it up to above £500. Even at this instant [he is writing in the thick of the Great Plague] it is worth £400, when the sale is at worst." Williamson, always Lord Arlington's right-hand man, now intervenes, and does not appear to advantage. He chose to understand L'Estrange's numerous complaints as relating to the "News-book" or Gazette, and politely offers him a "salary from the King of £100 a year, which shall be paid through my hands without [you] being put to move the Exchequer for it. If I taxe it too lowe, you must blame yourselfe." And Lord Arlington recommends compliance, as L'Estrange's wisest course.

L'Estrange's account of his services.

"Touching your Lordshipp's proposall of my relinquishing my right in the Newsbooke," replies L'Estrange, "upon a consideration express: It is certaine that both in gratitude and justice your power over mee is without limitts, but this let mee offer withall, that it would utterly ruine mee." And again, in a subsequent letter, he remonstrates pathetically thus:—"In the first place, I am to throw up my house, turn off my servants, and satisfy a debt of neare £3000, ... contracted in the King's service, beside the expense of my private fortune. .... It may be a second consideration, my Lord, the quality of my employment: *It was to teaze and prosecute the whole rabble of the faction*, which I have done to such a degree that I have drawn upon my head all the malice imaginable. And can it be that I am now to be delivered up . . . for a sacrifice?—with the brand of a foole upon mee into the bargain! Thirdly, your Lordship very well knowes that the Newes-book was given mee to ballance my service about the presse, and in doing my work, be judg, my Lord, if I do not deserve my wages." He adds, too, that by outfacing so dreadful a pestilence, and persevering with his service in London "even till the plague came into my own family," . . and nearly "eighty men in the printing trade had died of it," he thought he had earned a different reward. But expostulation was fruitless. The press had been bridled for the time, and the bridler must now be content to take what he could get. The reward, after all, was congruous with the service. Williamson was made Editor of the Gazette, and he set about his new labours with characteristic energy and success.*

Scarcely less curious is the account which Sir Joseph's Chief Clerk for News-letter writing gives of the daily budgets which were sent into the country; of the clerks by whom they were prepared, and the correspondents to whom they were addressed; and of the "allowances" received for the duty. It does not appear that Williamson himself derived any profit from this source. Nor did all the persons who received news-letters pay for them. These "correspondents" were of all ranks in society. Among them appear the Duke of Ormond, the Archbishop of Dublin, Lords Allington, Scudamore, Widdrington, Carlisle, and Leigh; the Deans of Durham and Carlisle, Sir William Curtin [Courteen], Sir William Dalston, and the Mayors of several provincial towns. Among the less known names are those of persons who were themselves employed as "intelligencers" at particular places, and who were paid, or partly paid, by the communication of the general news on certain days of every week. Besides the superintendent of the office, four clerks ("before Mr. Charles, my Lady

The Office for News-letters.

* *Dom.*, Charles II, S. P. O., cii, 99, &c.; ciii, 28; cxxxiv, 103, 117; cxxv, 49; cxxxv, 8, 24; clx, 149.

Portsmouth's gentleman, came into it,") were employed in writing the letters. The yearly payments of those who received the letters, by subscription, varied from six pounds to four pounds, and the aggregate receipt to from £170 to £200, which was divided amongst the clerks. "My Lady Portsmouth's gentleman not being able to write more than four letters a day, the business," says the Superintendent, "will lye much heavyer upon us all." There was a rival news-letter writer, Henry Muddiman, whose letters were at convenient times stopped at the Post Office. Many of them are now amongst the State Papers. Muddiman is said to have received from some of his subscribers as much as forty pounds a year.* Williamson's subscribers had their news at easier rates. Sometimes "a year is paid when there is two due. Others pay only something when they return to town, . . or pay not [at all]."† For the greater part of a century to come this profession of news-letter writer was still to flourish.

This account of the news-office is addressed to its proprietor when he was already Secretary of State.‡ In the fourth year of his Secretaryship, Sir Joseph found himself very unexpectedly in the Tower, whither the House of Commons had sent him, at a moment's warning, in the heat of a debate about Popish Recusants, to whom the Secretary—so it was charged—had given illegal commissions. The King's wrath was great, and he summoned a Council for the next morning. "His Majesty," say the

* *Dom.*, Chas. II, clx, 149.

† Ib., Various, Bund. 129, No. 164 (Unbound papers).

‡ 23 Oct., 1674. By some oversight, this paper has been classed and described, as relating to the State Paper Office itself. Perhaps, the old endorsement, "*The State of Your Honour's Paper Office*," occasioned this mistake. Or Williamson's private business may have been actually carried on there.

Williamson's imprisonment in the Tower, and his release.

Minutes, "having acquainted the Lords with the reason of the Councill's meeting, the Earl of Craven proposed that the King should send for the House of Commons to speak to them, and at the same time to send for his Secretary out of the Tower, and then tell the House he had done it."* This course was supported, on the ground that the Commons have power of imprisonment in matters of privilege only, by the Bishop of London (Compton) and others, and adopted by the King. He sent for the Commons to the Banquetting House, and told them—"I will deal better with you than you have dealt with me, and I therefore do acquaint you that I have sent for my Secretary." On their return, they drew up a Remonstrance, setting forth the heinousness of Williamson's offence, but without effect. Up to this date, his name is of frequent occurrence in the debates.† For a long time afterwards, it does not, I believe, occur at all. At the end of the session, he resigned the seals,‡ thinking, probably, that the stakes were getting too high for a prudent man to continue the game.

His marriage and his benefactions.

In December, 1678, Sir Joseph Williamson contracted a splendid alliance with the blood royal, and acquired a considerable fortune, by his marriage with Catherine Stuart (widow of Henry, Lord O'Brien), granddaughter and eventually heiress of Esme Stuart, sixth Duke of Lennox and third Duke of Richmond, K.G., and Baroness Clifton, in the Peerage of England, in her own right. This marriage had no issue, but it enabled Sir Joseph to testify his gratitude to Dr. Langbaine, by a liberal bequest to that kind

* *Minutes of what past in Council*, &c. (MS. Addl., 15643), f. 50.

† Comp. *Parl. Hist.*, iv, 1038.

‡ He was not, as Mr. Courtenay in his able *Life of Sir William Temple* states him to have been, dismissed by the King. Nor is there any foundation for Rapin's oblique insinuation that he retired in con-

patron's descendants, and to Queen's College, by a multitude of benefactions, both by gift in his lifetime and by legacy, amounting in the whole to more than eight thousand pounds. He also left a noble benefaction of five thousand pounds to Rochester (for which city he had sat in four parliaments) for the foundation and endowment of a mathematical school, the recent rebuilding of which, by the way, was made the pretext for needlessly destroying—in the foolish and reckless manner so characteristic of our age—much of the ancient walls of Rochester. Nor did he forget the remote Cumbrian village which was his birthplace. The visitor to Bridekirk may still see the church-books, and the church-plate, which keep alive the names both of the Secre-

sequence of a corrupt bargain with Lord Sunderland. The sale of the Secretaryship was the established practice of the time. Williamson had given for it £6000, in 1674. He received for it £6525, in 1678. There seems always to have been misunderstanding and jealousies between Williamson and Temple, and there is reason to think that these jealousies had sometimes an evil influence on important negotiations. (See *Holland Correspondence*, S. P. O., 1674-76; *Life of Temple*, i, 358, 423, 452, 482, 489; ii, 5, 84, &c.) They may have had a double origin. Temple was the son and grandson of men conspicuous in public life. Williamson had come to London as a boy in service, to seek his fortune. They had been competitors, in a sense, for the Secretaryship—*i. e.*, as far as Sir William Temple's temperament permitted him to be any man's competitor for anything. And, finally, their mental characteristics were oppugnant. Temple worked fitfully, indulging at intervals the luxurious fancies of a fine and fastidious gentleman. Williamson, even when he had grown rich, worked pertinaciously, with all the plodding assiduity of a poor scholar. And I may add, that while Temple has been eminently fortunate in his biographers, Williamson has had no biographer at all. The curious volume, however, which records the proceedings of the Cabinet of 1679-80 (quoted above, as Add. MS. 15643) was unknown both to Courtenay and to Macaulay. It modifies several minor statements, both of the careful biographer, and of the brilliant essayist. Nor can any one, I think, read it, without doubting the assertion (in which both agree) that Temple's famous Council of Thirty was intended, by its projector, to transact all sorts of business, without the intervention of any Committee, even for mere details.

tary of State, and of the humble Vicar, his father. He was a benefactor to the Library at St. Bees, and to the Company of Clothworkers. His gratitude to his tutor, Dr. Thomas Smith, he had shown long before by procuring his elevation —much to the good parson's own surprise, it is said—to the bishopric of Carlisle. Among the multitude of other men who were at various times befriended by Williamson, were Dr. Lancaster and Dr. Joseph Smith, both fellow-Cumbrians, and both afterwards Provosts of Queen's, and, in their turn its benefactors. One feels a special pleasure in recording the good deeds of a man whom an unusual measure of worldly success failed to harden.

Classification of the Papers in 1682.

Notwithstanding his many other employments, Williamson kept in view the improvement of the Paper Office, although he is far from having the merit of instituting all those precautions for recovery of lost documents, and security of existing ones, of the necessity of which he had had ample and personal experience. But he caused numerous inventories to be made, some of which are now before me, though they, too, have wandered widely from their proper place of deposit. Other papers, which have remained in the Office, show that the twelve classes, of Wilson's time, had increased to nineteen classes under Williamson, and that the papers, in 1682, were still contained in two rooms, besides closets. The headings of classification run thus:— I, England; II, Scotland; III, Ireland; IV, Spain; V, United Provinces; VI, Flanders; VII, France; VIII, Italy; IX, Germany; X, *Military;* XI, *Ecclesiastical;* XII, *Criminal;* XIII, *Household;* XIV, *Parliament;* XV, *Offices;* XVI, London; XVII, Jersey; XVIII, Guernsey; XIX, Wales.*

* *Dom.*, Var. (Unbound papers), B. 129.

Sir Joseph Williamson died in 1702, bequeathing his transcripts of State Papers, his MS. collections on Political Affairs, and his Official Papers generally, to the Paper Office, at the head of which he had been for more than forty years. He bequeathed his general library, both of books and MSS., to Queen's College, but, probably by an oversight on the part of his executors, some of the MSS., which plainly should have come to the State Paper Office, went to Queen's; but the collection which did arrive is of considerable extent and value. It comprises State Papers of all the reigns from Elizabeth to William and Mary inclusive, the number of bound volumes being 282, besides a large series in bundles.* John Tucker, who succeeded Sir Joseph in the keepership,† has made a caustic comment on this bequest, to the effect that many of the books which the testator bequeathed to the Office, he had first taken away from it. But there needs no large experience, either of literature or of life, to teach a man that statements of that sort are anything rather than evidence of fact. Tucker found that the office had been neglected in the late years of his predecessor's life, and that to bring it into reasonable presentability, would make the keepership by no means an agreeable sinecure.

Williamson's bequest to Paper Office.

Scarcely, indeed, was he settled in his post, before troublesome inquiries were made into its condition, and at length a Select Committee of the Lords was formally appointed. Tucker stated to them, sweepingly, that "nobody having been employed in this office for twenty years past, the papers are in confusion and disorder," and that he had himself "been at the expence of a

The Lords' Committee of 1705-6.

* *Report of T. Astle and others* (*First Report on Public Records*, i, 68).

† June, 1702, and by patent, during his Majesty's pleasure. All previous keepers had been appointed for life.

clerk constantly employed in sorting them, . . under proper heads."* The Committee reported, on the 4th March, 1706, (1) That more room and more presses ought to be provided for the Office. (2) That the "Miscellany" Papers should be completely digested under heads, and all papers be bound up in volumes with proper indexes. (3) That a Catalogue should be made up of the volumes, referring to the presses in which they are placed. (4) That few papers had been delivered into the Office by Secretaries of State, since the year 1670, except those left by Sir Lionel Jenkins, and that many papers of preceding periods were also wanting,—more especially certain sections of "Foreign Correspondence," between 1641 and 1660. (5) That, although there was in the Office a complete set of Warrant Books, from 1661 to 1679, yet they were those only of Mr. Secretary Nicholas, of the Earl of Arlington, and of Mr. Secretary Williamson; there being none of any other Secretary of State, since the beginning of King Charles the Second's reign.† An Address to the Queen, in accordance with these recommendations, was then presented.

An Office of "Collector of S. Papers" established

There is nothing said in this Report, or in the Address, of the need of a new Officer, but not long after their entry on the Journals, the office of "Collector and Transmitter of Papers of State and Council" was created, with a salary of £600 a year.‡ It was first granted to Edward Weston, and, subsequently, in succession to John Couraud, Edward Rivers, John Ramsden, and Charles Goddard. In other respects, if even in that, the recommendations of the Lords' Committees were not efficiently carried out.

* *Domestic*, Var., S. P. O., Bund. 129.

† *Lords' Journals*, xviii, 135.

‡ *Domestic*, Various, S. P. O., Bund. 130, p. 318.

When, in the year 1719, the Lord Chancellor Parker, afterwards Earl of Macclesfield, called the attention of the House of Lords to the state of the Public Records, and caused a new Committee of Inquiry to be appointed, the Paper Office was not included in the Order of Reference.

Enlargement of the Paper Office.

As far as is now apparent, the chief result of the inquiry of 1705 (irrespective of the new Collectorship), was the allotting and fitting up of a portion of the Lord Chamberlain's apartment at the Cockpit, to the enlargement of the office. It was then that the room long known as the "Middle Treasury Gallery" was first appropriated to the reception of papers.*

The Office of "Transmitter" or Collector of Papers, in the form actually given to it, proved to be a mistake. Instead of being the mere feeder of the existing office, and a check upon the misappropriation of Papers, it was absurdly made the means of creating a divided place of deposit, and a divided control. Eventually, instead of diminishing old evils, it formed a new one. But of that in its order.

The Keepership of the Paper Office becomes a sinecure;—

Tucker was succeeded in the Keepership by Mr. Hugh Howard (18th February, 1714), who had, at first, a patent "during pleasure," but afterwards a re-grant for life. From the time of Mr. Howard, to that of Sir Stanier Porten, inclusive,—a period of nearly eighty years,—the history of the *original* office is a history of neglect and of removals, in which part of the papers were capriciously tossed about from room to room (in order to increase or to alter the accommodation of official persons), and another part was left in the chamber over the old or "Holbein

* *Dom.*, Various, B. 131 (*Lord Chamberlain's Warrant*; *Report of Sir Chr. Wren*, &c.).

gateway" of Whitehall, which speedily acquired a double destination. It became, at once, a State Paper Office, and a pigeon-house. When, in 1763, an officer of the Board of Trade needed to refer to some documents of the age of Charles I, he applied to the Privy Council Office. Nothing was known there, he says, of any Paper Office, other than that of the "Transmitter" appointed by Queen Anne, but a venerable clerk had a dim recollection that he had heard, in his youth, of the existence of some old books in the room over the gateway, and suggested a search, which—after many adventures with decayed staircases, locksmiths, flocks of pigeons, and "accumulations of filth,"—proved eventually to be successful. The story is told by an Under-Secretary of State, who gravely records that on hearing of the discovery, Mr. George Grenville, with far-sighted regard for the public service, *created* an Office "for the preservation of State Papers."* A little before the date of this "discovery," another Under-Secretary (Mr. Andrew Stone) was actually "Keeper of State Papers," and of course received the salary of that office. At the very time of the discovery, it was held by a Commissioner of Customs, Mr. Porten, afterwards Sir Stanier Porten, also Under-Secretary of State, in his turn. This gentleman when examined, long subsequently, by the Commissioners on the Public Accounts, said:—"I found my office a sinecure, and I have allowed it to continue so." The Commissioners, without further inquiry, report the Paper Office as one "to which no duties are attached," and which, therefore, may usefully be abolished.

And the Office a Pigeon-house.

The Transmittership of the Paper Office.

What Mr. Grenville really did, in 1763, was, substan-

* *Dom.*, Var., Bund. 131. Referring to Mr. Pownall's Statement in Knox's *Extra-Official State Papers* (1789), 12, 13.

Commission for methodizing the Papers.

tially, an imitation of the example of 1713. As there was already a Keeper, who had, practically, no custody, and a "Transmitter of Papers," who did *not* transmit them, Mr. Grenville issued a commission to three gentlemen (all of them holding other and numerous offices and employments) "to methodize, regulate and digest the Papers of State." After a brief interval, the new Commissioners faithfully followed the old precedents. The persons appointed were Sir Joseph Ayloffe, Bart., Dr. Andrew Coltee Ducarel, and Thomas Astle, Esq. During the first three years (1764-66) they made several reports to the Secretary of State, which are still to be seen at the Rolls House. After 1766, no such report is discoverable. When the Commission had existed continuously for about *thirty-seven years* the then Commissioners, (Thomas Astle, Thomas Astle, Junior, and John Topham)* reported to the House of Commons (1), that "*with respect to the time which may be required to make complete Catalogues and Indexes throughout these two Offices, it cannot be ascertained;* because *each* transmission of Papers *will of course call for more time and labour;*"

State of the Offices in 1800.

. . . . (2) that [as respects the old office,] "*the business of methodizing and digesting . . . can only be carried on during the summer months;*" and, finally, that [as respects the new or Transmitter's office,] "the House is old and ruinous throughout, and the overflowing of the river . . . . renders the lower apartments *so extremely damp, as to be wholly unfit for the preservation of Papers and Records.*"† A story like this is not a whit the less instructive for being, in 1864, somewhat old. I add, therefore (after examining every original document on the subject which is accessible), that this statement was made after these Commissioners—

* *First Report on the Public Records of the Realm* (1803), 68, seqq.

† *Ibid.*

one of whom had personally continued a Commissioner during the whole period of thirty-seven years—had received upwards of twenty thousand pounds, for "methodizing and digesting the State Papers;" and that there appears no reason whatever for thinking that one word would have been publicly uttered by them on the subject, but for the appointment of Lord Colchester's Committee on the state of the Records of the Realm. These Commissioners and their then deceased colleagues appear in our Biographical Dictionaries as "eminent antiquaries." Mr. Astle, (who for a long period was Keeper of Records in the Tower as well as Commissioner of the Paper Office, and Commissioner of the Augmentation Office, and Co-Editor of the Rolls of Parliament,) was singled out, (I observe, in passing) in one of the more recent of those publications, for special eulogy as the bequeather of a noble collection of MSS. to the late library of the Duke of Buckingham, at Stowe. Partly by various purchases, and partly by gifts from friends, Mr. Astle, it seems, had acquired a most extensive and remarkable series of Records and State Papers, many of which had once belonged to the Public Departments and Repositories. And amongst them are documents of the highest value. He had also acquired many Calendars of Papers and Records. All of them—public documents, and calendars of public documents, alike—were bequeathed to the then Marquess of Buckingham, and are now, I believe, in the fine library of Lord Ashburnham. A mere catalogue of these State Papers and Records would occupy some hundreds of pages. It is in perfect keeping, to find that Messrs. Astle and Topham, when asked by the Committee of 1800, What can be done for rendering the use of the Records in your custody more convenient to the Public? replied— "These being private Records and

Papers of State and Council, we humbly conceive that they can only be inspected by His Majesty's Ministers or under their particular order."

Facts like these are obviously essential to any truthful history of the matter in hand. But they have another value. They suggest, most forcibly, how large is the debt of gratitude which we all owe to the Langdales, the Romillys, and the Hardys, of our own day.

At the date of Lord Colchester's inquiry (1800) the Paper Office at the Treasury contained about 3500 volumes, besides a vast mass of unbound and unsorted papers. The earliest records in this office, so far as they were then known were of the year 1246; the latest, of the year 1706 or 1707. The Transmitter's Office, in Middle Scotland Yard, contained about 3307 volumes or bundles, also in addition to a mass of unarranged papers. In this latter office there were papers of as early a date as 1570, but the bulk began in the later years of Charles II. It excites no surprise to find that the partial attempt at an arrangement in either office was at that date greatly worse than the old arrangement, which had subsisted in Thomas Wilson's time; and, of course, the newer "arrangement"—so to call it—differed considerably in the two offices. In the older office, the "classes" were fifty-eight, twenty-two of which related to Foreign affairs. In the newer office, they were seventy-four, forty-three of which related to Foreign affairs. The arrangement of this last-named division was very inaccurate and arbitrary, but as the "classes" were geographical names, it was capable of being understood by dint of study. But no amount of learning or of study would enable an inquirer to understand the arrangement of the Domestic papers. It must, therefore, have been very gratifying to know that

Arrangement of the Offices in 1800.

"*we* [the methodizers]" are so well acquainted with the situation in which the papers are placed, ... that *we* can advert upon any occasion to such evidence and authorities, as may be wanted by His Majesties Ministers."* The headings of the classes themselves were such as these:—"*Correspondence with Ambassadors*, 1530-1677;" again, "*Letters from Persons residing in Foreign Parts*, 1657-1706;" and, once again, "*Ambassadors*, &c., 1509-1706." There was a class entitled "*Merchants and Merchant Ships, Foreign Trade*, &c., 1572-1608;" and another class, entitled, "*Trade, Domestic and Foreign*, 1562-1690;" a class—"*Army and Military Affairs*, 1586-1705;" and another, "*Militaria*, 1586-1705;" and so on. To comment on such a method of "methodizing, regulating, and digesting" State Papers would be to waste time. The commission was eventually superseded, but not without much difficulty and a hard fight, in the same year in which the inquiry in the House of Commons had taken place.

Appointment and labours of Mr. J. Bruce.

As the early history of the Paper Office lies very much in the biography, and the personal reminiscences, of Sir Thomas Wilson; and that of its middle period in the biography and the bequests of Sir Joseph Williamson; so the history of its last period—as a separate office—is, to a great extent, comprised in the narrative of the labours and efforts of Mr. John Bruce, the last holder but one of the old keepership, as constituted by Henry VIII. Mr. Bruce, towards the close of the last century, was a Professor in the University of Edinburgh, when he attracted the attention and patronage of the then powerful "Minister for Scotland," Mr. Henry Dundas, who gave him, first, a post under the India Board, and then the Keepership of Papers (15 Nov.,

* *First Report on the Public Records*, ut supra.

1792), as the successor, after an interval, of Sir Stanier Porten. Mr. Bruce was a man of literary tastes, of indefatigable industry, and of special aptitude for what is called (for want, perhaps, of a vernacular equivalent) *précis*-writing. His best efforts in this direction, although printed, are comparatively little known, because printed, at first, only for the use of the Government. Two important works, however, on the History and Politics of British India,* were published; one of them as early as 1793. The privately printed books treat of the Balance of Power; of the Measures taken for Defence of the Country against threatened Invasion, in the days of the Armada, and on some subsequent occasions; on the Renewal of the India Company's Charter; on the Union of England with Scotland; and on other important subjects. These reports rendered yeoman-service to the Administration of the day, and are still valuable contributions to the literature of Politics. It is interesting to observe in Mr. Bruce's correspondence with the Ministers, that he has often to complain of being obstructed in his tasks, by the difficulty of access to those very papers of which he was himself Keeper by the King's Patent.

State of the Paper Office in 1800.

The State Paper Office, therefore, in the closing years of the last century, presented the edifying spectacle of a National Repository, the head of which, with a salary of £160 a year, found difficulty in getting at its contents, for administrative purposes; the official "Transmitter" of which, with a salary of £600 a year, kept the Papers away; and the

* *Historical View of Plans for the Government of British India* (1793); and *Annals of the East India Company* (1810). Mr. Bruce had published at Edinburgh, many years earlier, a book entitled *First Lessons in Philosophy*. In his later years he sat in Parliament, and took an important share in the discussion on the renewal of the East India Company's Charter.

official "Methodizers and Regulators" of which, with aggregate salaries and allowances amounting to about £700 a year, kept the Papers without the advantage of Calendars, but with the advantage of occasional irrigation by the surplus waters of the Thames. When, by dint of repeated reports and applications, the Keeper of the Papers had at length obtained the united efforts of Mr. Pitt, Mr. Dundas, and the Duke of Portland, to put an end to this state of things, and to make the Keepership at once an efficient and a responsible office, Lord Grenville, then Principal Secretary of State (who had steadily patronised the Methodizers and resisted the new plans), very politely and very pressingly urged on Mr. Bruce's acceptance—the *Consulate at Hamburgh.**

Re-organization of the Office in 1800.

Eventually, however, all obstacles were surmounted, and the office was reorganized (May, 1800). Mr. Bruce received a new Patent, with a gross salary of £660 (then producing little more than £500 net), and with an establishment of clerks and servants, with allowances, by Treasury warrant, amounting, in the aggregate, to £470 a year. The Keepership was made a useful and responsible office, but, for a time, the transmittership continued to be an office independent of the Keeper. The commission of 1763 was, as I have said, revoked.

It illustrates the depth of oblivion into which the early history of the office had fallen, to find that in the recitals of the new Patent four of the *recorded* Keepers

* *MS. Correspondence of Mr. Henry Dundas and the Duke of Portland, &c., with Mr. Bruce,* S. P. O. I have seldom met with more amusing reading than this. The drafts are often preserved, as well as the letters. When Mr. Bruce was worn out and probably a little exacerbated with official manœuvres and delays, Mr. Dundas would sketch out for him a diplomatic letter, to take the place of a too straightforward one.

are left out, and one name is added which has no right there. Mr. Bruce himself, even after many searches, made Sir Thomas Lake to be Keeper in Henry the Eighth's time, and to have had but two successors before Williamson (who died in 1702), expressing, very naturally, surprise at their longevity. Astle, in his turn, reports to the House of Commons (1800) that the office of Transmitter was created in 1741. That office had (up to 1800) been held in succession by Edward Weston, John Couraud, Edward Rivers, John Ramsden, and Charles Goddard.

Erection of the late State Paper Office in the Park.

In 1819, the office in Scotland Yard was pulled down, and the papers were removed thence to a house in Great George Street. The papers of the old office remained in the Treasury Gallery. In 1833, the late well-known Paper Office, in Saint James's Park, (built expressly for their reception,) was completed; the papers were at length combined, and their arrangement and calendaring vigorously pursued. In 1820, Mr. Bruce was succeeded by the late Mr. Henry Hobhouse, the last "Keeper and Registrar of the King's Papers, concerning matters of State and Council."

On the 10th of June, 1825, an important step for increasing the public utility of the Office was taken by the issue of a royal Commission, which recites that the Papers of State "have been in great measure, [it would have been more strictly accurate to have said in *some* measure] arranged and indexed," and empowers certain Commissioners therein named, "to consider which of them, [namely, of "Our Papers and Records,"] may fitly be printed and published with advantage to the public, and to proceed to print them accordingly. This Commission was renewed in 1830, in 1837, and in 1842. Under its auspices, the valuable although incomplete series of *State Papers of King Henry the Eighth*, extending to eleven volumes, quarto, appeared between the years 1830 and 1850. It is an admirable contribution towards the history of that memorable reign, but will receive important augmentation and improvement by the detailed Calendars now in course of publication, under the Editorship of Mr. Brewer.

Increase of the Establishment.

The editing of this first selection of State Papers, and the preparation of Calendars, involved an increase of the Establishment; and this became the more needful, on account of the transfer of Papers in increased quantities from the various departments of State. Part of this accumulation was drafted to the Public Record Office, in November, 1845, and the amalgamation of both Offices was, in the same year, recommended by the Treasury, but not then carried into effect. In the year 1848-9, the number of clerks in the State Paper Office had been increased to nine, and the annual expenditure to £2680.

Free admission of literary inquirers to the Paper Office.

Ultimately, a Treasury Minute of the 8th of August, 1848, approved by the Secretaries of State on the 14th September, and by the Master of the Rolls on the 24th October, in that year, made the Office a branch of the Public or General Record Office, created under the provisions of the 1st and 2nd Victoria, c. 94, as will appear more fully in the succeeding chapter. This important change was soon followed by regulations for the systematic admission of Literary Inquirers, without payment of fees; and by the gradual publication of admirable Calendars of the contents of the State Paper Branch. No boon of equal value has ever been conferred by public authority on Literature, and more especially on Historical Literature, in England. But any details on this head belong more fitly to the history of the Record Department at large.

In 1862, the entire contents of the State Paper Branch were removed to the new Repository, and the building itself was pulled down, to make room for the new erections of the Treasury. It had existed barely thirty years.

Of the general arrangement of those contents, and of the relation they bear to other masses of Records, from which they were so long severed, some notice will be found in an Appendix to the present volume. Of the new Calendars of State Papers, so far as they have yet been given to the Public, mention is made in the concluding section of the next chapter.

CHAPTER IX.

HISTORY OF THE PUBLIC RECORDS OF THE REALM.

When a man, though a native of this Island, comes fresh to peruse ...a piece of its ancient History,...he is like one newly landed in a strange country. He finds himself in another climate. He observes many things strange and uncouth, in language, laws, customs, and manners............But there are some persons who seem habitually disposed to speak meanly of all parts of learning which are not directly lucrative. They are apt to say, "*Of what use are these old antiquated things? Give us what is more suitable to the age we live in;*" and such like. But if we examine these allegations, they will, I suppose, be found to have no force. Every part of learning is of some use............History may be said to be twofold, ancient and modern. The former consists of Antiquities, and cannot, even in thought, be separated from them....The knowledge of Antiquities is a part of Historical learning, and cannot be impugned without impugning History itself.

MADOX, *The History of the Exchequer*, xiii.

If there be still reason to regret that no clear and available account of the growth, transmission, and specific characters, of our Records can be found in any one existing book, there is, I suppose, no room for doubt that the deficiency is owing rather to the abundance than to the paucity of the materials. The mass, indeed, of the books *about* the Records seems to have become almost as appalling, as had been that strange superfetation, upon the *Classing* of the Records, of an uncouth legistic terminology, which, in union with many other like impediments, for a very long

Nomenclature of the Records.

period impoverished our historians, in order to enrich our lawyers. It is formidable to look on the long row of vast folios in which the annals of the Records lie imbedded. It is more formidable still to look, with the humility that befits ignorance, on the long row of mysterious designations, under which the contents of those Records have sometimes been skilfully concealed. Who has not, at some time or other, shrunk in dismay from the *Arrow Bundles*, the *Cardinal's Bundles*, the *Pot Bundles*, and the *Stool Bundles*;—the *Misæ Rolls*, the *Nichil Rolls*, the *Nonæ Rolls*, the *Pipe Rolls*, and the *Ragman Rolls*;—the *Monstrans de Droit*, the *Ouster le Mains*, the *Originalia*, the *Parliamentary Pawns*, the *Black Books*, the *Red Books*, and the *Pye Books*?

To these difficulties, arising, first, from the bulk of the merely descriptive and narrative Record Reports and Returns to Parliament, and, secondly, from the awful-looking nomenclature, were long added other difficulties yet more deterring. Only a few years have elapsed since the Records kept within the Metropolis alone, had to be sought in some twenty different parts of London, ranging East and West from the Tower to the Abbey, and North and South from Pentonville* to Lambeth. Documents of one kind were kept in many places. And in all these places, as David Casley wrote to Professor Ward, a hundred years earlier, "they are sharping for fees."† Worst of all, there were often neither Calendars nor Indexes. Or, when these did exist, and had been made by public officers, they were treated as private property. They were usually, like the documents to which they

Former Difficulties of Access.

Want of Calendars.

* For even to this very modern locality Records often found their way during the operations of the first Record Commission.

† Letters to John Ward (*Ward MSS.* in B. M.).

referred, open only to a golden key. And the key had to be applied to a whole series of locks, in due succession.

These things being so, there is as little cause to marvel that the Records have had no Historian, as to marvel that so few of our Historians had any Records. Both facts have a common origin.

The History of the Records, whenever it shall be adequately written, will too often be a history of losses. And yet, various and long-continued as these have been, our public archives, after all, are not (there is good reason to believe) surpassed by those of any country in the world. Our losses, by all sorts of neglect, have been great, but we have lost comparatively little by the spoils of war. The contents of the new repository may, in a sense, be said to reach from William the Norman to Victoria; and to include evidences which will throw the strongest light on every branch of our social polity. They are now in course of being systematically arranged and calendared, and have been most liberally opened to all competent inquirers. Many, as we all know, are the authors who have already profited by this liberality. But many also are the fields of research, in respect of which authors to come may say, with Lucretius,—

Extent and Value of the Records preserved.

> Avia Pieridum peragro loca, nullius ante
> Trita solo, juvat integros accedere fonteis
> Atque haurire....

Results like these have been attained only by a long series of laborious individual efforts, which well deserve to be chronicled as a series of arduous, persistent, and eminently disinterested public services. To recount them adequately—by whomsoever the task may eventually be undertaken—will need, not a chapter, but a volume.

In attempting even some slight survey of the subject, it will be needful to break it up into divisions. As the matter shapes itself to my own mind, four main epochs seem to stand out saliently in the annals of the Records of the realm. There is, first, the period of gradual accumulation, in several separate and, in their earliest stage, nomadic repositories; secondly, the period of increased separation, of neglect, and of plunder, with occasional efforts at improvement; thirdly, the period of partial aggregation, of partial arrangement, and of premature publication; fourthly, the period of complete aggregation, of thorough arrangement, and of wise and liberal publicity.

Four Epochs of the Records.

These periods are obviously very unequal in duration; they sometimes overlap each other; yet they will be found, I think, to have a really distinctive character, and to facilitate review. With them may fairly be connected some prominent names, occurring in the story. The earliest names which we meet with are names only. But of Bishop Walter Stapledon, of Arthur Agarde, of William Bowyer, and of William Lambarde, in the period of early growth, we can in some measure retrace the labours. William Prynne did not become a Keeper of Records until he was far advanced in the evening of his life, but he had long before been a student of them, and he saw almost the beginning of the epoch of gross neglect and plunder. It would have needed a patriarchal longevity to have seen also its end. With the long-delayed period of partial reform, the name of Charles Abbott, Lord Colchester, is bound up, almost as closely as are with various stages of the current period of complete reform, the names of Sir Harris Nicolas; of Henry Bickersteth, Lord Langdale; of Sir John Romilly; and of the present Deputy Keeper of the Records, Mr. Hardy.

Some prominent names in the Story.

Some brief account of these four distinctive epochs in

the story, will be followed by an attempt to characterise the main contents and arrangement of the new Repository, in both its chief departments. But this I place in an Appendix, at the end of the volume.

§ 1. THE PUBLIC RECORDS IN THEIR EARLY PERIOD OF GROWTH AND OF SEPARATE CUSTODY.—NOTICES OF THE LIVES AND LABOURS OF WALTER STAPLEDON, BISHOP OF EXETER; OF ARTHUR AGARDE; OF WILLIAM BOWYER; AND OF WILLIAM LAMBARDE.

SOME of the earliest of existing Records partake of that mingled character, partly administrative, partly judicial, which has always been so influential on the *management* of the Records. Some such admixture seems to have begun with the practice of "record" itself. In days, indeed, when the same officer discharged very multifarious functions, and the same Court dealt with causes the most dissimilar, it must needs be that the same repository should contain documents of diversified character, and even the same membrane be made to chronicle very incongruous matters. Thus, in some early records,—as, for example, in the Misæ Roll of King John,—we meet in close proximity entries which relate to grave affairs of State, and other entries which relate to the most minute and humble personal necessities of the monarch. That same Misæ Roll serves to shew that many Records were wont to be carried from place to place, in attendance on the King. From entries in it of payments to the Sheriffs of London and Middlesex for their charges, on certain occasions, in transporting the rolls—*e.g.* from London to Northampton—it would seem that although the Exchequer had already its usher, clerks, and roll-writers, as well as its Chamberlains

Nomadic character of the early Records.

and Chancellor,* there was, as yet, no one officer exclusively charged with the entire custody of the Rolls. At this period the annals of the Records are, in fact, identical with the annals of the King's person, of the "King's Court," of its branch, the "King's Exchequer," and of the King's itinerary. For both *Curia Regis* and *Scaccarium* moved with the Monarch, and, under John, very pilgrim-like, indeed, must have been their life. When at length the Exchequer became a fixture, it became the first "Record Office" of the realm. But the exact date of this change in the office cannot, it seems, be determined.† Nor can the date either of the earliest rolls originally preserved in it, or of the division of its repositories into (1) *Chapel* and (2) *Treasury*, each of them (for a time) containing different classes of records, be precisely fixed. "To the Chapel," says Sir Francis Palgrave, "the King's *Chancery* had always been annexed; and the registration or enrolment of the documents, authenticated by the Great Seal, ... produced the rolls or records which constitute the nucleus of that repository. The *Treasury* contained the records of the Courts of Justice, *and* whatever more immediately concerned the property and personal engagements of the sovereign."‡ After a while, it also contained, as we have seen, the humble beginnings of the Royal Library.

* Richard Fitz-Nigel (Treasurer to Rich. I), *Dialogus de Scaccario*, I, c. 5.

† Fitz-Nigel, in the Dialogue already quoted, says that Rolls of Henry I were preserved in the Exchequer in his day [*frequenter in veteribus Annalibus Rotulis Regis illius invenies scriptum*...]. (Ib., i, c. 7.) One famous roll of the 18th of that monarch is still extant. An Exchequer clerk, Alexander de Swerford, who compiled the *Liber Rubeus*, about 1220, says expressly that none of his contemporaries had seen any rolls of the Conqueror's time.—"*Nec annalia sua*" (Regis Willielmi I) "*temporibus meis a quibusdam visa sunt*" (f. 47, *a*).

‡ Palgrave, *Antient Kalendars*, &c., Introd., xv.

The Records of the Treasury of the Exchequer.

To this "Treasury of Records" its first efficient organization was given, in the year 1323, by Walter Stapledon, Bishop of Exeter, and Treasurer of England. Bishop Stapledon occupies a place in English history as the munificent founder of Exeter College, first called Stapeldon's Inn, and as one of the chief builders of Exeter Cathedral.* He also deserves honourable memory for his care of the Records; his earnest remonstrances against loose practices, which had already, in the fourteenth century, imperilled their safety; and his evident anxiety to make them useful. It was, too, in the zealous discharge of his official duty, as Treasurer of the Exchequer, that he incurred the popular hatred which led to his murder by a riotous mob.

The Life and Character of Stapledon.

Walter Stapledon was born in the parish of Monkleigh, in Devon, probably about the year 1270. He was educated at Oxford, where he became Professor of Canon Law; was made Precentor of Exeter Cathedral, and Rector of Aveton Giffard. In November, 1307, he was elected Bishop of Exeter, and approved by the King. He received the Papal confirmation early in 1308,† and was enthroned with great splendour‡ at the end of that year. Exeter Cathedral was then in course of being rebuilt, and the new bishop promoted the work with characteristic ardour. The fabric rolls§ shew that he gave to this object the sum of eighteen

* Stapledon's Register, preserved at Exeter, is amongst the more remarkable documents of its kind. From a passage in it which contains a curiously minute description of the person of Queen Philippa at nine years of age, founded upon an official "inspection" (*Inspeccio et descriptio filiæ comitis Hanoniæ*, are the Bishop's own words), it would seem that the marriage which proved so potential in shaping English history was contemplated as early as 1319. Dr. Oliver has translated it in his *Lives*. The Bishop had a considerable library, a full catalogue of which is also preserved in Exeter Cathedral.

† Patent Rolls and Roman Rolls, quoted in Hardy's Edition of Le Neve's *Fasti*, i, 371.

‡ *Exeter Monasticon*, 323.

§ *Exeter Fabric Rolls*, MS., quoted in Dr. Oliver's *Lives of Bishops of Exeter*, 56.

hundred pounds, — a donation that would scarcely be matched by the gift of as many thousand pounds now, and respecting which there exists local evidence that it had a most stimulating effect on the liberality of his contemporaries. His episcopal zeal was shewn not less conspicuously in his visitations of his clergy.

The four Royal Treasuries of the Exchequer.

Early in the fourteenth century we find occasional mention of no less than *four* Royal Treasuries as already existing. One or two of these can now be identified only by the aid of tradition and conjecture. But it seems to be established that the most ancient of the four was that venerable room in Westminster Abbey which is frequently designated, on Records of the time of Edward III and his successors, as "the King's Treasury in the Cloister of the Abbey of Westminster, adjoining to the Chapter House."* This is a massively vaulted chamber of great antiquity, and may well have formed part of the structure of Edward the Confessor. It was the scene of that daring burglary in the year 1313, for connivance at which the monastic community was so severely punished. The second of the Westminster Treasuries was, probably, that described in records as "the Treasury adjoining to the Court of the Receipt of the Exchequer," in the old Palace, and popularly known, in later days, as the "Tally Court." Here Domesday and some of the Papal Bulls were long preserved. At what date the Chapter House itself became a Royal Treasury is uncertain. In the reign of Edward III it was, as is well known, the meeting place of the House of Commons. Eventually it became the chief Treasury of Records, and, as far as Westminster is concerned, absorbed

* *Memoranda of the Treasury*, 19 Edw. III, f. 1, &c., 6 Hen. IV, f. 38, verso, &c.

the contents of all the other Treasuries. But, as a Treasury, it was preceded by the crypt of the Temple Church, which seems to have been a Repository of Records prior to the nineteenth year of Edward I (1291). At that period the Temple was called the "New Temple," to distinguish it from the earlier seat of the Order, which stood on the site of the present Lincoln's Inn. In 1291, the King addressed a writ to his Treasurer, William de Marchia, commanding him to open a chest in his "Treasury at the New Temple; to take therefrom certain Rolls of Chancery; and to send them to the King, then in Scotland."* The records thus delivered were returned to the Temple, by the King's command, in the following year (1292), and, with the keys of the Chancery chest, were given in charge to John de Langton, "Keeper of the Rolls of the Chancery of Our Lord the King."†

The King's Treasury at the New Temple.

The Tower of London made a Record Repository.

The earliest evidences of the preservation of Records in the Tower of London are merely incidental. In the *Pleas of Parliament* of 33 Edward I (1305) directions are recorded for searching various rolls in order to obtain testimony in a certain case of the Prior of Goldyngham, and amongst these are mentioned "the Rolls of Scotland which are kept in the Tower of London."‡ From an entry, in the same year, on the Close Rolls, it may, perhaps, be inferred that Records were first kept in the Tower as appertaining to the King's Wardrobe. On the 6th November, 1305, the King directs the Treasurer and Chamberlains of his Exchequer to deliver all Papal privileges granted to him or to his progenitors, then in his Treasury, to Robert de Cotingham, Comptroller of his Wardrobe, that the same may be kept in the Tower of

* Close Roll, 20 Edw. I, m. 13, dors. † Ib. (Note in margin).

‡ *Placita Parliamentaria*, 33 Edw. I, p. 284.

London, under the seals, jointly, of the said Comptroller and of Adam de Osgodeby, Keeper of the Rolls of the King's Chancery."* It is only when we reach the reign of Edward III that we find express mention of "the King's *Treasury*, under the Great Hall in the Tower of London."† From the Close Roll entries of 1292 and 1305, already cited, the long list of the recorded "Masters of the Rolls" takes its start.

Origin of the Mastership of Rolls.

Of John de Langton's first appointment to that office no record remains;‡ but he is mentioned, under the same title of *Custos Rotulorum Cancellariæ Domini Regis*, as early as 1286 (14 Edw. I).§ Nine years earlier there occurs a writ directed to the Chancellor, "*and to the Keeper of the Rolls*," containing the reference of a petition. Long before this, again, incidental mention of the office is found in Chancery proceedings. In its origin, therefore, it was simply the senior "Mastership in Chancery," to which the custody of documents had been annexed by immemorial usage. The Chancellor, says Fitz-Nigel, has the custody of the Rolls "by a deputy" (*per suppositam personam*).‖ The precise demarcation between Chancellor and Treasurer, as respects authority over records, is one of the many obscure points in our legal antiquities.

Langton became Chancellor on the 17th Decmber, 1292; and in 1296 he presided at the famous Parliament of Berwick, which lent a temporary sanction to the subjugation of Scotland. His successor in the custody of the Rolls was not appointed until October, 1295, when the

* Close Roll, 33 Edw. I, m. 3.

† Palgrave, *Antient Kalendars*, Introd. i, cxxvii.

‡ Hardy, *Catalogue of Lord Chancellors*, &c., x.

§ Patent Roll, 14 Edw. I, m. 12 (sched.).

‖ *Dialogus de Scaccario*, lib. i.

office was conferred on Adam de Osgodeby.* There is no evidence of anything having been done either by this Keeper, or by his successor William de Ayremynne, for the methodizing of Records. Osgodeby was succeeded by Ayremynne in 1316.† The first recorded steps in this direction were taken by Bishop Stapledon in 1321.

Bishop Stapledon's measures for the improvement of the Records.

Stapledon had been made Treasurer of the Exchequer in February, 1320. His appointment to office was quickly followed by the issue of a writ of Privy Seal (14 Edw. II) for the methodizing and due ordering of the rolls, books, and other documents, "of the times of the King's projenitors, . . . then remaining in the Treasuries of the King's Exchequer, and in his Tower of London."‡ This writ was followed, in December, 1322, by another, which more specifically directed the Treasurer and Chamberlains of the Exchequer to classify, *and to calendar*, the Papal Bulls, Charters, and other Muniments, then remaining in the Treasuries of the Exchequer, in the King's Wardrobe, and in other places.§ From this Commission came the remarkable inventory of 1323, known as "Bishop Stapledon's Calendar."

The Treasurer prefaces his work by remarks which throw light on some of the causes of that disorderly condition of the Exchequer Records which had attracted his attention on his entrance into office. He condemns particularly the practice which had accrued of needlessly transferring the Records from the Wardrobe to the Chancery, and from the Chancery to the Exchequer, and then from the Exchequer to the Treasury, and so on; and

* Close Roll, 23 Edw. I, m. 6, dors. The MS. List of Masters of the Rolls, contained in the Cotton volume *Vitellius*, C. 17, begins with Osgodeby.

† Ib., 10 Edw. II, m. 28, dors.

‡ Ib., 14 Edw. II, m. 22.

§ Ib., 16 Edw. II, m. 19, dors.

His Classification of these Records (in 1323).

proceeds to arrange all the documents then contained in the principal Treasury, in twenty-four classes, as follows:—(1) Papal Bulls, "according to subjects," in twenty-six sections; (2) Deeds and Charters relating to lands conveyed or surrendered to the Crown of England, or to the Royal Family; (3) The like, relating to grants of lands by or from the Crown; (4) The like, between subjects of the Crown of England; (5) Exemplifications of Statutes; Confirmations of the Great Charter; Deeds relating to Bishops; (6) Acquittances relating to Rome; (7) Miscellaneous Acquittances;* (8) Memoranda and Miscellaneous Documents relating to the affairs of England; (9) Wills of the Kings of England, and Papers relating to the Royal Household; (10) Papers relating to Indulgences and to other Ecclesiastical affairs; (11) Extents and Perambulations of Manors and Forests in England; (12) Documents relating to Wales and to Welsh affairs, in various subdivisions; (13) Documents relating to Ireland, in various subdivisions; (14) Documents relating to Scotland, also in various subdivisions; (15) Documents relating to the Netherlands;† (16) Papers relating to the Earldom of Bar; (17) Brabant Papers; (18) Sicily Papers; (19) Ponthieu Papers; (20) Flanders‡ Papers; (21) Norway Papers; (22) Castille§ Papers; (23) Aragon Papers; (24) Burgundy Papers. Such was Stapledon's classification of the contents of the Treasury of the Exchequer towards the close of the reign of King Edward the Second.

Details of Stapledon's Calendar of the Exchequer Records.

The Calendars framed in accordance with this arrangement are carefully compiled. The subdivisions of classes are usually designated by the letters of the alphabet. The documents are numbered. They were lodged in a variety

* "Acquietanciæ diversorum pro Rege."—*Kalendarium*, 85.

† In Stapledon's MS., "*Hollandia.*"

‡ Ib., "*Flandria.*"

§ Ib., "*Hispania.*"

of receptacles, such as iron-bound chests and coffers, or "forcers;" bags and pouches, sometimes made of canvas, but more usually of leather; tills; skippets (or boxes turned on a lathe); and hanapers. These receptacles were, for the most part, *portable*, and had signs or labels of various kinds; sometimes mere letters; sometimes monograms, or coats of arms; sometimes rebusses of the names of office clerks; not infrequently, symbols of a hieroglyphical sort. Thus, papers relating to rebellions would be marked, suggestively, with a gallows; papers relating to marriages, with clasped hands; papers on the woollen manufacture, with a pair of shears; documents about Peter pence with a key; documents relating to remote countries with a Saracen's head of great fierceness; and so on. And these marks are copied into the margins of the Calendar. Occasionally, the scribes indicate their possession of reasonable leisure by the grotesque elaboration of these figures. Sometimes, they evince a certain genius for political caricature. Many of the ancient chests and pouches still remain. Some have been first opened in recent years, having been found in the very condition in which they were delivered to the Treasurer of Edward of Carnarvon more than five hundred years ago. Nor is it without interest to remember that it was of this same unfortunate monarch that a most curious (perhaps, of its kind, an unique) enrolment of private letters was discovered, in the Chapter House, still more recently.*

Bishop Stapledon met his premature and violent death whilst he was in the immediate discharge of his duty to

* See a note (by Mr. F. Devon) of the contents of some of these letters—written when Edward II was our first "Prince of Wales"—in the Appendix to *Ninth Report of the Deputy Keeper* (1848), pp. 246--249.

Stapledon's Murder by the London populace in 1326.

the King and the realm. He is recorded to have been busied at Exeter with the affairs of his diocese, towards the end of September, 1326. When the invasion under Isabella and her paramour Mortimer began (in Suffolk, 28 Sept.), he had probably already returned to London; for, four days afterwards (2 Oct.), we find him entrusted with the charge of the city, during the King's absence. But the Queen's army was approaching, and a body of disaffected citizens, with the usual admixture of thieves and vagabonds, was soon in open insurrection. On the 15th of October, as the Bishop was riding towards his own house at noon-day, "clad in the kind of armour which we commonly call 'aketon,'" says the Chronicler,* and—observing the formidable aspect of the tumult—made hastily, for Sanctuary, towards the north gate of St. Paul's,† he was surrounded by the rioters, pulled from his horse, dragged to "the Cheap," and beheaded. His body was cast into a pit in a neighbouring, but then disused, cemetery. Such is Walsingham's account of this event, and it accords in substance with that given in the French "Chronicle of London,"‡ although with several circumstantial variations. Some six months afterwards, the body was removed to Exeter, and honourably buried in the Church to which the murdered prelate had been an ornament and a great benefactor. It is probable that this murder prevented the full realization of his plans as a

* "Indutus autem fuit Episcopus quadam armatura quam *aketon* vulgariter appellamus."—Walsingham, *Historia Anglicana*, i, 182 (Riley's Ed.).

† "Not remembering that, as the Prophet Jeremy has said, '*Evil shall break forth from the North.*'" This strange conceit occurs in another account, more circumstantial (but perhaps of later date) than the printed ones. It will be found in the Cotton MS., *Vitellius*, C. 17, f. 5, verso.

‡ *Croniques*, Cott. MS., *Cleopat. A.* 6. There is yet another account, with more considerable variations, in that Chronicle of William de Pakington, which Leland translated from the French.

Founder, either at Oxford or at Exeter. But he had done more than enough to vindicate his place in the roll of the true Worthies of England.

The value of Bishop Stapeldon's labours at the Exchequer will appear saliently if his Calendar of 1323 be compared with the earlier and clumsy Registers or 'Books of Remembrance' ('*Libros de Remembrances*' is the title by which they were usually known), compiled some thirty years earlier, and still to be seen at the Rolls House. He followed up the improvements he had made at Westminster by causing the appointment, in July of the same year, of Robert de Hoton and Thomas Sibthorp "to put in order the King's Records at the Castles of Tutbury, Pontefract, and Tonbridge; *those contained in the House of the Dominicans* of London; and also such as had recently been brought into the Tower.* The Convent of the Dominicans, it may be added, was at Baynard Castle within the City, and the King had, for a time, kept his Court there. In the year of the Treasurer's murder, these officers were commanded to deliver their schedules of arrangement, and likewise the keys of the chests and coffers, to the Treasurer and Chamberlains of the Exchequer.†

The 'Books of Remembrancea;' temp. Edw. I.

It is probable that some part of the White or 'Cæsar's' Tower was the first place of deposit of the Records sent to the Tower of London, and that they remained there until that part of the grand old fortress which they had long occupied was allotted by the Council to be the residence of the illustrious captive of Poitiers, John, King of France. An entry on the Close Rolls, dated in April, 1360, shows

The first removal of the Records in the Tower.

* Patent Roll, 16 Edw. II, pt. 1, m. 28.

† Close Roll, 19 Edw. II, m. 26.

that the "servant of the Rolls of the King's Chancery" had then a warrant for his charges in effecting the removal of the rolls,* thus occasioned. Another entry records instructions to the Clerk of the Works at the Tower to make the necessary adaptations for their reception in their new abode.† And a like entry occurs in 1362.‡ The precise building is not indicated by name, but there can be little doubt that it was at this date that the well-known octagonal tower—sometimes called the 'Hall Tower,' sometimes the 'Wakefield Tower,' but more frequently the 'Record Tower,'—was first appropriated to the reception of the Rolls and other muniments of Chancery. This

The 'Tower of the King's Records.'

'Tower of the Kyng's Recordes,' as it was designated early in Henry the Eighth's reign, consisted of two stories. It was in the upper room, according to popular rumour, that Richard III made that "bloody supper in the Tower," the tradition of which helped as materially to blacken his memory in old times, as its want of proof has helped to whitewash him, in some measure, in our time.

Continued Itinerancy of the Rolls.

But although the Records, and especially the Records of Chancery, were thus provided for more carefully than heretofore, they continued to make frequent journies in attendance on the King, the Council, and the Courts. Thus, in all the reigns from Edward I to Edward IV, inclusive, we meet with frequent warrants for the removal of Rolls from London to York, and other places. Usually, writs are directed to certain Officers of Chancery, commanding them to produce the Records on a day fixed, and other writs are directed to some of the Religious Houses, apprising them of the king's need "of a strong and steady horse, to carry

* Close Roll, 34 Edw, III, m. 33. † Ib., 34 Edw. III, m. 15.
‡ Ib., 36 Edw. III, m. 25.

his Rolls of Chancery," and requiring them to furnish a competent animal accordingly.* In other instances, certain functionaries are directed by the King to seize "such and so many horses and carts," as may be sufficient for the conveyance of the Records from London to York,† or elsewhither, as the case might be. But notwithstanding such aids the costs to the Treasury of these transfers were sometimes large. Thus, in April, 16 Richard II (1393), the Keeper of the Hanaper is allowed the sum of one hundred and five pounds, sixteen shillings, and sixpence, for conveying the Rolls to York, and reconveying them to London.‡

Claim of the Commons in 1372, for undisturbed access to Records.

The year 1372 (46 Edward III) is notable in Record annals for the claim, then first distinctly asserted, to an unimpeded use of the Records, in due form, by all the lieges. The Commons in that year pray the King, that whereas Records and everything in the King's Court ought to remain there for perpetual evidence, and for the aid of all those whom they concern; and whereas, of late, the officers have refused "to make search and exemplification, . . . may it please you to ordain by Statute, that search and exemplification shall be made for all persons,"§ &c. And the petition was granted. Five years later (1377), Edward the Third, only a few weeks before his death, laid a noble foundation for that great General Repository of Records which is now, after the lapse of nearly five centuries, in course of gradual erection, by granting to the then Master of the Rolls, William Burstall, and to his successors for ever, the House or Hospital for Converted

* Close Roll, 28 Edw. I, m, 7, dors.; Ib., 6 Edw. III, m. 26, dors.; Ib., 7 Edw. III, part I, m. 12, dors.

† Patent Roll, 15 Rich. II, m. 7.

‡ Close Roll, 16 Rich. II, m. 10.

§ *Rolls of Parliament*, ii, 314.

Jews (*Domus Conversorum*), and the land and other endowments belonging to it. Burstall, like several of his predecessors in the Mastership of the Rolls, had previously enjoyed the office of Warden of the Converts.

Foundation and objects of the House of Converts.

The House of Converts had been founded by Henry III, in the 17th year of his reign (1233), to encourage and reward Jewish conversions.* It received several subsequent grants and endowments. The practice, indeed, seems to have been established in that reign that any act of oppression, more outrageous than usual, on the Jews at large, should be accompanied by some gift to the Converts. In 1272, on complaint of abuses in the appropriation of the income, the Founder directed inquiry to be made by the then Warden, John de Saint Dennis, and the Mayor of London, jointly.† In 1320, the complaints were renewed. Some of the Converts alleged in a Petition to Edward the Second that they had not for three years past received any alms, or any grant from the Exchequer, which privation, they add, "has caused the death of many of the said poor Converts;"‡ but they seem to have met with no relief, other than the reference of their petition to their Warden, William de Ayremynne, who was then also Master of the Rolls. On the expulsion of the Jews, generally, from the Kingdom, thirty years before (*i.e.*, in 1290,) the ordinary increment of the inmates had of course been arrested, but the charity was extended to other poor; and occasionally a Jewish convert from abroad seems to have been admitted.§

* According to Madox, the original enrolment of this grant is lost. The grant does not appear even in the new edition of the *Fœdera*, but was printed by Holinshed in 1587 (*Chronicles*, iii, 1281).

† Patent Roll, 56 Hen. III, p. 1, m. 19.

‡ *Rolls of Parliament*, i, 378. Another petition, undated, occurs at p. 465, in the same volume,

§ *e. g.*, Close Roll, 30 Edw. III, m. 13,

And thus the House continued in its original constitution, but in gradual decline, until the year 1377, when Edward III annexed it to the Rolls,* in perpetuity.

Subsequent confirmation of the Gift.

The gift was confirmed by Act of Parliament in the first year of Richard II. And it was again confirmed, on the appointment of John de Waltham (afterwards Bishop of Salisbury and Lord Treasurer), to the Mastership of the Rolls, in 1381.† But it appears that for a long period a few occasional converts drew their small pensions from the Rolls Estate.

That small section of our English domestic History with which we are here concerned, like other and greater sections, seems for a long while to have been thrown into deep shadow, by the all-engrossing demands of the Wars in France, and of the bitter strife of the rival Roses at home. The Records must needs have had their share in the perils and calamities of so disturbed a time. Few and slight are the notices indicative of care about them,‡ which are again to be met with, until we reach the days, and almost the latter days, of the Tudors. But, on the other hand, if we look at the bulk, and at the variety, of the Plantagenet documents which have survived, it will surely be felt that the extent of our actual possessions is a far more reasonable cause for wonder, than the amount of our probable losses.

* Patent Roll, 51 Edw. III, m. 20.

† Ib., 5 Rich. II, part 1, m. 22.

‡ But amongst these few notices are some of a kind which would scarcely, perhaps, be looked for. Thus, in the 24th year of Henry VI (1445) occurs a petition to the king, praying him to cause the careful transcription of the Red Book of the Exchequer, and of other important records, because (amongst other reasons), such "bokes and rolles beth in parcell of so small scripture," &c. Cotton MS., Vesp. C. 14, f. 496. Comp. the Catalogue entitled *Scaccarii Regii Westmon. Codd. MSS.*, in Harleian MS., No. 694, f. 209.

Custody of the Judicial Records.

After the reign of Edward III, the practice of the ultimate delivery of the Judicial Records into the Exchequer, by the judges, appears to have suffered a long interruption. In the 15th Henry VI (1436) the Chief Justice is directed to deliver those which had accrued, up to the reign of Henry IV, "to be kept in our Treasury;" but in 1439 the Commons petitioned that the rolls which had been so delivered, in obedience to the King's writ, should be carried back to the Courts. The petition was refused.*

Transfers of Chancery Records to the Tower.

In proportion as the Rolls, more directly in the custody of the Master, accumulated at the Rolls House, the practice of removing the accumulation, from time to time, to the Tower seems to have fully established itself,† yet without fixed rules. Doubtless, the Tower was originally chosen, mainly as being a place of special strength and safety. The jurisdiction of the Master over the Record Keepers seems never to have been adequately defined. Sometimes—as in the case of John Alcock, in the reign of Edward the Fourth—the newly created Master was himself appointed, by one and the same writ, to the specific custody of the Record Repository in the Tower (. . . . *necnon custodiam* Domus Conversorum *pro habitatione sua, ac cujusdam* Turris infra Turrim nostram Londinensem *pro custodiâ dictorum Rotulorum, ... damus et concedimus;*)‡ but a grant in this form is exceptional. In later reigns there were many conflicts about jurisdiction, and about relative interests in fees and dignities; at one time, between the Tower Record Keeper and the Chamberlains of the Exchequer; at other times, between the same functionary and the Master of the

* *Rolls of Parliament*, v, 29.

† Close Roll, 11 Edw. III, part 2, m. 23. Ib., 14 Edw. III, part 2, m. 10, dors.

‡ Patent Roll, 11 Edw. IV, part 1, m. 24 (29 April, 1471).

Rolls. Some of these will be important to our subsequent story.

From other repositories, also, Records were from time to time transferred to the Tower. Thus, for example, in 1461 (39 Henry VI) "sundry great chests of Records" belonging to the Court of Common Pleas were removed thither from the Priory of Saint Bartholomew, in West Smithfield.* But at the date of Bowyer's Report to Lord Burghley (1564?) no Records of later date than the end of the reign of Edward IV had, it seems, been received.

Enlargement of the Treasuries at Westminster.

In the Westminster Treasuries, meanwhile, the accumulation of documents had come to be so considerable, that in the reign of Henry VIII it was found necessary (it is said) to acquire certain houses or chambers adjacent to the Palace, known by the "names of Paradise, Hell, and Purgatory, together with other tenements adjoining thereunto, for conserving and disposing the Rolls and other Records of the Exchequer."† I quote this official statement, although it will not, perhaps, be found to tally very well with subsequent evidence.

Measures for the improvement of Record Offices under Queen Elizabeth.

Under Elizabeth, many important measures for the preservation and well-ordering of the Records were taken, at various times, and were zealously prosecuted by the several labours of William Bowyer, of William Lambarde, and of Arthur Agarde. Bowyer was a laborious and learned, but somewhat litigious, officer. He was recommended to the Queen by Sir Thomas Parry, and also by the Marquis of Winchester, then Lord Treasurer, whose favour he had won

* Bowyer, *MS. Notes on Records*, preserved amongst Lord Burghley's papers, in Lansd, MS., No. 113, f. 111.

† Auditor's Patent Book, No. 13, pp. 96–106. (*Materials for History of Public Departments*, p. 147, note.)

by drawing and emblazoning, in a sumptuous form, the Paulet pedigree;* and early in 1567 was made Keeper of the Records in the Tower, having previously served as Deputy Keeper to Edward Hales, his predecessor, for about seven years. Whilst yet deputy, he had got embroiled with Edward, Lord Stafford, one of the Chamberlains of the Exchequer, who had himself laboured hard to improve the condition of the Tower Records in the days of Queen Mary. In an undated memorial, addressed to Cecil, Lord Stafford reminds him that a commission had been issued by the Queen to Lord Shrewsbury, to Cecil himself, and to some others (at Stafford's own instance, it may be inferred), to inquire into the causes of certain removals by which the Records had suffered injury, and to take order for the preparation of "a perfect Inventory." Stafford proceeds to state that by these Commissioners a key of the Record Tower was given to his custody. In making an Inventory, he adds, "I have travailed, to my great pains and charges. . . . I have made repertories of every matter from King John's days until Richard III, and of Charter Rolls, Patent Rolls, and Parliament Rolls, from Edward III to Richard III; and, for the more speedy service, I have made sundry Registers; . . . . and have caused a book of the delivery and return of Records to be kept."† The "Keepership," at this date, must have been an easy office.

The labours on the Records of Edward, 19th Baron Stafford.

The Chamberlain's narrative bears the obvious marks of good faith. He seems to have worked for love. And he carefully discriminates what he advances on his own know-

* Winchester to Cecil, 11 Apr., 1567. *Dom.*, Eliz., S. P. O., xlii, 43.

† Stafford to Cecil, 8 January, 1564 [?] S. P. O., *Dom.*, Eliz., xxxiii, 2, and Lansd. MS., No. 113. The latter is the original, as it is endorsed in Lord Burghley's hand. Stafford was the nineteenth Baron of his house, and was the lineal representative of the Stafford Dukes of Buckingham.

ledge, from what he takes on trust. His inaccurate statement that whatever disorder had previously existed was caused "by reason the Master of the Rolls, for the time being, hath appointed the keeping of the Records to one of his servants, and delivered him the key thereof, without taking any Inventory what they found or what they left, and so might such a Keeper do what him list with the Records, without controlment," is prefaced by a cautionary "As they now say." That the Master had *not* appointed, regularly and uniformly, the Record Officers, was precisely one of those causes of complaint and conflict which constantly gave trouble, and sometimes hindered needful reform.

On this occasion, the disputes continued a long time. Bowyer contended, against Stafford, that only one man should have a key to the Record Tower; and also, against the Master of the Rolls, then Sir William Cordell, that the Keeper was and ought to be an independent officer. Lord Winchester supported him strenuously,* and in 1567, obtained the Queen's warrant for the transfer to the Tower of the Parliament Rolls, Patent Rolls, Charter Rolls, Close Rolls, Fine Rolls, Bundles of Escheats, Inquisitions, "and all other Rolls and Records whatsoever of our Chancery," of the reigns of Richard III, Henry VII, Henry VIII, and Edward VI.† But the warrant was not executed.

Warrant for Transfer of Chancery Records to the Tower.

At this period, some increased accommodation for Records was provided at the Tower, but the repository itself was in a dilapidated condition. It was hard to harmonise the conflicting requirements of lawyers and of soldiers. And, in the Tower, the lawyers were wont to go to the wall. Long before Bowyer's appointment, a mass of

State of the Record Tower.

* Winchester to Cecil, S. P. O., *Dom.* Eliz., xlii, 43.

† Warrant, 9 Eliz., ib., 74.

documents had been hastily moved, for some garrison purpose, and it had been utterly forgotten, says Lord Stafford, whither they had been carried, "until Master Hobby, searching for a place *to put gunpowder in,*" found the lost Records, "whereof no small number were eaten with lime of the walls;" and apprising the Keeper of his discovery, had them brought away. Thus, to the other anxieties of the Record keepers was added, in the middle of the sixteenth century, that proximity of gunpowder and of muniments, which was fated to be the occasion of some racy correspondence between the Duke of Wellington and the Master of the Rolls, almost in the middle of the nineteenth century. But, in 1568, the more immediate anxiety was to get the Record Tower made weather-proof. It is amusing to find that in July of that year, the Queen herself, the Lord Chief Baron, and Mr. Chancellor of the Exchequer, had a solemn conference on this stone and mortar question, which conference, after protracted deliberation, was ended by the Queen saying: "I would gladly that these repairs were made, *if time and treasure were ready for it.*"* But ——

The Gunpowder question.

Bowyer's Keepership; and his Successors.

Bowyer had, like many other men, to struggle at once with his work and with the impediments to working. He did strive; and, having the advantage of the previous labours of Stafford, he brought the Tower Records into a far better condition than that in which he had found them. He remained Keeper, until his death in 1581. He was succeeded by a man of much less energy, Michael Heneage. After Heneage, came the most eminent man, perhaps, who has ever held the specific custody of the Records in the Tower, William Lambarde. His appointment to it came late in life, but he worked with a will; and so achieved

* Winchester to Cecil, July, 1568, S. P. O., *Dom.*, Eliz., xlvii, 17.

more in two years, than his predecessor had achieved in nearly twenty. And it was his good fortune to have the opportunity of presenting some of the results of his labour to Elizabeth in person, and to hold with her a conversation which is, I venture to think, as characteristic of the "man-minded" chief interlocutor, as almost anything of its kind that has been handed down to us.

Lambarde was the son of a London alderman, was born in October, 1536, and was admitted into the Society of Lincoln's Inn in 1556. His first publication—a collection and translation of the Anglo-Saxon laws—appeared in 1568, under the title, Ἀρχαιονομία, *sive de priscis Anglorum Legibus libri*. It was dedicated to Sir William Cordell, Master of the Rolls. That this first collection of our early laws was exceedingly imperfect is the necessary consequence of the fact that the best MSS. were then utterly unknown. But Lambarde's work, with the additions of Whelock, remained for a century and a half the one generally accessible source of information on the subject, and was in great measure the basis of the labours of Wilkins. It was reserved for Mr. Thorpe, in our own day, to be the first to build upon a new foundation.

Life and labours of Wm. Lambarde.

In 1570, Lambarde married into the Kentish family of Multon, and settled at Westcombe, near Greenwich, the manor having become his own. He was made a bencher of his Inn in 1578, but from 1570, until his first appointment to a Chancery office in 1592, his time seems to have been divided mainly between the study of antiquities, and the local business of his county. He had early formed the design of a work which would have substantially anticipated Camden's *Britannia*, although on another plan. But his modesty was not less remarkable than his learning. On

His plan of general Description of Britain.

hearing of Camden's project, and of the progress he had made in working it out, Lambarde communicated with him; obtained some part of the manuscript of the *Britannia* for perusal, and then wrote to him thus: "In the reading of these your painful Topographies, I have been contrarily affected: one way, taking singular delight and pleasure in the perusing of them; another way, by sorrowing that I may not now, as I wonted, dwell in the meditation of the same things that you are occupied withal. And yet I must confess that the delectation which I reaped by your labours recompensed the grief that I conceived of mine own bereaving of the like; notwithstanding that in times passed I have preferred the reading of Antiquities before any sort of study that ever I frequented."* But to the project which Lambarde abandoned, in favour of Camden, we owe the valuable *Perambulation of Kent*, a book that has made its author known to many, who know little of him otherwise, and the merits of which are durable. Originally intended as a mere chapter of the *Dictionarium Angliæ Topographicum et Historicum*, Lambarde amplified it into a separate work, and exhorted other students of Antiquity to take their respective Counties in hand in like fashion, "whereby both many good particularities will come to discovery everywhere, and Master Camden himself may yet have greater choice wherewith to . . enlarge the whole [kingdom];" and he made his own special conversancy with Kent the occasion of another liberal testimony to Camden's merits. "What praise you deserve in all," he continues, "I can best tell by Kent, wherein, howsoever I have laboured myself, I learn many things by you, that I knew not before. . . . . To be plain, I seem to myself not to have known Kent, till I knew Camden."† But Camden,

His letter to Camden.

* Cotton MS., Julius, c. v, f. 25.

† Ib.

in his turn, says that Lambarde has described Kent with so much felicity as to have left little to those that come after him.* When Lambarde abandoned his original design, he placed his collections at Camden's service. They remained in manuscript until 1730, when they were at length published from the author's autograph. Lambarde's exhortation was not thrown away. He became substantially the progenitor of the goodly line of our County Historians.

Lambarde's foundation of the College of Queen Elizabeth.

The diligent antiquary was also the open-handed but prudent and politic benefactor. In 1576—the very year of the publication of the volume on Kent—Lambarde founded and liberally endowed an Hospital at Greenwich, to be called "*The College of the Poor of Queen Elizabeth;*" the first steps towards its establishment having been taken two years before. Ten pensioners were to be supported during his own lifetime, and twenty, for ever, after his death. The Master of the Rolls, and the Wardens of the Company of Drapers, were made, by the Charter, a body corporate for its government, as "the President and Governors of the College of Queen Elizabeth." In 1720, and again in 1791, some additional benefactions were left to the Charity. In 1817, the house built by Lambarde was rebuilt, at a cost of nearly five thousand pounds, most of which was defrayed by the sale of timber on the College estate.

Lambarde's legal works.

Lambarde's principal publications, after the *Archaionomia* and the *Perambulation*, are legal hand-books designed, chiefly, to methodise and simplify the law for the practical use of its non-professional officers. His *Eirenarcha, or, Of*

* Camden, *Britannia*, § Cantium, Introd. (......"*Adeo graphice justo volumine descripserit ut curiosa ejus felicitas paucula aliis reliquerit,*" &c.)

the Office of Justices of Peace, and his *Duties of Constables,* show their worth and their timeliness by the number of editions through which they have passed. His own zeal in the discharge of magisterial duty, as Chairman of the Justices for the Western Division of Kent, is borne witness to by a series of twenty annual "Charges," delivered from 1581 to 1600. His official connection with the Records began in 1597, when Sir Thomas Egerton, then both Master of the Rolls and Lord Keeper, made Lambarde his Deputy as Keeper of the Rolls and of the Rolls House. The ability he displayed in the duties of this office were made known to the Queen, who, at Greenwich, was his near neighbour, and who honoured him with an interview. On such an occasion his stately presence would be of no disadvantage to him. Elizabeth, even in 1600, would look none the less graciously on a zealous servant, for the personal merits which in earlier days had won for him the designation of "*the handsome Man of Kent.*" In that year she made him Keeper of the Records in the Tower. He set zealously to work on calendaring, and in August, 1601, submitted to the Queen herself the indexes he had made. These he had first given to Lady Warwick, that she might show them to the Queen, but Elizabeth told her Ladyship to carry them back. What passed at the subsequent interview Lambarde has carefully narrated.

On his presenting to the Queen "Pandects of all her Rolls, Bundles, Membranes, and Parcels, that be reposited in Her Majesty's Tower of London," the Queen, he tells us, said, "You intended to present this book unto me by the Countess of Warwick, but I will none of that; for, if any subject of mine do me a service, I will thankfully accept it from his own hands." Then, opening the book, she added, "You shall see that I can read," and so, with an audible

The Conversation on the Tower Records between Q. Elizabeth and Wm. Lambarde.

voice, read over the Epistle, &c., carefully minding her stops, as her auditor admiringly notes; then she turned over the leaves from the time of King John to that of Richard III, pausing now and then to inquire the precise meaning of certain technical terms, such as '*Oblata,*' '*Litteræ Clausæ,*' '*Rotulus Cambii,*' and the like; saying she would be a scholar in her age, and thought it no scorn to be learning during life. Lambarde's explanations were patiently listened to; and then the Queen went on with the book. Coming to the name of Richard II, she exclaimed vivaciously—"*I am Richard the Second, know you not that?*" Such a wicked imagination was indeed, said Lambarde, attempted "by a most unkind gentleman,—the most adorned creature that ever your Majesty made." "He that will forget God," replied the Queen, "will forget his benefactors. *That tragedy was played forty times in open streets and houses!*" Elizabeth, continuing to turn over the leaves, asked, "What is '*Præstita*'?" Lambarde expounded the term as meaning monies lent by Her Majesty's Progenitors to their subjects *for their good,* but with assurance of good bonds for repayment. Ah, said the Queen, "so did my good grandfather King Henry the Seventh; *sparing to dissipate his treasure or lands.*"

The sad business of Essex was evidently still agitating Elizabeth's thoughts. Turning suddenly from profitable loans to dark memories, she asked Lambarde, "Have you ever seen any true picture of Richard the Second's countenance or person?" "None," said he, "but such as be in common hands." "Lord Lumley," continued Elizabeth, "who is a lover of antiquities, discovered one fastened on the back side of the door of a base room, which he presented unto me, praying with my good leave that I might put it in order with his ancestors and successors. I will command Thomas Knyvett, Keeper of my Gallery at Westminster, to show it unto thee."

Then, resuming her questions about rolls, she asked him if '*Rediseissins*' are "unlawful and forcible throwing of men out of their possessions?" Yea, answered Lambarde, "and therefore these be the Rolls of fines, assessed and levied upon such wrong doers." "In those days," rejoined Elizabeth, "force and arms did prevail; but now, *the wit of the fox is everywhere on foot, so as hardly a faithful and virtuous man may be found.*" Finally, she commended Lambarde for his great pains about the Records. "I have not," she added, "since my first coming to the Crown, received any one thing that brought with it so great delectation unto me;" and, being now called to Prayers, *she put the book into her bosom*, and, "having from first to last forbidden me to fall on my knee before her, she ended the interview with a 'Farewell, good and honest Lambarde.'"* One can well conceive the emotions with which the worthy antiquary left Greenwich Palace, and hastened home to write down the conversation, whilst the Queen's pithy and gracious words were yet ringing in his ears.

Death of Lambarde.

Lambarde's death must have been very sudden. In his account of the interview with Elizabeth there is nothing which indicates any consciousness of failing health.† But he survived this final honour only fifteen days, dying on the 19th August, 1601. By his last Will, he made a useful bequest to the Drapers' Company, for the purpose of establishing loans, without interest, to its poorer members,

* Additional MSS. in Brit. Mus., 15664, ff. 226, 227 [A transcript of Lambarde's MS.].

† In a letter to Lord Burghley, written twelve years earlier (4 Oct., 1589), he speaks of his "decay of sight," which makes his labours on the Records the more honorable to his memory.

to aid them in their industry. He was buried at Greenwich, where a monument was raised to his memory, which, on the rebuilding of the church (1718), was removed to Sevenoaks, the seat of the Lambarde family. Some of his numerous writings yet remain in manuscript. His *Pandecta Rotulorum* found its way, like so many other documents of a similar nature,* into the Library of Mr. Thomas Astle, and by him was bequeathed to the Duke of Buckingham. Everything that he did is as strongly marked by conscientiousness and humility, as by learning and skill. The productions which have given him an honourable place in our literary history grew out of the strenuous performance of the duties of the day. Few men have worked out more consistently the old maxim—

Spartam quam nactus es, hanc exorna.

The next Keeper of the Tower Records was Sir Roger Wilbraham, of whom in that capacity nothing is known, beyond the fact of his appointment. He surrendered the office in June, 1603, and was succeeded by Robert Bowyer, who to some extent continued the labours of his earlier predecessors. Henry Elsing, better known in his office of Clerk of the Parliaments, was conjoined with Bowyer in his Patent, which had the formal confirmation of the Master of the Rolls in December, 1604.† But the true story of the Records has to be taken up in another quarter.

Lambarde's Successors at the Tower.

Arthur Agarde, Deputy Chamberlain of the Exchequer from the year 1570 to the year 1615, was almost exactly contemporary with Lambarde, although he survived him

* Amongst them other Calendars of Records in the Tower, compiled by Michael Heneage and others, and signed by Lambarde.

† *Docquet Book*, Jas. I, Dec. 23, 1604 (Rolls House).

Career of Arthur Agarde.

fourteen years. Their pursuits, and for a time their official functions, were closely similar, but there is not, I believe, any indication of their intimacy. Agarde, like Camden, Cotton, Spelman, and Selden, was a conspicuous member of that early "Society of Antiquaries," which has been mentioned in a preceding chapter.* It is uncertain whether or not Lambarde belonged to this Society.† Both Agarde and Lambarde rendered eminent service as Record Officers, but while Lambarde had only four years in which to work in that department, Agarde had forty-five years. Born while Henry VIII was still in his vigour, he lived through more than half of the reign of James I, and was the life-long friend and fellow-labourer of Sir Robert Cotton.

His Labours at the Exchequer.

His close friendship for Cotton has, indeed, been lately made the occasion of casting a stigma on Agarde's fame, as well as on Cotton's, which I believe to be, in both cases, undeserved. That, however, will be most fitly dealt with, when we come to the biography of Sir Robert Cotton himself. Born in 1540, of a respectable Derbyshire family, Arthur Agarde became at an early age a Clerk in the Exchequer, and by Sir Nicholas Throckmorton was made Deputy Chamberlain. To the duties of that Office his energies were thenceforth devoted. His relaxation seems to have consisted mainly in the composing discourses on some crucial subjects in our English archæology, which were read from time to time to his brother antiquaries at their periodical meetings.

The Compendium of Records, of 1610.

Agarde's *Compendium of the Records in the Treasury* was not entirely completed until 1610. In 1631, it was printed for public use. It is drawn up with great perspicuity, and includes many quaint and curious illustrative remarks.

* Chapter VII, p. 160.

† The lists differ considerably. Lambarde's name occurs only in one, and that I believe the least authentic.

Like all early works of its kind, it makes no attempt to classify the documents described, more minutely than they were classed by their actual arrangement and sequence in the repositories themselves. Like its compeers, therefore, it is what would now be termed a press-catalogue, or inventory. It is prefaced by "A distinguishinge of the Threasauries." There were then four of them, which are thus enumerated: (1) The first Treasury, in the Court of Receipt; (2) The second Treasury, in the New Palace at Westminster; (3) The third Treasury, in the late dissolved Abbey of Westminster (in the old Chapter House); (4) The fourth Treasury, in the Cloister of the said Abbey. Then follows an earnest exhortation to his successors, "in the name of God, for the service of the Prince, satisfying of the Subject, and discharging of their own duty with a good conscience," that they would "observe some instructions, . . learned and noted by long experience, . . both for the preservation of the same Records and the ready finding of them."

The four great enemies of Records are, he proceeds to say, Fire; Water; Rats and mice; Misplacing. These require a four-fold diligence. Against Fire, he commends the continuance of the Records in vaulted rooms. Against Water, he reminds the officers of the necessity for thorough examination, and reparation, when needful, after any "great glut of rain, snow, or tempest." Against Rats and mice, he enforces the necessity of strong boxes, chests, and presses, and of periodical inspection of their contents. As to Misplacing, he thus exhorts the Record Keepers to come: "Misplacing is an evil that riseth by the Officer that produceth the Record for the search or service; and it is an enemy to all good order, and the bringer in of all horror and inconvenience among Records. . . . If one be thrust

The great enemies of the Records.

into another's bag, or misplaced in its King's time, . . it is impossible to find anything certain; yea, and the officer shall be discredited, when it shall be pleaded against him, '*Nul tiel record.*'" Another and important remark which immediately follows will require notice hereafter, for its bearing upon the recent allegations against Sir Robert Cotton.

Details of Agarde's Inventory.

The Inventory proceeds to describe the principal Records of each Treasury, beginning with *Domesday* and the *Black Book*, and it mentions, incidentally, the various calendars and "breviates" which Agarde had himself prepared of many important classes of documents. Its value is enhanced—in a certain sense—by the marginal notes which subsequent officers of the Exchequer, and more especially Peter Le Neve, have inserted, indicating sometimes that they had, in their due custody, the documents and calendars so inventoried, but too often that they had "never seen" them. Eminently curious is the "Calendar of all the Leagues and Treaties, between the Kings of England and other States, as they are placed in the fourth Treasury at Westminster," which concludes the series. These are arranged, tabularly, under the names of the countries treated with. The earliest document entered is dated in 1190; the latest, in 1597.

It is another and conspicuous proof of the good order into which the Records, generally, had been brought towards the close of the reign of Elizabeth, that in the Remembrancer's Office at Westminster a series of Calendars was kept of the Records *in the Tower of London*. It is not apparent by whom this useful provision was made for searchers, but such a series seems to have been available in 1592.

Agarde died (22nd August, 1615) five years after completing his *Compendium*, which he had carefully secured to the use of his successors, and for the public service. He was buried in the Cloister of Westminster Abbey. By his last Will he directed that eleven other MSS. on Exchequer affairs, which he had prepared for his own use, should be placed in the Exchequer Office, on payment of a small sum to his Executors. His general collections in archæology he bequeathed to his dear friend Sir Robert Cotton. Camden has honoured him with the epithet "a most excellent antiquary." Selden says of him: "Mr. Agarde was a man known to be most painful, industrious, and sufficient," in matters of Antiquity. He has thus that acceptable tribute —the praise of the praiseworthy.

Death and Bequests of Agarde.

With the Bowyers, the Lambardes, and the Agardes, of Elizabeth's days, and their honourable labours, I close this slight retrospect of the History of our Records, in its first period. There had doubtless been many losses and much occasional neglect. But, on the whole, this first period is characterised by strenuous effort to preserve and to systematise the memorials of our Legislation,—the materials of our History,—the evidences of our ancient and hard-won Liberties. The very cumbrousness of the formalities and technicalities which enwrap our national muniments, and thus add to the toilsomeness of research amongst them, also add—under one point of view—to their significance and value. For these very technicalities bear witness to our English reverence for law, and love of ancient usage. It would be hard to tell what we owe as a Nation to the practice of traditional, minute, and almost indiscriminate "enrolment." Nor is it an accident in our History that so many of the eminent statesmen and patriots who have stood in the van, in our days of peril, have also been "black-letter lawyers."

§ 2. History of the Public Records in the period of increased separation and of gross neglect.—Losses during the Civil Wars.—Life and labours of Prynne.—Committees of the House of Lords.—The "Methodizers" of 1764.

To the ordinary causes of neglect and loss, arising from that occasional succession of an indolent and unskilful man to a zealous and able one, which seems to be an incident inseparable from human affairs, whether great or small, were added, under the Stuarts, causes more potent still. Favouritism and corrupt bargaining became habitual in the filling up of all kinds of State appointments. The Civil Wars occasioned, first, hasty removals of Records and State Papers from place to place; then, the multiplication of repositories, already too numerous; finally, the actual destruction of valuable Records,—sometimes, by the mere accidents of warfare; at other times, of set purpose. And to the losses which thus accrued were added severe losses by fire.

Conflicting Jurisdiction as to Records in the Tower.

The conflicts, also, about jurisdiction over Records became increasingly a source of mischief. The dispute between Sir William Cordell and Bowyer had led to no settlement of the question. It was revived in 1604, between Edward, Lord Bruce of Kinlosse, then Master of the Rolls, and Peter Proby, who claimed an independent custody over all the Records in the Tower, as successor of

Sir Roger Wilbraham. The Lords of the Council, after referring the matter to the Judges and receiving their opinion, reported thus:—The possession of the Records of Chancery ought, they say, to be delivered up "unto the Master of the Rolls, or to such as his Lordship shall appoint to receive the same." But "whereas there are divers other Records remaining in the Tower, that have been removed thither from the King's Bench, the Common Pleas, the Exchequer, and other Courts of His Majesty ..... the custody of which ... doth not appertain to the Master of the Rolls, but is and ought to be at His Majesty's pleasure to order and dispose of, we think it meet that .... the custody of the foresaid Records not appertaining to the Chancery be not otherwise disposed of than by His Majesty's warrant." They suggest, however, the possible expediency "that the Master of the Rolls do make suit unto His Majesty to obtain . . a grant . . of the keeping of the said Records, not of the Chancery;" and, finally, reciting the purchase by Proby from Mrs. Heneage, the widow of a former keeper, of certain Calendars, "and other instruments," they recommend the payment to him of two hundred and fifty pounds, "upon the delivery of the said Records and Books."*

Remembrancership of Records.

In 1617, an attempt was made to create a new office called "General Remembrancer of Matters of Record," to be held, jointly, by three Patentees, avowedly "for the ease of the King's subjects in their searches," but more probably to give birth to a new and lucrative system of fees. This scheme failed, as did also an attempt in the following reign, to resuscitate the grant.† It made no change in jurisdic-

* *Domestic Papers*, MS., S. P. O., James I, ix, 14, &c.

† Ib., Chas. I, cxlviii, 57.

tion, and no reduction in the number of the Record Repositories.

Burning of Records of Six Clerks' in Chancery.

The burning of the Six Clerks' Office, in December 1621, occasioned a severe loss of Records. A certain Six Clerk named Tuthil, having (according to the account we have of the calamity by an eye-witness of it, Sir Simonds D'Ewes), "out of a little base niggardliness, neglected to mend the hearth of his chimney, which was cracked, some of the fire .. got through .. to the woodwork, .. and so firing that chamber, was the occasion of burning all the Six Clerks' Offices." The Council did what could be done towards repairing the mischief by issuing a Proclamation for re-enrolments, but much of the loss was irretrievable.*

To narrate, in detail, the various losses of Records which accompanied the progress of the Civil Wars would be both tedious and profitless. The results will sufficiently appear in subsequent passages of the story. The attention of the Houses of Parliament was repeatedly called to the subject, at various stages of the contest, but with no substantial advantage. Thus, in 1643, the House of Commons ordered the Office of Clerk-Keeper of Records in the Tower to be "sequestrated into the hands of John Selden," and with the assent of the Lords it was sequestrated accordingly. But Selden's vast claims on the gratitude of posterity do not include any direct service in this department. Again, in 1647, the House of Lords ordered that "all sequestrated Evidences and Records" should be delivered to the Registrar for the Sale of the Bishops' Lands. This order was the source of additional mischief. Part of these Records were kept at Westminster; part of them in

Parliamentary Ordinances respecting Records.

* *Journal*, &c., in Harleian MS., 646, f. 63; *Collection of Proclamations*, S. P. O., No. 100.

a house in the Old Jewry, others were lost.* Four or five years later, Hugh Peters proposed a method of dealing with the Records generally, which would have been swift and final. In his curious tract entitled, *Good Work for a Good Magistrate,* under the heading "A Short Model for the Law," after recommending a system of public and parochial Registration, both of Lands and of Wills,—"This being done," he continues, "it is very advisable to burn all the old Records; yea, even those in the Tower, the monuments of tyranny." But it is fair to acknowledge that this silly outburst of ignorance occurs in a piece, which, in its treatment of several other and weighty subjects, indicates an acute and vigorous intellect. In relation to such matters as Public Works, the proper incidence of Taxation, Prison Discipline, Copyright, the Rewards of Invention, he was in advance of his age.† In matters of technical jurisprudence, and in regard, especially, to the right province of legislation, he was almost on a level with Jack Cade.

Hugh Peters on Records.

From the terms of an order of the House of Commons, made 2nd November, 1647,‡ it has been strangely supposed that the good policy of a single General Record Repository for the whole kingdom, was recognised by the Long Parliament, whilst yet scarcely out of the heat of its struggle with Charles. But a more attentive examination of those terms, will, I think, make it plain enough that what was

Supposed Ordinance of the Long Parliament for a General Repository.

* *Journals of the House of Commons,* iii, 291, 728; *Journals of the House of Lords,* vi, 285; ix, 440.

† Thus, in 1651, he advocates an extensive system of canals; the embankment of the Thames: the abolition of imprisonment for debt, in company with severely repressive measures against fraudulent bankruptcy; the universal substitution of Salaries for Fees of Office; and many other changes, which in our own generation have been carried out, or partially carried out.

‡ *Journals of the House of Commons,* v, 348.

then contemplated was nothing more than a collection, into one place, of those Records and documents which had been seized, as part of the estates of "delinquents." If further evidence of the fact be needed, it will be found in the Interregnum Books, preserved in the State Paper Branch at the new Rolls House.

Other Record incidents in the Interregnum.

Between this date and that of the Restoration, the principal notices which occur of the fortunes of the Records, lie in two other entries on the Journals of the Commons. In 1651, that House directed that the Master of the Rolls, for the time being, should have the responsible superintendence of the Record Office in the Tower, and that William Ryley should continue as clerk under him.* In 1656, it directed that certain Records which had accumulated in rooms above the Parliament House, should be removed to the house called "the King's Fish House."† For a very long period, indeed, the course pursued whenever an accumulation of Records created inconvenience, was simply to establish a new repository, in almost any place that might chance to offer, and with little or no regard either to accessibility or to safekeeping. The records in the custody of "the King's Fishmonger" figure conspicuously in the Reports of Committees of Inquiry in the days of Queen Anne and of King George the First. They were records of high historical value, being, for the most part, the archives of the famous Court of Wards and Liveries.

Removal of Records from Scotland to the Tower of London.

After the surrender of Edinburgh Castle to Cromwell, in December 1650, he gave to the Lord Register of Scotland, Archibald Johnston, passes for the safe conveyance of the "Public Writs and Registers of the Kingdom of

* *Journals of the House of Commons.* vi, 617.

† Ib., vii, 445, 448.

Scotland," and they were placed on shipboard accordingly, but, despite the passes, were captured by the Parliament's ships, and brought to London, where they were lodged in the Tower.* In 1653, on complaint of the Scottish Parliament, that of England ordered a severance of Public Records and Papers of State from Registers and Deeds concerning the right of private persons, with a view to the retention of the former class, and the return to Scotland of the latter, but it was not until 1657 that the Ordinance was carried into effect.† After the Restoration, the documents which had remained were again claimed. In December, 1660, Ryley petitioned the King for a reward for his "extraordinary pains in examining a hundred and seven hogsheads, twelve chests, five trunks, and four barrels, of Records and Papers belonging to Scotland, now delivered to the Deputy of Sir Archibald Primrose, Register of Scotland."‡ How far this formidable-looking task was rewarded, if at all, I find no evidence. The unlucky Scottish Records were returned—by intention—to their proper abode, but their mishaps pursued them, and they suffered shipwreck, with no small damage; thus experiencing a like fatality to that which is said, traditionally, to have attended a former transfer and former return of Scottish Records, in Plantagenet days.

* Ayloffe's statement (or rather Astle's), in the Introduction to the *Calendars of Ancient Charters* (p. 59), is a mere travesty of the facts. It begins thus: "Cromwell, *after the Battle of Worcester*, having *ravaged Scotland*, caused the Records...of that kingdom to be removed to the Tower of London." There are here three distinct assertions, and each of them is inaccurate.

† *Domestic Papers*, MS., S. P. O., Chas. II, xxiv, 419. Thurloe's *State Papers*, i, 117. Whitelocke, *Memorials of the English Affairs*, 490.

‡ *A Brief Register of Parliamentary Writs*, Pt. iv, Dedicatory Epistle. [Prynne's "Brief Register" extends to 1470 closely printed pages].

The appointment to the Tower Record Office of William Prynne.

William Ryley was succeeded, in the custody of the Tower Records, by William Prynne, the "Cato of the age," as Charles the Second called him. One does not wonder that Charles could not hear Prynne's name mentioned, without a smile or a jest. Two more antithetical men never, it is probable, stood face to face on English ground. Prynne had had a long acquaintance with Records in almost every form. He had studied and quoted them with reference to all sorts of topics. He had been himself the subject-matter of many records which mark the nadir of English jurisprudence. But before he became a Record Keeper, he had passed his sixtieth year. Yet he achieved something in their arrangement and cataloguing which, incomplete as it necessarily was, well deserves memorial. He could not fail, while breath was in him, to continue those endless compilations which have won for him the epithet "voluminous Prynne," but he could honestly boast that he made progress in his self-imposed tasks "at vacant hours borrowed from my natural rest and repasts, without the least neglect of my other and public services." That his labours might be unbroken upon, it was his plan to work, in the old Record Tower, with a tray of bread, cheese, and ale, at his elbow; and his learned successor, Sir Francis Palgrave, was inclined to think that, occasionally, his calendars bore testimony to the nappiness of the beverage. It is a suggestive picture. That grizzled head which is so studiously bent, from morn till eve over the musty rolls of the Plantagenets, had been thrice mutilated in the pillory; had been imprisoned in ten fortresses; had, in that very Tower of London, been driven, when deprived for a season of pen and ink, to express its crowding thoughts by scratching them on the stone walls; had uttered many vehement if not very coherent speeches in the critical days of the

Long Parliament; had, in fine, given birth to a hundred and sixty several treatises,—some of them books of a thousand pages apiece,—before it began to struggle with its seven years' weary labour on the Records of the Tower.

Prynne was born at Swainswick, near Bath, in 1600; became a commoner of Oriel in 1616; and a student of Lincoln's Inn, in 1620. His first publication, *The Perpetuity of a Regenerate Man's Estate*, appeared in 1627, and brought him immediately into conflict with the ruling powers. With him, it will be seen, thinking and study long preceded publication, but, having once begun to print, he knew no pause. And almost every fresh book was a fresh trouble. The famous *Histriomastix* appeared in 1633, but much of it had been printed nearly three years before. Bishop Laud, now at the threshold of his Archbishopric, had been grievously offended by Prynne's previous books, but the punishment he had then been enabled to inflict, fell more upon the printer than the author. Now, he hoped to wreak full vengeance upon both, and also upon the unlucky licenser; for the offensive books had come out with the *imprimatur* of Archbishop Abbot's Chaplain. Laud, there is good reason to think, carried the volume with his own hands to the King, pointed out obnoxious passages, and put a malevolent interpretation upon doubtful ones.* An unfortunate entry in the Index—"*Women Actors, notorious* —," which especially and naturally excited Charles's wrath, from the fact that the Queen herself had recently (for the first time) performed in a Court masque, could not well have been aimed at royalty, since proof was adduced that the

Prynne's Life and Labours.

* *Domestic Papers*, MS., S. P. O., Charles I, cxli, No. 17; cxlii, 22; cxliv, 10, 48.

The Histriomastix and its punishment.

book, with its index, was actually published before that performance took place. But King and Prelate were implacable. And, in the Star Chamber, although the voices were the voices of the judges, the words were the words of King and Prelate. Very significant is the language of Lord Cottington, Chancellor of the Exchequer:—"If Master Prynne should be demanded what he would have, he liketh nothing; no state or sex; music and dancing are unlawful, even in Kings; no kind of recreation, no kind of entertainment, no, not so much as hawking: all are damned. . . . Master Prynne would have a new church, new laws, and new entertainments. God knows what he would have. He would have a new King!" Such was the style of a Star Chamber charge, under Charles the First. "I do condemn Master Prynne," continued Lord Cottington, to stand in the Pillory in two places, . . and that he shall lose both his ears, one in each place; . . . and, lastly —nay not lastly,—I do condemn him in five thousand pounds' fine to the King. And lastly, to perpetual imprisonment." And the other judges echo Lord Cottington. One of them was even for increasing the fine to ten thousand pounds; and would have had his forehead branded. Prynne in vain entreated mercy; besought the Council to become his mediators with the King for the mitigation of his ruinous fine and corporal punishment. He had already suffered a long and severe imprisonment, before trial, under a warrant of the Council issued by the King's command.* His sufferings were made a jest by the courtiers: "Master Prynne," they said, "is become so enamoured of dancing that he will dance a gaillarde on the

* *Domestic Papers*, ut supra, S. P. O., ccxlii, 50; ccxlv, 6; ccxlvi, 108; cclx, 120; cclxiii, 46; cclxvi, 60. Rushworth, *Collections*, ii, 220. *State Trials*, iii, 562—586.

loss of his ears." The University of Oxford deprived and expelled him. The Society of Lincoln's Inn disbarred him. It appears, curiously, that by the bequest of some Puritan lady, a copy of *Histriomastix* had been given to Sion College Library, in the short interval between its publication and the trial. The Star Chamber endeavoured, vainly, to suppress the book, wherever it might be met with.

The merits and demerits of the Drama were of real and momentous interest to Englishmen, but the interest was ill-appreciated in Prynne's day. A busy, conspicuous, and in some points of view an estimable section of the public, shared many of Prynne's opinions about it, but neither he nor they represented English feeling on that question. The subject which next brought Prynne into the Star Chamber and into the Pillory, stirred English feeling to its depths.

The Trial of Prynne, Bastwicke, and Burton, in 1637.

The growth of ecclesiastical tyranny had become as manifest as the growth of puritanical fanaticism and puerility. Each had fed the other. Both, together, were daily imperilling the very existence of that Church to which in earlier, as in later, days, everything that is best and deepest in English culture and in English policy had been so largely indebted. The excesses and follies of a rabid Puritanism were becoming only too evident. But they were not, as yet, the crying evils of the day. The unchecked dominance of the Church Courts; the supremacy, over all literature, of a Church Censorship; the repression of errors of opinion by fire and sword, must have proved fatal to English freedom. Whatever their mistakes and their excesses, Prynne, Bastwicke, and Burton, when they stood together at the bar of the Star Chamber, to answer to charges of libel, after a vain attempt by the Crown

Counsel to expose them to the utmost penalties of High Treason, stood there as the champions of the Liberties of England.

Prynne's present offence—the addition, that is, to the standing offence of his continuing to breathe vital air—lay in the writing, during his imprisonment in the Tower, of two pamphlets on Church questions. The one was *A Dialogue concerning the Sabbath's Morality;* the other was called *Newes from Ipswich*, and stigmatised, in terms of gross virulence, some recent acts of Matthew Wren, Bishop of Norwich, and of other prelates. Here it will suffice to quote one small but most significant incident of the trial. In the course of it, the Lord Chief Justice Finch, looking earnestly on Prynne, said, "I had thought Master Prynne had no ears, but methinks he hath ears," which caused, says the narrator and eye-witness, the Lords present to take the stricter view of him; and for their better satisfaction, the Usher of the Court was commanded to turn up his hair, and show his ears; upon the sight whereof the Lords were displeased that there had formerly been no more cut off; and uttered some disgraceful words of him. Lord Cottington again was first to pronounce judgment—"I condemn these three men to lose their ears in the Palace Yard; to be fined five thousand pounds a man to His Majesty; and to perpetual imprisonment in three remote places, . . namely, in . . . Carnarvon, Cornwall, and Lancaster." "I," added Lord Finch, "condemn Prynne to be stigmatised in the cheeks with the letters S. L.,* for a 'seditious libeller.'" To which all the Lords agreed.

Prynne's Second Trial.

* Which he himself used to interpret into *Stigmata Laudis* :—

"Stigmata maxillis referens insignia Laudis
Exultans remeo, victima grata Deo."

PRYNNE'S *Comfortable Cordials*, p. 15.

The scene at Whitehall at the execution of the sentence on these three men, on the thirtieth of June, 1637, was, in a very special sense, the precursor of another sad scene at Whitehall, on the thirtieth of January, 1649. The executioner, we are told, "cut deep and close to the head, so as the blood ran streaming down upon the scaffold, which divers persons standing about the pillory seeing, *dipped their handkerchiefs in*, as a thing most precious; the people giving a mournful shout."*

Prynne's Imprisonment at Mount Orgueil.

Prynne, who could never decently control his temper or restrain his pen when engaged in controversy, seems always to have shown patient firmness and moderation under actual suffering. During his first imprisonment, Simonds D'Ewes tells us—"When I went to visit him in the Fleet, I found in him the rare effects of an upright heart and a good conscience, by his serenity of spirit and cheerful patience."† And such, it seems, was his behaviour during his three years' imprisonment in the solitary but grand and romantically-seated old Castle of Mount Orgueil, on the coast of Jersey. He won friends, too, in his prisons. Jailers, Wardens, Lieutenants of the Tower, Governors of Jersey, seem uniformly to have conceived respect for the laborious, rugged, and much enduring man. His Jersey imprisonment he celebrated, or as he would himself have preferred to say, improved, in a long poem on "Rocks, Seas, and Gardens."‡ There is, as might be expected, not the smallest spark of Poetry in this production, but it shows a wonderful familiarity with all parts of Holy Scripture, and there is not a single quotation from any uninspired author, in the whole book,—which, for Prynne, is a marvel indeed.

* *A New Discovery of the Prelates' Tyranny* (1641) passim. *State Trials*, iii, 711-770.

† D'Ewes, *Journal*, Harl. MS. ut supra.

‡ *Mount Orgueil; or, Divine and Profitable Meditations*, 1641.

Traditional speech about him is not yet, in Jersey, quite extinct.*

Prynne's return to London in 1640, in company with Henry Burton, one of his fellow-sufferers, who had joined him on the road, was like a triumphal procession. "Never here," says Robert Baillie, "such a like show. . . . . Some of good note say [that there were] above four thousand horse, and above a hundred coaches; . . . with a world of foot, every one with their rosemary branch." Well may he add, "This galled the bishops exceedingly."† This public reception was soon followed by one of the most curious, and also one of the least creditable, incidents in Prynne's life. In regard to his conduct towards Laud,—had he been put on his defence of it,—it would have been useless for him to have striven to make private vindictiveness wear the mask of public duty. It is too plain that much as he may have learnt from the Bible, he had failed to learn some of its most obvious lessons.

Prynne's conduct in the trial of Archbishop Laud.

The startling effect produced on Laud's mind and demeanour when, on that trying morning on which he was called upon to sum up the main points of his long Defence against the charges aimed at his life, he saw that "every Lord present had a new thin book in folio, in a blue coat," containing extracts from his own "Diary," has often been referred to. It was Prynne's act, and bore but a too close resemblance to acts by which Prynne himself had grievously suffered. What Prynne had endured for conscience sake had been rewarded, not only by shouts and rosemary branches, but by an eager readiness to return him to Parliament, on the part of several constituencies. He took

* That, at least, is the impression I have retained of a visit paid to Mount Orgueil many years ago.

† Baillie, *Letters and Journals* (Bannatyne Club), i, 277.

his seat for Newport Pagnell in 1642, and in the following year bore a prominent part in the Archbishop's impeachment, as one of the chosen Managers for the Commons. That he should strain every nerve to put down the Archbishop's policy was, with his views, a plain duty. That he should descend to stratagem and surprises in order to shed the blood of the defeated Prelate, already tottering to the grave, is a deep stain on his memory.

The way in which Prynne obtained Laud's Diary and other papers, to be used for his surer condemnation, is thus described by the Archbishop himself in the *History of the Troubles and Tryal,* written during his imprisonment:—

"The manner of the search upon me was thus: Mr. Pryn came into the Tower, with other searchers, so soon as the gates were open. [This was on the 31st May, 1643.] He made haste to my lodging, commanded the warder to open my doors, left two musketeers sentinels below, . . and one at the stair-head; with three others, which had their muskets ready cocked, he came into my chamber, and found me in bed. . . . . He falls first to my pockets to rifle them; and by that time my two servants came running in, half ready. . . . . . *He took from me twenty and one bundles of papers, which I had prepared for my defence;* . . . . . the Scottish Service-book, with such Directions as accompanied it; a little book or Diary, containing all the occurrences of my life, and my Book of Private Devotions; both these last written through with my own hand. Nor could I get him to leave this last, but he must needs see what passed between God and me,—a thing, I think, scarce ever offered to any Christian. The last place which he rifled was a trunk which stood by my bedside. In that he found . . . . a bundle of some gloves, . . . and caused each glove to be looked into. Upon this, I tendered him one pair of the

Laud's account of the seizure of his private papers by Prynne.

gloves, which he refusing, I told him he might take them and fear no bribe, for he had already done me all the mischief he could, and I asked no favour of him. So he thanked me, took the gloves, bound up my papers, . . . and went his way."* Prynne pursued his fallen enemy with great bitterness to the end. He saw so little to regret in that bitterness that, after the lapse of nearly five years, he said, in the House of Commons: "I brought you off with honour in the case of Canterbury" [the word "Bishop" would have choked him] "when you were at a loss, and cleared the justness of your cause, when it was at the lowest ebb."

Prynne's course during the Commonwealth.

Under the victorious Parliament, under the Council of State, and under Cromwell, Prynne was repeatedly in conflict, and in disgrace. Even with his brethren of the Presbyterian party he seems to have parted company. "Prynne and the Erastian Lawyers are now our *remora*," writes Robert Baillie, in September, 1645.† Had his tastes lain that way, he had again ample opportunities of studying English antiquities, in our old Castles, as he had already studied them in our old Records. Dunster Castle, Taunton Castle, Pendennis Castle, are among the prisons in which at this period of his life he was by turns confined. At length, with the other secluded Members, he sat in the restored Long Parliament, and also in the "Healing Parliament" of 1660. He pleaded zealously for the Restoration; and sat in Charles the Second's first Parliament, where, however, he had to ask pardon in his place for a pamphlet offensive to the House. When Charles was asked, "What shall be done with Prynne, to

* *Troubles and Trial* (*Works*, by Bliss, iv, 25, 26).

† *Letters and Journals*, ii, 315.

keep him from falling foul of the Bishops?"—"Let him pore over the Records," said the King. He was made Keeper at the Tower, with a salary of five hundred pounds a year, and Charles ordered that his Patent should pass without fees. It is charmingly characteristic of the mode of transacting public business under the "merry monarch," to find another five hundred a year granted, at the same time, to a certain William Bryan, as a person "to whom the King *intends* the office of Keeper of Records in the Tower."*

Prynne's keepership had its difficulties at the threshold. The Lieutenant of the Tower had profited by the interval of vacancy, to put one of his own subordinates into the Record Keeper's house. Poor Prynne had to represent to the King, by petition, that he and his helpers "in the duty of sorting, transcribing, and tabulating the Records, have not even a fire near at hand, to warm and dry themselves."†

Prynne again at the Tower.

What sort of a task this was, after the accumulated neglect and confusion of the Civil Wars, Prynne has himself depicted for us: "No sooner received I your royal Patent," he tells the King, "for the custody of your ancient Records in your Tower of London, even in the midst of my parliamentary and disbanding services, . . but I designed and endeavoured the rescue of the greatest part of them from that desolation, corruption, confusion, in which . . . they had, for many years bypast, lain buried together in one confused chaos, under corroding, putrifying cobwebs, dust, and filth, in the darkest corner of Cæsar's Chapel in the White Tower, as mere useless reliques not worthy to be calendared, or brought down thence into the office amongst

State in which he found the Records there.

* *Docquet Books*, MS., S. P. O., Charles II, Mar., 1661, p. 100.

† *Domestic Papers*, MS., S. P. O., Chas. II, lxvi, 154.

other Records of use. In order thereunto, I employed some soldiers and women, to remove and cleanse them from their filthiness, who, soon growing weary of this noisome work, left them almost as foul . . as they found them. Whereupon, immediately after the Parliament's adjournment, I and my clerks . . . spent many whole days in cleansing and sorting them into distinct, [but] confused heaps, in order to their future reducement into method, the old clerks of the office being unwilling to touch them, for fear of . . . endangering their eyesights and healths by the cankerous dust and evil scent. In raking up this dung-heap," continues Prynne, "according to my expectation I found many rare ancient precious pearls and golden Records; . . . with many original Bulls of Popes (some of them under seal), Letters to and from Popes, Cardinals, and the Court of Rome; . . besides sundry rare antiquities, specially relating to the Parliaments of England, . . and no less than ninety-seven parcels of Original Writs of Summons [from Edward I to Henry VI,] . . confusedly intermixed with many thousands of other Writs and Records." And he proceeds to present to His Majesty's "royal view," a Chronological Catalogue of the Parliamentary Writs thus newly discovered, together "with those formerly kept in the Record Office."*

Prynne's labours on the Records.

Last works and death of Prynne.

Death put a term to Prynne's long and diversified labours in 1669. The last of them was the most formidable of all. It is entitled *An exact Chronological Vindication of our English Kings' Supreme Ecclesiastical Jurisdiction*, and was never completed, although four folio volumes are extant, the last and unfinished volume in an unique copy. The great Fire of London occurred whilst this

* *Brevia Parliamentaria* (1662) Epistle Dedicatory.

enormous book was in the press, and destroyed, it is said, all but seventy copies of the first volume, and a large portion of the second. The fourth volume is known only by proof sheets of the first four hundred pages, which found their way to the Library at Stowe, and at the Stowe Sale were purchased for the Library of Lincoln's Inn, at a cost of three hundred and thirty-five pounds. Prynne's books are less uncouth and abnormal than they look, but his style and diction are unspeakable. Yet they did their work in their day. Booksellers were found to venture three or four hundred pounds on a single volume. Thirty-three years after his first publication—and at that date his faults must have been at least as well known as his merits—when a powerful party needs an exponent, one of its shrewdest leaders turns to Prynne, as to a penman of established fame, and imagines him equal to "the crushing of the high and proud Episcopalians."* Some painstaking arithmetician has, I believe, computed that Prynne wrote or compiled, and printed, about eight quarto pages for every working day of his life, from the day when he reached man's estate to the day of his death. Several of his productions were translated into foreign languages. Some of them have become extremely scarce, without owing that merit entirely to the trunkmakers. Strype searched through London for a book of Prynne's which had had two editions, and could only obtain it at Cambridge. Whilst he sat for Bath, Prynne himself collected them for a Library in the Abbey Church. At his death he bequeathed a nearly complete set to the Society which had once disbarred him, but had long been proud of his renewed fellowship; and in its chapel he rests from his labours.

* Principal Baillie to James Sharp (*Letters and Journals*, iii, 400).

Keepership of Sir Algernon May.

Prynne was succeeded at the Tower by Sir Algernon May, who retained the office until 1702. It is significant to find him stating to a Committee of the House of Lords, in 1681, that the King then owed him three thousand pounds, or six years' salary; but the royal cash-books of that day show that it was difficult enough to find money for Duchesses of Portsmouth, and Duchesses of Cleveland, without the Treasury worrying itself too anxiously about the claims of Record Keepers and Clerks. In 1685, Sir John Trevor became Master of the Rolls. He found the repositories under his more immediate control in a very unsatisfactory condition. These had increased to ten or even to eleven, exclusive of the repositories at Westminster and at the Tower. The Records of the "Petty Bag" Office, and those of the Six Clerks' Office, which ought periodically to have been transmitted to the Rolls' Chapel, were detained, partly from arrears in enrolment, partly for the increase and diversion of fees for searches.* And they were not only detained, but were ill-arranged and ill-kept. Each Six-Clerk had his particular record-room, and some of these rooms were cellars. Sir John Trevor caused some improvements of detail to be made, but seems to have struggled in vain with the main abuses. On the appointment, in December 1703, of a Committee of the House of Lords to inquire into the state of the Records, generally, he submitted a report narrating what he had done or attempted, and describing each several repository as it then stood.† It is from that report, and from the proceedings of the Committee, which was reappointed from time to time, until 1719, that the best account of the state of the Records and of their administration, as they were in

Sir John Trevor's Account of the Records, 1685-1703.

* Trevor, *An Account of the Records*, Lansd. MS., 319, ff. 107—112.

† Ibid.

the last century, is to be gathered. The able and accomplished Charles Montague, Lord Halifax, was the leader in this inquiry.

At the date of its commencement the Tower Records were in the immediate custody of William Petyt, a Bencher of the Inner Temple, and an antiquary of considerable learning and ability, who had first been appointed to assist in their arrangement in the year 1689. He succeeded Sir Algernon May, as Keeper, in 1702. He held the office only five years, but appears to have discharged its duties with some diligence. He formed, too, a considerable Library, including a valuable and extensive series of collections on English history and antiquities, partly derived from the Records; and he bequeathed the whole *to the Public*, leaving to his executors a discretionary power as to the manner of carrying out his intentions, of which power they availed themselves by giving the Library to the Society of the Inner Temple, stipulating, however, for free public access. Petyt published many treatises on legal antiquities. His posthumous work, entitled, *Jus Parliamentum; or, the ancient power, jurisdiction, rights, and liberties of Parliament, revived and asserted*, retains, I believe, its value and authority.

Life and Writings of Petyt.

In reporting on the Tower branch of the Record service, the Lords Committees of 1703-4 say that they found the Records there in good condition; that Petyt had fairly transcribed most of the old calendars, but that a great number of early Rolls remained without any calendars or abstracts; that the "confused heaps," or some of them,—which had so troubled poor Prynne,—still remained in Cæsar's Chapel; and that the Keeper ought to have an allowance for "a considerable number" of competent clerks. But a hundred years was yet to elapse, before

Lords' Report of 1704.

even an approximation to an adequate establishment, really fitted to grapple with the work, in its entirety, would be provided. In other respects, large improvements were made under Lord Halifax's continued superintendence.*

The Records in "Fish Yard."

In 1709, the renewed Committee further reported that a large quantity of Records, belonging formerly to the Court of Wards, lay neglected, and in a perishing condition, "in a Fishmonger's House," near Westminster Hall. The lead had been stolen from the roof; the windows had been broken; the rain "had corrupted and destroyed" many documents; and, finally, "the Fishmonger had recourse *to search them*, at pleasure, or to let anybody go in, and do as they pleased; . . . . and it is to be feared many of the Records are embezzled."† On the same occasion, the Committee also reported that "there are two places (containing Records) near Westminster Hall, called, 'The Treasuries of the Court of Queen's Bench,'" under one of which Treasuries there was a wash-house and a stable; the other Treasury being "a low, damp place, fitter for a cellar than the use it is put to." Very similar is the account given of some other Record Repositories.

The State of the Rolls' Chapel.

It does not appear that this Committee made any report specifically on the Records in the Rolls' Chapel and subordinate offices. Sir John Trevor endeavoured to prepare a way for better arrangements there, by issuing his warrant, in 1712, for the removal to the Tower of a large accumulation of Chancery documents, but the authorities at the Tower objected by alleging the want of space for their

* *Journals of the House of Lords*, xvii, 555, 574, 637; xviii, 69, 135, 318.

† *Journals*, ut supra, xviii, 715, 716.

reception; and the transfer was not effected for twenty-seven years. In 1717, Sir Joseph Jekyll succeeded to the Mastership. He caused his official house to be pulled down and rebuilt. During the demolition, a mass of utterly neglected Records was discovered in a disused room. Sir Joseph also rebuilt (under the powers of an Act of Parliament passed in 1661) many of the houses on the Rolls estate. He rebuilt them in a substantial and costly fashion, expending, it is said, between thirty and forty thousand pounds, under the impression that he was empowered to grant leases for forty-one years, and that his heirs would retain a beneficial interest, in conjunction with his successors, and in consideration of his outlay. This circumstance, combined with an unusual bequest in his Will, led, long afterwards, to a very singular application to Parliament. Sir Joseph Jekyll, after providing largely, as he believed, for his relatives, bequeathed certain considerable sums in East India Stock and South Sea Stock, to the King, his heirs and successors, "to be applied to the use of the Sinking Fund." When it was discovered that twenty-one years' leases, only, could be granted, the position of Sir Joseph's residuary legatees was so materially altered that they sought and obtained from the Legislature a sum of £13,580, out of the proceeds of the Stock bequeathed for the lessening of the National Debt, by way of compensating them for their loss.*

The Mastership of Sir Joseph Jekyll.

His bequest to the Crown.

This bequest, I think, was no mere craze. Sir Joseph Jekyll had lived through a period, *not* honourably distinguished in our annals as respects the disinterestedness or the purity of public men. He had sat in Parliament for almost forty years,—years more than usually fraught with lessons to a thoughtful man. He could not imagine that a

* *Case of the Residuary Legatees of Sir J. Jekyll* (in Brit. Mus.).

sum of twenty-five or thirty thousand pounds would, of itself, avail much in lessening the public burdens. What he had himself received from the public was the wages, not of a sinecure, but of a laborious office. That fact, he might not unreasonably though vainly hope, would give point and pregnancy to his example.

The Parliamentary inquiries of 1719 and 1731.

Two other Parliamentary inquiries into the state of our Records preceded the memorable inquiry at the close of the eighteenth century. The first of them, in 1718-19, was obtained by the influence of the Lord Chancellor Macclesfield; the second, in 1731, grew out of the partial destruction of the Cottonian Library by fire. Lord Macclesfield's inquiry dealt more especially with the Treasuries at Westminster and at the Tower, but it led to no permanent improvements; did not even succeed in overcoming the obstinate pertinacity with which the Board of Ordnance continued, at the Tower, to stand in the way of such improvements. The inquiry of 1731 was more general. It came then to be apparent that the one essential preliminary to real progress in the matter was the lessening of the number of separate repositories and of conflicting Keeperships. The fact was recognised, but the reform was not effected.

The importance of such a measure was, indeed, pointed out and enforced by circumstances, in almost every conceivable way. Multitudes of valuable Records, actually in public custody, were notoriously becoming more and more widely scattered, and were daily perishing through neglect. But others, long since freed from such custody, were continually in course of active destruction. Often such losses would attract no attention; but often, too, an accident would bring them under public notice. Thus, for instance, an historian chances to hear that ancient-looking papers are getting distributed at a cheesemonger's shop, and he buys there an original Privy Council Book of King Edward VI. Or, an auctioneer stumbles into another cheesemonger's, to find that the worthy tradesman has just made a bargain, in the course of business, and at the price of ten pounds, for a mass of State Papers, collected by Sir Julius Cæsar in the days of James the First, and vast enough to enwrap the cheese and butter of a dozen years to come. More curiously still, the temporary expedients resorted to, from time to time, as this abuse and the other came to be detected, were made the sure seed-plots of another crop of abuses, to arise thereafter. Thus, a fire at Whitehall, early in the seventeenth century, having caused the hurried removal of a large number of Records of great value, as we are told, to the Pell Office in the Exchequer,—an office with which they had nothing to do, and where they were wholly overlooked,—they are, on their discovery, early in the eighteenth, given by a Committee of the Lords into the charge of Garter, King at Arms, to be put into order. Forty years afterwards, Garter dies, and a warrant is issued which recites the receipt of information that certain "valuable Records belonging to the King's Majesty" are "concealed in the house of the late Garter, King at Arms, in the county of Surrey," and directs their seizure by a King's messenger. Another whole generation elapses, and then it is discovered, by accident, that these very Records remain in the "custody" of the venerable messenger, who had had a royal warrant for transporting them from Surrey in his youth. Such, by sample, was the administration of the Record service in the last century. One repository and one control,—and the systematic preparation of Calendars for the public use, and for the public use alone,—were

Dispersion and destruction of Records, in the last century.

obviously the sufficient and the only remedies. But a vast complication of vested interests in fees of office stood in the way. And it was left for Lord Langdale and his fellow-workers, in our own day, and after infinite pains, to effect the reform so long and so manifestly needed.

The Methodizers of 1763—90.

The formal appointment of "Methodizers" expressly charged to "arrange and regulate" certain classes of Records in July 1763, continued in force until 1790. It appears to have entailed an expenditure of between six thousand and seven thousand pounds. The Methodizers were our old friends of the Paper Office, Sir Joseph Ayloffe, Thomas Astle, and Andrew Coltee Ducarel. Their commission extended to the Records of the Court of Augmentation, and to those of the King's Remembrancer, and of the Lord Treasurer's Remembrancer. Its product was, in the former, nineteen volumes of Calendars, with Indexes of Places. None of them had any Indexes of matters; only two of them Indexes of persons. What had been done in "arrangement and regulation" will be sufficiently apparent from the following passage in the Report of the Committee of Inquiry of 1800: "In the Augmentation Office, there are about two hundred bags of Records, of which the general contents are known to the officer, but there is no Calendar of them, nor any Index whatever."* As to the King's Remembrancer's Records, it may be stated, on the same authority, that twenty classes of them were in 1800 wholly unarranged; and that the "other valuable Records

* *First Report on the Public Records of the Kingdom* (1800), p. 12. It is curious (by the way) to find, again, among the multitude of Record documents which were by Mr. Astle's bequest, contained in the late Library at Stowe, Calendars of Augmentation Records, but whether or not these were merely transcripts of the Calendars made for the Public, I am unable at present to ascertain.

which, together with the preceding, form the whole of the Records belonging to the King's Remembrancer's Office, . . are equally unserviceable to the public [as the unarranged], for want of proper Calendars and Indexes."* And, finally, as to the Records of the Lord Treasurer's Remembrancer, it does not appear that the Methodizers had done anything whatever. That office had been twice burnt down, once when it was kept in Ivy Lane, near to St. Paul's (1666), and again, in the Inner Temple (1684). The Remembrancer who reported in 1800 found a great part of his Records, when he came into office, "heaped together in chests in his Record Rooms at Westminster, in great confusion, ... and they continued in the same confused heaps," he says, "until they were [once more, but far from finally,] removed to Somerset Place."† The migrations of our various Records have, indeed, been far more numerous than the fires, and perhaps scarcely less destructive.

It must be added that the ill success of Mr. Grenville's scheme of 1763 was the necessary result of intrusting an arduous and extensive task to men—however eminent in learning and ability—whose energies were almost as widely scattered as the Records they had to work upon. In addition to his other multifarious pursuits, Mr. Astle was for nearly thirty years Keeper of the Records in the Tower. He was really a man of eminent knowledge, but of no concentration of effort, and accordingly his Keepership, like his "Methodizing," is only a little more memorable than the brief and obscure periods of office of his immediate predecessors at the Tower, Shelley, Hay, Polhill, and Topham, the last named of whom had been the next

* *First Report on the Public Records of the Kingdom* (1800), 143-145.

† Ibid., 156.

successor to Petyt. Yet Mr. Astle, as it appears,* added forty-five Calendars and Indexes (together) to the collection which he found. In other respects, from Petyt to Lysons, —if the evidence of the contemporaries of the latter, as to the state of the Records at his entrance into office, is to be accepted,—proof of any conspicuous improvement in their condition is wanting.

§ 3. The Records in their period of partial aggregation and of premature publication. —Lord Colchester's Committee of 1800, and its results.—The Commissions on the Records.— The Labours of Samuel Lysons, and of Henry Petrie; of John Caley, and of Sir Harris Nicolas.—Mr. C. Buller's Committee of 1836.

The Conversation on the Records of C. Abbot and H. Addington, in 1799.

When Mr. Charles Abbot (better known now as the late Lord Colchester) took his morning ride with Mr. Speaker Addington, in October, 1799, and, as they jogged along, discussed the state of the Records, the notorious confusion of many of the offices, the long lapse of time since Parliament had inquired into the subject, and the course which a new Committee must shape for itself, in order to be practically useful, he made a remark to the Speaker which, though it was doubtless at the moment true, is strikingly in contrast with what came to be the truth almost immediately afterwards. "The stock of information," he said, "about Records is gradually declining."† Every year,

* *Report* of 1800, p. 11. *Domestic Papers*, MS., S.P.O., 'Various.' The Report speaks of Mr. Astle's "great and exemplary diligence and liberality."

† *Diary*, 1 Oct. 1799 (i, 188, 189).

probably, that has elapsed, since that conversation took place between the then Speaker and his successor in the chair, has made some notable addition to the number of patient students of the Records. Lord Colchester could scarcely have foreseen the full amount of self-imposed labour and anxiety that he was incurring. Yet he was anxious to have the assistance, in his contemplated inquiry, of the great man at the helm. Addington proffered to open the subject to Pitt, and when he had so done, reported to Lord Colchester that Pitt's answer was, in substance, "*Non equidem invideo, miror magis.*"

Course of the Inquiry.

Lord Colchester, nevertheless, boldly faced his work. He began, very judiciously, by requiring a written return to an elaborate series of questions from every Record Keeper in the realm. The returns thus made show that, at the beginning of the present century, the number of Metropolitan Repositories of *ancient* Records had increased to *thirty-six.* This number is exclusive of repositories the contents of which were limited to Records and documents connected with merely recent and current business. It is also exclusive of Libraries into which Records had entered merely by gift or by purchase. Including these and the provincial repositories of various kinds, the total number from which returns were obtained *exceeded three hundred.* The Welsh repositories, the contents of which were nevertheless important, were not included in the inquiry. The total number of Record Offices from which the Committee of 1732 had obtained returns was eighteen.

Report of 1800 as to the general condition of the Repositories.

On the general condition of the principal repositories the Committee reported that it had seen with satisfaction the state of many of the Buildings, and the regularity of their internal arrangement; particularising the Tower, Chapter House, Rolls Chapel, and the Chancery Offices adjacent to the Chapel, as, in these respects, the best. Many other offices, it reported, were exposed to the most imminent risk of destruction by fire, especially the ancient buildings adjoining to Westminster Hall. As to the large and crowded repositories at Somerset Place, the Committee states that papers "were perishing daily by damp in the vaults;" that the Records of the Lord Treasurer's Remembrancer's Office "were exposed equally to all these complicated risks, and were, in the mean time, absolutely inaccessible for want of space."

Measures of Improvement suggested.

On the more important point,—the Measures of Improvement to be suggested to Parliament,—the Committee lays stress chiefly on (1) the purchase for the Public of such Calendars and Indexes as were deemed to be private property, and the provision of new ones, where needed; (2) on some improvements of detail in the establishments and in the duties of office; (3) on the printing of some of the principal Calendars and Indexes, "and also of such of the original Records, hitherto unpublished, as are the most important in their nature, and the most perfect in their kind." The Committee proceeds to point out certain Calendars and Indexes, which it regards as especially important for publication; and then the Records, the full or partial publication of which it also recommends. These latter belong to five classes: (1) Surveys, Political or Ecclesiastical; (2) Judicial Proceedings; (3) Unedited Statutes; (4) Parliamentary Proceedings; (5) State Papers. Pope Nicholas' Taxation of 1291, the *Nonæ Rolls* of 1341, the *Nomina Villarum* of Edward II, with its continuation, are among the individual Records which the Committee thinks should be printed in their entirety; together with a systematic edition of the ancient law writers, and a continuation of the *Fædera* of Rymer and Sanderson.

Printing of Calendars.

Printing of Records.

Record Buildings.

On the cardinal points of Building and Transfers, the Committee dwells but lightly. It enumerates some repairs of existing buildings and some additions to them as essential; and glances at the mischief of such a multiplicity of Record Offices, and then proceeds:—"No general transfer of the Records of these several Repositories from their present local situations could be desirable, *unless* it were for the purpose of establishing a General Repository," either for those Public Papers and Records which cease, gradually, to be in use for the current business; or, for the Registration of private conveyances; in either of which cases the "General Register House for Scotland would be a useful model for imitation."*

Record Transfers.

Results of Lord Colchester's Report of 1800.

The plans for publication proved to be the most acceptable part of this Report. And experience showed that they were, in the main, premature. Not that it would have been good policy to have made all publication, even of integral Records, wait until the whole arrear of the ancient documents had been reduced into order; still less, to have postponed the publication of such of the existing Calendars as were really complete. But it should have been laid down, as the one basis of all Record work, that thorough arrangement and gradual aggregation—so far as that was then possible—were the primary duties and aims of the department; that complete and accessible Calendars were its next business; and that the publication of Records, however important, must be subordinate to those cardinal requirements. The proceedings of the successive Commissions,† from 1800 to 1831, were, in great degree, modelled

* *Report*, ut supra, p. 13.

† Six in number, and issued in the several years 1800, 1806, 1817, 1821, 1825, and 1831. The first Commission consisted of twelve persons, the last of twenty-five.

on Lord Colchester's Report. Those Commissions rendered several public services. They laid the groundwork of some valuable improvements to come. But this grave defect, together with a total want of real Parliamentary responsibility, and of wise economy, hampered them throughout.

Composition of the Record Commissions.

And to these sure sources of comparative failure was added another, scarcely less productive. The various Commissions included the names of many men eminent in literature and in the Civil Service, but not one of them was able to give his persistent and undivided attention to Record business. The control of that business passed, substantially, into the hands of the Secretaries of the Board, and the very Secretaries had prior, various, and conflicting duties, which did not, however, always prevent them from interfering with the duties of other Record Officers,—duties lying totally apart from their own sphere.*

And, finally, none of these Commissions conferred upon the Commissioners any real control over the buildings in which the Records were deposited, or over the officers to whose charge they were entrusted. It resulted, therefore, quite inevitably, that the Record buildings continued to be incommodious and insecure; that the migrations of Records continued to be frequent, costly, and destructive; that the diversity of internal regulations and the oppressiveness of fees, in the various offices, continued always to obstruct and sometimes to defeat the purposes for which Records are preserved. At length, however, the Commission of 1831 gave express power to *inquire* into the duties and emoluments of the offices; and into the alterations which might beneficially be introduced. But, before its report on this head (made in 1837) could be considered by Par-

The special duty imposed on the Commission of 1831.

* See the *Minutes of Evidence on Record Commission* (1836), pp. 88, 299, 300, 301, 307.

liament, the last of the Record Commissions was permitted to expire by efflux of time after the demise of the Crown, without renewal. The duty of inquiry had already, for practical purposes, passed to the Commons' Committee of 1836, appointed, on the motion of Mr. Charles Buller, to examine the working and results of the Commission itself.

Labours, at the Tower, of Samuel Lysons.

In the interval, certain improvements of detail accrued in some of the Record offices from the exertions of individual officers. Mr. Samuel Lysons deserves honourable mention on this head, for his labours on the unarranged portion of the Records in the Tower, and for his partial preparation for the press of a series of early Royal Letters of great interest (the basis of later labours, the results of which have yet to be given to the public), as well as for other and better known, but not more meritorious, contributions to our British History and Antiquities.

There is, at first sight, a discouraging sort of monotony about the story of the Records. Labourer after labourer appears on that small nook of the vast arena on which it is appointed for man to strive with his work. Some of them are soon appalled at the difficulty of their task. Others grapple with it vigorously. In the Record Tower, we have seen Lord Stafford, Bowyer, Lambarde, Prynne, Petyt, trying hard, one after the other, to bring order out of chaos. Two or three centuries roll on. And, after all those successive labours, Lysons, in 1803, finds a chaotic mass of documents, lying in neglect and in filth, and calling aloud for busy hands, and a clear head, to make them serviceable to the Historians to come. There have been eight or ten generations of workers struggling with the task, in turn; nevertheless, if a David Hume of the nineteenth century, about to narrate our early history, had

Anecdote of David Hume and the Records.

then been brought face to face with some of his best materials, he might still have said, as the Hume of the eighteenth is reported to have said,—in similar circumstances, and with notorious results,—"Ah! my Publisher won't wait."

Meanwhile, the real progress had been greater than the apparent. Mr. Lysons was not easily frightened at the look or the extent of his work. His successors in the Keepership there had always enough to do both in arrangement and in calendaring, but neither of them, I believe, found merely chaotic heaps of Records to fight with. Nor was it at the Tower that skeletons of cats were, in recent days, found embedded among Records. The Tower chaos was, at length, substantially vanquished.

Notices of Mr. Lyson's literary career, and of his chief productions.

Born in 1763, at Rodmarton in Gloucestershire, and educated in the Grammar School of Bath, Samuel Lysons early began the study of the law, but was not called to the Bar until 1798. In the interval he had practised as a Special Pleader, but archæology had always a stronger hold of him than law. He had unusual skill, too, as a draughtsman—in the artistic sense of the word—and thus those topographical researches which more particularly occupied his leisure gratified at once his love of art, and his love of literature. His first publication, entitled *Views and Antiquities in Gloucestershire*, appeared in 1791, and was continued by several consecutive works, especially by the *Account of Roman Antiquities discovered at Woodchester, near Minchin-Hampton*, published in 1797. He took an important part, conjointly with his brother, Daniel Lysons, in the well-known *Magna Britannia*, intended to comprise an alphabetical series of topographical descriptions of all the British counties, but which human limitations—quite as frequently forgotten in the planning of literary works, as in the ardour of pursuits less reflective—permitted them only to carry from "Bedfordshire" to "Devonshire," inclusive. This portion of their large undertaking was published between the years 1803 and 1822, in six volumes. The brothers also united their labours in the *Britannia Depicta* (1806-1818, in six parts). To both these works, Samuel Lysons contributed with his pencil as well as with his pen. But his chief production is the splendid work entitled *Reliquiæ Britannico-Romanæ* (in three volumes, colombier folio), published between the years 1813 and 1817, on which Mr. Lysons had expended six thousand pounds, as well as much of the leisure hours and vacation time of twenty-five years. It is a notable fact, which has its bearing on the subsisting interests as well as on the mere curiosities of Literature, that Mr. Lysons was forced to make this noble book less complete than it would otherwise have been,* by the provisions of *An Act for the Encouragement of Learning.* The "encouragement" which this Statute would have extended to the author of the *Reliquiæ Britannico-Romanæ*, had he carried out his original plan, consisted in exacting from him eleven copies of a book, the cost price of which was estimated at fifty guineas a copy, to place them, without compensation, in Libraries, some of which were,—and are,—to the Public, as effectually sealed as was that walled-up Library, which a little while ago was one of the invisible lions of Grand-Cairo. Mr. Lysons died, unmarried, but beloved by a large circle of friends, in June, 1819, after holding the Keepership of Records for nearly sixteen years. The last, but by no means the smallest, service which he rendered to the Record Department was the introduction to it of Mr. Thomas Duffus Hardy, who, more than forty years afterwards, became virtually his successor in the custody of the

The *Reliquiæ Britannico-Romanæ*

* *Minutes of Evidence on the Copyright Act,* 1818.

Tower Records, after their removal to the new General Repository. His immediate successor at the Tower was Mr. Henry Petrie, of whom hereafter.

The Secretaryship and Sub-Commissionership of John Caley.

In the working of the early Record Commissions, Lord Colchester took an active part for several years. But he had numerous competing claims on his time. And, as I have had occasion to remark already, the practical working of the Commission fell almost totally upon the Secretary. For thirty years (1801—1831) that office was held by Mr. John Caley, who had been connected with the Record Service for almost twenty previous years, having been introduced to it by Thomas Astle,* with whom a slight acquaintance had ripened quickly, under the genial influence of the gift of a curious manuscript, casually met with at a stall. Caley was first employed in the office at the Tower. In 1787, he was made Keeper of the Records in the Augmentation Office, and in 1818, Keeper of the Records in the ancient Treasury of the Exchequer, better known as the Chapter House Record Repository, at Westminster, with a salary of four hundred a year, and other emoluments. Here he succeeded a well-known man—"old George Rose."

Career and labours of the Right. Hon. George Rose

Mr. Rose had fallen into the Record Service as fortuitously as his successor, but had made it the stepping-stone to an eminent official career, diversified by several respectable contributions to literature, and especially to the literature of Politics. He had begun life in the humble capacity of a chemist's apprentice. He had then been captain's clerk on board a man-of-war. But not finding that he was likely to get on in the Navy, he obtained a situation at the Chapter House, and by that resolute labour which always

* *Gentleman's Magazine*, N. S. ii, 320.

characterized him, acquired great knowledge of Records. What we misname chance, gave him the opportunity of displaying this knowledge to Lord Marchmont, who was Chairman of a Committee of the House of Lords, appointed to consider of the best means of publishing the *Rolls and Journals of Parliament*. This was in 1767. Rose's superior officer, who had been summoned to attend the Committee, was absent. Rose attended for him, with other Record Officers, whose knowledge of Records did not appear to the Committee to have risen with their rank. Rose was made Editor of the *Rolls and Journals*, with a handsome salary; became soon after Keeper of Records; and rapidly won favour by the union of discretion with ability. At last, a man, high in office, asked him what he was looking forward to in life, as the object of ambition. He replied, "To be Clerk of Parliaments." "Have you no more ambition than *that?*" rejoined his noble interlocutor. Mr. Rose took the hint; attained considerable eminence in Parliament, as well as in political office; and acquired a large fortune. Nor did he live entirely for himself, and for the party to which he rendered such long, varied, and conspicuous service. His name is closely connected with the foundation of our Savings' Banks, the full national advantages of which have yet to be developed.

John Caley's industry, too, seems to have been considerable, though desultory. His current reputation in literary circles was great. But his contributions to literature were worthless, and his labours on the Records,—considered as a department of the public service,—very small indeed. He was, however, a very "clubable man." Who does not know the type? Bustling, but dignified, after his fashion; self-important, but courteous in manner; knowing everybody, and known by everybody; dining at all sorts of public dinners, and full of engagements to private ones; belonging to all kinds of Societies and coteries, and ever ready to propose his friends; talking much about Literature, and cultivating it too,—exactly as a market gardener cultivates cabbages. Men of that stamp were able, in Mr. Caley's time, to make petty labours and very moderate attainments go a great way. The genus is by no means extinct, but its feeding-ground is much contracted.

Diversity of Mr. Caley's Record functions.

To the functions of Keeper of two Record Offices, and Secretary of the Record Commission, Mr. Caley added those of Sub-Commissioner, and of Editor or Co-Editor of fourteen of the publications of the Commission. He was also the real Treasurer and Expenditor of the Board, and had a practically uncontrolled power of borrowing money, on the credit of parliamentary grants to come.* This plurality of function had the conspicuous merit of keeping the service compact, and for a time peaceable. If you make the superintended and the superintendent the same man, you may reasonably hope that they will not quarrel. The extraneous public, unfortunately, did not find the arrangement so unexceptionable. But, at the Record Commission, it lasted for more than thirty years.

General working of the Record Service under the Commission, 1830-31.

The general working of the system at this period may be briefly summed up thus:—The number of metropolitan Record Repositories had been reduced, but it still amounted to twenty-one, irrespective of libraries and of offices containing only the Records of current business. At the Tower and at the Rolls Chapel, pre-eminently, and at some other offices in less degree, great improvements in point of arrangement and security had been made, but in every

* *Minutes of Evidence*, 1836, Q. 7843—7849.

instance those improvements had been checked by the nature of the buildings. In other offices, and important ones, the Records continued to be unarranged, filthy, and practically almost useless. Large masses of valuable Records were still kept in vaults in which no man could work without peril of health and life, exposed to damp and vermin. In all the offices the system of inordinate fees for searches and extracts continued to prevail. If eleven rolls or rotulets had to be produced at the bar of the House of Lords on twelve successive days, the charge for producing each of them was twelve guineas, or one hundred and thirty-eight pounds in all. Meanwhile the most precious documents were carried to and fro the private houses of Keepers and Clerks, at their pleasure, and sometimes remained absent from the proper repositories for years, exposed to even worse usage than that arising from the vermin of the vaults.* Indexes and Calendars, made by salaried officers, were regarded as private and marketable property; were kept from public use, while the officers were living, and were sold to private purchasers when they were dead. At John Caley's sale, for example, twenty-five volumes of "MS. Indexes to, and Extracts from, Records

* "I have known," said a witness of long experience, to the Committee of 1836, "a search [at the Augmentation Office] to be prolonged to a fortnight, as I had first to call upon Mr. Caley, and ask him to produce me the Minister's Accounts of such a Religious House. In a few days, he would produce me two or three. If I found they would not answer my purpose, he would be obliged to send for more from Westminster, and then there was the same delay again; and probably those produced last would lead to another search for Conventual Leases; ......all, no doubt arising from Mr. Caley not being on the spot."...... "Bags of Records were kept in Mr. Caley's house...in a very careless manner,...thrown under presses and trampled upon." ......" Mr. Caley never would allow any access to his Calendars; *or to any Records, except those sent for, to his private house, for the purpose of inspection.*"—Evidence of Mr. Hewlett, ut supra, Q. 785, 788, 789, 807.

in the Augmentation Office," were sold for two hundred and twenty-five pounds. In addition to these, eighty-two volumes of *Collectanea* from the Records were sold for four hundred pounds. When Mr. Caley died in 1834, he had been fifty years a Record officer; had, during many of his thirty years' Secretaryship, enjoyed emoluments amounting to about eleven hundred pounds a year; and since his retirement from that office, in 1831, had received, as the salary of a merely nominal Inspectorship, a pension of five hundred pounds a year.* But he bequeathed no contributions to our Historical Literature, and no Indexes to our Record Offices.

The Record Commission of 1831.

The Commission of 1831 was an unquestionable improvement on its predecessors. Its effect upon the Record publications will be noticed presently. But the Board was still composed, in great part, of men already overburthened with other duties. The weight of the business was still thrown upon the Secretary, now Mr. Charles Purton Cooper, Q.C., who began by urging, with more vigour, perhaps, than caution, a multiplicity of reforms of detail. As so often happens, one extreme had led to its opposite. The former Secretary had been an epitome of the abuses of the old Record system, but had possessed great knowledge of Records; the new Secretary was the antagonist of many of the old abuses, but had all his Record knowledge to learn. Before three years were over, the Board and several of the Officers; the Secretary and several of the Editors, were in open hostility. Despite the dryness of the subject, the story is not a dry one. It has its amusing, as well as

* *Minutes of Evidence*, ut supra, 32; 410-467; 527; 867; 881; 918-920; 1523-1529; 3871-3989; 7819; 8139. See also the *Report on the mode of remunerating Sub-Commissioners*, May, 1831, pp. 4, 5.

its painful and instructive episodes; but there is no need to tell it now. Those discussions and paper wars promoted, potently, the recent and pregnant reforms. And in that fact lies all their present importance.

That they did promote those reforms, effectually, is mainly owing to the exertions, made in very different spheres, of an eminent lawyer, and of an eminent antiquary. Lord Langdale's labours connect themselves, more especially, with the passing of the Public Record Act, and with the erection of the General Repository. Those of Sir H. Nicolas, with the Committee of 1836, and with the discussions which long preceded it.

The life and labours of Sir N. H. Nicolas.

Nicholas Harris Nicolas was the son of a Commander in the Royal Navy, whose great grandfather had been one of the many French exiles, the loss of whose skill and energies by France proved very notably to be England's gain. From Abel Nicolas, the emigrant of the close of the seventeenth century, came several gallant officers who fought for England in the eighteenth and nineteenth centuries, as well as the distinguished writer who made important additions to our historical literature, and worked effectively, for the public, in many other ways. Sir Harris Nicolas was born in 1799, passed several years in the Navy, and served as midshipman on an occasion, in the war of 1815, in which one of his brothers acquired naval distinction. His marriage, in 1822, with a descendant of Elizabeth's Secretary Davison, gave him an interest in the fate and memory of that unfortunate statesman, and so led, in 1823, to the first of a very long series of writings. He had already began to keep his terms at the Inner Temple, and was called to the bar in 1825. From the publication of his *Life of Davison* to the year of his death, not one year passed without the appearance of some useful book from his untiring pen. His professional labours were restricted to Peerage Cases before the House of Lords, so that in law as in letters almost his whole energies were given to some branch or other of historical, biographical, or antiquarian research. In getting up his books, as in getting up his Peerage claims, he laboured strenuously to be thorough. Rapid as was their succession, they always displayed honest industry, a vigorous intellect, a graceful diction, and a sincere love of literature. He could not always choose his subjects, but he chose them more frequently than is usual with those who write to live. His public spirit; his eager impatience of the continued existence of known abuses; and his impulsive way of throwing, instantly, a hard-hitting pamphlet at the head of anybody whom he knew, or believed, to be keeping them alive, sometimes made for him active enemies, and were often injurious to his personal interests. But those who knew him best were well assured of the integrity and generosity of his motives, however they might regret that his finer qualities were not tempered with more of that discretion and deliberation which would have increased their force, and would have made their possessor a more prosperous man. It will be long before his beaming face, his hearty greeting, his genial conversation, his varied knowledge, and his liberal readiness to impart it, will fade from the memory of those who regret his loss.

The literary Works of Sir N. H. Nicolas.

Sir H. Nicolas' *Synopsis of the Peerage*, his Memoir on the *Scrope and Grosvenor Roll*, his *Life of Hatton*, his *Despatches of Nelson*, his *Testamenta Vetusta*, and his *Proceedings and Ordinances of the Privy Council*, (with the remarkable prefaces which added so largely to the value of those Council Records,) are original, and will be enduring gifts to English History. His *Chronology of History* is an admirable text-book, although it has had but three editions since its first appearance, as *Notitia Historica*, in 1824. When he died, in August, 1848, he was busily employed on two considerable works. One of them was a collection of the St. Helena papers of his old friend, Sir Hudson Lowe, with a vindicatory biography of that officer. The subject was a very unpromising one, and there is no reason to think that such a book would have added anything to Sir Harris Nicolas' literary reputation. But the other—a *History of the British Navy*—was admirably suited to his powers, and the portion which has been given to the public (under many disadvantages) warrants the belief that a good book on a great subject has been lost to us, by his almost sudden death at the age of forty-nine.

Sir Harris Nicolas' labours in Record Reform.

In his labours to reform the Record service, Sir Harris Nicolas had been engaged several years before the renewal and modification of the Commission in 1831. He had himself experienced, on innumerable occasions, the vexatious obstructions which the old Commissions had kept at nurse. His ground of controversy was the firmer, inasmuch as he had often been working to promote Record studies, at his own cost, while other men, paid by the public, were working to impede them. In this direction, he urged the necessity of reform, both in the *Quarterly Review* and in the *Retrospective Review*, repeatedly. But his most effective weapon was the *Observations on the Present State of Historical Literature*, addressed to Lord Melbourne, then Home Secretary, and published in 1830. The points most strongly pressed in that pamphlet are (first) the necessity of entirely remodelling the Commission, by limiting its numbers, composing it, mainly, of men practically familiar with the work to be performed, paid for the devotion to it of their time and energies, and directly responsible for its performance; and (secondly) the further necessity of destroying the fee system,* the three-hours-a-day attendance system, and the private index system, and making the offices thoroughly accessible and serviceable to the public, at whose cost they are supported. These, and several correlative measures, Sir Harris Nicolas urged with all his might, in season and out of season; in conversation and correspondence with statesmen, as well as in his better-known appeals to public opinion, through the press. In their advocacy, he challenged all assailants. In the ardour of the fight, he sometimes mistook his adversaries, but he was never struck down in the mêlée. It was, in large measure, owing to his efforts that the Committee of 1836 was appointed, under the chairmanship of Mr. Charles Buller, and was enabled to prosecute its inquiry to a good issue. He worked throughout this long controversy most untiringly, and, of necessity, not without falling into occasional errors. He lived only long enough to see the beginnings of a thoroughly reformed Record service. Other men have entered into his labours.

Publications of the Record Commission.

The first publication, of an original record, by the Record Commissioners, was the *Taxatio Ecclesiastica Angliæ et Walliæ, circa* A.D. 1291, which appeared in 1802. This record was the regulator of all our taxation, until nearly the middle of the sixteenth century. On several points of

* For copying the *Scrope and Grosvenor Roll*, one hundred and eleven pounds was charged in 1828. This was for a simply literary purpose. Indeed, that roll can be applied to no other purpose. The Keeper and Clerks were then in receipt from the Public Purse of £1440 a year.

subsisting Church polity—in relation to revenue—it is still the highest extant authority. This was followed by the *Testa de Nevill, sive Liber Feudorum*, of the reigns of Henry III and Edward I;—the great *Valor Ecclesiasticus* of Henry VIII;—the *Rotuli Hundredorum* (Henry III and Edward I), rolls abounding in curious matter, illustrative of our political, biographical, and commercial history;—the *Rotuli Scotiæ*, from Edward I to Henry VIII;—and the *Inquisitiones Nonarum*, of the reign of Edward III. These important Records, together with several Calendars to portions of the more ancient Rolls of various classes, both at the Tower and at Westminster, appeared under the authority of the several Commissions antecedent to 1831. To the same period belong a new edition of the *Statutes of the Realm*, from Henry I down to the accession of the House of Hanover, with indexes, both alphabetical and chronological;—the commencement of a new edition of Rymer's *Fœdera*, carried, however, only from the Conquest to the year 1383;—and a valuable, but also unfinished, collection of *Parliamentary Writs, and Writs of Military Summons*.

Nearly all these Records—the exceptions will be noted—appear to have been judiciously selected, and some of them were edited with ability. The Calendars are conspicuous exceptions, in both respects. They, pre-eminently, were premature publications; so imperfect in their contents, and so ill-edited, as to be almost useless. The careful and well-considered republication of the *Fœdera* was then, and is at this moment, a crying want; and the want is a national reproach. It is certainly untrue that the great deficiencies of the previous editions could have been adequately supplied by any mere supplement. It is plainly discreditable to the country that for several purposes of historical

The editing and cost of the Record publications.

reference, the Hague reprint of Rymer—imperfect as it is—is a more ready and more useful book than either of our English editions. But, none the less, the new edition commenced by the Record Commissioners was a premature and ill-advised publication. Ample evidence to justify this assertion may be found in the blue-book of 1836, as well as in the work itself. Moreover, one grave objection applied in common to all, or to nearly all, the publications of the various Commissions prior to 1831, which their obvious utility could not countervail. Their cost of production was inordinate. To meet it, other and more essential branches of the service were impoverished. Certain instances of manifest and glaring wastefulness brought a scandal upon the Commission. And a considerable arrear of debt was created. The natural result followed. Several excellent works, undertaken by the Commission of 1831, remain to this day unfinished.

Had the prodigality consisted merely in the too-liberal payment of half-a-dozen editors, there would have been little wisdom in making a stir about it. The rewards of literature, and especially of historical literature, are and will continue to be meagre enough. It had a startling sound in the House, when the facts were told that the three volumes of the *Fœdera* had cost the Public thirty thousand pounds;—the two volumes of the *Parliamentary Writs*, seventeen thousand pounds;—the eleven volumes of the *Statutes of the Realm*, fifty-nine thousand pounds,—transcription, printing and editing, together. But a little reflection on the character of the work, and on the previous studies and labours of the compilers; and a little comparison of the rewards attained by the most fortunate of eminent archæologists, with those attained every day by eminent lawyers, or eminent Civil-Service men, would soon have abated the virtuous indignation of members. The real mischief was that some of those who did least work got most pay; and that among some of the overpaid Record-men were to be found the most obstinate maintainers of the worst abuses in the Record Offices. If part of the liberal pay fell to a Sir Francis Palgrave, the author of the invaluable *History of Normandy and of England;* a still larger part of it fell to a John Caley, the author, as we have seen, of nothing, save of almost innumerable impediments to English history.

The "Report" and "Appendices" on the Fœdera.

The Commission of 1831 checked much of this wasteful expenditure. It introduced a less cumbrous form of book. It lessened the cost of the publications to purchasers. It took greater pains to secure competent editors. Two Commissioners—Dr. Copleston, Bishop of Llandaff, and Mr. Edward Protheroe—laboured with unusual assiduity to unite economy with efficiency in this, as in other departments. But, on the other hand, the Commission, or its Secretary, launched into an extravagant outlay in connection with vague and undigested plans for resuming the *Fœdera*, and were especially lavish in obtaining transcripts from Continental repositories, and in printing them, even before it had been ascertained whether the documents copied abroad were not already enrolled at home. And these inquiries were so prosecuted as rather to impede than to assist the most valuable of all the publications relating to our early history, which had ever, at that date, been undertaken, at public expense,—namely, Mr. Petrie's *Materials for the History of Britain*, commenced, in its ultimate form, in the year 1822, but planned and worked upon five or six years earlier.

It is not a new fact in any department of the public

service to find very notable labours and improvements originated outside the doors. The Exchequer, the Post-Office, the Board of Trade, could bear striking testimony on this head. In the Record department we have met with repeated instances already. Mr. Petrie's services afford another and conspicuous example.

Labours of Henry Petrie.

Henry Petrie began his career as a dancing-master at Stockwell, near London, where he lived and died. Dr. T. F. Dibdin, the well-known writer on bibliography, amongst his other elegant pursuits, chanced to study under Mr. Petrie's violin. The ambition of the master already looked beyond the best possibilities of success in equipping even fashionable divines for pre-eminence in a quadrille, and by the gratitude of the pupil he was introduced to Lord Spencer, who encouraged him to apply himself to literature. To Lord Spencer it is owing that Mr. Petrie's daring plans of doing for Britain what Bouquet and his colleagues had done for France, and Muratori for Italy, were brought, at first, under the consideration of a few distinguished promoters of learning, and, ultimately, under that of Parliament. Lord Spencer, too, procured for Mr. Petrie, in 1819, the Keepership of the Tower Records, on the death of Mr. Lysons, who had first encountered his successor as one of a crowd of auditors, standing about the excavated Roman antiquities at Bignor, and listening to the explanations of their discoverer.* Petrie, it is said, startled the learned dissertator by some shrewd remarks, which seemed too apposite to come from a bystander, quite unknown to the assembled pundits.

The "Materials for the History of Britain."

In 1822, the then Chancellor of the Exchequer, Mr. Vansittart (afterwards Lord Bexley), proposed in the House of Commons that an Address should be presented

* *Gentleman's Magazine*, N.S., xviii, 661.

to the King, praying that measures should be taken "for the publication of a complete edition of the Ancient Historians of this Realm."* In November of that year, the Record Commissioners were instructed to take such measures, and they entrusted the chief preparation of the work to the able and enthusiastic antiquary who had planned it. In the primary collection of Chronicles and Excerpts, Mr. Sharpe, the translator of William of Malmesbury, was conjoined with Petrie. In the collection of the Anglo-Saxon Laws and Institutes, Mr. Price, and afterwards Mr. Benjamin Thorpe, were employed.† And to Mr. Thorpe is mainly due the credit of producing the excellent volume, published in 1840, under the title, *Ancient Laws and Institutes of England.* The corresponding volume on Wales, published in 1841, was first entrusted to the late Mr. Humffreys Parry, but his death occurred before he had made any substantial progress in the task. It then fell to Mr. Aneurin Owen, who in his preface warmly acknowledges Mr. Petrie's valuable assistance in his labours. As long as health and vigour were spared to him, Mr. Petrie proceeded with his peculiar share of the vast enterprise. But when (in 1832-3) sickness had brought its inevitable hindrances, unwise and wanton interferences (in 1834) multiplied them, and needlessly wounded the natural feel-

* *Parl. Hist.*, 2nd Ser., vii, 1737-1740.

† "Had the work not been suspended, it is probable that Mr. Petrie might have lived to witness the completion of several successive volumes. After the publication of the first, the series would have gone on rapidly, as several works were nearly ready for printing; but the suspension of the undertaking completely paralysed his efforts."—Hardy, *Materials for the History of Britain*, General Introduction, p. 42. The known expenditure of more than three thousand pounds on "Transcripts," unframed "Reports," and "Appendices," about the Fœdera, none of which are publicly available, save by accident, will scarcely be regarded as public compensation for a fact like this.

ings and the reasonable pride of one who was not only a zealous public servant, but a public benefactor. Mr. Petrie, it may be added, resolutely refused to accept any remuneration until he should have completed his first volume—a thick folio containing the matter of eight or ten large octavo volumes—and, without doubt, was over-fastidious in his anxiety to make the book thoroughly worthy of its subject, and of the auspices under which it was to appear. And thus, as if by a combination of untoward influences, the formal completion (chiefly by supplying needful illustrative and prefatory matter), even of the first volume, fell into other but able and reverent hands. Mr. Petrie died, in March, 1842, in his seventy-fourth year. Mr. Duffus Hardy published the "*Monumenta*," or "*Materials*," by command of the Queen, in 1848. It was therefore the third of the published volumes which have grown out of Mr. Petrie's original plan of 1818, and out of the Instructions given to the Record Commissioners in 1822.

Recommendations of the Commons' Committee, of 1836;

The chief recommendations of the Committee of 1836 comprised, first, the creation of one General Repository, and they founded their particular proposal on Lord Langdale's recommendation of the Rolls Estate, as the proper site of such a Repository; secondly, the creation of one general Custody; thirdly, the framing of a new Commission, few in numbers, and paid; fourthly, the entrusting to such a Commission powers to continue the publication of valuable and complete Records, as a function subordinate to care and arrangement; to control the composition of modern Records; and to destroy useless Records, under due precaution; and, fifthly, increased facilities of access.

The Commissioners, in their *General Report to the King in Council*, of 1837, also recommend a "plan of general deposit," in one or in several buildings, constructed purposely for the reception of Records, and prospectively with a view to their gradual but certain increase, but without interfering with the custody of judicial records "relating to recent or pending proceedings." They further recommend that the "control and direction of Records should be entrusted to a single person," having no other avocation, with a sufficient establishment of Clerks. The number of officers, they say, "should be in strict proportion to the care and labour to be performed; their duties should be adequately defined; their payment should be chiefly, if not entirely, by salaries; and the fees should be reduced to a fair and moderate scale." And further, with reference to the site of the new Record House:—"It appeared to us that a portion of the Rolls Estate would afford a most desirable site for a General Repository."* On this one cardinal point, therefore, competent opinion would seem to have been, in 1837, fully agreed.

and of the Commissioners in their General Report(1837).

§ 4. History of the Records in their final period of thorough aggregation and arrangement. —Labours of Henry Bickersteth, Lord Langdale.—The passing of the Record Act.—The new Rolls House.—The improvements made by Sir John Romilly.—The *Chronicles and Memorials of Britain.*

But the path to one adequate and well-governed Record Repository, was still variously obstructed. There was yet to be needed many a conflict, and much wearisome labour, in order to the removal of the remaining impediments. To

* *General Report to the King in Council,* xiii-xv.

this work Lord Langdale addressed himself. His first act (14th January, 1836) as Master of the Rolls had been the disinterested resignation of all personal interest in the Rolls Estate, that might stand in the way of its devotion to the Record Service.* His evidence, as Master, before Mr. Charles Buller's Committee, was strongly in favour of the reforms which its Report ultimately recommended. His earnestness as a Law-reformer had been repeatedly shown on former occasions, and had already borne good fruit.

The Commission on the Records, it will be remembered, expired by efflux of time on the 20th December, 1837, King William IV having died on the 20th of June. At the request of the Home Secretary, Lord Langdale acted as its Executor, "taking temporary charge of the business which had been entrusted to the Commissioners, and of the books, &c., lately under their care," and adhering to the subsisting estimates.† Mr. Cooper continued to act as Secretary until March, 1838, when a letter from the Home Office notified to him the cessation of his Secretaryship. Lord Langdale was not more distinguished for public spirit than for the feelings of a high-bred gentleman. "I know nothing," he wrote on this occasion, "which in my opinion makes it just to dismiss Mr. Cooper in a manner which seems to disgrace him; and the business of the late Record Commission is not in such a state as to make the loss of the information which he possesses immaterial."‡ Lord John Russell directed his Secretary to assure Lord Langdale, in reply, that "he had not the least idea of conveying any censure"§ on Mr. Cooper.

* *Minutes of Evidence*, 4476-4564.

† Hardy, *Memoir of Lord Langdale*, i, 459.

‡ Hardy, ut supra, ii, 115.

§ Ib., 117, 118.

Mr. Charles Buller gave the natural parliamentary sequence to his Report of 1836, by proposing to the House of Commons, in May, 1837, a measure for vesting the custody of the Records in one responsible Officer; finding that to be a less difficult, and a far more promising, course, than to use pressure on the Government for creating a new and carefully restricted Commission. But he proposed that the new Officer should be nominated by the Treasury, and be removable at its pleasure.* This was a plan open to several obvious objections. But there is no need to follow the discussions and negotiations which ensued. Ultimately a new Bill, with many modifications, was drawn by Mr. Drinkwater Bethune, and was at length, after further amendment, approved by Lord Langdale; but it did not pass into a law until the 14th of August, 1838.

Analysis of the Record Act of 1838.

The *Public Record Act* (1 and 2 Vict., c. 94) was passed "to establish one Record Office, and a better Custody; and to allow the free use of the Records, as far as stands with their safety and integrity, and with the public policy of the Realm."† It enacts (1) that the Records shall be in the custody of the Master of the Rolls; (2) that those of the Tower, Chapter House, Rolls' Chapel, Petty Bag Office; of all the Exchequer Offices; and of the Courts of Chancery, Admiralty, Queen's Bench, Common Pleas, and Marshalsea, together with those of certain recently abolished Courts of Wales and of the Palatinates, shall be at once transferred to the Master's custody; (3) that the Queen in Council shall be empowered to transfer other Records to the like custody, from time to time, at pleasure; (4) that future accumulations of Records shall,

* Hansard, 3rd Ser., xxxviii, 463-465.

† *An Act for keeping safely the Public Records* (Collection of Public General Statutes, 1 and 2 Vict., 777-784).

from time to time, be similarly transferred, with the approbation of the Lord Chancellor; (5) that the Master of the Rolls shall have full powers to order the cleansing, arranging, and calendaring, of Records, and to take other needful measures for their security and utility; (6) that the Master of the Rolls, with the approval of Her Majesty, shall appoint a Deputy Keeper of the Records; (7) that the Treasury shall appoint sufficient Assistant Keepers, with other needful Officers and Servants, removable at pleasure by the Master of the Rolls, on report to the Treasury; (8) that the Treasury shall provide needful buildings for the reception and safe custody of all the Records; (9) that a Public Record Office shall be established, and that all places containing Records shall be taken to be branches of such office, and all persons having charge of Records to be Officers thereof; (10) that the Master of the Rolls shall have power to make rules, and to appoint a scale of fees, and to dispense with fees; all rules and regulations being from time to time communicated to Parliament. The other clauses of the Act provide for the printing and sale of Records, and of Calendars of Records; empower the Secretary of State to present Record publications to public institutions, and the Treasury to purchase private calendars and indexes; provide for compensation for the losses of existing officers, and direct an Annual Report, by the Deputy Keeper, to be made to the Queen, and to be laid before Parliament.

Steps taken by Lord Langdale, in execution of the Record Act.

On the 14th December, 1838, Sir Francis Palgrave, then Keeper of Records at the Chapter House, and already connected with the Record service, as Officer or as Editor, during nearly seventeen years, was appointed by Lord Langdale to be first Deputy Keeper, under the Act; and

Mr. F. S. Thomas, of the State Paper Office, was made Secretary of the Records. Then began what for a while seemed to be an interminable correspondence, about the erection of a suitable General Repository. The question had been complicated by an ill-advised project for applying —adapting was impossible—the Victoria Tower, and even some portion of the roof of the new Houses of Parliament, to the reception of the Records. This seems to have become by adoption a pet project of the Treasury, and it clung tenaciously to life, long after all argument about it was at an end. Great as were the knowledge, the disinterestedness, the patience, and the perseverance, of Lord Langdale, all these qualities were needed to the full, in the negotiations which ensued. And they had a second and not less arduous field in the settlement of the Fees and Compensation questions. The story of both controversies has been told, partly by Sir F. Palgrave, in his early Reports as Deputy Keeper; partly by Mr. Hardy, in his *Memoir of Lord Langdale*, and, by the latter, with special clearness and ability. It is needless, here, to dwell long upon either.

Lord Langdale's great public service, in regulation of Record Fees.

But on Lord Langdale's great service in the regulation of fees something must be said. The fees for searches ranged in amount from two guineas to ten. The calendars were usually worded in an equivocal and misleading way, expressly to whet the searcher's appetite. Fresh searches brought new fees. If a paragraph of a few words only in the long-sought document would fully answer the patient searcher's purpose, he could not have it. To the essential line or two were united, with Mezentian rigour, hundreds or, perhaps, thousands of dreary lines, that brought no information to the searcher, but brought, in some cases, a hundred guineas, or so, to the officer. It is still remembered that on one such occasion, when, after payment of multitudinous fees, caused by the ingenious construction of the Calendars, and by other cognate circumstances, the precious paragraph was at length disinterred, and the weary and well-nigh disheartened fee-payer asked, finally, how much a copy of that paragraph would cost, the obliging functionary turned over the membranes, made his mental calculation, and in a gravely official tone, replied, "*One hundred and forty-five pounds, Sir.*"

This clever system Lord Langdale overturned, not by the abolition of fees, but by their strict regulation. Individually, he was favourable* to entirely free access. But considerations (1) as to the protection of Records from indiscriminate searches, and (2) as to the relative equitable claims of law-inquiries and literary inquiries, induced him to hold his hand, even in respect to the researches of students. That great claim to their gratitude was to be acquired only by Sir John Romilly, at a subsequent period. Lord Langdale, however, made the fees so low† that they ceased, in all cases affecting property, or dignities, to be obstructive. And he enforced the most rigid impartiality in literary matters.‡ To these great claims on public gratitude, he added many others. New and good Calendars; increased and regular hours of attendance; improved arrangement of Records; these and other advantages were by no means the spontaneous growth of the Record Act. They, like the ultimate provision of an admirable Repository, were the results of Lord Langdale's arduous labour. But these were not *all* the results. There have been many men who have worked energetically in the improvement of our public institutions, and whose efforts have been attended with bril-

Appreciation of Lord Langdale's labours by Record Officers.

* Hardy, ut supra, ii, 149, 151.

† Namely, a shilling *a week* for using calendars and indexes, and a shilling a week for the inspection of a roll or bundle, however large, with the power of copying the whole contents in pencil.

‡ See an instance in Hardy, ii, 150, note.

liant success. They have been public benefactors, and have well deserved the public testimonials and honours awarded them. Their work done, they have at length retired; but it has been noted more than once or twice, that such men, when taking their leave, have occasioned no deep emotions in those who have worked under them; no voices have been agitated, in giving the parting salutation; no eyes moistened, in taking the farewell look. Exactly the opposite of this occurred to Lord Langdale, when he went the round of the various Record Repositories on the 26th of March, 1851, to say "Good bye" to the officers and servants, to whom it had long become an ambition so to discharge their duties as to win his approval; whose endeavours he had wisely counselled and generously appreciated; whose grievances he had been always ready to listen to, and, if he could, to redress. Mr. Hardy, in the excellent memoir which he published of his "old Master," in 1852, has told us, touchingly, what on this occasion were his own feelings and those of his subordinates at the Tower. At the other Record establishments, he adds, "Lord Langdale left regret and sorrow behind him." He survived this leave-taking only three weeks, dying at Tunbridge Wells, on the 18th of April, 1851, in the sixty-eighth year of his age.

Sir John Romilly succeeded Lord Langdale at the Rolls. His mastership, as it respects the Records, has been distinguished by an achievement even more important than the great boon conferred upon literature, in his first year of office, by opening their stores with absolute freedom for literary purposes. Sir John Romilly has laid the foundation of a series of the monuments of British History, maturely planned, well edited, and economically produced, which, if it be continued with the spirit and the

The Records under Sir John Romilly.

judgment that have hitherto governed it, cannot fail to deprive Englishmen of all occasion for envying France its Bouquet; Italy, its Muratori; Denmark, its Langebek; or Germany, its Pertz.

Progress of Transfers.

Meanwhile, the contents of fifty-six Repositories—for to that number the offices of Record, prior to the passing of the Record Act, amount, when to those already described in these pages are added the various petty receptacles of current judicial documents—were gradually aggregated and methodized. The new Rolls House, the final sanction of which Lord Langdale's utmost exertion had failed to obtain until 1850,—so that he had not even the gratification of laying the foundation-stone of the edifice he had so truly founded,—was began in the year of his death. But he had sanctioned the definitive plans prepared by Mr. Pennethorne;* had witnessed the progress of the preliminary excavations; and had enjoyed a compensatory gratification in his knowledge of the worthiness of the hands into which the duty of prosecuting his labours would fall. The first stone was laid by Sir John Romilly in the summer of 1851. The first block of the new building was finished in the course of the year 1854.† Its cost, including subsequent fittings, was £88,490.‡ A second block is now (1864) in active progress. The two blocks together comprise, according to the original plans, ninety several depositories (or their equivalent), each seventeen feet by twenty-five feet, and fifteen feet high. Their cubical accommodation for Records amounts, according to the estimate which accompanied those plans, to about 228,000

Erection of the New Repository.

* *Estimates of Civil Services*, 1850. viii, p. 12.

† *Sixteenth Report of Deputy Keeper*, 1854-5, pp. 27, 28.

‡ *Correspondence relative to the Public Records*, 1862 (Sess. Paper Coms., No. 318), p. 22.

feet,* after deducting corridors and other open spaces, but is now liable to some further deduction on account of a larger provision of search-rooms, and other appurtenances, than was at first contemplated. When the building was commenced, the cubical contents of the Records then actually in the charge of the Master of the Rolls was estimated roughly at 160,000 feet,† subject, of course, to immediate and constantly accruing increase. Since that date the actual transfers of Records have, year by year, exceeded all anticipation.‡ How necessary a liberal *contingent* allowance of press room and shelf space becomes, in planning a Repository such as this, may be illustrated by the fact that in the eleven years from 1851 to 1861, inclusive, the actual increment of documents to the new Rolls House, from sources wholly unforeseen when the plans for 1850 were prepared, and, for the most part, additional to those provided for in the Record Act, was equal, at least, to the *yearly* addition of ten thousand folio volumes of the size of an average volume of Parliamentary Papers, when bound into the customary sessional series, as they stand in the Library of the House of Commons.

Character of the New Record Building.

The plan of taking a little room twenty-five feet by seventeen as the *unit* of the new Record building, by the simple multiplication of which (or by some near approximation to that), the whole accommodation required for a mass of public archives far vaster than was ever before accumulated in any country, must be provided, was of course instantly fatal to all ideas of grandeur of internal effect. What such an assemblage of national documents, from the Conqueror to Victoria, well arranged and displayed

* *Estimates*, ut supra, 10, 11. † Ib.

‡ *Correspondence relative to the Public Records* (1862), pp. 23, 24.

(as far as Records could ever be displayed at all, consistently with safety) in a series of well-proportioned halls, would have presented to the eye and to the imagination, can be sufficiently comprehended by any one who has seen the noble Reading Room of the British Museum. But, unfortunately for the architect of the new Rolls House, the exacting and jealous vigilance with which Records must be secured, now that they are, at length, really in custody, precluded even the conception of such a scheme. Small fire-proof receptacles were laid down, on the best authority, as the one primary and indispensable condition of true safety. Anything of architectural beauty must be external, not internal. That Mr. Pennethorne's exterior will, eventually, have both beauty and grandeur is certain. But its true proportions will not be seen, until five several blocks of building, of which only the second is yet in hand, shall have been reared. Those who look upon that ultimate building will see the result of the joint endeavours of a Master of the Rolls to King Edward the Third, and of a Master of the Rolls to Queen Victoria. But for Lord Langdale's labours, the Records would still have been housed in several, if not in a multitude, of widely-scattered repositories. But for William Burstall's suit to King Edward for the *Domus Conversorum*, the General Repository,—when at length provided,—would have been a clumsy, ill-arranged, and almost inaccessible Tower, eked out, in course of time, by a long series of garrets, in which the Records, after their innumerable adventures, and hair-breadth escapes, would have been again exposed to extremes of temperature, and placed at the mercy of undiscovered fractures in long ranges of roofing;—the most fortunate of them, meanwhile, being consultable only under conditions eminently disadvantageous to inquirers.

The history of the execution of the Record Act of 1838 is told, ably and completely, in twenty-two annual Reports, by the late Sir Francis Palgrave—the first of which was made on the 15th of May, 1840,—and in three subsequent annual Reports by Mr. Hardy, who succeeded Sir Francis Palgrave on the 8th July, 1861, and made his first Report to the Queen on the 22nd January, 1862. They narrate a long series of zealous labours performed, at small cost to the public, by an establishment strikingly disproportionate both to the tasks it has accomplished, and to the existing demands upon it. The Records are by no means the only things that have been transferred to the new Rolls House. Large consignments of public documents of recent dates have brought with them a multiplicity of duties, heretofore performed by officers of the several departments in which those documents accrued. Thus, in 1842, an Assistant Keeper was, at the request of the Treasury, appointed to survey the vast accumulation of Treasury documents at Whitehall. This survey, extending at intervals over several years, led to large transfers from Whitehall to the Rolls House in 1846.* In 1851, 1852, and 1853, came additional papers, bound and unbound, equivalent to at least twelve thousand volumes more. In 1854, came about *twenty-four tons* of Records from Wales and Chester; followed, in 1855, by a hundred and sixty tons of War Office Papers, removed from Whitehall Yard, which, after laborious examination by a Committee, were reduced, by selection, to *a hundred and five tons.* The Admiralty took up the movement in 1857, and ultimately contributed about *two hundred and thirty-five tons* of papers, for perma-

Sir F. Palgrave's Reports as Deputy Keeper, 1840-61.

Transfers from the Public Offices.

* "Documents which have...already...very great historical value... and would have perished, but for their transfer." Palgrave, *Ninth Report of Deputy Keeper* (1848), p. 9.

nent preservation, after the elimination of a hundred and sixty-five tons, which it was found could be dispensed with, and be converted more usefully into pulp.* The War Office continued its transfers, in that and subsequent years, with a vigour worthy of its first beginnings. The Colonial Office, the Foreign Office, and the Home Office, have since followed suit with vast masses of their respective papers; and such transfers will continue. Meanwhile, the Commissioners of Patents have made large demands on the Record service, for assistance in their important operations; and the "Literary Inquiries" have grown so rapidly that within the ten years, 1852-1861, no less than 104,746 documents were consulted, at 13,123 several visits, exclusive of the innumerable references to calendars and indexes. Yet the establishment which, as respects *officers*, comprised thirty-six persons, and cost £8122, in 1844,† amounts still to but thirty-six officers, costing £10,893 in 1864.‡

Edmund Burke, on one of the many occasions in which his genius converted a pamphlet on a passing question into

* Hardy, *Twenty-third Report of Deputy Keeper* (1862), p. 8.

Comparative Establishment in 1844 and in 1864.

† 1844.		
	No. of officers.	Amount of yearly salaries.
(1) ROLLS HOUSE:—		
Deputy Keeper...........	1	788 : 0 : 0
Secretary	1	400 : 0 : 0
Assistant Keepers	8	2760 : 0 : 0
Clerks.......................	22	1940 : 0 : 0
(2) STATE PAPER OFFICE:—		
Keeper	1	} 1974 : 0 : 0
Assistant Keeper.........	1	
Clerks.......................	2	
Extra allowances	...	260 : 0 : 0
Total............	36	Total £8122 : 0 : 0

an immortal contribution to English literature, said, incidentally, "Mere parsimony is not economy. Expense, and great expense, may be an essential part in true economy." But the differences of opinion between a great statesman and a small functionary are differences that are sure to be constantly obtruding themselves. Sir Francis Palgrave had learnt, during his long connection with the Record service, the importance of promoting, on all opportunities, the preparation of calendars and indexes;—the small attractiveness of such work in itself;—the spur that is given to it by the natural pride which all sorts of labourers in literature feel at attaining the dignity of print;—the certainty that what is written for the press will be written with some measure of increased care;—the additional certainty that researches will be usefully promoted by partial and quickly produced indexes in print, pending the slow production of matured ones. Accordingly, he made it a practice to append to his Reports, from year to year, brief but most valuable lists of various important classes of Records, theretofore little known. Those lists were of great utility to literary inquirers. They have given to Sir F. Palgrave's annual reports permanent value. But a functionary, in another department, scandalized at the profligate expenditure of new ink and new paper on the

The Indexes to Records appended to Sir F. Palgrave's Reports.

Comparative Establishment in 1844 and in 1864.

‡ 1864.		
	No. of officers.	Amount of yearly salaries.
ROLLS HOUSE AND STATE PAPER OFFICE, combined:—		
Deputy Keeper	1	936 : 0 : 0
Secretary	1	700 : 0 : 0
Assistant Keepers	10	2884 : 0 : 0
Clerks	24	6373 : 0 : 0
Total	36	Total £10893 : 0 : 0

description of a musty heap of old parchments, conferred with other sages of like calibre, and caused the discontinuance of Indexes, the merits of which are attested by the constant use that is still made of them.* They form one instance, among a multitude, of Sir F. Palgrave's zeal in discharging even the merest routine duties of his department.

But, in this direction, all previous labours have been eclipsed by the admirable series of *Calendars of State Papers*, commenced in 1854, and of which twenty-six volumes have already been published, according to the plans and under the direction of Sir John Romilly. The amalgamation of the Paper Office with the Rolls Repository now enabled the Master of the Rolls to give completeness to the new series of Calendars, by incorporating identical but long-severed classes of papers; and to give it striking literary interest, as well by widening the scope of the Calendars, as by extending their limits to more recent times.

Sir John Romilly's series of Calendars of State Papers.

Sir John Romilly also saw that to carry out his plans effectively there must be either a large increase of the establishment,—a matter involving many prospective difficulties,—or the co-operation with the Record Officers of literary persons, familiar with Records, but unconnected with the service. With the approval of the Treasury, the latter alternative was chosen. Mr. Brewer was appointed to calendar the Papers of the reign of Henry VIII; Mr. Lemon, to calendar those of the three subsequent reigns; Mr. Bruce, to calendar those of Charles I; Mrs. Everett Green—the accomplished authoress of *Lives of Princesses*, and other well-known historical works—those of the reigns

* For instance, of the *Baga de Secretis* (prepared by Sir Francis himself); of the Royal and Miscellaneous Letters at the Tower (prepared by Mr. Hardy); of the Treasury documents (prepared by Mr. W. H. Black), and of many others.

of James I and Charles II. Other calendars of Scottish, Irish, Colonial, and Foreign Papers, were committed respectively to Messrs. H. C. Hamilton, Markham Thorpe, Sainsbury, and Turnbull; to the last of whom, on his regretted resignation, the Reverend Joseph Stevenson, a veteran in Record service, succeeded. The Calendars which appeared after 1858 are better than those which preceded that date—and, indeed, leave nothing to be desired—but all of them are valuable. And they are in steady progress.

Many are the plans which at various times have been formed for a comprehensive series of our early historians and annalists. Archbishop Parker, Camden, Sir Henry Savile, and probably many other early editors of select Chroniclers, pondered such schemes, but had to content themselves with certain comparatively small contributions, "rescued from the dirt;" as Savile tells us, in one of his prefaces. Two centuries afterwards, it was the frequent subject of the meditations, and was probably the last theme of the consecutive thought, of Edward Gibbon. When Mr. Petrie's plans were interrupted, after so many years of labour, the English Historical Society was formed, in the hope that it might be enabled to pursue them with better issue in another shape. But there, also, what was accomplished is only a sample of what was hoped for. Seven years only have elapsed since Sir John Romilly framed, definitively, the scheme of the *Chronicles and Memorials of Great Britain and Ireland, during the Middle Ages*, and obtained for it the approval of the Treasury, but already that proposal has effected more for British History—if what is actually doing be added to what is fairly done—than all the previous plans and efforts taken together.

The "Chronicles and Memorials of Britain."

Sir J. Romilly's plan of 1857. To avoid all possibility of prejudicing the new series of annalists by an immature pre-arrangement, Sir John Romilly proposed that each work or series of documents should be treated independently; should be confided to a competent Editor, who should deal with it, whether it were original or not, as if he were then editing it for the first time, forming his text from an accurate collation of the best MSS., prefixing to it an account of those MSS. and of the author; and adding to the text such notes and remarks only, as would establish its correctness, exhibit important variations, and clear up its chronological difficulties; together with all needful glossaries and indexes. The Treasury Minute, warmly approving this plan, bears date 9th February, 1857, the First Lord being then, as now, Lord Palmerston.

The first work published in pursuance of the scheme was John Capgrave's *Chronicle of England*, edited by the Rev. Francis Charles Hingeston, M.A., which appeared at the end of the same year. This work was now printed, for the first time, from a manuscript in the Public Library of Cambridge. Capgrave's Chronicle. Capgrave was born in 1393. He begins, as usual, with the Creation, and names, more frequently than is usual, both the sources whence he draws the earlier and fragmentary portions of his story, and the authorities on which he relies in the subsequent narrative. From the year 1216 to 1417 his work becomes, especially, a History of England, and is a substantial contribution to that history. It enters minutely into the circumstances which attended the murder of Richard the Second, and the usurpation and death of Henry the Fourth, and preserves some minor incidents of which the author was an eyewitness. His English chronology, Mr. Hingeston tells us, is on the whole precise and accurate. The book is dedicated to

Edward the Fourth, whose obtainment of the crown Capgrave survived but three years, dying in 1464. Doubtless his sickness and death brought his Chronicle to an end at an earlier date than he had intended. In 1858, another book of Capgrave's, the *Liber de Illustribus Henricis*, was first given to the world, under the same editorship, and here Mr. Hingeston had the satisfaction of treading in the steps of Mr. Petrie, who had partially prepared this work for publication—in the *Materials for the History of Britain*—from the fine Cotton MS. (Tiberius A. VIII), adopted, as the best of the two known manuscripts, by the ultimate editor. This work is of course, in great part, a compilation, but a most interesting one. It describes, for the greater glorification of Henry VI, the lives of twelve famous Henries,—six of them Emperors and six of them Kings of England. In treating the latter half of the subject there is much that is original. For the Emperors, Capgrave founds chiefly on Martinus Polonus, and on Godfrey of Viterbo. For the earlier Kings, on Henry of Huntingdon, on Walsingham, and on Higden. As he comes down to his own times, his personal experience and that of his contemporaries are largely drawn upon.

His "Book of Illustrious Henries."

The *Chronicon Monasterii de Abingdon*, edited by Mr. Stevenson in two volumes was the second publication. This Chronicle embraces a period of five hundred years; traces the history of a great Benedictine monastery from its foundation in the seventh century to the accession of Richard the First; adds largely to that minute local information which forms so important an auxiliary to History; and presents a fair type of English monasticism in its influential period. It has, the editor tells us, the great merit of substantial and unquestionable veracity. It narrates to the members of the Berkshire community the

The Chronicle of Abingdon.

words and deeds, the hopes and the fears, the good and the evil fortunes, of the men who had reared their Abbey, gathered its possessions, and built up its influence. The author evinces an acquaintance with several of the Latin poets, but shows less familiarity with earlier chronicles, closely bearing on his subject, than might be looked for. Two manuscripts are known, both of which had belonged to Sir Robert Cotton, and both are of the thirteenth century. "Claudius, B. VI," Mr. Stevenson regards as a revised edition of the other, and from that he prints.

The Metrical lives of Edward the Confessor.

The Abingdon Chronicle was followed by three several *Lives of Edward the Confessor;* edited by the Rev. Henry Richards Luard, of Trinity College, Cambridge, none of which were before known to the public otherwise than by occasional notices and extracts. The first of these is metrical, is written in Norman French, resembles closely in its style the *Estoire des Engles* of Geoffrey Gaimar, already printed by Petrie in the *Materials,* and is entitled *La Estoire de Seint Aedward le Rei.* Its groundwork is the *Vita Sancti Edwardi Regis* of Ethelred, or Alured, of Rievaulx, and other writings of the same author, but with many additions and modifications introduced by the versifier himself, partly from sources not now traceable, partly from other chroniclers. This poem Mr. Luard prints from a Manuscript in the Public Library at Cambridge, which formerly belonged to Bishop Moore of Ely. His second *Life of St. Edward* is also metrical, and founded upon Ethelred's work, but, like that, is in Latin; and is preserved, in the Selden MS. 55, at Bodley's Library. It is a production of the middle of the fifteenth century, and is perhaps a favourable specimen of the Latinity of that period. Speaking, in an exordial address to Henry VI, of that undying theme, the degeneracy of the times, the writer has a curious reference to "Piers Plowman"—

> ......Tantaque simplicitas nostris succrevit in annis,
> Quod vulgi plus sermo placet, quem dictat *arator*
> *Vulgari lingua,* quam mellica musa Maronis;*

and then proceeds to glorify the old poets for preserving the fame of vanished empires. The third biography of the beloved Confessor is partly in Latin verse, partly in prose. Humphrey Wanley appears to have thought (groundlessly) that it might, perhaps, have been written by Eadmer, but Mr. Luard, who has edited these pieces with admirable pains and skill, is unable even to offer a conjecture as to the author's name. He shows that the tract is the production of a contemporary of King Edward and of Harold; that it contains a strikingly original view of the character of Godwin; and that one or two later chroniclers have been considerably indebted to it, although no modern historian has ever used it save John Stow. The MS. used by Mr. Luard is "Harleian, No. 526," and unique, but unfortunately, written—a circumstance far from being unique—by a scribe who would have deserved more of our gratitude had his oscitancy been less. Yet to his labour, careless as it was, we owe a remarkable illustration of a period of history which can never lose its interest for Englishmen.

Bartholomew Cotton's *Historia Anglicana,* extending from the year 449 to 1298, is another publication, adding largely to the value and originality of Sir John Romilly's series, which has appeared under the care of Mr. Luard. It was published towards the end of 1859, and the special pains which its editor took to distinguish Cotton's original

* Luard, 362, lines 27—29.

matter from his borrowed matter, and also to affiliate, as far as was possible, the borrowings upon their true authors, has made this work a model to be followed by succeeding editors. The special value of Cotton's history lies in its account of portions of two reigns—those of Henry III and of Edward I, whose contemporary he was. In describing the events of the years 1264-1279, and of the years 1285-1298, more particularly, the good monk of Norwich—known to us only by this book—has made a substantial and enduring gift to our national stores. In common with most cultivated Englishmen (whatever their date) he had a strong *county* feeling, as well as a national feeling, and accordingly Norfolk events and personages have their special and due prominence in his later pages. The same characteristic is found in the additions which he has made to Malmesbury's account of English prelates,—the groundwork of Cotton's *Liber de Archiepiscopis et Episcopis Angliæ*. Cotton has been quoted by many historians, during the last century and a half, and by some of them to good purpose, but it remained for Mr. Luard to print him, in his entirety, in 1859.

Luard's Edition of Bartholomew Cotton.

Meanwhile, three other eminently important contributions to British History had been made in this series by Mr. Brewer's publication of the *Monumenta Franciscana*, gathered chiefly from Thomas Eccleston and Adam de Marisco; and of the principal works of Roger Bacon;—by Mr. Turnbull's edition of Hector Boece's *Buik of the Croniclis of Scotland*, in the metrical version of William Stewart;—and by Mr. Riley's very curious *Munimenta Gildhallæ Londinensis*, intended to embrace, ultimately, the *Liber Albus*, the *Liber Custumarum*, and the *Liber Horn*.

Adam de Marisco, the beloved friend of that great

English prelate, Robert Grostete, has, by an extensive correspondence (which has survived many dangers solely in the Cottonian MS., "Vitellius, C. VIII"), supplied considerable materials towards the history of the Franciscans in England, a subject very scantily noticed in direct treatises yet extant. He also rendered a notable service to literature in his own day when, as we know by the *Annales* of Nicholas Trivet, he persuaded Grostete to bequeath his Library to the Franciscans of Oxford. Marsh's letters, interesting on many accounts, are combined in Mr. Brewer's *Monumenta* with the treatise *De Adventu Fratrum Minorum in Angliam* of Thomas de Eccleston,* and with a Register of the London Franciscans, also preserved amongst Sir Robert Cotton's MSS.† All these works are now published for the first time, and form a valuable addition to previous knowledge. But still more important is the collection—yet to be completed—of the unpublished works of Roger Bacon, whose true place in philosophy, and in English history, has never been, and could not be, ascertained, until the labour now committed to the able hands of Mr. Brewer should first have been accomplished. The materials lie widely scattered, and some of those which are known to exist are not, perhaps, even yet fully accessible. But, already, a large stride has been taken towards the supply of a conspicuous defect in our literature.

The Monumenta Franciscana of Mr. Brewer.

By the publication of the *Buik of the Croniclis of Scotland*, a minor want has been supplied,—one felt, doubtless, by a much smaller class of students, but very fitly provided for in Sir John Romilly's comprehensive scheme. William Stewart's metrical version of Boece's Chronicle was made by the express command of King James the Fifth; is the

Stewart's version of the Scottish Chronicle of Boece.

* Cotton MS., Nero, A. IX, and MS. at York Cathedral.

† Vitellius, F. XII.

only metrical Scottish Chronicle which is known to exist, except Wynton's; and has been edited by Mr. Turnbull, from a manuscript in the Public Library of Cambridge.

The *Munimenta Gildhallæ Londinensis* belong to a class of Records which in former official publications had been almost wholly disregarded. They were known to very few even among professed antiquaries. Stowe, Rymer, and Strype, had each made such use of them as was compatible with their own specific purposes as writers, and with the jealous restrictions which, in the days at least of Rymer and of Strype, limited the access. In our days, the Corporation of London has been very liberal, but the only man who preceded Mr. Riley in devoting much labour to the acquisition of some real familiarity with the contents of its Record-room, seems to have been the distinguished French antiquary, M. Jules Delpit. These municipal Records throw light upon a multitude of subjects, which, at a first glance, might seem remote from civic affairs. The history of our foreign alliances, of our foreign wars, and of our national taxation, are here illustrated, as well as the growth of trade, the progress of arts, and the history of those mediæval guilds and mysteries which were so curiously interwoven with the various phases of political and social life, no less than with the development of municipal liberties.

The Guildhall Records.

Mr. Riley's published volumes include (1) the *Liber Albus*, compiled in 1419 by that John Carpenter, Town Clerk, who became, four centuries after his death, founder of the City of London School; (2) the *Liber Custumarum*, compiled in the reign of Edward the Second, and probably about the year 1320; and they are to be followed (3) by the *Liber Horn*, compiled by a City Chamberlain of that name, in 1311. The 'White Book' is an elaborate collection of the duties of civic officers; of the procedures in civic courts; of transactions between the King and the corporate body; of City Charters; of rates and imposts; and of the local regulations, of all kinds, touching trade and citizenship. The great bulk of this book is in Latin, but a small portion of it is in Anglo-French. The writing is throughout modern Gothic, but in at least half a dozen different hands. The compiler's original plan was not fully carried out. He had purposed to digest, in his final division ("Book IV"), the contents of a series of earlier books belonging to the Corporation, but finding that to be a graver labour than he had anticipated, he calendars them instead of digesting them. The 'Book of Customs' begins with Fitz-Stephen's famous *Description of London*, which is followed by some extracts—from the curious encyclopædical work of Dante's tutor, Brunetto Latini, called *Le Trésor*—on the duties of magistrates. Then comes a vast compilation of charters and ordinances, and of regulations, both royal and municipal, for various arts and trades; then writs, precepts, and enrolments of many kinds,—some relating specifically to London, others of a more general scope; followed again by charters and accounts of ceremonies. Among these diversified contents, nothing perhaps is of more general interest than the incidental account of the "*Festival of the Pui*,"*—a brotherhood which had been established in London, late in the thirteenth, or early in the fourteenth century, by foreign merchants, chiefly, as it seems, natives of Picardy or Gascony. Such institutions were at that period widely spread over France and some parts of the Low Countries, but Mr. Riley is

* The name is derived, immediately, from a famous shrine of the Virgin (*Notre-Dame du Puy*) at Le Puy in Auvergne. In its nature, the Society was partly religious, partly literary, and partly provident.

able to quote authoritative testimony to the fact that the document preserved in the *Liber Custumarum* is both fuller, and more ancient, than any of the foreign documents of like character at present known to have survived. Finally, the occasional illustrations of mediæval life and manners which occur in all these Guildhall books are innumerable, and the editing of those which have already appeared is exemplary.

The *Political Poems and Songs, relating to English History*, edited by Mr. Wright in 1859 and 1861, widely different as are their form and origin from those of the London records, have a somewhat similar value as vivid illustrations of a departed social polity, in addition to their obvious utility for philological purposes. The period they cover extends from the accession of Edward III to the death of Edward IV. Other illustrations of the history of the fifteenth century—illustrations derived from the pens of men who were eminent actors in its great events—are given in this series, in the *Royal and Historical Letters during the reign of Henry the Fourth*, edited by the Rev. F. C. Hingeston; and in the *Letters and Papers illustrative of the Wars of the English in France, during the reign of Henry the Sixth*, edited by the Rev. Joseph Stevenson.

The Miscellaneous Collections of Poems, Letters, and Tracts.

Letters are not History, and the choicest conceivable collection of them would be a very poor substitute for History, but they are unquestionably among the most precious and life-like of its rough materials. In the *Memorials of Henry the Fifth*, Mr. C. A. Cole has collected some interesting biographical tracts by various writers. Very curious is the juxta-position of three versions of the same career, taken from quite opposite points of view. Yet one Henry more is brought under new light in the *Historia Regis Henrici Septimi* of Bernard André, published in company with several other pieces, all of them written by Henry's ministers or contemporaries, under the editorship of Mr. James Gairdner. The same period has also received useful elucidation by the *Letters and Papers of the reigns of Richard III and Henry VII* of the same editor.

But it is not only amongst letters, political songs, and miscellaneous tracts connected, more or less directly, with the great names and the grand march of History, that contributions have been levied for the "Chronicles and Memorials." The new researches have been carried much farther afield. As a great poet can find deep thoughts in the meanest flowers, so a good historian can find precious material in the most despised superstitions of a long-past age. Mr. Cockayne has rendered eminent service to future historians by his volumes entitled, *Leechdoms, Wortcunning, and Starcraft, of Early England.* He has drawn, too, for all his readers quite other lessons than those of a complacent self-satisfaction at our own vast progress and wonderful cleverness, from the very omens and exorcisms, the charms and the incantations, of our benighted ancestors. The cultivation of natural science, the state of arts, the degree of acquaintance with classic authors, and the growth of religious ideas, among the Anglo-Saxons, are only some of the topics which receive elucidation in Mr. Cockayne's book, and its preface. The larger and most curious portion of his first volume is derived from the blackened ruins of the once magnificent manuscript in the Cottonian collection, entitled, *Herbarium Apuleii Platonici,** amplified and illustrated, however, from many other sources.

Cockayne's "Leechdoms of Early England."

Nor has the specially religious history of the country been overlooked in Sir John Romilly's Collection. The *Fasciculi Zizaniorum Magistri Johannis Wyclif cum Tritico,*

* MS. Cott. Vitellius, C. III.

Works illustrative of the History of the Church.

ascribed to Thomas Netter of Saffron Walden, and *The Repressor of over-much Blaming of the Clergy*, of Bishop Reginald Pecock, contain matter for a strikingly vivid picture of two several stages in the long conflict of the Reformers before the Reformation. Netter's work has been edited by Mr. Shirley, from a Bodley manuscript which once belonged to Bishop Bale, and which is interspersed, more lavishly than usefully, with his notes, variations, and extracts. The editor's introduction contains a brief but excellent view of Wycliffe's life and labours, and in a subjoined note he has put in a clearer light than heretofore existed, the facts which bear on the old controversy as to the two John Wycliffes, and their respective careers.

Bishop Pecock's "Repressor."

Pecock's *Repressor* is by far the most remarkable theological production of the fifteenth century. Its English is more like that of the fourteenth than like the English of his contemporaries. No editor could well have had a more difficult task than Mr. Babington undertook in editing this work from the only known MS.,—now preserved in the Public Library at Cambridge,*—which seems to be the very copy exhibited before the Archbishop, in the proceedings that led, ultimately, to its author's degradation, and to the compelling him, with his own hand, to put fourteen of his works into the fire at Paul's Cross; but the task has been so performed as to give to these volumes an incidental value, for the philological student, scarcely inferior to their intrinsic value as materials of our Church history.

Whilst large contributions have thus been made to British History, in the widest sense of the term, the special object of publishing a comprehensive series of "Chronicles" has been steadily pursued. To do this effectually, it is as

* Kk. iv. 26.

necessary to republish, after thorough revision, the annalists who were edited by Parker or Camden in the sixteenth century, by Gale or Fulman in the seventeenth, or by Hearne in the eighteenth, as it is to give to the world in plain print a chronicler hitherto known (thoroughly) only to the readers of manuscripts, or one but recently disinterred from entire oblivion. The old texts, even of the most eminent editors, abound in corruptions. They rarely show anything of the sources whence the annalist drew his materials. They not unfrequently issue the same matter under different names. Many of them, nevertheless, can with difficulty be purchased even at high prices. In the new series, both classes of Chroniclers have gone on abreast. To the originals above mentioned, John of Oxnead, Richard of Cirencester, and the anonymous Monk of Malmesbury who compiled the extensive epitome of general history known, sometimes, as *Eulogium Temporis*, but more usually called *Eulogium Historiarum*, have been already added. Oxnead (after an exordium about Hengist and about King Arthur) begins his narrative with the anointing of Alfred, which he dates in 872, and continues it to the year 1293. He is printed by Sir Henry Ellis from a Cotton MS., believed by the editor to be unique, but of which another copy has (since 1858) been discovered. From a manuscript in the library of the Duke of Newcastle, some important additional paragraphs have been printed, as an appendix to Sir H. Ellis' work, but the text of that manuscript is more corrupt than the Cottonian text. Cirencester's *Speculum Historiale de Gestis Regum Angliæ* begins with Vortigern, and ends with the defeat of Harold. This Chronicle is edited by Mr. Mayor, from a manuscript in the Public Library at Cambridge. The Monk of Malmesbury has been published by Mr. F. S. Haydon, of the

Other Chronicles now first printed.

Record Office, from a manuscript of the fourteenth century, —apparently in the author's autograph, —belonging to Trinity College, Cambridge. The chronicler derives his matter from a multiplicity of sources, and in dealing with these Mr. Haydon had the disadvantage of preceding Mr. Luard's edition of Bartholomew Cotton, but the editor has bestowed great pains on their identification in the introductory prefaces, as well as on the collation of his text with the other known manuscripts, and he has treated with much ability some interesting correlative questions. From a MS. bequeathed by Sir Matthew Hale to Lincoln's Inn, the narrative is brought down to the year 1490, but this portion had been previously printed. Two other original chronicles tell the stories, respectively, of Saint Peter's Abbey at Gloucester, and of the Abbey of Evesham. The latter, narrated chiefly by Abbot Thomas of Marlborough, is especially notable for its obvious honesty, its manly tone, and (as far as respects Abbot Thomas' portion) its pleasant contrast in point of style to the ordinary run of monkish annalists. Mr. Macray has edited it, chiefly from a manuscript* in Bodley's library.

The *Eulogium Historiarum.*

Foremost among those reprinted chronicles which, from their editorial treatment, come before us almost with the freshness of originals, are Mr. Luard's edition of the *Annals of Margan, Tewkesbury,*† *and Burton*, Mr. Stubbs' *Chronicles of the Reign of Richard I*, and Mr. Riley's *Saint Albans' Chronicles*, beginning with Walsingham, who is now printed partly from an Arundel manuscript at the Heralds' College, partly from the Royal manuscript, 13. E. IX. Mr. Stubbs' first volume, entitled *Itinerarium Peregrinorum et*

Revised Chronicles.

* MS. Rawlinson, A. 287.

† These Tewkesbury annals, however, appear for the first time from Cotton MS. Cleopatra A. VII.

Gesta Regis Ricardi, by Richard, an Augustinian Canon of London, is our old acquaintance "Geoffrey Vinesauf," in more accurate form. It is now, I hope, becoming widely known that not a few of the prefaces to the "Chronicles and Memorials" are, by themselves, excellent reading. In Mr. Stubbs' hands a mere Introduction to Richard the First's *Itinerary* has become a vigorous epitome of the internal history of the Crusades and of the Kingdom of Jerusalem, as well as the most life-like portraiture of Richard's own character which can be met with; and, in his appendix to that Introduction, the editor has printed, for the first time, a curious account, written by an eye-witness, of the siege and capture of Lisbon by the Crusaders in 1147. This he prints, like the *Itinerary*, from a Corpus Christi manuscript* at Cambridge. Mr. Thorpe's reprint of the *Anglo-Saxon Chronicle* exhibits, in parallel columns, the texts of six manuscripts, four of which six, with two others, had belonged to Sir Robert Cotton; one is the Corpus Christi manuscript,† the oldest which has come down to us. The remaining MS. is the beautiful Laudian volume, which its owner gave to Bodley. They all end at different times, but all appear to have been copied, substantially, from an earlier manuscript, which has perished. Mr. Thorpe has added an excellent translation and indexes.

Neither Wales nor Ireland has had to wait long for its special share in this collection of the materials of British History. Two works on Ireland are in the press; three

* Osbernus *de Expugnatione Lyxbonensi*, MS. Corp. Christ. Coll. Camb. 470. The Itinerary is from MS. C. C. C. C. 129. Gale's edition was from a MS. in the Public Library at Cambridge.

† Formerly *S. XI.*, now No. 173.

relating to Wales have already appeared, namely, the *Annales Cambriæ*, and the *Brut y Tywysogion* ("Chronicle of the Princes"), both edited by the Rev. John Williams ab Ithel; and the "Giraldi Cambrensis *Opera*," edited by Mr. Brewer. The *Annales* are supposed, by their editor, to have been originally compiled in the tenth century, and continued, by several hands, to the year 1288. To the *Brut y Tywysogion*, Mr. Williams has prefixed a general account of Cambrian Chronicles and Legends, but the reader who should be deterred by the vagueness and utterly unhistorical tone of that preface, and especially by its marvellous beginning,* from his intended perusal of the "Chronicle of the Princes" itself, would do that work an injustice. It begins with A.D. 681 and extends to 1282. The text is founded on a complete copy of the Chronicle which occurs in the well-known Welsh Miscellany at Jesus College, Oxford, called *The Red Book of Hergest.* Mr. Brewer's edition of Gerald de Barri is characterized by his usual care and thoroughness, and contains in its preface the best extant life of a man who has had several biographers.

Works relating to Wales.

In Mr. Hardy's *Descriptive Catalogue of Materials relating to the History of Great Britain and Ireland*, the eminent and enduring utility of the task accomplished, when compared with its inherent and repelling discouragements, creates an unusual claim to the gratitude of students. The want must certainly have been felt a thousand times.

* "The voice of tradition would not lead us to suppose that the ancient Britons paid any very particular attention to the study of chronology *previous* to the era of Prydain,...which is variously dated 'from the year 1780 to 480, B.C.' *Prior to that time*, the recollection of events depended upon the popularity of ... songs," &c. But for the context, this would read like a bit of quiet satire on Welsh archæology.

But now, for the first time, the effort to supply it has been wisely directed, and perseveringly prosecuted. Mr. Hardy's book is one of that small and enviable class which is sure to prove the seed-plot of good books to come. His published volumes carry the main Catalogue from the Roman Period to the Norman Conquest. The forthcoming volume continues it to the commencement of the fourteenth century. His plan is one which presents the needful information respecting each book in the compactest form. It exhibits (1) the name of each manuscript work in the chronological order of its latest recorded event, or as nearly in approximation to that as is found to be ascertainable in the few cases of uncertainty; (2) the name of each repository, whether at home or abroad, in which a copy of it is known to exist, and the size, date, and local reference, or press-mark, of every copy, with (in most cases) the words in which it begins, and the words in which it ends. Then follows, in all important and practicable instances, (3) the literary history, and (4) a critical summary of the historical value, of each manuscript. The student who has ever seriously attempted to carry out such a plan for even a single work of mark, the copies of which lie far apart, can form some idea of the literary skill, the varied research, and the persistent energy necessary for its execution on the scale of Mr. Hardy's "Descriptive Catalogue" of the entire sources of our mediæval history, scattered as they are all over Europe. The difficulty of the task has been increased largely, and the utility of the product more largely still, by the inclusion of those Lives of Saints in which so much of legendary matter is bound up, inextricably, with historical matter of high value. In his Introduction, Mr. Hardy has shown, both pleasantly and clinchingly, how often the very legend itself enwraps some vital truth of history.

Mr Hardy's Descriptive Catalogue of Materials of British History.

Historical value of the Lives of Saints.

The long series of historical works—produced within seven years—which has thus been so inadequately glanced at is, it must be borne in mind, but an incidental result of that great reform in the administration of our Records which I have now endeavoured to describe and illustrate by examples. If the value, both direct and indirect, of these *Chronicles and Memorials* be compared with the smallness of their cost of production—three thousand pounds a year,—regret at the misdirection of some portion of a much more lavish expenditure in bygone years, will perhaps be qualified by the reflection that past mishaps have served as buoys and soundings into safer channels. And the time, no doubt, will come when it will be seen that *some* of the suspended labours of the old Commissions are well worth resuming, under cautionary checks. Although by a petty and false economy, the source of which is well known, and is in nowise connected with the Record Administration, the price of the new series of volumes has been raised to buyers;* more than twelve thousand volumes, in the whole, have been already sold.

Sale of the *Chronicles and Memorials.*

Another important boon has been conferred on the lovers of historical literature, in the production, under the direction of Sir Henry James, but by the joint labours of Record officers and of Ordnance Survey officers, of photozincographs of *Domesday Book.* This work was completed at the beginning of 1864. And, in the same year, the transfers of Records to the one custody of the Master of the Rolls, provided for by the express enactments of the Record Act, have been very nearly completed.

Reproduction of Domesday Book.

* Namely, to ten shillings a volume. It was originally eight shillings and sixpence, so that a poor student could, usually, buy one of these volumes, for ready money, at a fraction above seven shillings. Now, under favourable circumstances, he must pay about the full original price.

CHAPTER X.

THE LIFE OF THOMAS PARKER, EARL OF MACCLESFIELD;—THE LIFE OF NICHOLAS JOSEPH FOUCAULT;—AND THE LIBRARY AT SHIRBURN CASTLE IN OXFORDSHIRE.

Thou art not, [*Shirburn*,] built to envious show
  Of touch, or marble; nor canst boast a row
Of polish'd pillars, or a roof of gold;
  Thou hast no lanthorn, whereof tales are told;
Or stair; or courts; but stand'st an ancient pile,
  And, those grudg'd at, art reverenc'd the while.
Thou joy'st in better marks,—of soil, of air,
  Of wood, of water,—wherein thou art fair.
Thou hast thy walks for health, as well as sport;
  Thy Hill, to which the Dryads did resort,
Where Pan and Bacchus their high feasts have made,
  Beneath the broad beech, and the chestnut shade,

BEN JONSON.

As the traveller crosses the wooded ridge of the Chilterns, and descends into the vale of Oxford,—whether from Stokenchurch or from the little hamlet of Greenfield,—Shirburn lies almost immediately beneath him. The now thickly sheltered house is one of the few castellated and still moated buildings, in England, which have been adapted to the requirements of modern comfort, without any—or with scarcely any—sacrifice of external congruity. Castellated in 1377, when part of the existing structure was already a building of respectable antiquity, it passed successively, and by many vicissitudes, through the families of De Lisle, Beauchamp, Talbot, Quatremaine, Fowler,

The Castle and its Successive Owners.

Chamberlayne, and Gage, until it was purchased by the Lord Chancellor Macclesfield from Thomas, Viscount Gage, at the beginning of the last century.

Brunetto Latini's visit to Shirburn in the Thirteenth Century.

There occurs in a letter of Brunetto Latini, the tutor of Dante, and author of the once famous didactic poem entitled *Il Tesoretto*, a curious passage in which he recounts a night spent at Shirburn Castle towards the close of the thirteenth century, when he was on his way from London to Oxford.* He seems to have retained a grateful memory of Shirburn, as his safe resting-place after a journey, made tedious by bad roads, and perilous by the robbers who then, and long afterwards, infested the Chilterns. Here, too, early in the following century, the barons met to form, under Thomas Plantagenet, Earl of Lancaster, their league against the Despencers,—a league which proved fatal to the leader. And here, three hundred years later, a stand was made for Charles the First against Fairfax, by a lady of the Chamberlayne family, with sufficient

* "Our journey from London to Oxford was, with some difficulty and danger, made in two days; for the roads are bad, and we had to climb hills of hazardous ascent, and which to descend are equally perilous. We passed through many woods, considered here as dangerous places, as they are infested with robbers; which, indeed, is the case with most of the roads in England. This is a circumstance connived at by the neighbouring Barons, on consideration of sharing in the booty, and of these robbers serving as their protectors on all occasions, personally, and with the whole strength of their band. However, as our company was numerous, we had less to fear. Accordingly, we arrived the first night at Shirburn Castle, in the neighbourhood of Watlington, under the chain of hills, over which we passed at Stokenchurch. This Castle was built by the Count of Tanqueville, one of the followers of the fortunes of William the Bastard, Duke of Normandy, who invaded England, and slew King Harold in a battle, which decided the fate of the Kingdom. It is now in the possession of the said Earl," &c. I owe my knowledge of this passage to the kindness of Lady Macclesfield, who has compiled from various sources a most interesting little MS. volume, containing many notices of the early history of Shirburn.

resolution to necessitate an attack by the Parliamentarians, of which the traces are still visible on the battered doors.

The Evidences of these Chamberlaynes, who in the fifteenth and sixteenth centuries were possessed of very extensive estates in Oxfordshire, Berkshire, Sussex, and four or five other English counties, were carefully compiled by a certain Richard Chamberlayne, in the reign of Henry VII, and are still preserved at Shirburn Castle. Towards the close of the reign of Elizabeth and the beginning of the reign of James, a series of calamitous incidents brought this large, widely spread, and stanchly Roman Catholic family down to a very small remnant. One Chamberlayne perished in a voyage between Tripoli and the Isle of Cyprus. Another, who had taken part in the Rebellion of the North, died in exile in Flanders, leaving children, all of whom died without issue. A third was killed at the siege of Rouen. A fourth was killed in Ireland. Ultimately this family came to be represented by two sisters, and coheiresses, the survivor of whom carried Shirburn to Sir Thomas Gage, of Firle, by whose son it was sold to Lord Macclesfield.

The misfortunes of the Chamberlaynes.

Thomas Parker, son of Thomas Parker of Newcastle-under-Lyne, was descended from the Parkers of Park Hall, an ancient family of Staffordshire, and was educated at the Grammar School of Newport, and at Trinity College, Cambridge, where he matriculated on the 9th of October, 1685. In May, 1691, he was called to the Bar by the Society of the Inner Temple. He quickly attained to a considerable practice;—partly by his reputation for hard reading and thorough mastery of the Common Law; partly by a peculiarly graceful and winning oratory which early procured for him the complimentary nickname of

Parentage and education of the Lord Chancellor Macclesfield.

"Silver-tongued Parker." Within ten years of his call, Thomas Parker was already the leader of the Midland Circuit.

Tutchin's Case.

The cause that first drew upon him the general attention of the public was a libel case, known to lawyers as *The Queen* against *Tutchin,* the defendant being the publisher of a paper, famous in its day but now utterly forgotten, called *The Observator.* Parker's speech at this trial (November, 1704) marked him out, not merely as an able lawyer and eloquent advocate, but as a man eminently qualified for public life. Within a few months, he became both Recorder of Derby and its representative in Parliament. In June, 1705, he was made Queen's Serjeant. In 1710, the House of Commons nominated him to be one of the Managers on the memorable impeachment of the silly zealot Sacheverell,—one of the many men who have attained a temporary prominence, simply by the possession of an inordinate faculty of scolding, and an unusual recklessness of consequences.

Trial of Sacheverell.

Sir Thomas Parker was, for life, a thoroughly stanch and conscientious Whig, of the old school, and as thoroughly a devout and dutiful son of the Church of England. He abhorred Sacheverell's slavish doctrine, and probably thought that firebrands were sometimes none the less dangerous for being in the hands of fools. He threw his heart into the prosecution, and made a deep impression on all who either heard his speeches or read them. He was almost immediately raised—over many heads—from the rank of Serjeant to the Lord Chief Justiceship of England (March 13, 1710), and within six months the Chancellorship was pressed on his acceptance, but, at that time, firmly refused.

Under the Regency Bill, Sir Thomas Parker was made one of the Lords Justices of the Realm, appointed to carry on the government until the arrival of King George the First. He contributed materially, by his energetic and statesmanlike conduct, to keep down the many plots and intrigues then concocted for disturbing the Hanoverian succession. His firmness and vigilance gave him an unquestionable claim to public gratitude, and as unquestionably sowed the seed of some bitter private animosities. By George the First he was, on the 10th of March, 1716, created Baron Parker of Macclesfield. He powerfully supported the King's claim—occasioned by the unhappy differences between the Sovereign and the heir apparent—to exercise a certain control over the education and the marriage of his grandchildren; and by the course he took on that question also, actuated, as there is abundant reason to believe, simply by a sense of public duty, Lord Parker incurred another animosity, in a high quarter, which was destined to exert a sinister influence on his own fortunes, at a long subsequent period.

Public Life of Lord Chancellor Macclesfield.

The Chief Justice was made Lord High Chancellor of Great Britain on the 12th May, 1718; was created Earl of Macclesfield on the 5th November, 1721, and also became Lord Lieutenant both of Oxfordshire and Warwickshire.

His Chancellorship.

Of Lord Macclesfield's eminent scholastic acquirements, devoted love of literature, and munificent encouragement of men of learning, I shall adduce some evidence hereafter. But here it may be fitly noted that among the earliest congratulations which he received, on his elevation, were those of his old associates, the Master and Fellows of Trinity, a deputation of whom he entertained at Kensington, within a few days of his acceptance of the Great Seal.

A complete series of his note-books as Chancellor is preserved at Shirburn. Even unskilled and profane eyes may be permitted to deduce from them their obvious testimony

Testimony to his eminence as an Equity Judge.

to his laborious and systematic industry in the collection and analysis of evidence. But it will be enough to quote the emphatic words in which one of his own successors in the marble chair—a man not prodigal of his laudation—has summed up the general judgment of Westminster Hall upon the Chancellorship of Lord Macclesfield: He became, writes Lord Campbell, "one of the greatest Equity Judges who ever sat in the Court of Chancery. . . . . None of his judgments were reversed. His authority upon all points, whether of a practical or abstruse nature, is now as high as that of Nottingham, or Somers, or Hardwicke."*

The Sale of Masterships in Chancery.

Unhappily, Lord Macclesfield permitted and encouraged the continuance of an ancient but gross abuse, in the sale of Masterships in Chancery. The practice of selling that office to the best among qualified bidders was then a considerable source of the Chancellor's income; and Lord Macclesfield allowed it so to continue under certain new and adventitious circumstances—in themselves and their causes beyond the range of his control—which had the inevitable effect of *increasing* the public detriment from a practice which must always have been more or less injurious. From the madness of the South Sea speculations of that day, in which so many statesmen were deeply concerned, Lord Macclesfield himself stood wholly aloof, but several Masters in Chancery dabbled in them, not only with their own moneys, but with those of the suitors. Public losses and an enormous scandal necessarily resulted, and Lord Macclesfield was impeached in the House of Commons—by 273 against 164 votes—of corruption in selling offices, against the sale of which a long-forgotten

Lord Macclesfield's impeachment.

but unrepealed statute was astutely disinterred. He resigned the Great Seal; was tried and convicted by his

* *Lives of the Chancellors*, Fourth edition, vi, 22.

Peers, and sentenced to pay a heavy fine to the King. A motion to incapacitate him from holding future office in the State was made and negatived. This trial took place in May, 1725.

Papers still exist at Shirburn which display Lord Macclesfield's inmost thoughts under this heavy blow, and at all its stages. They bear the most conclusive marks of being intended for no eye save his own, but accident has preserved them. They also show most evidently that Lord Macclesfield's offence was simply the continuance of an abuse, ancient, systematic, and notorious. The practice of selling some minor Chancery Offices was even continued to a period within the memory of persons now living. But it is true, nevertheless, that a man of Lord Macclesfield's mental power, and of his exalted aims in life, ought to have given his whole energy to its suppression. He knew the increased temptation which its continuance must needs put in the way of sordid men. He omitted that duty, and men infinitely beneath him, in morals and in public usefulness, as well as in intellect, were permitted to be the instruments of his punishment. But he was still, as he had ever been, a better as well as a greater man than those who most loudly triumphed in his fall from power. In his retirement into private life he carried with him the full possession of his mental faculties, the undiminished zest for good literature, the correspondence, the esteem, and the love, of some of the best men of that age. He could, in those solemn hours in which a man stands in the immediate presence of his conscience and of his God, rejoice (though with Christian humility) that during fifteen years of judicial life, no judgment of his had ever been stained by any tinge of corruption. Nevertheless, and of neces-

What the Offence of the Lord Chancellor Macclesfield really was.

sity, he went down to his grave—as regards all earthly matters—in comparative gloom.

The behaviour of Geo. the First.

King George the First showed his sense of the inner springs by which some at least among the actors in this impeachment (visible or invisible as may have been their agency) were impelled, by declaring to his ex-Chancellor that he should insist on defraying the heavy fine out of the privy-purse. But death prevented the completion of that purpose. Another incidental event is still more weighty and significant. Lord Macclesfield was succeeded on the woolsack by Lord King. His successor received a salary of £6000 a year, and *an additional sum of twelve hundred pounds a year, out of the Hanaper Office*, expressly "*in consideration of the sale of offices in the Court of Chancery having been adjudged to be illegal.*"* To comment upon that fact would be to weaken it.

The compensation of succeeding Chancellors.

It is recorded of Lord Macclesfield that on the last day of his sitting in Chancery—with the full knowledge of the plans of his enemies, and of the course which had been resolved upon by that consummate master of statecraft and intrigue, his colleague Walpole,—he went into the examination and decision of an intricate point of equity † with such entire self-possession and concentration of his eminent faculties, that his decree on that final occasion became a valuable precedent, which has repeatedly governed the decisions of subsequent Chancellors. Lord Campbell records this characteristic fact with some astonishment. Could the eye of any reader of the *Lives of the Chancellors* fall on the private meditations I have ventured to refer to,

Lord Macclesfield's last decree in Chancery.

* Campbell, *Life of Lord King* (*Lives of the Chancellors*, Fourth edition, vi, 95).

† In a certain case of *Martin* versus *Nutkin*.

that reader would feel no astonishment at all. The Chancellor knew that however blameworthy his neglect to put down an old abuse, the ill effects of which passing circumstances had unexpectedly aggravated, he had administered justice between man and man, as "ever in his great taskmaster's eye." And in that humble consciousness he found both strength and consolation.

The parallelism observable in the careers of four eminent Chancellors.

Lord Macclesfield died on the 28th April, 1732, in the sixty-sixth year of his age. Despite the one grave fault of his public life, he was a true patriot, as well as a consummate lawyer; a humble-minded Christian, as well as a statesman of lofty and varied parts. He was, in a word, both a great and a good man.

Such are the principal incidents in the public life of the Lord Chancellor Macclesfield. One can scarcely recount them without a thought suggesting itself of the curious parallelism in tastes, in certain peculiarities of character, and in calamity, which links together the careers, otherwise so diversified, of four Lord Chancellors,—all of whom were pre-eminent for mental gifts. For the combination of natural vigour of intellect, and versatility of parts, with breadth of culture and of sympathies, it would not, perhaps, be easy to pitch on a fifth Chancellor, who is quite worthy of being classed with Bacon, Clarendon, Somers, and Macclesfield. Great, indeed, are the differences of birth and of early education, greater still the difference of *degree* in the mental capacity, of these four Chancellors. To one only among mortal men has it been accorded to use, within the straitest limits of truth, the lofty words:—"I have taken all knowledge to be my province." But the four had more in common than they had in divergence. They are more alike in faculty and in power, as well as in misfortune, than any other four English lawyers that could readily be grouped together. All the four raised themselves to the marble chair, in the face of unusual, although diverse, difficulties. All the four were eager in the pursuit of wealth, and lavish in its expenditure. All were the disciples, the promoters, and the life-long lovers, of Literature. All were eminent jurists, but all took as keen an interest in politics and statecraft as in law. All rendered brilliant political service, at critical conjunctures of British affairs. All were men of frank and outspeaking temper, and somewhat disdainful of those politic arts which, if they do not exempt the user from enemies, do often extract from enmity its power to sting. All were impeached of corruption, in Parliament. And all, save only Somers, went to the grave in the gloom of a great downfall.

Character of the Parliaments in which Bacon, Clarendon, Somers, and Macclesfield, were severally impeached.

And the parallelism does not stop there. The epochs of those four impeachments were, all of them, epochs that stand out saliently in our Annals, for the unusual bitterness and ferocity of party conflict. The Parliaments that impeached those four Chancellors extend over a period of more than a century, crowded with events and with vicissitudes, but those four Parliaments agree in being among the most utterly unscrupulous of all the political assemblies which figure in our national story. They all belonged to times in which some of the most worthless and most contemptible of men lived prosperously in high places, and went down to their graves, not only unimpeached, but adulated and toadied to the last.

Is it, perhaps, something more than a possibility that not alone the faults, the mistakes, the omissions, or the crimes, but also the distinctive merits, and the intrinsic greatness, of Bacon, of Clarendon, of Somers, and of Macclesfield, may have had a good deal to do with their several impeachments? The "*State Trials*," no less than the "*Statutes of the Realm*," are a mine of information for English History, and one—I venture to think—which hitherto has been but partially and feebly worked.

There is ample evidence that Lord Macclesfield was an ardent lover and a liberal promoter of good Literature. That assertion, indeed, runs in the teeth of one of the many strong—and reckless—statements * which detract so seriously from the merits of the *Lives of the Chancellors*, but it is none the less true. Happily for his memory, the papers of this Lord Chancellor, as well as his books, have been preserved, with unusual fidelity, and they are papers of a kind which, to the seeing eye, depict the man, in his habit, as he lived.

First, however, a word or two needs to be said of the share of Lord Chancellor Macclesfield in founding the fine Library which now adorns Shirburn Castle. We have all seen, occasionally, important Libraries, which afforded no tittle of evidence that their collectors had any claim to be called lovers of Literature:—

Varieties of the genus "Collector."

> ...Indocti primum, quanquam plena omnia gypso
> Chrysippi invenias: nam perfectissimus horum est,
> Si quis Aristotelem similem, vel Pittacon emit,
> Et jubet archetypos pluteum servare Cleanthas.

Men of that stamp do not belong exclusively to the age of Juvenal, nor is it needful to travel so far as to Rome, in order to get a look at them. But Lord Macclesfield was a Collector of another sort. He had inherited books from his father, and was himself a book-buyer throughout his busy life. Thus, whilst yet at the Bar, he had become the

The Collection of the Lord Chancellor Macclesfield.

* "He despised authorship...He wanted...the love of Literature."—Campbell, *Lives of the Chancellors*, iv, 561, 562 (1849).

owner of a Library of considerable worth, not merely in the department of Law, but in the departments, also, of Classical Literature, of Theology, and of History. Many of his printed books contain copious manuscript notes. He seems habitually to have read with pen or pencil at hand, but most usually his annotations were made on loose sheets or slips of paper. What remains of these notes would have sufficed to show that his studies were quite as diversified as were his books.

His encouragement of learning.

When raised to the Bench, Lord Macclesfield (then Lord Chief Justice Parker) became conspicuous as an encourager of learning, and as the open-handed patron of learned men. Bishop Warburton (in a characteristic passage which I met with recently in his MS. Correspondence with Dr. Thomas Birch) bears testimony on this point, easily to be corroborated, if need were, from many other sources:—"I believe," he says,—writing many years after Lord Macclesfield's death,—"the flatteries to Chancellors never rose so high as to the three last [Parker, King, and Talbot], and yet, for all that, the last, and perhaps the first, *of our times*, who was a real Mæcenas, was Parker."*

His acquisitions at the Sale of Foucault's Library.

On acquiring Shirburn Castle, one of Lord Macclesfield's earliest cares was to furnish it with books. He appears to have made considerable purchases both at home and on the Continent, more especially at the sale of the fine Library of Nicholas Joseph Foucault, an eminent French administrator, who will have a claim to some personal notice hereafter. Many of the choicest books at Shirburn bear Foucault's book plate, and form the foundation on which the present Library has been built.

The papers and books at Shirburn that more particularly

* *Warburton to Birch*, January, 1739, [1740, N. S.], in BIRCH MSS. in the British Museum, No. 4320, p. 162.

evince the keenness of the interest in literature, and in the fortunes of learned men, which characterised the Chancellor during the whole of his life, are of three kinds: (1) his own collections from different sources on a great variety of literary and scientific topics; (2) the books that were presented to him, with acknowledgments of the aid that he had extended to their respective authors; (3) portions of his Correspondence, after his fall from power, which show the mode in which his enforced leisure was employed.

The Papers of the Chancellor Macclesfield preserved at Shirburn.

His manuscript collections are so multifarious, and often so elaborate, that they seem to indicate an almost equal interest in Theology, in the Mathematical Sciences, in Philology, and in Polite Letters. They evince systematic and persevering labour, as well as wide research. Some of them seem to imply plans of publication, which must have been obstructed, either by the smallness of the span of life which remained to him, after his fall, or by other causes. As it proved, the *Memorial relating to the Universities*, printed by Gutch (in the *Collectanea Curiosa*), is the only treatise of his which has been given to the English public. For that "short and plain account of our Constitution, and of the changes it has undergone," the want of which he recognised at the close of the seventeenth century, the public had to wait till the nineteenth.

But in the Manuscript Library lately at Stowe there was a treatise by Lord Macclesfield on the Succession, which has not been printed. Its full title reads thus: *An Account of a Conference concerning a Scheme for establishing, by Act of Parliament, that in the Succession to the Crown, the Male Descendants of His Majesty shall, in all cases, be preferred to the females, and that the Princes his Descendants, not yet born, shall not hold the Kingdom of Great Britain and His Majesty's dominions in Germany, in case of a younger*

Lord Macclesfield's Treatise on the Succession to the Crown.

Brother or male of a collateral line, that might hold those Dominions in Germany, but that in such case they should go to such younger Brother. And to this manuscript King George the First's "opinion," written in French, was annexed.*

Other MSS. of Lord Macclesfield collected at Stowe.

In the same Library was also contained an extensive series of manuscript collections made by Lord Macclesfield on many political and politico-historical subjects; as, for example, on Corporations; on Universities; on the Correspondence and Conspiracies of the Jacobites; on the Office of Chancellor, and the Sale of Offices; and on the Guardianship of the Kingdom by Regencies and Lords Justices; together with various topographical collections on Derbyshire and Staffordshire. All these, together with the Treatise on the Succession, are now, it is believed, in the Library of Lord Ashburnham. Portions of Lord Chancellor Macclesfield's correspondence are also there, having been included in the purchases at Stowe. Other portions are in the State Paper Office and in the British Museum. A still larger portion remains at Shirburn, and of this I shall have occasion to speak hereafter.

Names of some among the authors whom he befriended.

Among the authors whose works and publications were in various ways encouraged and promoted by the first Lord Macclesfield, may be named Sir Isaac Newton; Dr. Richard Newton, Founder of Hertford College at Oxford; Bishop Zachary Pearce; Thomas Hutchinson; Dr. Bernard Mandeville; Elizabeth Elstob, the eminent Anglo-Saxonist;

* I have searched the State Paper Office, not only amongst the documents of the Home Department, now accessible under the ordinary regulations, but—by the obliging permission of Lord Russell—amongst those of the Foreign Department, yet have not succeeded (perhaps only from the want of Calendars) in finding any copy of this "Account," or any papers relating to it.

Richard Bradley; Peter Des Maizeaux; Thomas Madox; William Jones, F.R.S., and Daniel Defoe. One of the latest of his personal labours was the collation of Sir Isaac Newton's *Observations on Daniel and on the Apocalypse*, from two distinct and very different MSS., but the task remained incomplete, and Newton's work was not given to the world until 1733. In the letters which the Earl wrote at this period of his life, he repeatedly speaks of literary pursuits as affording him his chief solace, next after the consolations of Religion and the affection of his family; and it is evident that he prepared for the last change with great piety, calmness, and resignation. He died in London, but was buried at Shirburn.

The Library of N. J. Foucault.

I have said that the most considerable book purchases of the first Lord Macclesfield seem to have been made at the sale of the Library of Nicholas Joseph Foucault. But I am unable to give the date of those acquisitions. Several of the largest known collections of sale catalogues have been examined, fruitlessly, in the hope of ascertaining when and where the sale occurred. Nor is there any mention of this sale, or of any Foucault catalogue, in the list of such documents prefixed to the *Manuel du Libraire*, or in the larger and more recent list given by M. Gustave Brunet, in his admirable *Dictionnaire de Bibliologie* of 1860. Foucault's library, as well as his fine collection of antiquities, was one of the lions of Paris, at the beginning of the eighteenth century. It is mentioned by Germain Brice, the Paris topographer (in 1717); by Le Long, in the *Bibliothèque Historique de la France* (in 1719); and by President Hénault, in his *Mémoires*. M. Baudry (who has recently edited, under the authority of the Minister of Public Instruction, and as part of that noble series of Inedited Documents concerning French History, which, until the days of Sir John Romilly, was a standing reproach to Englishmen, Foucault's own Memoirs,) is of opinion that the library was dispersed, after Foucault's death, in 1721. Yet a comparison of two passages in Le Long,—one in the text, and the other in the subsequently printed preface—seems to prove that it must have been dispersed in his life-time.* Be that as it may, the very choicest of his books appear to have been brought to Shirburn, but I have seen a few volumes containing his book-plate at Blenheim Palace, and elsewhere. His career is remarkable.

The career and character of Foucault.

Nicholas Joseph Foucault was born at Paris in 1643. He was the son of an official man, who had the ear of Colbert, and who obtained for the youth, at the age of twenty-two, an appointment as secretary to a commission on law reform. His subsequent and protracted official life, as one of the King's Intendants, was passed successively, at Montauban, at Pau, at Poitiers, and at Caen. He seems always to have distinguished himself for ability and energy, and also for a wise moderation, as far as respects secular politics, in trying times. But it was Foucault's chief misfortune to be largely mixed up with the execution of those unscrupulous measures for the extinction of the Reformed Churches throughout France, which grew out of the senility of Lewis XIV, and the consequent revocation of the Edict of Nantes. His part in that unholy crusade was to cajole into abjuration as many of the Huguenots within his reach as were cajolable, and if possible to terrify the rest. He was certainly not a man who would, of himself, have counselled deeds of blood, but he cannot be acquitted of the heavy

* *Bibliothèque Historique*, Edit. of 1719, p. 88, and preface. Compare with this the new edition, 1768, by Fevret de Fontette, p. 406.

crime of having countenanced them. And this stain on his memory is the deeper, because he was at all times a student of history, and a cultivator of literature. He knew something of what the world owed to free thought and free speech. He knew something of the penalties which, in one form or other, are sure to be exacted from those who seek to destroy such freedom. His name will continue to have a place in the history of learning, from the fact that to his instrumentality it is due that more than one important book—theretofore lost—was given to the world. To find amongst these discoveries the now famous treatise of Lactantius *De Mortibus Persecutorum* (which he met with in the Abbey of Moissac), reads like an irony of Providence—if such a term be allowable—on the criminal folly of which he had made himself the tool.

Boulainvilliers' tirade against Foucault's devotion to literature.

Foucault's devotion to literary pursuits was so great, and so notorious, that when his eminent contemporary publicist, the Count of Boulainvilliers, in preparing his *Etat de la France*, had to pass in review a series of Memoirs on the condition of the several provinces of the kingdom, which had been drawn up (in 1698) by their respective Intendants, and found Foucault's Memoir on Normandy to be slight and perfunctory, he instantly laid the blame on the author's overweening love of books,* and apostrophised him indignantly for losing such an opportunity of signalising himself in his official duty. Yet Foucault's long and remarkable correspondence with Colbert and with Louvois shows abundantly that he was a zealous public servant; and he has left

* "L'amour de l'Etude et des Lettres."—*Etat de la France* (1727), 11. Boulainvilliers adds that he has found no other example of neglect, arising from *that* cause, and he continues: "This example excites my indignation the more, since I little expected it from the Intendant of Caen. Is the love of country so extinct among us, that so enlightened an administrator as he is should, in his Official Report, give not the smallest proof of his capacity?" &c.

many conspicuous marks of his administrative career. The Academies he founded, and the improvements he introduced into the Colleges of Nancy, of Cahors, and of Poitou, may be laid at the door of his love of learning. But he also developed much of the industrial capabilities of the districts entrusted to him, improved their fiscal systems, promoted many useful public works, and encouraged many benevolent institutions.

Proofs of Foucault's administrative ability.

Nothing, however, in Foucault's varied career is more interesting to Englishmen than the curious record he has left of a conversation with King James the Second, held in his own house at Thorigny, near Caen, in 1690, when the royal fugitive was on his way from Ireland to his asylum at St. Germains. The poor King then extended to Foucault the advantage of some instructions in contemporaneous history from royal lips. Among other characteristic utterances, James imparted to his shrewd but polished auditor, the facts that he still possessed the universal love of his subjects, and that nothing save the terror inspired by the Dutch mercenaries had hindered him from being restored by acclamation. James left Thorigny, delighted with his reception; and, as soon as he was gone, Foucault described—quietly but keenly—to a distant friend, the smiling self-complacence with which the royal fugitive had asserted, in June, 1690, his popularity with his subjects, and the certainty of his future triumph. These letters have been overlooked by Foucault's biographers, but they are printed in Sirtema de Grovestins' *Histoire des Rivalités Politiques entre les Puissances Maritimes et la France*,* and they did not escape the lynx-eyed research of Macaulay.†

Foucault's conversation with James II.

* VI, 229—232.

† And, since the passage in the text was first written, they have been reprinted by M. Baudry, in the *Documents inédits sur l'Histoire de France*, ut supra.

Collection of George, 2nd Earl of Macclesfield.

To the Chancellor's collection, large additions were made by George, second Earl of Macclesfield, who succeeded his father in 1732, and died in 1764. Earl George's tastes and pursuits were pre-eminently mathematical, and his attainments in that direction were considerable. He became President of the Royal Society in 1752, and, in the same year, took a prominent part in the measures for the alteration of the calendar. To him belongs the distinction of maintaining, at Shirburn, the only astronomical Observatory in England, which, according to the testimony of the then Astronomer Royal himself,* was adequately supplied with instruments. His book-acquisitions were not confined to mathematical subjects, but embraced both history and polite literature. Besides the collection which he made for Shirburn, he formed a Library,—small, yet of considerable value, and including many fine manuscripts,—at his house in London, but this town library, in pursuance of his testamentary arrangements, was sold by auction, in January, 1765.

Library of Wm. Jooes, Esq., F.R.S.

The celebrated Library of William Jones, F.R.S., an eminent mathematician, and the father of a man still more eminent in many departments of knowledge and of labour, was bequeathed by him to the second Lord Macclesfield in 1749. Its character was diversified. It included a choice collection of Bibles in many languages. It contained what, in its day, was a large and remarkable collection of books on Linguistics, embracing treatises on human speech in general;—Dictionaries of all kinds;—Grammars and other systematic works;—the productions of those early language-reformers who anticipated, but in a milder form, some of the "phonetic" absurdities of our own day;—together with

* Dr. James Bradley to George, Earl of Macclesfield. (*Shirburn MSS.*)

many of the works of those who have attempted to invent a "universal character;"—and—not least in curiosity—a series of primers and alphabets, some of them printed in obscure towns in remote corners of Europe. It also contained a collection of Welsh MSS., including many of high antiquity, the formation of which had been begun by the Rev. Samuel Williams, Vicar of Llandyfriog in Cardiganshire, in the reign of Charles II, and continued by his son, the Rev. Moses Williams, Vicar of St. Mary's, Bridgewater, who strove, unsuccessfully, to preserve his acquisitions in the surest manner by printing them; and by whom the conjoined collection appears to have been bequeathed to Mr. Jones. Moses Williams obtained some valuable transcripts from the ancient Library of the Vaughan family which was long preserved at Hengwrt, in Merionethshire,* but has been recently inherited by Mr. Wynne, of Peniarth. Other Welsh MSS. passed to Jones from the hands of Lewis Morris, an antiquary of some note in the earlier part of the last century. But the most conspicuous feature of Mr. Jones's Library was its series of printed books, and of MSS., on the Mathematical and Physical Sciences.

Jones's acquisition of the Mathematical MSS. of John Collins;

In this department Mr. Jones had acquired—apparently about the year 1708—the manuscript collections of John Collins, an intimate friend of Newton, and one of the early members of the Royal Society. Amongst them he found an

* With a recklessness of statement, unsupported by evidence, which, as will appear after, has curiously abounded in relation to the literary treasures now assembled at Shirburn, Lewis Morris has charged Williams with the acquisition by dishonest means of a portion of these MSS. In a note to a MS. letter of John Morgan to Moses Williams, he writes thus (in 1748): "Some he bought, some he begged, and stole a great many, and they are all now in the hands of William Jones, of London." What is otherwise known of Williams renders this charge highly improbable.

extensive correspondence on scientific subjects between the most eminent mathematicians of the age, and some important mathematical tracts in Newton's autograph. From this collection was first published (in 1711), under Jones's editorship, the *Analysis per quantitatum series, fluxiones, ac differentias;* and also, in great part from it (in 1712), the celebrated *Commercium Epistolicum,* which, together, secured to Sir Isaac Newton his rightful fame as the discoverer of the infinitesimal calculus, after a lapse of time between invention and publication that led to a bitter controversy, and for awhile threatened to place the laurel, wrongfully, on a foreign head.

To the collection thus acquired, Mr. Jones was enabled, by his close friendship with the great discoverer, to make the precious addition of many other papers from Newton's hand, so that at Shirburn may be seen Newton's own notes on the controversy with Leibnitz, as well as rough draughts of portions of the *Principia.* And his subsequent additions thereto.

The assiduity with which Mr. Jones collected, even from distant countries, all the important publications on the mathematical and physical sciences of which he could get tidings, seems not to have been greater than the liberality with which he was wont to communicate what he possessed for the promotion of scientific studies. Such, at all events, is the concurring testimony of many authors who speak of their obligations to his library. The frequency of such acknowledgments in the prefaces and dedications of contemporary works might well have suggested further inquiry to some of the writers who have successively repeated the assertion that Mr. Jones gave his MSS. to Lord Macclesfield, under the "singular injunction of not even showing them to any person whatsoever." None of these writers seems to have thought it worth while to look at the Jones's liberal admission to his Collections during his lifetime;

And his alleged restriction of such access, after his death.

will itself. Other writers, who say nothing of any such restriction, speak of the "dispersion" of Mr. Jones's papers,* and even assert, circumstantially, that his Library "was sold by auction, in 1801."†

Mr. Jones's will was proved in August, 1749. All that relates to the matter in hand is comprised in these few words:—

Terms of the Bequest.

> "Also I give and bequeath to the Right Honourable George, Earl "of Macclesfield,...my Study of Books, as they stand in my "Catalogue, together with such additions as I may hereafter "make thereto, and I request his acceptance thereof as a testi-"mony of my acknowledgment of the many marks of his "favour which I have received."‡

No conditions whatever are imposed on the bequest. So that there is the same sort of foundation for charging Mr. Jones with a 'puerile desire to obstruct the usefulness of his MSS. after his death, as there is for asserting that his Library has been sold.

Nichols' statement as to the loss of a Mathematical MS. entrusted to Ld. Macclesfield for publication.

By Mr. Nichols, the compiler of the well-known *Literary Anecdotes of the Eighteenth Century*, the last-named assertion has been combined with another and circumstantial statement that the manuscript of a work "intended to serve" as a "general introduction to the sciences," was prepared by Mr. Jones for the press,—was fairly copied out by an amanuensis, was entrusted to Lord Macclesfield for publication,—"as well for the honour of the author, as for the benefit of his family, to whom the property of the book belonged,"—and has been carelessly lost. Mr. Nichols

* Hutton, *Mathematical Dictionary*, 2nd edit., § "Jones."

† Nichols, *Literary Anecdotes of the XVIIIth Century*, i, 64.—"Jones's books, which had occupied the side of one of the galleries at Shirburn Castle, were sold by auction, in London, in 1801."

‡ MS. Register of Wills proved in the province of Canterbury, 1749, No, 252.

was in doubt "which is most to be censured, the destruction or loss of Mr. Jones's manuscript, or the dispersion of his Library from the family of his learned and munificent patron."* The striking scrupulosity with which what seem to have been the roughest, smallest, and most fragmentary of Mr. Jones's MSS.—extending even to useless jottings of figures, and to diagrams made on scraps of paper—have been preserved, makes it more than probable that this assertion also is simply a blunder. And the probability is increased by the circumstance that there is at Shirburn a MS. volume by Mr. Jones, bearing the less ambitious title of "*Mathematical Tracts*," and fairly written in the hand of an amanuensis, which has the appearance of having been intended for the press.

However this may have been, the Jones collection, taken as a whole, is among the most precious portions of the Shirburn Library. Some of its rarities will be more specifically indicated hereafter.

A fourth collection accrued, not long afterwards, when Sir Thomas Clarke, who had been Master of the Rolls for many years, and who was an attached friend of the Macclesfield family during three generations, bequeathed to Thomas, third Earl of Macclesfield, a small library, consisting chiefly of books on theology, history, and law. Like so many other of the eminent lawyers of that and of the preceding ages, Sir Thomas Clarke had a predilection for Theological studies, and many of his divinity books, as well as of his law books, abound in MS. notes in his autograph. Library of Sir Thos. Clarke.

To Thomas, third Earl, was also bequeathed in the year 1791, an extensive collection of books on the Arts of War, Military Library of Genl. G. Lane Parker.

* *Literary Anecdotes of the Eighteenth Century*, i, 463—465.

and on the subjects allied therewith, which had been formed, during many years, by the Testator, Lieut.-General the Hon. George Lane Parker, a younger son of George, second Earl of Macclesfield. This collection had been brought together with great pains and research. It comprised the best books on military matters,—and pre-eminently on the Arts of Strategy, Fortification, and Gunnery,—which had appeared up to nearly the close of the last century, as well in the French, Spanish, Italian, and German languages, as in English. It also included many valuable works on ancient and modern history.

Elimination of Duplicate Volumes.

By the union of so many separate collections a Library was at length formed, which amounted in the aggregate to more than 20,000 volumes. But a considerable number of duplicate, and even of triplicate volumes necessarily resulted. Most of these were from time to time weeded out, and were sold by auction; those which had accrued by the union of Mr. Jones's Library with that of the first and second Earls in the year 1764; and a subsequent and larger portion in March, 1794. Some duplicates still remained, but most of these were removed in 1819. The present number of volumes in the Library is about 13,000, namely, of printed books, 12,677, and of MSS. (taking the yet unbound ones at an approximation), about 260 volumes. The collection is arranged in these six classes:—I. *Theology and Philosophy*. II. *History*. III. *Politics*. IV. *Sciences and Arts*. V. *Literature*. VI. *Polygraphy*. The catalogue is in two parts:—I. Subjects. II. Authors,—and it extends to six volumes in folio. Both parts are alphabetically arranged.

Present Extent of the Collection.

The Mathematical MSS. at Shirburn.

In addition to what has been already said of the collection of Mathematical MSS. at Shirburn,—when speaking of its origin,—it must here suffice to remark that it contains, in Newton's autograph, his *Tractatus de Quadratura Curvarum*, and other papers "*Concerning Curve Lines;*" a paper *De natura Acidorum;* rough "*Notes on Light and Colours;*" Forty-four letters (wholly in his hand), addressed to Collins, Halley, Oldenburgh, and Boyle; with copies of other letters written by him, and with some of the replies; many papers by Oughtred, Briggs, Hooke, Machin, and Wallis; with original letters of Bishop Seth Ward, Flamsteed, Barrow, Cotes, James Gregory, Hooke, Wallis, among other English Mathematicians; and of Borelli, Fermat, Huyghens, Auzout, Pardies, and Maupertuis, among Foreign Mathematicians. A partial selection from these has been published, under the editorship of the late Dr. Rigaud, in the volumes known as the "Macclesfield Correspondence." It contains, too, portions of the rough draft of the *Principia*, also in Newton's own hand.

Of the Linguistic MSS., the most valuable are the Latino-Basque (or Latino-Cantabrian) *Dictionary* (unfinished), and the Basque *Grammar*, of Pierre d'Urte, together with a translation of the Books of *Genesis* and *Exodus* into Basque, the whole extending to seven volumes, in folio. That language is remarkable, alike for the important place it occupies in the study of Comparative Philology, and for the fewness of the documents and grammatical appliances which are available for its mastery. The most eminent philologists agree in assigning to Basque a very high antiquity, a wide geographical range, a marvellous aptitude both for verbal deflection and for syllabic combination, and pregnant affinities with languages which are usually looked upon as too remote to have anything in common. The Basque proverb which embodies the popular opinion of the difficulties which that language presents to extraneous students,

Basque or Cantabrian MSS. of Pierre D'Urte.

goes the length of asserting that it tasked the energies of a Certain Personage himself, for seven years, without success. Be that as it may, there can be no doubt that in the Basque MSS. at Shirburn—as in the Welsh—lies much valuable material hitherto unused. That these manuscripts have not, as yet, been turned to better account has arisen from no lack of liberality on the part of the noble family to which they belong. Access to them has, in several instances, been generously accorded, for literary purposes. And of the Basque MSS., indeed, some brief account was long since given to students by Mr. Samuel Greatheed, in the *Archæologia;* whilst of a certain portion of the Welsh MSS., good use was made by the Editors of the *Myvyrian Archaiology of Wales*, whose third volume was dedicated to the then Earl of Macclesfield, in acknowledgement of his liberality. On both occasions, however, the examination was very inadequate and fragmentary, and there were no catalogues to assist the searchers. By the present Earl, that defect has been supplied.

History of the Basque MSS.

It seems probable that the D'Urte MSS., like some of the Welsh, passed through the hands, successively, of Dr. Edward Browne, of Edward Lhuyd, and of Moses Williams, before they reached those of William Jones. All these antiquaries were evidently attracted to Basque by more or less perception of its importance in Comparative Philology, and more especially of its possible value in elucidating the origin of those ancient British tongues in which they were chiefly interested.

The Special Treasures among the Welsh MSS.

Amongst the Welsh MSS. of the Macclesfield Collection nine volumes stand saliently out as of pre-eminent curiosity and value. All of these, as to their contents, are either Miscellaneous or Poetical manuscripts. One of them is a Roman Catholic Primer compiled shortly after the Reformation.

Another, a transcript of Lives of Saints, with other tracts, compiled, from ancient sources, in the year 1628, partly by a certain Roger Morys, of the Vale of Clwyd, and partly by Thomas Evans, of the Vale of Edeyrnion (between Bala and Corwen), to whom the volume belonged. Four volumes bear, in common, the title "Miscellaneous Collection" (*Didrefn Gasgliad*). Another miscellaneous volume is entitled "The Red Book of Talgarth" (*Y Llyvr Cóch o Dalgarth*); another, compiled in 1456 by Griffith Owen, is without any collective title, but begins with a translation, from the Latin, of "The Book that is called *The Mirror of Obedience*," sometimes ascribed to Pope Pius III. The two principal poetical collections—out of thirty-six in all—are entitled, respectively, "The Long Book of Shrewsbury," and "The Chief Book of the Bards" (*Prif-lyfr y Beirdd*). All of these volumes merit a detailed account, but a brief description of some of them must suffice, although I have the advantage of some excellent illustrative notes, prepared by Mr. R. Owen, of Jesus College, after a careful examination of these Welsh MSS. in 1862.

The Primer is entitled "A Godly Book" (*Llyfr Duwiol*), and is written in a strange compound of Welsh with English. Thus a morning prayer, called "A wholesome Exercise," is headed not "*Arfer iachus*," but "*Arfer holsom*" (fol. 31); and (at fol. 81) the words "the Nations of the Gentiles" are translated, not "*Poblodd o'r Cenhedloedd*," but "*Naseiyne o'r Gentles*," and a like barbarous but very curious diction runs through the volume. And the history is as notable, sometimes, as the style. The passage from which the last-quoted phrase is taken is a sort of epitome of early church history. It ends thus:—

A Welsh Primer, temp. Elizabeth.

"From Rome the faith spread among other nations. And thus it came also into the land of us the Cymry, or Britons, from Pope Eleutherius, in A.D. 180; to the Saxons, from Pope Gregory the First, in A.D. 590."

"Didrefn Gasgliad," formerly E. Lhuyd's.

The *Didrefn Gasgliad*, in four volumes, belonged to Edward Lhuyd, and is mentioned in his *Glossology*. The first and second of these volumes contain a copy of the *Brut y Brenhinoed* ("Chronicle of the Kings") with variations and additions, and with curious rubricated titles, but it is imperfect. This is followed by a most interesting Welsh translation of the "Travels of Brother Oderic of Portenan [Pordenone] into India and the remote East," . . "translated by Sir David Vychan of Glamorgan, at the command and request of Rhys ap Thomas ap Einiawn, his master." The Franciscan Oderic was born in 1286, and his travels began about twenty years after Marco Polo's return. He went across Armenia into Persia, visited Java, Ceylon, and Thibet; and doubtless owed the honour of his ntroduction, probably in the 15th century, to the Welsh baron, to the popularity of his Order amongst Welshmen. They possess no translation either of Mandeville or of Polo. Among other interesting contents of the remaining volumes of this Miscellany is a series of Welsh fables, strikingly illustrative both of the social condition and of the theological opinion of the period.

"Lyvr Côch o Dalgarth."

The *Red Book of Talgarth* is chiefly, but not exclusively, theological in its contents. It is a fine manuscript on vellum, and was given to Moses Williams by John Powell, of Talgarth, in 1719. Some of the tracts of which it is composed are found also in the "Book of the Hermit of Llandewi" (*Llyvr yr Aner o Llandewi Brefi*), now in the Library of Jesus College. Very striking are the poetical description of a trance into which a certain monk fell one Trinity Sunday after Matins, and a translation into Welsh of the *Veni Creator Spiritus*. And amongst other curiosities is a theological dialogue between the Emperor Hadrian and "Ipotus, a spiritual man;" Ipotus being our old acquaintance Epictetus, turned monk, and conversing with Hadrian, "much in the same style," says Mr. Owen, "as we may suppose Alcuin to have done with Charlemagne in the School of the Palace." This volume also contains a Welsh version of "*The Gospel of Nicodemus*," which seems to differ considerably from the usual text.

The "Prif-lyfr Beirdd."

The beautiful "*Chief Book of the Bards*" (containing 772 pages, folio, on paper), is one of the finest extant collections of Welsh Poetry; was compiled by several hands; is written, notwithstanding that circumstance, with great care and elegance; contains works of Poets who,—if we take the usual chronology and accept Aneurin, Taliesin, and Llywarch Hên, as genuine bards of the sixth century,—flourished during twelve hundred years, inasmuch as it begins with Aneurin and ends with Alban Thomas; and contains much that appears to be both valuable and unprinted. Among the historical poems are conspicuous two ascribed to old Llywarch, the first of which narrates the death of Geraint ab Erbin (the "Sir Geraint" of the *Idylls of the King*), and the other that of the Condidan, "Prince of Shrewsbury," mentioned in the Saxon Chronicle, who fell at Cirencester in the sixth century. There are many Lancastrian poems in this volume which commemorate events in the wars of the Roses, and some of which glorify in extatic terms poor Henry VI, and those who adhered to his cause. A poem of later date preaches the duty of a new crusade to the Holy Land, and exhorts—of all men—Henry VII to be its leader. Another, addressed to Henry VIII, the "crowned kinsman of North Wales" (*coronog câr i Wynedd*), predicts that he will be Emperor, "if he wait awhile," and exhorts him, also, to "take a large force, visit the Holy Land, and subdue fell Turkey."

Another poem that may be called half-historical, narrates the author's experiences at Rome, in the middle of the fifteenth century, when he visited it as a pilgrim. He describes the churches, the rood-lofts, the 'stations,' and the reception of "many thousands of pilgrims," by Pope Calixtus III. There is also, in this volume, a sort of petition in verse, drawn up on behalf (or in wicked mockery) of a simple-minded Abbess of Saint Clair's, in Pembrokeshire, praying the gift of an ape—"a sprite resembling a lay-brother" (*ac ysprayd Uur gwas brawd Uyg*)—that it may "send awe into the young men," and so be a safeguard to the nuns. But the curiosities of these Welsh Manuscripts abound, and enough has been said to serve as sample of their quality.

The Laws of HowelDha.

The Welsh Collection also embraces a notable series of MSS. of the Laws of King Howel the Good,—a document of great value, philologically as well as historically. Most of the sixteen copies of that Code, of which this series consists, are of course comparatively unimportant, being transcripts by modern hands. Three copies, however, are of considerable antiquity and authority. There is also an abstract of the Code, and a volume of notes upon it.

Other Juridical MSS. at Shirburn.

The other juridical and political MSS. include the entire series of Note Books, and a considerable portion of the Public and Private Correspondence, of the Lord Chancellor Macclesfield, with many of his most eminent contemporaries. Another portion of the Correspondence was, it seems, stolen from Shirburn many years ago; at length found its way, as I have had previous occasion to mention, into the Duke of Buckingham's Library at Stowe, by the bequest of Thomas Astle; and at the Stowe Sale was, together with the Political Collection already described, among the purchases of Lord Ashburnham. There is also a curious collection of Diplomatic Cyphers made by Dr. John Wallis during the Civil Wars; and a copy of the *Fleta, seu Commentarius Juris Anglicani*, covered with manuscript notes, for a new Edition, by Sir Thomas Clarke.

The Shirburn Library having never been described,—scarcely even mentioned,—until now, I append to this chapter some notices of the more conspicuous among its rarities, not hitherto enumerated. And I follow the order into which the books were classed in 1861.

Remarkable Books at Shirburn, in the Class "Theology and Philosophy"

Amongst the choice Editions of the Holy Bible, with which the Class "THEOLOGY" begins, the first place is due to the earliest or 'Complutensian' Polyglott (1514-17). The Shirburn copy once belonged to Cranmer, and bears his autograph. From him it passed to John, Lord Lumley, who died in 1609. Of its subsequent history there is no indication. The copy of Bishop Walton's Polyglott has the Lexicon *Heptaglotton* of Castell, which is rarer* than the Bible itself, on account of the partial destruction of the impression. Among other biblical works of importance occur a fine copy of the first edition of the *Greek* Bible, printed by Aldus in 1518; a copy of Cardinal Caraffa's celebrated edition of the Old Testament in Greek, based on the *Codex Vaticanus*; and a copy of Koburger's *Biblia Latina* of 1477, printed at Nuremberg, in choice condition, with richly illuminated initial letters, and with many MS. notes in a nearly contemporary hand. Amongst the other choice Editions of the Vulgate Bible are those of 1481, of 1482 (printed by Reinhardt and Philippe, at Lyons); and of 1483. The Copy of Cranmer's *English* Bible of 1540 is imperfect, as are most of the few copies which have survived the wear and tear of the early use in Churches, and the subsequent perils of the Marian suppression. The so-called "Vinegar" Bible, best known for its curious misprint, but intrinsically

* But by no means so rare as it has been sometimes stated to be. Prior to the sale of duplicates in 1794 there were at Shirburn *four* copies of this Lexicon.

more remarkable for its beauty, is also here. The first edition of the Bible in *Welsh* (1588), and that of the New Testament alone (1567) in the same language, are both of extreme rarity.

Of the remarkable series of versions in the languages of Northern Europe, the following merit special notice: (1) The earlier *Bohemian* Bible, of 1577, and that in the version of the Moravian Brethren, printed (1579—1661), at Kralitz, at the private press of Count John de Zarotin; (2) the *Windish* Bible of 1584, translated by Dalmatin, on the basis of Luther's version; (3) The second Edition of the *Icelandic* Bible, printed at Hoolum, in 1644; (4) The first Edition of the *Sclavonic* Bible, printed at Ostrow, in 1581; (5) The *Lettish* Bible, translated by Glück, of 1689; (6) the *Hungarian* Bible of 1612; and (7) Luther's *Saxon* version in the Edition of 1596. His *German* version is also here in the Wittemberg Edition of 1546-47. The great rarity of the Moravian and Lettish Bibles above mentioned, notwithstanding their comparative recency of date, arises, I believe, in the one case from rigid suppression by the Austrian government; in the other, from the destructive effects of an inundation at Riga.

The exceedingly scarce *Spanish* Bible of Cassiodoro de Reyna, printed in Switzerland in 1569, and known from the printer's device as "The Bear Bible," is also at Shirburn, together with that curious translation of the Scriptures, professedly into the same language, made by Dutch Jews established at Ferrara, and rendered so faithfully from the Hebrew —'*palabra por palabra*'—as to be scarcely intelligible, it is said, to Spaniards. Far more remarkable than either of these is the precious MS. translation of the Books of Genesis and Exodus into the Labortan dialect of the *Basque* previously mentioned. This MS. derives especial importance from the fact that the Old Testament has never been printed in Basque.*

Portions of the Bible in various languages.

Among other choice editions of *portions* of the Holy Scriptures may be enumerated the Polyglott Psalter of Giustiniani, Bishop of Nebbio, printed at Geneva in 1516; the Aldine *Greek* Psalter of 1497; the Diglott Testament—*English* and Erasmian *Latin*—of 1550; the *Anglo-Saxon* and *English* Gospels of 1571; the *Arabic* and *Latin* Gospels of 1591; and the Epistles in *Italian*, with the Commentary of Bruccioli, printed at Venice in 1544. At Shirburn may also be seen a translation

* A complete Basque Bible has indeed been asserted to exist (*e. g.*, "Man hat eine Bibel in dieser Sprache," Zedler, *Vollständiges Univl. Lexicon*, iii, 624. "Plusieurs personnes ont parlé d'une Bible Basque et ont dit l'avoir vue à Rome," Fleury Lécluse, *Grammaire Basque*, 18). But nevertheless it is certain that no such Bible has been printed, nor is any complete translation in MS. now known. The New Testament in French Basque was printed at Rochelle in 1571.

of the "Epistles and Gospels," as used by the Church of England, into *Welsh*, printed at London in 1551, which thus preceded the entire New Testament by sixteen years, as the latter preceded the complete Bible by a period of twenty-one years. Here also the very rare *Acta* is *Apostolorum Græco-Latina*, printed by Hearne from the Laudian Codex.

Liturgical Books.

There are many liturgical and ritualistic books of great interest in this library besides that Welsh one of 1551, which has been mentioned. For example:—The *Horæ...secundum usum Ecclesiæ Sarum* of 1531;—the Greek *Horæ...secundum consuetudinem Romanæ Curiæ* of 1528; the Salisbury *Primer* of 1556; the Hungarian Liturgy of 1610; a vellum copy of the Swedish Liturgy, which seems to have belonged to King Charles XII; a Commentary on the Athanasian Creed by Petrus de Osoma, printed at Paris by Ulrich Gering (the Caxton of France, but a Caxton with partners); and also a notable series of versions of the Lutheran Catechism into most of the languages of Northern Europe.

Rare Tracts in Philosophy.

Among the conspicuous books which come within the section "Mental and Moral Philosophy" the following are of special curiosity:—A very rare edition of the "Tablet" (Πιναξ) of Cebes, with other tracts, by Plutarch and Xenophon, printed at Rome in the type of Calliergi; a remarkable series of the mystical tracts of Giordano Bruni; and a copy of the Aristotelian tracts printed at Alost, in 1474, by John of Westphalia and Thierry Martens. This last-named work is of such excessive rarity that its very existence has been called in question. "It is quoted by Maittaire," says an eminent authority on such matters, M. Weiss,* "but no other bibliographer has seen it." Maittaire's books, it may be added, were sold in London in 1748. Tracts like this were, in that day, deemed of such small account that they were not specified in the sale catalogues, but lumped together in lots.

Choice Books in the Class "History:" (1) Geographers.

Of the many remarkable books in the Class "History," I can mention but a few. Conspicuous among geographical works are the first Editions of Ptolemy (1) in the Latin version of Jacobus Angelus (Vicenza, 1475) and (2) in the recension of Nicholas Donis (Ulm, 1482), with its extraordinary coloured maps, and illuminated initial letters, and with many MS. notes in a nearly contemporary hand;—and the first Editions—all of them by Aldus—of Strabo, 1516; of the *Onomasticon* of Pollux, 1502; and of Stephanus of Byzantium (Περι πολεων), also printed in 1502.

(2) Chroniclers.

Among the many choice Editions of Mediæval Chronicles are (1) that of Gaguin, on vellum, with beautiful miniatures (Paris, Galliot Du Pré, 1514)—which, on vellum, is so rare that Van Praet mentions only one copy; (2) the *Legende des Flamens, Artisiens et Haynuyers* (First Edition, 1522); (3) that of Monstrelet, printed by Antoine Verard about

* In the article "Martens (Thierry)" in the *Biographie Universelle*.

1500; (4) that of Jacques de Guise, in the French version of Lessabée (Paris, Galliot Du Pré, 1531); (5) the precious Froissart, as translated by Lord Berners, of 1525, printed by Pynson and Middleton; (6) the *Cronycle of England with the Fruyte of Tymes*, printed by Wynkyn de Worde, in 1520; (7) the *Chronicle of Briteyn*, of 1569; (8) the superb Holinshed of 1586—with cancelled leaves; and (9) a curious specimen of early Rouen typography in an edition almost unknown of the *Croniques de Normandie*, without date, but probably printed between the years 1495 and 1500.

Of the remarkable MS. Chronicle entitled the "Book of Hyde," I have elsewhere given some brief account. There is also at Shirburn an unprinted and unfinished English Chronicle, on Vellum, extending from the fabulous ages to the year 1293. It begins with an abridgement of Geoffrey of Monmouth, omitting the prophetical seventh book, and with this abridgement it incorporates a chronology of Popes and Emperors. The second division of this Chronicle carries the history from the "dispersion of the Britons" to the reign of Edward the Elder. The third, from that period to the accession of Edward the First in 1272. The fourth division narrates the events of Edward's reign, and, as far as regards the text, is taken wholly from Nicholas Trivet. It breaks off abruptly. The second and third divisions are derived from very varied sources. Throughout are interspersed copious intercalations and marginal additions, with occasional directions to a subsequent scribe, which seem to indicate that this manuscript became the text of a later Chronicle. It is of the fifteenth century, and before it came to Shirburn passed successively through the hands of John Rivers, Thomas Potter, and William Jones. Of its earlier history there is no account. It is almost wholly different from the Chronicle of John Beaver, which also begins (in the same words, *Æneas cum Ascanio*), with an abridgement of Geoffrey, and covers nearly the same period. With the unprinted Chronicle in Trinity College, Oxford (No. 10), formerly belonging to David Powel, I have not as yet been able to collate it. They will probably be found to have, at the least, a common origin. Mention must also be made of a copy of the first and rare edition of the Epistle of Gildas, *De Excidio et Conquestu Britanniæ*, undated and without name or place of printer, but known to have been printed in 1525, under the editorship of Polydore Virgil. This rhapsodical tract is more notable for the controversy it has occasioned than for any intrinsic worth. A manuscript copy is amongst the Welsh MSS. at Shirburn, bequeathed by Jones.

The Printed Historic Tracts.

The printed Historical Tracts at Shirburn are numerous and valuable. They include many on the War of Independence in the Netherlands—one of which has a manuscript note that seems to be in the hand of Lord Burghley; on the defeat of the Spanish Armada; on the dawning

History of the American Colonies; and on the Voyages and Discoveries of early Adventurers in other parts of the world. Amongst the many "Collections of Voyages" are fine copies of those of our own Hakluyt and Purchas; of that of Ramusio, printed by the Giunti at Venice; and of the still more celebrated and very rare collection of De Bry. This section of the class "History," and the sections allied with it, include many other conspicuous books, but I cite only the *Comentarios de los Incas Reyes del Peru...y Historia del descubrimiento...y como lo ganaron los Españoles* (in the original edition, printed partly at Lisbon, partly at Cordova, in the years 1609—1616); and the *Sanctarum Peregrinationum in Montem Syon, ad venerandum Christi Sepulcrum in Jerusalem, atque in Montem Synai...Opusculum*, of Bernard de Breydenbach, with its most curious wood-cuts, printed at Mentz in 1486. Collections of Travels.

What has been said of the sources whence the MATHEMATICAL portion of this Library accrued has shown already that its printed as well as its manuscript treasures are manifold. In the section "Arithmetic" they include several books so rare as to be unnoticed in Professor De Morgan's long and elaborate list,* and many more which he knew to exist, but had failed to get sight of. The first Edition (1494) of the *Summa de Arithmetica* of Lucas Pacioli di Borgo is almost as notable when regarded as a fine specimen of printing, as for its place in the history of the Science of Numbers,—a place due to it, not indeed as the first printed work on Arithmetic (which some writers have erroneously asserted it to be), but as being really the first work printed on Algebra.† This Shirburn copy has finely illuminated initial letters. Here, too, is a precious copy, with the autograph of Bacon, of Bishop Tonstall, *De Arte Supputandi*, in the rare first edition, printed by Pynson, in 1522. This copy has also many MS. notes which seem to be in Bacon's hand. Choice Books in the Mathematical and Physical Sciences.

The section "Geometry" opens with a series of texts, versions, and commentaries, of Euclid—ninety in number—which include the first edition (1533) of the Greek Text; the Latin version, with various commentaries, of 1516, edited by Lefebvre d'Etaples; the first edition of Commandinus' version; and the first edition of the Arabic version of Nasireddin. Here, also, is the curious volume of Antonio Capella, entitled, *Divina Proportione*, printed at Brescia in 1509, and illustrated with diagrams after Lionardo da Vinci;—an edition of the treatise *De Triangulis omnimodis* of John Müller of Königsberg (*Regiomontanus*), printed in 1533, and so scarce as to be unknown alike to Müller's biographers, and to De Murr, Delambre, and other writers on the bibliography

---

* *Arithmetical Books from the Invention of Printing.*

† De Morgan, ut supra.

of Mathematics;—and an extensive collection of Geometrical Tracts, many of which are of the highest value and rarity.

Notable books in Astronomy.

In "Astronomy" occur (1) a series of editions and versions of Ptolemy's *Almagestum*, embracing the first edition of the Greek Text, of 1538; the first edition of a version from the Arabic, different from that of Alhaçen, and printed in 1515; and the first known edition (1528) of the version made from the Greek by Trapezuntius;—(2) Copernicus, *De Revolutionibus Orbium Cœlestium*, first edition (1543), with MS. notes by John Greaves, Savilian Professor; together with copies of the subsequent editions of 1566 and of 1617;—(3) the Astronomical poem of Manilius, without any note of impression, but apparently printed about 1480;—(4) the Astronomical and Cosmographical Tracts of Cardinal Pierre d'Ailly, also without any note of impression, and almost unknown to bibliographers;—(5) several remarkable Astronomical MSS. of Richard Wallingford, Abbot of St. Albans, of Lewis Caerleon, and of Simon Bredon, all of them apparently of the fourteenth century;—(6) a volume of curious astronomical and astrological tracts, printed in London by Robert Wyer, without date, but probably about 1530;—(7) A very large Collection of Tracts on astronomical subjects, by various authors and of various dates, from the closing years of the fifteenth to the middle of the eighteenth centuries (printed in all parts of Europe),—no small proportion of which is of interest for the History of Astronomy, and some of which are not, it is believed, elsewhere to be found;—(8) A nearly complete series of the works of the great Astronomer, Hevelius—fifteen in number, and some of them printed at his private press—with his autograph notes of presentation to Henry Oldenburgh, Christian Huyghens, and others. Some of these derive their extreme rarity from the destruction of the greater part of the several impressions in a fire which destroyed Hevelius' house at Dantzic in 1679, just after the completion of his chief work the *Machina Cœlestis*, of which the fine copy at Shirburn is one of ten, all preserved, it is said, by their previous distribution as gifts from the author.

Other Choice books in Mathematics.

To a similar calamity, on a wider scale, is due the still greater rarity of another of the remarkable books, formerly belonging to Wm. Jones, and now preserved at Shirburn. Of Thomas Salusbury's *Mathematical Collections* the Shirburn copy is, indeed, not "rare," but "*unique.*" The printing of the work seems to have been spread over a period of at least six years, so that, although the first volume was issued in 1661, the second was still at press, when the Fire of London occurred in 1666. Each volume was in two parts, and the entire impression of the fourth part, containing, amongst other matters of intrinsic value, a Life of Galileo, appears to have perished, the sheets which were already in the author's hands only excepted. These sheets form part of the Shirburn copy, together with some unfinished proof sheets, as they came from the printer, a portion of the rough MS., and some letters containing information respecting Galileo, which had been communicated to the author from Italy during the progress of his work.*

Of the first edition of the works of Archimedes printed at Basil in 1544 two copies occur, each of which has important additions in MS. One copy came from the Library of the eminent Mathematician John Greaves, and is enriched with copious MS. notes and corrections from his hand. Another copy came from the Library of Sir Charles Scarburgh, who appears to have contemplated an edition of his own, and it contains MS. letters addressed to him by Wallis, with many additions to and corrections of the text. The curious physico-mathematical work of Robert Fludd (*Utriusque Cosmi, Metaphysica, Physica, atque Technica, Historia*) has many MS. notes in the hands both of the Lord Chancellor Macclesfield and of William Jones. In Sherwin's *Mathematical Tables* were recently found some letters of Halley relating thereto; and in a volume of Flamsteed's *Historia Cœlestis Britannica* was found some correspondence between Flamsteed and Newton relating to the famous controversy to which that work gave rise, together with the Award of Newton and others as arbitrators of the matters at issue between the author and the Representatives of Prince George of Denmark, at whose expense the first edition of Flamsteed's book had been printed. These Halley and Newton papers—being on loose sheets—are now arranged with the Mathematical and Mathematico-Physical MSS.

Books with MS. Notes and additions.

Of works in Natural History, may be noticed the *Hortus Indicus Malabaricus* (12 vols. fol. 1673-1703); the *Hortus Eystettensis* (original edition of 1613): the *Hortus Elthamensis*; the *Hortus Gramineus Woburnensis* (Fol. 1816); a set of the works of Conrad Gesner, and another of those of Aldrovandi; a fine copy of Dr. Martin Lister's *Historia Conchyliorum* (1685-92); and a copy of John de Cuba's curious Cyclopædia of the Natural History of Mediæval Times, translated into French, copiously adorned with woodcuts, and printed at Paris by Antoine Verard, about the year 1500, under the title: *Le Jardin de Santé.*

Choice Works in Natural History;—

The curiosities in the section "Arts and Trades" are less conspicuous than in other departments; but they include some rare books and tracts on the Plastic Arts; on Music; on Perspective; on Printing; and on Metallurgy. There is a fine copy of the *Arcano del Mare*—a work which belongs partly to Hydrography, partly to the Art of Navigation—of Robert Dudley, titular Duke of Northumberland, printed at Florence between the years 1647 and 1661, and of great rarity in a complete

And in Arts and Trades.

* The British Museum appears not to possess even the first volume of this remarkable book.

form; a copy of the *General and Rare Memorials pertayning to the perfect Arte of Navigation* (1577) of Dr. John Dee; and a precious copy of Sir Henry Wotton's *Elements of Architecture*, copiously annotated in the autograph of Sir Christopher Wren.

Choice Editions of Greek Classics.

Of the choice editions of Greek Classics,—which form section first of the class LITERATURE,—the Florence Homer—but the *Iliad* only—claims the first place; next to this may come (2) a fine copy of the Complete Works, in the rare edition printed at Rome, 1542-1550, with the Commentary of Eustathius and the Index of Devarius;—(3) the first edition of the works of Quintus Calaber, Tryphiodorus, and Coluthus, printed by Aldus in 1505;—(4) the Aldine Pindar with Callimachus, Dionysius, and Lycophron, of 1513;—(5) the superb Pindar printed at Rome by Calliergi in 1515;—(6) the excessively rare Aldine Theocritus, &c., of 1495;—(7) the first edition of the Dialogues of Lucian (1496), commonly ascribed to the press of the Giunti, but more probably printed by Lorenzo de Alopa; and (8) the collection of Gnomic poets printed at Paris in 1507, remarkable as the first dated Greek book which proceeded from a French press. Here also may be mentioned a diglott translation from Lucian, entitled, "*Necromantia, a dialog of the Poet Lucyan, for his fantesye faynyd for a mery pastyme,*" in Latin and English, printed by John Rastell about 1520, which is both scarce and curious.

Choice Editions of Latin Classics.

Amongst the conspicuous Latin Classics may be enumerated (1) the Ovid of 1492-1498, printed at Venice;—(2) the Lyons Ovid of 1513;—(3) the Aldine Silius Italicus of 1523 (containing, for the first time, the doubtful verses which begin "*Vidi constructas nostræ Carthaginis arces;*"—(4) A copy of the Paris Claudian of 1511, noticeable for its copious MS. notes in a 16th century hand;—(5) a copy of the Antwerp Virgil of 1575, interleaved with curious plates engraved after the illuminations of a MS. which is one of the show-books of the Vatican Library; (6) the excessively rare version of Virgil "into Scottish meter" by Gawin Douglas, printed in 1553; and (7) the firstfruits of the celebrated Venetian press of Nicholas Jenson, in the Letters of Cicero to Atticus, Brutus, and Q. Cicero, printed in 1470, and which is probably quite as well entitled to the epithet "Editio princeps" as the edition printed at Rome, in the same year, by Sweynheym and Pannartz, to which that distinction is usually given. The *Oratiunculæ Elegantiores ex diversis Marci Ciceronis Epistolis*, printed in Gothic type of the fifteenth century, is wholly without note of impression.

Amongst other tracts and books which, like that just named, may be regarded as curiosities of printing, must be mentioned the *Ars Oratoria, Ars Epistolandi, et Ars memorativa,* of Jacobus Publicius, with mnemonic woodcuts, in an edition of 1490, almost unknown to bibliographers; *Historia Daretis de Excidio Troiæ*, printed at Wittemberg, by Joannes Viridimontanus in 1512;—the *Isagogicus libellus in Eloquentiæ præcepta*, of Agostino Dati, printed at Paris by Ulrich Gering; the *Ars Epistolarum conficiendarum* of Guillermus Saphonensis, wholly without date or other note of impression;—the *De Arte Versificandi libri tres*, of Robert Gaguin, printed at the same press, probably about 1478; and the *Hystoria Destructionis Troiæ* of Guido delle Colonne, also without note of impression, but probably printed about 1480.

English Classics.

The rare editions of English Classics comprise (1) the *Venus and Adonis* of 1602, of which heretofore, according to the statement of Lowndes, two copies only were known to exist;—(2) the first edition of the *Paradise Lost* (1667, but with the reprinted title page in which the date is altered to 1669); (3) the first edition of *The Faerie Queene* (Part I, 1590; Part II, 1596);—the first edition of *Colin Clout* (1595);—the *Visions* and *Muiopotmos* of 1590; (4) the first edition of *The Advancement of Learning*;—(5) the first collective edition of Skelton's Poems (1568);—(6) the *Vision of Pierce Plowman, of* 1561, a copy which is enriched with curious MS. Notes, chiefly philological;—and (7) the rare Collected Works of Sir Thomas More, printed in 1557. And among Foreign Classics are observable a copy of the Aldine Petrarch of 1514, with the obnoxious political sonnets, not (as they are in so many copies) cut out, but erased with a pen, and subsequently restored in MS.;—copies of two out of the four rare editions of the *Quixote* which were printed in 1605 (those, namely, of Valencia and of Lisbon);—and the first edition (1617) of *Los trabaios de Persiles y Sigismunda.*

Foreign Classics.

Rare and Notable Works in Linguistics.

The Philological department also abounds—as might be expected from the prominence of that feature in the Jones Collection—in rare and remarkable books. On the Latin language we find (1) an abridgement of the work of Laurentius Valla, in a volume, without date or imprint, but which may, conclusively, be traced to the press of Gering, Crantz, and Friburger, the joint introducers of printing into France, and to a date at least as early as 1471;—(2) the *Promptorium Puerorum, sive Medulla Grammaticæ*, in the excessively rare first edition printed by Pynson in 1499; and also in the edition printed by Wynkyn de Worde in 1516. This work may be regarded as the first in the long list of Latin-English Dictionaries, and has been variously ascribed to Richard Francis, a Dominican Friar, and to "Galfridus Grammaticus," of whom nothing but the name seems to be known;—(3) the Vocabulary of John Stanbridge, also in editions printed by Pynson (1519); and by Wynkyn de Worde (1523); respectively;—(4) a series—nine in number—of the Grammatical Tracts of Robert Whittington of Lichfield, all printed by Wynkyn de Worde, between the years 1521 and 1524;—(5) an English "Orthography" by John Hart, Chester Herald (1569), merits remark as one of the earliest of the "phonetic" attempts to improve the language of Shakespeare. An "*Introductorie for to lerne Frenche trewly,*" by Gilles Du Wes, was written for the instruction of Queen Mary when a youth, and was printed about 1540-45. On the Welsh language there is a series of printed works, all of which are of great rarity, and some of them have copious MS. notes and additions. One of them is the first book printed (1546) in Welsh. Another is a grammatical treatise—*Dosparth byrr ar yrhan gyntaf i Ramadeg*—published by a Welshman, Dr. Griffith Roberts, at Milan in 1567.* Some Grammars of the same language occur amongst the Welsh MSS. There are also elementary books on the language of the Indians of New England. Among the Grammatical treatises on the Oriental languages occur Tissard's Hebrew Grammar of 1508—the first work printed in France which contains Hebrew characters—and the *Introductio in Chaldaicam linguam, &c., of* Ambrogio de' Albonesi, printed by Simonetta at Papia, in 1539, and of which some curious characteristics are mentioned by Ebert.

Works on Welsh Language.

A few books of miscellaneous contents have yet to be noticed. In the first rank amongst these is a superb copy, on vellum, of the *Natural History* of Pliny, printed at Rome by Sweynheym and Pannartz in 1470. This volume would rank among the choicest treasures of the richest libraries. Its interest is enhanced by a record of its history for the last three centuries. In the sixteenth, it belonged to an eminent collector and man of letters, François de La Croix du Maine, by whom it was given to Nicholas Michael Du Prat—"amicum suum integerrimum." From him it passed to a certain "Dns. de Savigni," who, in turn, presented it to the Library of the College of Jesuits at Caen in 1616. There it remained until 1794, when the community, "in æternum grati animi monumentum," gave it to their benefactor Foucault, from whose collection it passed, with so many other conspicuous and splendid volumes, into that of the Lord Chancellor Macclesfield.

The Vellum Pliny.

"*The Kalender of the Shepherdes*" is a singular medley of the Astrology, the Ethics, and the Poetry of the Middle Ages. It was originally compiled in French, by an unknown author, and contains astronomical tables which seem to fix its date at 1497. This edition of the English translation—which had previously appeared at Paris—was printed by Wynkyn de Worde in 1511. Its rarity is so great that there is no mention of it either by Dibdin or by Lowndes. "*The Dia-*

Kalendar of Shepherds.

* "In every place things often occur where they are least expected. I was shown a Welsh Grammar, written in Welsh and printed at Milan, I believe, before any Grammar of that language had been printed here."—Johnson to Sir Frederick Augusta Barnard, on the formation of a Library.

logues of Creatures moralized" is of Latin origin; is ascribed to the press of Rastall by Ames, but, according to Herbert, was printed on the Continent. The "*Margarita Philosophica*" may be described as a Mediæval Encyclopædia, printed in 1503, and copiously adorned with woodcuts. "*Les Parables maistre Alain*" is also precious for its curious woodcuts, and this edition (printed by Antoine Verard at Paris in 1492) is also of excessive rarity.

Dialogues of Creatures.

Margarito Philosophica.

Finally, must be mentioned the Caxton volume, entitled, *The Mirrour of the World*, "translated," as Caxton tells us, "out of Latin into "French, by the ordinance of the noble duke, John, of Berry and Au- "vergne, in...1245, and now at this time rudely translated out of French "into English by me simple person William Caxton, at the request, "desire, cost and dispense, of . . Hugh Bryce, Alderman and Citizen "of London." This precious volume is of the first edition; was printed in Westminster Abbey in 1481; and is the first English book which is illustrated by woodcuts. Only eight perfect copies of it are known to exist, and of these, three are in public libraries. A copy of it was sold by auction, in 1682, for five shillings. In 1812, a copy was sold, also by auction, for three hundred and fifty-one pounds.

The Shirburn Caxtons.

There is another beautiful Caxton volume which, as it has not been mentioned in its proper class, claims a word of notice here. This comprises the two treatises of Cicero, *De Senectute*, and *De Amicitia*, translated into English, from the French version of Premierfait. To these is added a translation of Buonaccorsi da Montemagno's "*Declamation of Nobility*," also translated from a French version, but originally written in Latin. The treatise *Of Friendship* and the *Declamation* were translated (as Caxton testifies) by that eminent lover of literature, John Tiptoft, Earl of Worcester. Only twelve perfect copies are known, seven of which are in public libraries. A copy was sold in the sixteenth century for three pence; another copy, in 1698, for four shillings and two pence. The last copy offered for sale—in 1857—produced two hundred and seventy-five pounds. It had adorned successively the libraries of Mr. Willett at Merly, of the Duke of Marlborough at White Knights, and of Mr. Watson Taylor in Wiltshire. It now belongs to Mr. Huth. These three treatises are usually regarded as forming a single volume, but the registers are duplicate, and it is probable that they were issued apart, as well as together. The Shirburn Caxtons are in choice condition, and have been recently put into suitable morocco coats, by Hatton of Manchester.

CHAPTER XI.

THE LIFE OF CHARLES SPENCER, THIRD EARL OF SUNDERLAND.—HISTORY OF THE SUNDERLAND LIBRARY AT BLENHEIM PALACE.

Andrew. Unload part of the Library, and make room
For th' other dozen of carts; I'll strait be with you.
Cook. Why, hath he more books?
And. More than ten marts send over.
Butler. And can he tell their names?
And. Their names! He has 'em
As perfect as his *Pater Noster*. But that's nothing;......
If all thy pipes of wine were filled with books,
Made of the barks of trees, or mysteries writ
In old moth-eaten vellum, he would sip thy cellar
Quite dry, and still be thirsty.—

The Elder Brother, Act I, Scene ii.

Like his almost life-long rival Robert Harley, Charles Spencer, third Earl of Sunderland, had an equally ardent passion for literature, and for the glorious strife of statesmanship. No man knew better how to enjoy and how to dignify retirement, and very few men have wrestled more strenuously to avoid it. Nearly twelve years of his short life were passed in high offices of State, and almost the half of that official period was spent under Queen Anne, who mortally hated him. The other half embraced those early years of the next reign, in which the contests of politicians too often resembled the combats of those ancient

Retiarii who fought with nets, as well as with sharp-pointed weapons.

Charles Spencer was the second but only surviving son of Robert, second Earl of Sunderland, and fourth Lord Spencer of Wormleighton, by the Lady Anne Digby. He was the grandson of the first Earl—twentieth in lineal descent* from Thurstan Le Despencer, Steward to King Henry I—who fell at Newbury, and of peerless Sacharissa,

Lord Sunderland's parentage and descent.

> "To whom a wild and cruel soul was given,
> More deaf than trees, and prouder than the Heaven;"

and seems to have inherited many of the brilliant qualities which are conspicuous in the lineage, both of the Digbys and of the Sidneys. He was born in 1673, and much of his early education was entrusted to a Genevese tutor of great ability, named Florival. He also studied at Utrecht.† As early as 1688, John Evelyn, who was very intimate with the Sunderland family, speaks of him as a "youth of extraordinary hopes, very learned for his age, and ingenious.‡ He was but twenty when Evelyn wrote to him:—"I was with great appetite coming to take a repast in the noble library which I hear you have lately purchased."§ Two years later the same agreeable writer diarizes thus:—"My Lord Spencer shewed me his library, now again improved by many books bought at the sale of Sir Charles Scarburgh, an eminent physician, which was the very best collection, especially of mathematical books, that was, I believe, [to be seen] in Europe, [and was] once designed for the King's Library at Saint James', but the Queen dying—who

Evelyn's character of him, in his youth.

* According to what seems to be the best authenticated of the Spencer pedigrees—that contained in Harleian MS. 3165.

† The earliest letters of his which I have seen were written to Evelyn from Utrecht. They are now preserved among the Additional MSS., B. M., 15949, 21-28.

‡ Ib. II, 279.

§ Evelyn, *Diary and Correspondence* (1850) III, 336.

was the great patroness of that design—it was let fall."*... This visit was made by Evelyn in March, 1695. In April, 1699, he again records Lord Spencer's purchase of "an incomparable library, wherein, among other rare books, were several that were printed at the first invention of that art," or were otherwise remarkable, as more particularly, "Tully's Offices, . . . a Homer, and a Suidas."†

Marriages of the third Earl of Sunderland.

The first marriage of Lord Spencer (January 12th, 1695) was to the Lady Arabella Cavendish, daughter and coheiress of Henry, Duke of Newcastle, K.G.,‡ and its issue was an only daughter, Lady Frances, who married Henry Howard, afterwards Earl of Carlisle, K.G. The Lady Arabella dying on the 4th June, 1698, Lord Spencer contracted a second alliance, in the following year, with the Lady Anne Churchill, second daughter and coheiress of John, Duke of Marlborough. This lady was as exemplary for her intellectual accomplishments and her Christian virtues as for that superb beauty which Lely has perpetuated. She appears to have been the one person in the world who always retained the unabated affection of Duchess Sarah, and who could at all times conciliate that haughty and impracticable temper, which was usually at

* Evelyn, *Diary and Correspondence*, 334. This Scarburgh collection also contained many curious tracts. (*Bibliotheca Scarburghiana* [1694], pp. 37-40.)

† Ib., 352.

‡ "You had not heard the news of my Lord Spencer's marriage from any one before me, had there not once been a rub in it...... She has £25,000, and ...a good report. I beseech God to give both them and us his blessing in this weighty affair, that she may prove every way a good wife for a very honest, worthy, goodnatured man, as indeed I think he is, without partiality."—*Countess of Sunderland to Evelyn*, 15 Oct. 1694. *Additional Manuscripts* in B. M. 15889. By a singular blunder of the former possessor of this MS., Mr. Upcott, a portrait of Anne *Churchill*, Countess of Sunderland, has been inserted as that of the writer of the letters.

least as formidable to friends as to enemies. Some touching memorials of her are preserved at Blenheim. A little before her death she wrote a farewell letter to her husband, to be given to him after the anticipated event, which concludes in these words:—"'Tis hard to part with one so much beloved, and in whom there was so much happiness as you, my dearest, ever were to me. My last prayers shall be to the Lord Almighty to give you all blessings in this world, and to grant that we may meet, happy, in the next." This excellent woman died on the 15th April, 1716. Marlborough's second son had died in infancy. His eldest son, a youth of great promise, died in 1703. His honours and chief estates descended (1722) to his eldest daughter, Henrietta, Duchess of Marlborough. Her only son, the second Lord Blandford, died before her, in 1731. On her own death, in 1733, the honours and entailed estates of the illustrious Duke passed, by virtue of the Act of 6th of Queen Anne, and of the Duke's testamentary dispositions—and after four intermediate deaths—to the Spencer line.

Lord Spencer entered Parliament in 1695, having been returned both for Heydon in Yorkshire, and for Tiverton in Devonshire. He elected to sit for Tiverton, and continued to represent that borough as long as he was a Commoner. In the great struggle on the Bill against Occasional Conformity, he sided with the opponents. His first public employment was as Envoy Extraordinary to Vienna, to congratulate the Emperor Joseph on his accession, and to offer, in the due diplomatic forms, the Queen's mediation on behalf of the insurgent Hungarians. Lord Sunderland (he had succeeded his father on the 28th September, 1702) set out for the Hague on the 6th of June, 1705; had

The Embassy to Vienna.

several conferences with the Duke of Marlborough, in whose company he visited the army; and then proceeded to Vienna. His negotiation was beset with many difficulties. The copious correspondence about it, preserved in the State Paper Office, shows that Lord Sunderland was soon led to the conclusion that no good result, as regards Hungary, could be attained at that juncture. "*Till* I came out of England," he wrote on one occasion, "I thought that we did abound in the passions of envy and malice more than any other nation."*

The dread of Lord Sunderland expressed at Vienna.

But, in truth, envy at home may well have had its direct share in increasing the difficulties abroad. Count Wratislaw's letters to Marlborough,† at this time, abound in expressions like these:—"I dread Lord Sunderland's inclination to establish a species of republic in Hungary." —"I dread the republican principles of Lord Sunderland, and the malicious spirit of Mr. Stepney, whom England has, by an unfortunate fatality, associated with Lord Sunderland in the mediation."—"I again repeat my apprehensions on the subject of Lord Sunderland, for Mr. Stepney will inflame him as much as possible; and as his Lordship is naturally devoted to the liberty of the people, he will perhaps act with more warmth than he ought;" with much more in a like strain. These "apprehensions," felt at Vienna, were, perhaps, of English growth. Lord Sunderland took an active part in the conferences at Tyrnau and at Presburgh. The Duke of Marlborough joined him at Vienna, and if but little was accomplished for Hungary, vigorous measures were agreed upon for the prosecution of the war against the common enemy. With a like purpose, the great Captain and the Envoy visited, in

* Foreign Correspondence, MS., S. P. O., *Germany*, vol. clxxxiv.
† *Blenheim Papers.* [Printed by Coxe.]

company, the Courts of Berlin, of Hanover, and of the Hague, in their homeward route.

Lord Sunderland a Commissioner for the Union.

After his return to England, he was made one of the Commissioners for concluding the Union with Scotland. It appears from a document in the Paper Office that it was Lord Sunderland who gave De Foe the employment which resulted in the remarkable account of that business which we owe to his pen.* Then followed the resolute effort of the Whigs to make Sunderland Secretary of State, in the room of Sir Charles Hedges, and in spite of the Queen's stubborn resistance.

The struggle to make Sunderland Secretary of State.

Anne's rooted antipathy to Lord Sunderland has been variously but not very clearly explained. Nor, indeed, does it seem to stand much in need of explanation. Both his opinions and his character were directly repugnant to hers. What they had in common, seems to have been a love of opposite extremes. And the man who was now to be turned out, to make room for Sunderland, had the inestimable merit, in the Queen's eyes, of belonging to no party in particular. The Duchess of Marlborough was foremost in pressing Lord Sunderland's claims. "To make a party man Secretary of State," remonstrated the Queen, "is throwing myself into the hands of a party."…. "Why must I be made so miserable as to be brought into the power of one set of men?" with much more in that familiar strain. Marlborough tried in vain to moderate the Duchess' zeal for their son-in-law. "I have really so much esteem and kindness for him," he wrote, "and have so much knowledge of the place you would have for him,

* To my Lord Sunderland's goodness I had many years ago been obliged, when I was, on a secret commission, sent to Scotland."—Defoe to Delafaye, *Domestic Papers*, MS., S. P. O., Geo. I, xii, 319, &c.

that I have my apprehensions he will be very uneasy in it."*

Lord Sunderland was appointed to the Secretaryship of the Southern Province on the 3rd December, 1706, after the contest of tongues and pens had continued nearly six months. His office was, as Marlborough had predicted, a very uneasy one. And the peculiar position in the Government of the Duke himself, and of the Lord Treasurer Godolphin, increased the discomfort. Their wish seems to have been to sit aloft, in proud independence, both of Whigs and Tories, and jointly to sway the balance to either side at pleasure. Of such trimming courses Sunderland was, perhaps, of all men living the most impatient, but ardent as was his opposition to it, he acted in close accordance with the counsels of veteran statesmen. The distrust between these near connections came at length to such a height that, for a brief interval, Sunderland and the great Duke were almost estranged. Towards the close of 1707 we find Marlborough writing to his wife:—"I send you back Lady Sunderland's letter, that you may read it once more; for I think it is plain they believe that Lord Treasurer and I have a mind to bring in the Tories, *which is very obliging.*" And, in 1708, Sunderland writes to the Duke of Newcastle:—"Affairs seem to grow worse every day at home. . . . . If there is not a just spirit shewn in Parliament, we had as good give up the game, and *submit to my Lord Treasurer and Lord Marlborough bringing in the Prince of Wales.*"† But this estrangement was very transient. Some part of Sunderland's correspondence at the same period is in a more hopeful strain. He characterises the Parliament of 1708 as "the most 'Wig' Par-

Sunderland's Secretaryship, 1706—10.

* *Blenheim Papers.* [Printed by Coxe.]

† Sunderland letters in the Lansdowne MS., 1236, f. 237.

liament that has been since the Revolution."* The Queen and her favourites watched, nevertheless, with eagerness for a pretext to dismiss him, yet dared take no step in that direction without cautiously feeling the ground on which Marlborough stood. An occurrence in Scotland, in the autumn of 1708, gave opening for a charge that Sunderland had exceeded his powers, and it became known that the Queen intended to deprive him of the seals. Marlborough instantly wrote to her:—"I did flatter myself that nobody could have prevailed with you . . to give me so great a mortification in the face of all Europe, at a time when I was so zealously endeavouring to serve your Majesty, at the hazard both of my reputation and of my blood."† This letter was written in the same week with that, above quoted, from Sunderland to the Duke of Newcastle. The political embroglio had the additional and curious complication, that whilst the management of the Navy was the thing most loudly condemned by the Whigs, the real administrator of naval affairs—under the titular Lord High Admiralship of Prince George—was Marlborough's Tory brother, George Churchill. "It is impossible," wrote Sunderland, in the Autumn of 1708, "to go on longer with the Court upon the foot things are at present. . . . The management of the Fleet is . . the most scandalous of all . . and is never to be cured but by the Prince's quitting. Whatever Council he has, George Churchill will in effect be always Lord High Admiral."‡ Marlborough's remonstrances delayed the striking of the blow at Lord Sunderland. Prince George's death prevented the public exposure of the schism in the administration.§

Marlborough prevents Sunderland's dismissal in 1708.

* Sunderland letters in the Lansdowne MS. 1236, f. 235.

† *Blenheim Papers.* [Printed by Coxe.]

‡ Lansdowne MS., 1236, f. 239.

§ "The death of the Prince has made so great an alteration in every-

Sunderland at length dismissed.

In the height of the Sacheverel folly, when several parts of England exhibited the spectacle of thousands of horsemen escorting a poor fanatic, and of the very roadside hedges being dressed up with flowers in his honour, it was determined to dismiss Sunderland from the Secretaryship, at all risks. "This is a resolution which I have long taken, and nothing shall divert me from it," were the Queen's words to Somers. In vain did Marlborough write:—"Such a step will in a great measure render me incapable of being useful to Her Majesty's affairs, either at home or abroad." Somers counselled him to restrain his indignation. "The most effectual way," said he, "of finally disappointing and punishing your enemies is to take no notice of what they do." The Whig leaders, collectively, addressed to Marlborough a remarkable letter to the same effect, conjuring him not to leave his great work unfinished. All the English ministers abroad received elaborate instructions that Sunderland's ejection had not arisen "out of the least unkindness or diminution of favour to the Duke of Marlborough,"* and similar assurances were even addressed directly, by the Queen's command, to foreign sovereigns.† The Tories were almost frantic with exultation. "Your Majesty is now Queen indeed," said the Duke of Beaufort. Observant bystanders of a cooler temperament made quite other reflections on the event. The Governor and Directors of the Bank of England presented an address to the Queen on the injurious effects of the Secretary's dismissal. "My Lord Sunderland," wrote De Foe, "leaves office with the most unblemished charac-

thing......that our friends press us to accommodate matters."—Sunderland to Newcastle, Lansdowne MS., 1236, f. 244.

* *Foreign Correspondence*, MS., S. P. O., *Germany*, vol. cxcvi.

† Ib., *Royal Letters*.

ter . . . of any statesman in the world." But Sunderland's own act on this occasion makes eulogy superfluous. The Queen, very conscious that the most zealous service from that quarter had been borne "with all the uneasiness imaginable,"* as long as the servant remained in office, signified her intention to bestow on him, now that she was rid of his presence, a pension of three thousand pounds a year. "No," said the ejected statesman; "I am glad your Majesty is satisfied I have done my duty. But if I cannot have the honour to serve my country, I will not plunder it."

One of the first acts of King George I was to confer on Lord Sunderland the office of Lord Lieutenant of Ireland, but he did not cross the Channel, although he held that great post, nominally, for nearly a year. In August, 1715, he became Lord Privy Seal, and shortly afterwards Vice-Treasurer of Ireland. In April, 1717, he was made, for the second time, one of the Secretaries of State. On the 16th of March following he became Lord President of the Council, and five days afterwards (21 March, 1718) First Lord Commissioner of the Treasury, which office he retained until the 3rd of April, 1721.†

Lord Sunderland's employments under George I.

The most salient events of Lord Sunderland's ministry at home, are the repeal of the Schism Act; the introduction of his colleague Stanhope's abortive Peerage Bill; and the long and bitter conflicts which grew out of the South Sea delusion. The first-named measure accomplished far less than the minister desired, but it was owing to his moderation and parliamentary skill that the Dissenters owed even that small instalment of relief. And, after a very few years

Chief measures of Sunderland's administration.

* These were Anne's own words to Godolphin on this occasion.

† *Treasury Minute Book*, S. P. O., xxiii, 43.

had passed, those disabling Acts which remained on the Statute Book became oppressive only in words. The object of the famous Peerage Bill was alleged to be "the settling the Peerage of the whole kingdom upon such a foundation as may secure the freedom and constitution of Parliament in all future ages." The most memorable thing about it, now, is that it led to a keen contest of the pen between Addison and Steele. It would undoubtedly have provided an adequate check to a possible or a remotely contingent abuse of royal prerogative, but it would have done this by certainly stripping the Peerage of some of its noblest functions. It is not the least scandalous incident of the party conflicts of that age that, to all appearance, the measure would have passed into law, but for the vigorous opposition of Walpole, who, six months later, was ready to support its re-introduction.*

The South Sea disaster, in which, or in its remoter consequences, so many reputations were wrecked, has left no stain on Lord Sunderland's character. He was a loser, not The South Sea disaster. a gainer, by the stock which he had purchased. And the emoluments of his high offices left him a poorer man, it has been authoritatively said, than he was when he entered on them. He was very covetous of power and of honour, but far from being covetous of money.

Whether in public or in private life, he was always liberal in his encouragement of literature. The noble library which he had begun almost in boyhood was the constant object of his solicitude, and of his open-handed

* In his able *History of England from the Peace of Utrecht*, (i, 547, 548) Lord Stanhope has shown that the defeat of his ancestor's Bill was owing to Walpole's opposition, and also that when he accepted office, in June, 1720, under Sunderland and Stanhope, Walpole was prepared to accept the Bill, too, substantially.

The formation of the Sunderland Library.

expenditure. He often experienced the truth of Selden's remark—"the giving a bookseller his price for his books has this advantage: He that will do so, shall have the refusal of whatsoever comes to the bookseller's hand." Humphrey Wanley's curious Diary shows with what jealousy the rapid growth of the collection at Sunderland House was watched by some neighbourly eyes. Thus, when recording a book-sale in 1721, he says:—"Some books went for unaccountably high prices, which were bought by Mr. Vaillant, the bookseller, who had an unlimited commission from the Earl of Sunderland. . . . The booksellers upon this sale intend to raise the prices of philological books of first editions, and indeed of all old editions, accordingly. Thus, Mr. Noel told me that he has actually agreed to sell the Earl of Sunderland six . . printed books, now coming up the river, for fifty pounds per book, *although my Lord* [Oxford] *gives no such prices!*" On another occasion he registers his belief that the same bookseller, Noel, had been offered "two hundred guineas to let the Earl of Sunderland have the preference, before all others, as to the buying of his old books."*

Description of the library, as it stood in Sunderland House.

Lord Sunderland's library was kept in his town house, which stood between Sackville Street and Burlington House, and with its gardens extended, in depth, from Piccadilly to Glasshouse Street. The library occupied a continuous series of five lofty rooms, one hundred and fifty feet in length, and lighted by two ranges of windows, and had galleries throughout its whole extent. It appears to have contained, in 1722, about twenty thousand volumes, of which more than a third were folios. According to a

* *Diary of Humphrey Wanley* [Librarian to Lord Oxford], Lansdowne MS., 771, ff. 50, 12, verso. See also, another MS. of Wanley's in the Lansdowne Collection, No. 677, ff. 9, 10.

contemporary estimate—the grounds of which I am unacquainted with—its cost had exceeded thirty thousand pounds. As far as regards printed books, it was undoubtedly the choicest library which had yet been gathered in England.* As far as regards choice and rare editions of the great authors of antiquity, it was then probably unsurpassed either at home or abroad. Yet this was not its main characteristic. It was, emphatically, the library of a statesman. It contained all the great sources of knowledge on the History and the Politics of all the States of Europe, and of some non-European States, in the best vernacular editions of the best authors, whose works had appeared up to the end of the year 1720. It also contained the finest and most valuable editions of the Holy Bible in many languages. It included many of the curiosities of mediæval literature, and the best editions of the classics of modern Europe. Lord Sunderland had also obtained—chiefly from Venice†—some very choice manuscripts, but at all times his favourite object was to collect fine printed books.

Sunderland in retirement.

Sunderland resigned office in April, 1721. With Walpole and Townshend he had never acted cordially, and their influence was now predominant in Parliament. His alleged intrigues with the Jacobite party rest, not on evidence, but on the rumours and the suspicions of political opponents. Those who may have occasion to undertake

* MS. Catalogues of the Sunderland Library (Blenheim MSS.), *passim*; Seymour [*i. e.* John Mottley?] *Survey of London*, II, 664.

† "I received a letter acquainting me that Mr. Smith, of Venice, has actually sold his MSS. (during his treaty with my Lord...) to the Earl of Sunderland for fifteen hundred pounds, and has received part of the money." Wanley's *Diary*, Lansd. MS. ut supra, f. 34. "I went to the Earl of Sunderland's to look into the MSS. his Lordship bought of Mr. Smith, of Venice, and to take some account of his Greek Manuscripts. —Ib. 70, verso.

the weary task of reading what is termed the "Hanover Correspondence" of that period,* will not, I think, derive from it such impressions of the motives and aims of the Walpoleites as to attach much weight to their unsupported aspersions. And it is certain that some of the still current accounts of the party conflicts of Sunderland's day—accounts which have been endorsed by great writers—rest, in essential points, upon the merest gossip. If the current versions be really the true ones, their truth has yet to be shown.

That interval of calm reflection between the strife of politics and the long rest, which one would fain think must be at least an object of desire to every statesman who is worthy of his calling, was in Lord Sunderland's case very brief indeed. He retained, in his retirement, the keenest interest in the old strife, and, as there is good reason to believe, no small influence on the mind of the sovereign. He died, after a short illness, on the 19th of April, 1722, and in the forty-ninth year of his age. Archbishop King, of Dublin, in a letter written a few days afterwards to his brother-prelate of Armagh, made a very natural reflection on the remarkable rapidity with which Death had thinned the ranks of Statesmen—"Halifax, Wharton, Burnet, Stanhope, Craggs, .. and now Sunderland, .. all snatched away by sudden and unexpected deaths."† It seemed almost to have been destined that the bitter rivalries of politicians should (to use Lord Stanhope's expressive phrase) be "closed up with coffins."

Lord Sunderland's death.

Very different was the reflection on the public loss which another contemporary hastened to note down in his Diary:

* In S. P. O., under the Heading "Regencies."

† King, Archbishop of Dublin, to the Archbishop of Armagh. Additional MSS. in Brit. Mus., 6117, ff. 73, 74 (15 May, 1722).

—"This day died the Earl of Sunderland, which I the rather note here, because I believe that by reason of his decease some benefit may accrue to this Library, *even in case his relations will part with none of his books.* I mean, *by his raising the price of books no higher now;* so that, in probability, this commodity may fall in the market; and any gentleman be permitted to buy an uncommon old book for less than forty or fifty pounds."* Such were Wanley's thoughts when one of his foremost countrymen was struck down, while yet in the full vigour of faculty and of ambition.

His surviving family.

Sunderland (whose eldest son had died in infancy) was succeeded by Robert, his second son, who became fourth Earl of Sunderland, but survived his father little more than seven years. He died in Paris, unmarried, in November, 1729, and was succeeded by his next brother, Charles, fifth Earl of Sunderland, and eventually second Duke of Marlborough. The fourth and last brother, John (the "Jack Spencer" who figures so conspicuously in the later correspondence of Duchess Sarah), became the founder of the present line of Spencers of Althorp. Earl Charles' two daughters by Lady Anne Churchill married, respectively, William, Lord Bateman, and John, Duke of Bedford. His three children by his third wife, Judith, daughter of Benjamin Tichborne, Esq., died in infancy.

Charles, fifth Earl of Sunderland, and second Duke of Marlborough.

Charles, fifth Earl of Sunderland, was a soldier, as well as a lover of books. He led the foot guards at Dettingen, and at the period of his death he was in active service in Westphalia. He succeeded to the honours of the Great Duke—after the extinction of seven intermediate lives—in

* *Diary of H. Wanley*, Lansd. MS., 772, f. 55.

1733, but did not succeed to the Marlborough estates, until the death of the Duchess Dowager in 1744. In accordance with the provisions which had been made in respect of that succession, he surrendered the Spencer estates to his brother. He continued to reside in Sunderland House, and took great interest in the noble library which his father had founded. His own additions to the collection were considerable, and include some books which figure among the special treasures of Blenheim. Amongst these are a finely illustrated copy of Clarendon's History, some choice books on Botany, and a copy of the noble Livy of 1470, printed by Vindelin de Spira, on vellum. But one other perfect copy, on vellum, is known to exist.* For this Duke, Bishop Hare drew up a brief *Manual of Bibliography*, illustrated with notes on the chief rarities of His Grace's own library.

The only Catalogue of the Library which had been made in the Founder's time was a mere Index, prepared, as it seems, by Paul Vaillant, the bookseller. In 1728, a Trust Inventory was prepared in three volumes, folio, under the direction of Bishop Hare. When the collection was removed to Blenheim it retained—speaking broadly—the arrangement which had been originally made in Sunderland House, so far as the very different construction of the rooms permitted. But, as respects the majority of the presses, only the contents of their *lower* shelves are in the great Library; those of the upper shelves being in another room, known at Blenheim as the "Bachelors' Row Library."

Arrangement of the Library at Blenheim.

In addition to the old Index compiled by Vaillant, there is a special and partial Catalogue of early editions, com-

* According to Brunet, only *one* perfect copy exists. But he was unacquainted with this Blenheim copy.

piled, I believe, by Dr. Nicholas Clagett, who was successively Bishop of St. Davids and of Exeter. King George III possessed another manuscript Catalogue of early editions at Blenheim, made by Jacob Bryant, and doubtless prepared with the express purpose of assisting in the collection of the Royal Library. This Catalogue is now in the British Museum.* There is, finally, at Blenheim, a very elaborate shelf-list, with appendices, made under the direction of Mr. Vaughan Thomas, in the years 1820-1822, in eighty volumes, quarto, but this is, of course, a mere inventory, and was drawn up for purposes connected with the administration of the Trust.

Its Indexes and Shelf-lists.

Jacob Bryant's memory is, in many ways, connected with the history of this magnificent library. He was the frequent guest of George, third Duke of Marlborough, whose friendship lasted as long as the life of the eminent scholar who had been his tutor at Oxford. The stores at Blenheim contributed to Bryant's works, and were augmented by his testamentary bequests. From his pen came the best portion of the text of the superb *Gemmarum Antiquarum Delectus* printed at the Duke's expense, towards the close of the last century. And many of the Blenheim books are enriched by his manuscript notes.

Connexion of J. Bryant with Blenheim Library.

But for untoward circumstances, a noble addition to the Sunderland Library would have been made by George, fourth Duke (1817—1840), the collector of the famous library at White Knights in Berkshire, and renowned in the annals of Bibliomania by his purchase, at the Duke of Roxburghe's sale in 1812, of the Valdarfer edition of

* MSS. K. Geo. III, Vols. 383 and 384. The first volume is an alphabetical catalogue of authors. The second, a shelf-list. The original slips, whence this Catalogue was made, were purchased for the Museum in 1838, and form the Additional MS. No. 11512.

The Marlborough Library at White Knights.

Boccaccio's *Decamerone*, at the price of two thousand two hundred and sixty pounds. The coveted volume is the only perfect copy of the Decameron, of 1471, which is known to have escaped those Florentine bonfires to which the alarmed auditors of Savonarola hastened to carry their books of amusement and ornaments of luxury, lest fires more terrible should await the owners. One of Boccaccio's admirers, it appears, could not make up his mind to the sacrifice, and bethought him of the expedient of lettering his treasure '*Concilium Tridenti*.' There was, and is, at Blenheim, another copy, wanting five leaves. The Roxburghe copy itself had been offered to Lord Sunderland for a hundred guineas, just a century before one of his great grandsons offered more than two thousand guineas for it, and was outbidden by another.

At White Knights was collected an extraordinary series of Missals, including the Bedford Missal (purchased for £698, in 1786), and another of books of Emblems. Amongst the editions of the Holy Scriptures was a copy of the second edition of Luther's version, on vellum, with others of great rarity and beauty. This collection included fine modern books as well as the choicest rarities of typography, and the bookrooms opened upon the loveliest of landscapes—

> "Through opening glades you saw a glittering scene,
> Lawns ever gay, and meadows ever green."

The library was dispersed in 1819. At that date, the keenness of competition amongst book-buyers was in check. The produce of the sale was scarcely fifteen thousand pounds. The collection had probably cost twenty-five thousand. That little Elysium in which the widest researches and the utmost refinements of arboriculture had been employed to heighten the prodigalities of Nature, was at length abandoned to the building speculators.

By the present Duke many important modern books have been added to his ancestral library, but they are kept apart. With the Sunderland library no additions have ever been incorporated, save those made by George, second Duke of Marlborough. Its aggregate contents are 21,800 volumes. Of these the superb great gallery—certainly one of the grandest rooms in Europe—contains 15,692. A few of the manuscripts are here, but the bulk of them is in the Second Library—arranged in wainscot presses—and in the Muniment Room. They are of the most varied character.

The Manuscripts at Blenheim.

First in interest comes a vast collection of the Correspondence of John, Duke of Marlborough, with Queen Anne, with the Lord Treasurer Godolphin, with the Earl of Sunderland, and with other English statesmen. Then follows the Duke's correspondence with foreign Sovereigns and Ministers of State, with Prince Eugene, and with the Electoral Family of Hanover. Much of Duchess Sarah's correspondence was, as is well known, destroyed by her own hands, but what survives of her collection of papers is here, as is also Lord Sunderland's own collection. There is also a remarkable series of military papers and plans illustrative of the great Duke's campaigns, and another relating to the building of Blenheim. Thus far, the Blenheim papers were known to, and largely laid under contribution by, Archdeacon Coxe.

But there are now at Blenheim twenty-eight volumes of the Duke's original letter books, which were wholly unknown in Coxe's time, and, indeed, were not discovered until 1842. These, at some unrecorded period, had been placed in one of a series of paper chests in a Muniment-room at Hensington, near Woodstock. The erection of a new muniment-room at Blenheim led to the examination of the Hensington chests and to the consequent recovery of these invaluable materials of history. The late Duke placed them in the hands of Sir George Murray, and they became the main foundation of the *Letters and Despatches* published, under his editorship, in 1845-46. Scarcely less curious was the recovery of the famous "pencilled note" written hastily on the field of Blenheim. This long-lost memorial of one of England's great days was found a few years ago in the leaves of a book on botany.

Discovery of the Letter Books of John, D. of Marlborough.

Amongst the manuscripts purchased by Lord Sunderland—other than those before-mentioned—are collections of papers on the history and politics of Spain and Italy, and some fine manuscripts of classic authors. Of later acquisition are some superb volumes of *Disegni* and of *Commissioni Ducali* by famous Venetian artists, which formerly belonged to Mr. Udny, British Consul at Venice.

Miscellaneous Manuscripts.

To enumerate the printed rarities at length would here be impracticable. It would need a chapter to itself, and that a long one. I can only attempt to indicate some of them, by samples.

The printed rarities at Blenheim.

The great series of *first* editions of the classic authors of antiquity amounts to nearly fifty several works, including many on vellum. It comprises the collective writings of Apollonius Rhodius, Apuleius, Aulus Gellius, Cæsar, Callimachus, Dioscorides, Euripides, Eutropius, Homer, Horace, Isocrates, Justin, Lactantius, Lucan, Lucian, Macrobius, Nepos, Phædrus, Plautus, Pompeius Festus, Sallust, Silius Italicus, Suetonius, Tacitus, Valerius Flaccus, and Valerius Maximus; the earliest *dated* editions of Livy and of Virgil, and the far-famed Zarottus Virgil, of 1472; for joy at the purchase of which (at forty-six pounds), Vaillant, Lord Sunderland's agent, threw up his hat in the auction room, as Wanley very grimly noted down for us, in his Diary.* This series also comprises the *Anthologia Epigrammatum Græcorum* of 1494; the *Astronomici Veteres* of 1499; together with many separate works—also in their earliest and choicest editions—of Aristotle, of Cicero, of Ovid, of the Plinies, of Plutarch, of Quintilian, and of Tacitus. In addition to these, there are many very early editions of the numerous classic authors, the precise date of whose first appearance in print is still matter of doubt and controversy. But rich as is the Blenheim Library in this coveted class of *Editiones principes et primariæ*, the extraordinary fulness of its collective *series* of the early editions of each great author, taken apart, is a note of its wealth more striking and conclusive still. In this particular, scarcely any private collection, I believe, can quite vie with it, except Lord Spencer's, —a collection which stands above all rivalry.

Early and rare Editions of Italian authors.

Amongst the rare editions at Blenheim of the great writers of modern Italy are conspicuous the Dante of 1472; the *Decamerone* of the same date (concerning Valdarfer's edition there is no need to add anything), and also those of 1516, 1522 (on vellum), and of 1527; the *Teseide* of 1475 (of such extreme rarity that a copy, not quite perfect, has sold for £160); the Petrarchs of 1470 and 1472; and the '*Satyræ*' of Francesco Filelfo, printed by Valdarfer in 1476.

Here, too, is a noble series of early and choice Bibles, beginning with the Mentz edition of 1462—the first Bible with a date—on vellum, and including fourteen editions printed from that year to 1490, together with the great Polyglot

* Lansdowne MS., 771, f. 50.

editions of the sixteenth and seventeenth centuries. The works both of the Fathers of the Church and of the chief writers of the Middle Ages are fine and numerous. Nor is the class of History less adequately represented. The Blenheim Library is scarcely worse provided in the curiosities and the chronological landmarks of that class, than in those standard histories, the collection of which from all parts of Europe was a special object of Lord Sunderland's care. There is a fine group of printed Mediæval Chronicles, including some that are marvels of typographic beauty. There are also a few superb books in Botany and in some other sections of Natural History, but they do not amount to a series. The weakest division of the library is that of Mathematics and Physics. The Poetry and the Criticism of Italy, France, and Spain,—up to about the middle of the last century—are usually present in their best editions. In English literature, the collection is respectable, but not rich.

Choice Works on Theology.

And in History, &c.

If we group together a few of the choicest rarities of printing, without regard to classification of subject, they will include,—amongst many others scarcely less worthy of mention,—the Durandus of 1459; the *Catholicon* of 1460; the Cicero, *De Officiis*, of 1465, on vellum; that of 1466; and the *Epistolæ ad Familiares* of 1467; the Subiaco Lactantius—the first book printed in Italy with a date—of 1465; the remarkable collection of tracts by various authors, printed by Ulrich Zell in 1467; Thomas Aquinas' *Secunda Secundæ* (Schoyffer), also of 1467; the Subiaco Augustinus of the same date; the Justiniani *Institutiones* (Schoyffer) of 1468; the Tacitus printed by Vindelin de Spira, probably in 1469; the Aulus Gellius (Peter de Maximis) of 1469; the Apuleius (uncastrated), the Lucan, and the Cæsar, of the same date, all printed by Sweynheym

Enumeration of a few of the special rarities of printing.

and Pannartz; the "Ex quo" *Vocabularium* (an abridgement of the *Catholicon*), printed by Bechtermütze at Elfeld, also in 1469; a Horace without any note of impression, printed with types resembling those employed at Schlussenried about 1469; the Livy (on vellum), the Virgil, and the Petrarch, of 1470, all printed by Vindelin de Spira; the Valerius Maximus of 1471, on vellum; the Laurentius Valla, and the *Liber de Remediis utriusque Fortunæ* of Adrian the Carthusian, both of the same date; and a most curious *Doctrinale* of Alexander de Villa Dei, wholly without note of impression, and certainly not of later date than 1471. It were easy, but needless, to continue the list, or to make another—which might as readily be a long one—of early printed books remarkable for certain points of peculiarity, as, for example, in respect of their illuminations, woodcuts, inserted water-colour drawings, early engravings, blooming capitals, and other specialities of illustration or of type. Many other books are notable for their bindings, former ownership, or manuscript notes. Eight Blenheim volumes, for instance, belonged to Jean Grollier. The series of Aldines contains many of conspicuous beauty, but, taken as a series, is surpassed in several other libraries.

Rare books at Blenheim of later date.

Among books of later date which are at once of special rarity, and of note in the History of Literature, Blenheim can boast fine copies of the works of Michael Servetus, of those of Giordano Bruni, and of the *Dialogos de Medallas, Inscriciones y otras Antiguedadas* of Antonius Augustinus, Archbishop of Tarragona. It has also, as would be expected, some noble large paper copies, and dedication copies, of books printed in Lord Sunderland's time, including the sumptuous Cæsar of 1712, dedicated to John, Duke of Marlborough. Of Servetus, it should be added, this collection possesses not only rare printed, but also manuscript works.

Finally, must be mentioned a copy of the excessively rare edition of the *Chronicle of England* (known, usually, as "Caxton's Chronicle"), without any note of impression, but printed with the types used in the *Speculum Christiani* of William de Machlinia.* I have been unable to find any mention of more than four copies of this edition, as known to bibliographers, and of these three are imperfect copies. Machlinia's Chronicle.

Taken as a whole, the collection at Blenheim may well be termed a magnificent library. And when the visitor calls to mind the short life and the intense devotion to politics of the statesman who collected it, the sight is likely to elicit almost as much of wonder as of admiration.

* Its collation is as follows:—Sign. *a*, in ten leaves, containing the table, and beginning thus:—"F[yrst] *in the prologue*"... Then, *B* to ȝ in eights; ꝛ, and *a a* to *d d*, also in eights. Then, *e e*, four leaves; ending with the words... "*com to the euerlasting lyfe in the blisse of heven.* amen." A full page has usually thirty-three, but sometimes thirty-four lines. Beginning and end—of the Chronicle—are identical with Caxton's edition of 1482. That has a colophon, but no prologue or table.

CHAPTER XII.

THE PUBLIC LIFE OF GEORGE JOHN, SECOND EARL SPENCER. —HISTORY OF THE SPENCER LIBRARY AT ALTHORP.

...... His honour,
Clock to itself, knew the true minute when
Exception bade him speak, and at that time
His tongue obeyed its hand. Who were below him
He us'd as creatures of another place,
And bow'd his eminent top to their low ranks,
Making them proud of his humility.

All's Well that ends Well, I, 2.

THAT old Despencer of the Plantagenet days who is recorded to have left behind him, amongst other and large possessions, a "Library of Bokes," must certainly have bequeathed his tastes with his blood. Besides three of the most conspicuous among English private libraries,—two existing and one dispersed,—collected by Spencers of the eighteenth and nineteenth centuries, we have evidence of minor but not undistinguished collections acquired by other Spencers. There is still at Althorp an old family collection, originally formed at Wormleighton, in Warwickshire, in the sixteenth century. There is also to be seen there the greater part of another collection, extending originally to some five thousand volumes, acquired by John, first Earl Spencer, from the executors of Dr. George, Head Master of Eton. In this collection brought from Eton was included a remarkable series of English tracts, which,

The Wormleighton Library at Althorp.

as it appears, is still preserved intact. Many of the rarer books of the George collection were exchanged from time to time, by the second Earl, for finer copies, as opportunity offered.

The George Collection at Althorp.

The author of the anonymous *Journey through England*, published in 1722, and usually ascribed to John Macky, narrates a visit paid to Althorp in the time of the founder of the present Blenheim Library—then lodged in those noble rooms of Sunderland House in London, which are mentioned in the preceding chapter—and says of the then Althorp collection (that, namely, which had been originally formed at Wormleighton), "the library is a spacious room; the books disposed in neat cases, and an antique busto over every case." Forty-three years later, Sir William Jones, then a youth of nineteen, luxuriated in the treasures of this library, as it had been enlarged by Earl John, and here a casual reading of Fortescue, *De laudibus legum Angliæ*, gave, it is believed, the decisive impulse to his choice of a profession. To Jones, in those days, the Althorp Library seemed already a splendid one. But if the books which preceded the earliest acquisitions of the second Earl could now be severed from the mass, they would doubtless look very insignificant. The "Spencer Library" of world-wide fame is, substantially, of his formation.

Early Accounts of the Althorp Library.

Both the great existing collections of the Spencers, when seen for the first time by those who care about books, are likely to leave impressions not soon effaced. But the impressions differ. The great library at Blenheim is so superb in its architecture and decoration as, in some degree, to dwarf the books. At Althorp the books produce their full effect. Several of the rooms are very handsome, but in all of them the books are, as they should be, salient.

Comparison of the Libraries at Althorp and at Blenheim.

And the long succession of rooms, with their variety of form and character, add perhaps to the charm. But, still more probably, lovers of books and of architecture will rest in the safe conclusion that each of these noble libraries has something which the other wants.

Descent of the Lords Spencer.

As I had occasion to note in the last chapter, the Lords Spencer descend from Lord Sunderland's youngest son, John Spencer, the favourite grandson of the old Duchess of Marlborough. Could the Duchess have had her will, England would have been deprived of some good statesmen. Among some letters and papers of hers preserved in Lord Macclesfield's library at Shirburn occur a curious passage or two, written in contemplation of her grandson's marriage. She took abundant delight in anticipating the future greatness of the younger branch, but insisted on making her splendid bequests contingent on the total abstinence both of John Spencer and of his sons from all public employments, and she would have entailed the abstinence with the estates, had English law given her the chance. The widow of Marlborough lived long enough to call the service of the Crown the "putting on of a fool's coat."

John Spencer married in 1734 Georgiana Caroline, third daughter of John Carteret, Earl Granville. John Spencer, the only son of this marriage, was created Viscount Spencer of Althorp in 1761, and Earl Spencer in 1765. He married Margaret, daughter of the Right Hon. Stephen Poyntz, and his only son, George John, the founder of the Spencer Library, succeeded him in the Earldom in 1783.

The second Earl Spencer was born on the 1st September, 1758. Few men have entered life under happier auspices of every kind. Fewer still have so completely and so

Youth and education of Lord Spencer — Tutorship of Sir Wm. Jones.

evenly realised the bright promises of a happy boyhood. He was but seven years of age when he was placed under the tutorship of William Jones—the future illustrious Orientalist—who, with the acquirements of an exceptionally studious man of thirty, was yet young enough and vivacious enough to unite, in an unusual degree, genial companionship with instruction. Tutor and pupil studied together at Wimbledon Park, at Harrow, and at Althorp; and together they made two continental tours, in the course of which they visited libraries as well as Courts. Jones cared little about "tall copies" or "large paper copies," but in more important points he had the tastes of a biographer as well as of a student. He seems, especially, to have had a keen zest for fine manuscripts. Towards the close of 1770 he resigned his tutorship, in order to enter upon his legal studies at the Temple. Dr. Heath succeeded to his charge; the pupil was not yet thirteen years old, but the best of the tutor's work was done. Jones and Lord Althorp corresponded frequently and cordially until 1783, when the former left England for his Indian judgeship. In one of the later letters of this correspondence, Jones assures Lord Althorp that his ancient affection had been "unchanged for a single moment," during an intimate acquaintance of some seventeen years. In many mouths such an assurance would be trivial enough. In Sir William Jones' mouth it was both a covetable testimony and a sure prediction. Lord Althorp had scarcely left Trinity College, Cambridge (to which he had proceeded from Harrow in due course), when he took his share of camp-life with the militia, then called out at Warley. Soon afterwards he made a third continental tour.

His subsequent correspondence with Jones.

Lord Althorp entered Parliament as member for Northampton in 1780, and bore his part in the overthrow of

Lord Spencer's parliamentary career.

Lord North's administration. He first addressed the House on the 30th November, 1781, in support of Mr. Thomas Pitt's motion for delaying the supplies. On the formation of the Rockingham ministry, March 27, 1782, he became a Lord of the Treasury. When Lord Rockingham's sudden death led to the remodelling of the Whig Government, under Lord Shelburne, he declined to continue in office. "I see and applaud the motive which must have induced you to resign an office which you were not at first much inclined to accept," wrote his old tutor to him on the occasion. In this first schism of the Whig party Lord Althorp followed Fox; in the next and memorable schism—ten years later—he was to oppose Fox, and to follow the Duke of Portland; but bitter as were the criminations and recriminations of that turbulent time, the perfect rectitude of Lord Spencer's motives was on both occasions admitted, even by those who disagreed most with his decision. He spoke in Parliament infrequently, and never acquired any conspicuous power of debate.* His great capacity for administrative labours was, as yet, unproved. But, already, no man carried with him more of the weight of personal character.

Ld. Spencer's Mission to Vienna.

The death of his father in 1783 (Oct. 31) removed Lord Althorp from the representation of the county of Surrey to the House of Lords. In 1794 he entered upon his first public employment, in the shape of a mission to Vienna, which bore no small resemblance to that of his ancestor, the third Earl of Sunderland, ninety years before. To rouse the Austrian government into vigorous co-operation against France, and not to buy its co-operation too dearly,

* Perhaps his best appearance in the House of Commons, was in seconding General Conway's motion for putting an end to the American war in 1782.

was the gist of Lord Spencer's instructions in 1794, as it had been of Lord Sunderland's in 1705. There was not, indeed, the smallest pretext for suspecting Lord Spencer of a "spirit of republicanism," but in other respects the impediments to a successful negotiation seem to have been pretty faithfully reproduced. Mr. Thomas Grenville was joined with Lord Spencer in this commission, and when reporting (in his private correspondence) the real posture of affairs, he found reason to say "there is no soul in the bodies of these men; none, at least, which is alive to the magnitude of the objects now at stake." But the negotiators did what could be done under such circumstances.

Whilst yet at Vienna, Lord Spencer was made Lord Privy Seal (16 July, 1794), which office he exchanged on the 20th December, 1794, for that of First Lord of the Admiralty, and at the Admiralty he remained for more than six of the most eventful years in British History. Lord Spencer's naval administration is immortalised by the great victories of Lord Bridport at L'Orient, of Sir John Jervis at Cape St. Vincent, of Duncan at Camperdown, and of Nelson at the Nile. His unwearied labours; his discriminating choice of commanders; his firm support of them when chosen, and his eager recognition of services which, up to that date, were certainly unparalleled in our annals, need not to be dwelt upon. But it was destined that Lord Spencer's qualities for naval rule should be tried by a much severer test than the utmost strain of war, and one which is, happily, without any parallel, either before or since. The mutinies of 1797 arose, in part, from causes for the continued existence of which Parliament must in fairness be blamed, even more than executive governments. When the original mutiny of the Channel fleet broke out, Lord Spencer hastened to hold a Board of Admiralty at

Lord Spencer's administration at the Admiralty.

The naval mutinies of 1797.

Portsmouth, and to confer with the best officers who were accessible. The real grievances of the seamen were redressed, promptly, fully, and frankly. It is doubtless matter of national reproach that any real grievances should have remained to be redressed under such circumstances. But the emergency was a surprise, the country was in the thick of war, and the real grievances of the sailors were complicated with very fictitious ones. The subsequent mutiny at Sheerness brought out this last-named fact saliently. Lord Spencer's memorable interview with Parker and his brother "delegates" showed him what the new mutiny was made of, and the firm resistance to the misled men at the Nore was as well-timed and as successful as the just concession to the Channel mutineers had been a month before. Unconditional submission was insisted upon. The most energetic measures were taken to prevent further mischief. And the bad leaven was at length effectually removed.

In dealing with that important branch of Admiralty duties, the construction of ships and the management of the dock-yards, Lord Spencer was most patient in considering proposed improvements and earnest in introducing them, when his judgment was convinced. He zealously promoted the improvements of Sir Samuel Bentham and of Sir Mark Brunel. The immense value of Brunel's block machinery had its first recognition from Lord Spencer, and the impediments which so long kept Brunel's just claims in check would have been speedily thrust aside—such, at least, is the opinion of Brunel's recent and able biographer, Mr. Beamish—had Lord Spencer continued in office. In his review of that knotty subject, Mr. Beamish comes to the conclusion that it was "only under the administrations of Lord Spencer and Lord St. Vincent that for many years any improvement had been attempted in the naval [constructive] department."* Lord Spencer, like other able administrators of that day, over-estimated the difficulties which stood in the way of the introduction of steam navigation, and so missed a grand opportunity, when Lord Stanhope made his early experiments, and submitted them to the Admiralty towards the close of the century. But, none the less, it was owing to Lord Spencer that the powers of steam were introduced (at length) into the dock-yards, for constructive purposes, in 1798.

Lord St. Vincent's eulogy of the indefatigable labours and of the extraordinary "extent of knowledge, both in the theoretic and practical parts of the naval department" which characterised Lord Spencer's term of office, express the conclusions of those who are best able to judge, and the assertion of the same high authority that "Lord Spencer's administration of the Admiralty had been the most auspicious to the honour of His Majesty's arms,"† of any then on record, has been amply endorsed.

Society at the Admiralty and at Spencer House.

Lord Spencer's naval administration has also its records of a minor but not insignificant kind. Some of the diarists of the day commemorate the splendid hospitalities of the Admiralty, where the bravery of the vanquished was as genially praised as the merits of the victors. Those hospitalities owed their best charm to his Lordship's marriage (at the outset of his public career, 6 March, 1781) with the Honourable Lavinia Bingham, eldest daughter of Charles, first Lord Lucan. Lady Spencer's eminent accomplishments and more than usual skill in those graceful arts which make a house attractive to visitors

* Beamish. *Memoir of the Life of Sir M. I. Brunel*, 52.

† Brenton, *Life and Correspondence of Lord St. Vincent*, i, 370, 413, 461, &c.; Tucker, *Memoirs of Lord St. Vincent*, ii, 112, &c.

of the most varied pursuits in life, rendered the Admiralty, in the closing years of the last century, and Spencer House during many subsequent years, very conspicuous in the social annals of London. Mackintosh, Rogers, Davy, Sir J. Banks, Thomas Young, Hatchett, Wollaston, Brunel, were intimate there, as well as great statesmen and great commanders. Nor was Lady Spencer less distinguished for her generous eagerness to assist struggling merit—as shown, for instance, in Brunel's case,—or for her impulsive and patriotic sympathy in the great achievements of her countrymen abroad.*

Lord Spencer's subsequent political career.

Lord Spencer retired from the Admiralty on the 19th February, 1801. In his estimate of the transactions which led to the Peace of Amiens, and of the value of the Peace itself, he differed widely from many of his political connexions, and still more widely, perhaps, from the great mass of his countrymen. But his words—uttered in the course of an animated speech in the House of Lords,—"I see in this nothing but a *precarious* Peace," were only too speedily justified by events. In the May of the following year and again in December, he made two other speeches on questions of foreign policy, and especially on the importance of keeping Malta,† both of which displayed great ability, clearness, and vigour. He remained out of office until the formation of the Grenville-Fox ministry ("all the talents") in February, 1806, when he took the seals of Secretary of State for the Home Department, and held them until the end of March, 1807. In accepting that office, and in retaining it on the subsequent modifications in the government occasioned by the death of Fox, he overruled his

* See, for an example, her glowing Letter to Nelson, *Despatches, &c.*, iii, 74.

† *Parliamentary History*, xxxvi, 161; 671-674: 1134, &c.

strongest predilections. Both predilection and special fitness naturally led him to look again to the Admiralty, with the duties of which he was so thoroughly familiar, and in which he had rendered such brilliant service. But the exigencies of party arrangements stood in the way. On the dissolution of the Grenville ministry, Lord Spencer finally retired from office. He continued to take an occasional part in the debates of Parliament. He devoted himself with conspicuous ability and energy to those local duties of a great landholder, with the efficient performance of which so much of what is best and most fruitful in English polity is connected inseparably. And in gratifying those literary tastes which formed his chief relaxation he had the enviable consciousness that here, also, personal enjoyment was closely linked with public advantage.

As a book collector, Lord Spencer began early in life, but not quite so early as some who were both his rivals and his friends. He had made occasional purchases before he was thirty, but the broad foundation of the Althorp Library, as we see it now, cannot be said to have got fairly laid until Lord Spencer acquired the choice collection of the Count de Reviczky, by purchase, in 1790. That collection at once raised the Althorp Library into importance, and influenced the character of the acquisitions which were most eagerly sought in after days.

Acquisition of the Reviczky Collection.

Charles Emanuel Alexander, Count Reviczky, was a Hungarian magnate of considerable fortune, born in Hungary, in November, 1737, and educated at Vienna. He seems to have possessed from his boyhood an exceptional aptitude for acquiring languages, and to have cultivated it during extensive travels both in Europe and in Asia. Besides the great languages of antiquity and the modern

Career and character of Count Reviczky.

tongues of ordinary attainment, he is said to have acquired thorough familiarity with the languages of Northern Europe, and with a majority of the languages and chief dialects of the East. He had not long returned from the travels he had planned for himself, when the Empress Maria Theresa sent him as her ambassador to Warsaw. Joseph II gave him similar functions, first in Berlin, and afterwards in London. He evinced great diplomatic ability, and appears always to have won attached friends, even, as at Berlin, under unpromising political circumstances. Probably the best idea of his character, and of his eminent accomplishments, is to be derived from his correspondence with Sir William Jones, who entertained a strong affection for him, and to whom his first introduction to Lord Spencer was probably owing. Everywhere, he made himself renowned as a collector of fine books, and especially of the curiosities and datemarks of printing. The chiefest characteristic of the Reviczky Library was its extraordinary series of the primary and most choice editions of the Greek and Latin classics. No collector has ever succeeded in amassing a complete series of first editions; but Reviczky, whose researches in this direction were incessant, made, or is believed to have made, a nearer approximation to completeness than any previous or contemporary collector. Next to these, it was his aim to gather such of the fine productions of the Aldine, Stephanine, Morelian, and Turnebian presses, as were not already included in the primary series; then, the Elzevirs, on all subjects; the 'Variorum' classics, both in quarto and in octavo; the Delphin classics; the choice editions of Baskerville, Brindley, Foulis, Tonson, and Barbou; and the curious tiny-typed productions of the press of Sedan. Of his classics of all sorts, and of his Elzevirs, the Count had himself

Special characteristics of the Reviczky Collection.

printed, under the pseudonym of "Periergus Deltophilus," a catalogue entitled, *Bibliotheca Græca et Latina.* This appeared at Berlin during his embassy in 1784, and, like the three supplements to it, subsequently printed, was restricted (I believe) to private circulation. Ten years later it was published, with additions. But the early and incomplete edition is chiefly prized by collectors. If it be true, as it seems to be, that Reviczky's health was already and very consciously failing him when he sold his library to Lord Spencer, he gave a curious and (in such dealings) an unusual instance of disinterestedness, in the conditions on which he insisted. He stipulated for a small sum in hand —one thousand pounds, it is said,—and an annuity of five-hundred a year. The bargain was made in 1790. The Count died, at Vienna, in August, 1793. But it is possible, of course, that he may have thought it as true of doomed men as of threatened men, that they sometimes live long.

Reviczky's likings and aversions in books.

One of Count Reviczky's peculiarities as a collector was an abhorrence of books with manuscript notes; no matter how illustrious the hand from which they came. To him, a "*liber notatus manu Scaligeri*" excited the same repugnance which he would have shown to the scribblings of a schoolboy on the fair margins of a vellum Aldus. This man of twelve languages, and of wide acquaintance with books and with statesmen, would say;—*I* am no scholar. I am simply a curiosity-seeker. What *I* prize in a fine book is the freshness and purity which show that the copy is still in the condition in which it left the printer, three hundred years ago. I confess, too, that a copy printed on vellum has a great attraction for me; nor am I at all insensible to the charms of "large paper," of "original binding," and other the like frivolities, so superbly disdained by great scholars.* Lord Spencer was by no means so intolerant as was Reviczky of manuscript notes, but he conjoined as thorough an appreciation of the external beauties of a choice book, with a just and keen estimate of its intrinsic merits. And the almost unrivalled beauty of condition of many of his later acquisitions made them quite worthy to occupy the same shelves with the cherished volumes of Count Reviczky.

After that great purchase, the owner of Althorp for some time contented himself with occasional, but very numerous, acquisitions at the sales by auction, or in the shops of the booksellers. He was a great patron of "honest Tom Payne" the second, and of Elmsly, the successor of Paul Vaillant, who had been the favourite bookseller of Lord Sunderland. At the sales, Lord Spencer was a liberal opponent as well as a liberal bidder. When Mason's books were sold, for example, in 1798, Lord Spencer agreed with the Duke of Roxburghe that they would not oppose each other, in bidding for some books of excessive rarity, but, when both were very earnest in their longings, "toss up, after the book was bought, to see who should win it." Thus it was that the Duke obtained his unique, but imperfect, copy of Caxton's *Hystorye of Kynge Blanchardyn and Prince Eglantyne,* which however came safely to Althorp fourteen years later, at a cost of two hundred and fifteen pounds;† the Duke having given but twenty guineas.

Lord Spencer's purchases at the Sales and of the Dealers.

Some of Lord Spencer's finest Caxtons he acquired by private purchase. His first Caxton acquisition at an auction was the second edition of the *Canterbury Tales,* bought at

Lord Spencer's Series of Caxtons.

* *Letter to the Abbé Denina.*

† MS. note by Lord Spencer at Althorp: and *Catalogue of the Roxburgh Library,* p. 176.

William Herbert's sale in 1795 for seven pounds. At Brand's sale, in 1807, he gave a hundred and eleven pounds for the *Knight of the Tower.* At the Roxburghe sale, in addition to the *Blanchardyn,* he acquired an imperfect copy of the *Speculum Vitæ Christi* for forty-five pounds; the second edition of the *Festial* for a hundred guineas; an imperfect copy of *Le Recueil des Histoires de Troyes* for a hundred and sixteen pounds; and a tolerable copy of the *Chastising of God's Children*—of which only eight copies are known to have survived—for a hundred and forty pounds. Lord Spencer's purchase of the library of Mr. Stanesby Alchorne, from its temporary owner, Mr. Johnes of Hafod, put him in possession of nine duplicate Caxtons, but most of them were more or less imperfect. The purchase, however, enabled him to improve his collection by the substitution, in some instances, of copies better than those he had previously possessed.

The Alchorne Collection.

The Alchorne collection had been offered to Lord Spencer, entire, in 1806, just as he had accepted the seals of the Home Department and when his thoughts were almost engrossed by public business. But he afterwards regretted his hasty rejection of the offer. Payne the bookseller made the purchase, and resold it, still entire, to Mr. Johnes. When the Roxburghe and Stanley auctions had shown the height to which the passion for rare books had grown, Mr. Johnes—who had then recently lost his only child—wrote to Dibdin: "I am an 'extinct collector' [alluding to the saying of the notorious John Wilkes, "I am an extinct volcano"]. . . . . If you can recommend me a purchaser for the Alchorne collection, I shall thank you. . . . . If Lord Spencer will give me *three* times what I paid, it shall be at his service." The terms were "mitigated," as Dibdin says, and the offer accepted. After a few advantageous exchanges and a few additions to the Althorp collection—including some fine specimens of the press of Wynkyn de Worde—the bulk of the Alchorne books was sent to Evans for sale by auction in the same year, 1813, in which it had been brought from Hafod. The rapid growth of the Althorp Library is shown, strikingly, by the fact that this was already Lord Spencer's fourth sale of duplicates. The nine duplicate Caxtons—seven of them imperfect—sold for £666. In the same year his Lordship gave, at the Merly sale, three hundred and thirty pounds for two Caxtons (*Book of Divers Ghostly Matters,* not quite perfect, and the second edition of the *Mirrour of the World.*) At Roberts' sale, in 1815, he bought a copy of the *Lyf of Saynt Katherin of Senis* for thirty-three pounds; and at Goldsmid's sale, in the same year, a copy of *The Royal Book* for eighty-five pounds.

Other Caxton purchases.

At the dispersion of the famous White Knights collection in June, 1819, Lord Spencer acquired a copy of the *Art and Craft to know to Die well*—one of the rarer Caxtons, only four copies being known—together with a slightly imperfect copy of the *Pilgrimage,* for a hundred and fifty-two pounds, and a copy of the *Propositio* for a hundred and twenty-six pounds. As a consequence of this sale, although not actually at the sale itself, Lord Spencer acquired, at the cost of seven hundred and fifty pounds, the memorable and unique copy of the Valdarfer Boccaccio of 1471, for which he had vainly offered two thousand two hundred and fifty pounds at the Roxburghe sale, seven years earlier. When examining the catalogue of the Duke's books and thinking over his intended purchases, Lord Spencer at first resolved to go as far, in pounds sterling, for the coveted Boccaccio, as the date of the year (1812) and no farther. But, before the sale came on, some passing

The White-Knights Sale.

circumstance or other brought him what he called "a windfall" of something more than four hundred and thirty pounds, and he added that casual gain to his former self-imposed limit, making its new amount the £2250 above mentioned. At that limit Lord Spencer stopped, precisely as he had resolved to do. When Lord Blandford again quietly added "*ten*," Lord Althorp urged his father to go on,* but Lord Spencer's courage and open-handedness were not more characteristic of him than was his steadiness of purpose. When (after his accession to the Dukedom of Marlborough) Lord Blandford's Berkshire Library was sold, and the Boccaccio was again under the hammer, Lord Spencer stopped at seven hundred pounds. The representative of Longman and Co. added fifty, and obtained the prize. *Then* Lord Althorp tried hard to induce his father to refuse to take it off their hands, at any excess over his own bid; but Lord Spencer thought it just to take it at cost price. The high rates of former years had brought their natural reaction; to be followed, as we have recently seen, by rates, for some classes of books, which make those of Roxburghe days look moderate in the comparison. The 'Boccaccio' will doubtless continue to be an exception by itself. It will not often happen that the owners of

* In a letter to Mr. Thomas Grenville, written almost thirty years after the event, the third Earl Spencer (the Lord Althorp of 1812) tells the Boccaccio story substantially as it is told in the text, but with a slight variation as to the figures, which the lapse of time may well account for. He corrects Dibdin's fantastically verbose account in some little particulars, and confirms it in others. The incident is a really memorable one for bibliography, and, as Dibdin was present, he might well be entitled to tell the story in his own words, but for his (inevitable) bombast about "swords, champions, ammunition, and blood." I suppose that if Dibdin's life had depended on telling a plain story in a plain way, he must have died immediately. Lord Althorp's letter is in the Grenville Library.

Althorp, Blenheim, and Chatsworth,* have set their hearts upon one and the same acquisition on the same occasion.

Lord Spencer received not a few curious proofs of the continental inferences which were drawn from the keen competition of English collectors at the Roxburghe and Stanley sales, and of continental ideas about English money-bags. In 1813, for example, a foreign owner of some rare books obligingly offered him a Mentz *Decretum Gratiani* for £240; and a Mentz *Bible* of 1462 for £450.†

At the sale in 1815 of the fine library of the Duke of Grafton, Lord Spencer acquired a very superb copy of Burnet's *History of the Reformation*, illustrated with a long series of additional portraits, for a hundred and six pounds. When the books of Mr. John Lloyd, of Wygfair in Denbighshire, were sold in the following year, he obtained two copies of the *Promptorius Puerorum*, printed by Pynson in 1499, for thirty pounds. For an imperfect copy of the precious Caxton volume, *The Noble Histories of King Arthur and of certain of his Knights*, he had to give three hundred and twenty pounds. No other copy of this volume is known to exist save the Harleian copy, now Lord Jersey's at Osterley Park. That copy passed from Lord Oxford to Osborne the bookseller, who sold it to Bryan Fairfax for five pounds. At the Fairfax sale—when the British Museum was already established, or virtually established—it was sold to Sir Francis Child, Lord Jersey's ancestor, for two guineas and a half. From that day to the occurrence of the copy sold at Wygfair, no copy had even been offered for purchase. No wonder that although the sale took place in Wales, in the depth of an inclement

The Wygfair Sale in Denbighshire.

* The Duke of Devonshire it is understood had resolved to go as far as sixteen hundred pounds, in 1813, for the coveted volume.

† *Bibliographical Decameron*, iii, 55.

winter, it attracted many and eager buyers. The local auctioneer was so inspired by the unwonted atmosphere in which he found himself that his ecstatic descriptions of the treasures he had to offer almost vie with those of Dibdin, and the proud results were recorded on a silver jug which, on fit occasion, may doubtless still court the admiration of the tourist.

Of this Caxton volume, too, something is to be told which is of greater interest than the circumstances of its acquisition. Ebert, in one of those snarling ebullitions which seem to have been a relief to him from the toils of bibliography, but which to his readers detract seriously from the unquestionable and eminent merits of his book, was once pleased to ask, "Of what utility to literature is the Spencer library?" The question admits of very many and very conclusive answers. Many enduring works have drawn largely on its stores. Many pleasurable associations in literary biography connect themselves inseparably with its history. Gibbon commemorated, seventy years ago, the delight with which he had examined its primitive treasures, "exhausting a whole morning among the early editions of Cicero." The author of that useful contribution to the curiosities of literature, as well as to the history of printing, the *Principia Typographica*, recorded, but the other day, the great and repeated obligations he lay under to the Althorp Library, not only for the use of books, indispensable to his task yet elsewhere unattainable, but for that conspicuous liberality with which Lord Spencer sent them more than once from Northamptonshire to London, merely for his accommodation. This Wygfair Caxton affords an individual, but not an exceptional, example of another kind. Its entire transcription enabled Southey to give to the public, in 1817, his *Byrth, Lyfe, and Actes of*

Services rendered to literature by the Spencer Library.

Kyng Arthur. To make a list of the obligations acknowledged by other authors would be to tell a very long story.

Acquisitions from Corporate and Public Libraries.

It was not only by liberal dealings* with booksellers and by spirited competition at the sales, that Lord Spencer continued to enrich his collection. If the guardians of a public or semi-public library were of opinion that they better discharged their duty, as trustees, by parting with some extremely rare but, in their present habitation, unused books, and by applying the proceeds to the acquisition of common but much wanted works of modern dates, he was always willing to acquire the rarities at their full value, and so to supply the means of multiplying the desired books of reference and of reading. But had Lord Spencer, personally, been the trustee of a corporate library, his own vote on such a proposition would certainly have been with the Noes. Had it fallen to his lot to deal, in Parliament, with such hypocritical and silly pretences as those which were employed a year or two ago to defeat the cherished purpose of Archbishop Tenison (under guise of promoting "*education*"), he would, I think, have branded the perpetrators with a quiet epithet or two not easily forgotten. The case of exchanging the books of Cathedral Libraries is less flagrant. But in one instance, at least, there is record of Lord Spencer's express approval of the decision of a Chapter majority against parting with the black-letter curiosities which had been given by a benefactor into its charge,—no matter how plausible the arguments for the exchange or how enticing the list of *desiderata* to be supplied. From the Cathedral Library

* The known examples are numerous. One only will be mentioned. Lord Spencer bought of Triphook a volume of old tracts for a few pounds. Finding afterwards that one of the tracts was printed by Caxton, he presented the bookseller with fifty guineas.

of Lincoln, however, there was obtained, in this way, through James Edwards the bookseller, three of the rarest "Caxtons" which are to be seen at Althorp.

Those choice volumes were part of the Library of a worthy Dean of Lincoln, Michael Honywood, who died in 1681, having in his life-time presented to the Chapter a noble collection of books, and a fitting receptacle (built expressly by Wren) for their preservation to the service of posterity. During his deanship, the old Chapter Library had been burnt, and by his munificence both books and building were more than restored. Of the Honywood collection at large, I hope to speak hereafter. It included seven Caxton volumes—three of which were wanting to the series at Althorp, namely, *The History of Jason*, probably printed in 1477, and of which three perfect copies, only, are known to exist; *The Historye of Reynart the Foxe*, probably printed in 1481, and of which four perfect copies are known; and *The Playe of the Chesse* (second edition), undated like the rest, but probably also of 1481. Of this second Chess-book only two quite perfect copies are extant. A copy was sold by auction in 1698, for eighteen pence; in 1798, for four guineas; in 1813, for a hundred and seventy-three pounds. The Lincoln—now Althorp copy—is slightly cropped and mended, but is substantially perfect. This first assault on the integrity of the Honywood Collection was made in September, 1811. Dr. Dibdin first heard of it by a letter* from Lord Spencer, announcing "a great piece of black-letter fortune," .... and "a proud day for the Library."

Purchases from Lincoln Cathedral Library.

Even the Dibdinian dialect breaks down under the

* Lord Spencer's letter is printed in Dibdin's *Reminiscences*, i, 488; Comp. *Bibliographical Decameron*, iii, 262—265; and *Northern Tour*, i, 104—117.

consequent emotions, when the precious volumes were (literally) embraced. And Dibdin made a raid at Lincoln on his own account, in 1813. A third quickly followed, but with only small booty. Many rarities yet remained—some of them encircled with suggestive pieces of string, by the Divine who was so persistently breaking the tenth commandment—but the fourth attempt was a failure. Dean Honywood's books have, since those days, been kept under stricter guardianship.

It is only fair to the then Lincoln Dignitaries to record that they, too, thought it a "proud day" for *their* library, when between four hundred and five hundred well-chosen volumes (many of them portly folios) in British History and Biography—such they were, for the most part—took the place of the dingy little pot-quartos which had made not a few bibliomaniacal eyes to glisten with more than wonted light.

Another and in some of its particulars a still more striking instance of the force of temptation occurred in 1818. Here the coveted treasures were not only books of extraordinary rarity, and rich in literary as well as in typographical interest, but they were of the sort which are as highly prized by Continental as by English bibliographers. And they belonged, not to a Dean and Chapter, but to a King.

Acquisition of two rare Virgils from the Royal library of Wirtemberg.

Among the many attractions of the Royal Library at Stuttgart were numbered in 1818 two Virgils, so rare as to be almost priceless. As in some other cases, the *second* edition of Virgil (1471) by Sweynheym and Pannartz, the printer of the first, is even scarcer than the Princeps. No copy of it was known to exist in England, although Scotland could boast of one. Of another edition (the place of printing of which is unknown), bearing the same date, the rarity is so great that there is only a single record of its sale. A metrical colophon hands down the bare name "Adam," as that of the printer, who is otherwise known only by an edition of Lactantius, also of 1471. This "Adam" Virgil was still in the primitive wooden coat which had been given him in the monastic abode, whence he had been taken to adorn the library of the Kings of Wirtemberg. Dibdin went to Stuttgart in bold quest of these books, despite their royal ownership. After many conferences with the King's librarian, M. Le Bret, the proposal was submitted to the King himself, and Dibdin had an audience, in which he dwelt, not unadroitly, on the magnificence of the Stuttgart Library in Theology, and its comparative insignificance in Classics, as affording a reason why a judicious exchange, which should give the means of supplying what was still lacking in the former class, at the mere cost of a couple of Virgils, would strengthen His Majesty's Library rather than weaken it. The King gave a general assent, provided the details of the exchange were made satisfactory to his Librarian. The terms were at length settled, for a round sum in francs, and a handsome copy of the *Bibliographical Decameron* was added to clinch the bargain. Dibdin bore the volumes in triumph to Althorp, where they swelled the number of distinct Virgilian editions *prior to the year fourteen hundred and seventy-six*, to the extraordinary number of fifteen. Of several of these only two, three, or four other copies are known to exist. Of the "Adam" Virgil, Van Praet said, when Dibdin placed it in his hands:—"Well, here is a book I have often heard of, but have never seen." Of a Brescia edition of Virgil of the year 1473, no other copy than that already at Althorp has yet been distinctly identified. The Virgilian series is now unmatched. Readers of literary history know sufficiently—whether they be also bibliographers or not—why such a series of the edition of a great Classic is important, in quite other points of view than that of bibliomania.

Other acquisitions made by Dibdin abroad.

In his homeward journey, Lord Spencer's zealous librarian procured a few choice vellum books at Nuremberg, and an extraordinary print or two, with dates—of the sort which perplex collectors. He made, too, some useful modern acquisitions in German and Austrian History. At Ratisbon, he tried his persuasive powers on the monks of a fast-decaying community, with purposes akin to those which had been pursued so successfully in other quarters. But the poor Jacobins of Ratisbon resisted temptations to which a Chapter of Lincoln and a King of Wirtemberg had succumbed. In earlier days, it had been otherwise. A Mr. Andrew Horn obtained some curious books from thence, towards the close of the last century, some of which are to be seen at Althorp.

Lord Spencer's Tour on the Continent in 1819-20.

In 1819, Lord Spencer himself made a "bibliographical tour" on the Continent. Among other special objects of research, he had at heart the perfecting of his fine series of the productions of Sweynheym and Pannartz. In Paris and in Milan he sought vainly for the Martial of 1473. He was told it could be seen in only one private library in Italy.

The moment he reached Rome he hastened to visit the booksellers, and soon found a copy, for which he had to give about twenty pounds. It carried his number of books from that famous press, printed prior to 1473, to thirty-two. Thirty-four are enumerated in the well-known letter of the Bishop of Aleria, and one of the thirty-four is not known to exist. So rare is the Martial, says Lord Spencer himself, that even Audiffredi knew it only by hearsay. Yet, curiously enough, within a few weeks he found himself the owner of two copies. This purchase at Rome made his series of the primary and choice editions of Martial perfectly complete. But it illustrates the difficulty of the pursuit to note that it took more than thirty years of collecting, on the Spencer scale, to complete the choice cradle editions even of Martial—insignificant when compared with those of the greater poets.

At Paris, it occurred to Lord Spencer that it was worth while to set at rest a question which had been raised by French collectors about the relative claims of his own celebrated "Saint Christopher" woodcut of 1423, and of another "Saint Christopher," in the French Royal Library. Dibdin carried the print over. The comparison left its claims as an unique survival untouched, but brought out the curious little fact that, on the wood, only the outline of the palm-tree fruit had been cut, the details being supplied by the pen.* The French bibliographers and collectors took advantage of Lord Spencer's visit to give him an entertainment, at once in his personal honour, and in honour of the bibliomania "all the world over." It went off brilliantly.

Acquisition of the Cassano-Serra Library.

But the most notable circumstance of this tour of 1819-20 was the acquisition of the entire Library of the Duke of Cassano-Serra, à Neapolitan, who had trodden very much the path of Reviczky,—with a special attention to the early productions of the press at Naples and throughout the Sicilies. Of the "fifteeners" of this collection, its owner had printed a catalogue as early as 1807. Seven years afterwards, he offered the entire collection to Lord Spencer for ten thousand pounds. That price was thought to savour too much of Continental inferences from Roxburghe Sale-catalogues, and the pur-

* *Bibliographical Decameron*, iii, 396, note.

chase was declined. Dibdin made an approximative estimate of the collection at current prices, which brought it only to about £7000. The books which had special attractions in Lord Spencer's eyes were (1) a copy, absolutely unique, of an edition of Horace, printed by Arnoldus de Bruxella at Naples, in 1474; (2) a Juvenal, in the small type of Ulrich Han, undated; (3) an Aldine Petrarch (1501), on vellum, with the manuscript notes of Cardinal Bembo. The Naples Horace is based upon the text of the Princeps, but has variations from manuscripts, the interest of which is well known by Mr. Babington's able collation. The Juvenal is supposed to have been printed before 1470. It closely resembles the Cicero, *De Oratore*, of 1468. Only three copies of it are known to have survived. The Aldine Petrarch is the copy which has been elaborately described by Renouard. Some of Bembo's insertions are of great curiosity. The Cassano purchase added, of course, a very large number of duplicates to Lord Spencer's collection, and made the very 1473 Martial, so eagerly sought for, a duplicate. And there is reason to think that could he have obtained the three volumes I have enumerated, and perhaps as many more, Lord Spencer would have been quite satisfied to have foregone the rest of the Cassano Library, fine as it was. For the first two in the list, the Horace and the Juvenal, alone, he actually offered the Duke of Cassano three thousand ducats. However, it was with great zest that he directed the embarcation of the *Quattrocentisti,* in bulk, on board an English man-of-war. Their arrival became a boon to many collectors.

The Sale of Spencer's Duplicates in 1821.

Lord Spencer knew his own collection so thoroughly that while he was yet at Naples he made a list of the principal duplicates which the Cassano acquisition would cause. Among them were the Mentz Bible of 1462,

Jenson's Bible of 1476, and his Pliny of the same date, all upon vellum;—five Sweynheym and Pannartz editions (including the princeps Virgil);—the Dante of 1481;—and the princeps Pliny. All these, with many others, were sold early in 1821, to the aggrandizement of the Grenville, Sussex, Heber, and Bodleian Libraries, as well as of many minor collections. The excessively rare *Teseide* of Boccaccio, printed at Ferrara in 1475, Lord Spencer presented to Mr. Hibbert, from whom he had received another choice, but less valuable, Boccaccio volume. At the Hibbert sale the *Teseide* sold for a hundred and sixty pounds.

In the course of his tour, Lord Spencer saw of course the best libraries both public and private that occurred within its limits, and in his correspondence with Dibdin he dwelt with particular satisfaction on the choice books he had met with in the collections of Counts Melzi and d'Elci. But he had now little to covet. From the Remondini collection he had obtained some fine Aldines; and he had made many occasional purchases, some of which improved his library without increasing it. To make a fine but imperfect book complete, he would not hesitate to buy two other imperfect copies, at the rate, perhaps, of fifty pounds for each. And if fortune put it in his power to benefit the collection of a friend, as well as to improve his own, his pleasure was increased. He never had the feeling, cherished by some eminent collectors, which found delight in putting two identical copies of an excessively rare book on his own shelves, expressly in order that neither of them should fill up a gap in the choice library of another collector. When he toasted "Bibliomania, *all over the world*," he meant what he said.

It is impossible to write about the Spencer Library—

Dibdin's writings on the Spencer Library.

and scarcely possible to visit it—without incurring obligation to Dr. Dibdin. His well-known books have had the curious fortune to keep their price, without keeping their reputation. They are lustily abused, and eagerly bought. Nor is the cause far to seek. Want of method, fantastic raptures about trifles, indiscriminate emphasis, inattention to minute accuracy, petty but provoking affectations in style, and wearisome repetitions of pointless anecdotes, are drawbacks which need very eminent merits to countervail them. That Dibdin had eminent merits is certain. But his works bring high prices chiefly because they are very decorative, and of small impressions. The author's acquaintance with books was large, and his love for them real. As a writer, he had powers which under due restraint might have become considerable. He had a highly cultivated taste in the arts of design. He had much industry. He had seen a good deal of the world, under varied aspects. But his mind seems always to have lacked the power of graduation. Much as he had mixed with society, his writings evince plainly that he could as little mark degrees in his estimates of men, as he could mark them in his estimates of books. The petty, the conventional, and the merely external qualities of both, so engrossed his attention, that the vital and intrinsic qualities usually escaped him. When he had to catalogue a library, magnificent in condition and binding, abounding in rarities, and affording ample means for artistic illustration, he did his work to the delight of the book-loving reader as well as to his own. When he attempted to guide other men, not in collecting fine books, but in choosing instructive and elevating ones, he showed plainly that he had been so busy about type and colophon, uncropped margins and morocco bindings, copies with proof plates and copies on vellum, as

Character of Dibdin's mind.

to allow the spirit of the author and the essence of the book to evaporate under his manipulations. In like manner, when you read his Reminiscences of the men with whom he had mixed in life, you are left in considerable doubt whether or not he quite understood the difference between two men, both of whom were "Roxburghians," and editors of black-letter rarities—Walter Scott and Joseph Haslewood.

His catalogues of the Spencer Library.

But, be that as it may, Dibdin's services to the Spencer Library are eminent and enduring. He loved the master, and he loved the task. He has sometimes described books inaccurately. He has more frequently described them with tiresome and frivolous garrulity. But, in the main, his work was honestly and zealously done. With a little more method and a good deal more of plainness, conciseness, and proportion, his Catalogues would have been perfect models. As it is, the *Bibliotheca Spenceriana*, the *Ædes Althorpianæ;* and the *Descriptive Catalogue of the Cassano-Serra Library*, constitute a more valuable contribution to bibliographical knowledge, in the technical sense of that term, than has been made by the aggregate labours of any three among other English bibliographers who could be named. Those works have made Lord Spencer's fame as a collector, and the merits of his library, matters of ordinary knowledge to all lovers of books throughout Europe, America, and Australia. They have made the paths smoother for all future labourers in the rugged bibliographic field. They have both gratified and spread a wise taste for fine printing. And the faults which attach to them are precisely such as are wont to be most keenly censured by people who, in like circumstances, would have been incapable of doing so well. In other ways, too, Dibdin rendered good service in his day.

Notices, of Dibdin's life; and of his other labours.

He was born at Calcutta in 1776, being the son of Thomas Dibdin (the "Tom Bowling, darling of our crew," of his brother Charles Dibdin's famous song), a captain in the Indian Navy. He lost both parents before he was five years of age, and the only recollection of either that he retained in after-life was the sad memory of the lowering of his father's coffin over the ship's side into a boat. He was educated in England, under the guardianship of an uncle,—first at Reading and at Stockwell, and then at Saint John's College, Oxford. Some of the years of early boyhood—years which often colour a lifetime—were passed with an aunt who treated him, he has said, with capricious dislike verging upon hatred. To so many early misfortunes, he added that of having a considerable claim upon the Nabob of Arcot, which brought nothing but delusive hopes. In his schoolboy days he showed the due taste for out-of-doors sports, mingled with a special love for scribbling letters. No books seem to have fastened on his attention in play-hours, but he was deeply impressed with those *plates* after Stothard, which have charmed so many youthful eyes, in Harrison's *Novelist's Magazine*. At St. John's he began essay-scribbling, instead of letter-writing, and before he was twenty had the delight of seeing himself in print, in the pages of the *European Magazine*. Very soon afterwards he printed some juvenile poems (1796), of which he subsequently destroyed such copies as he could lay hands on. Intended at first for the bar, passing circumstances led him to take holy orders, but, unfortunately, the only thing for which he had shown strong predilection was authorship. He was ordained in December, 1804, having already published two editions of his *Introduction to the Knowledge of Rare and Valuable Editions of the Classics*. This was, in its day, a really valuable book. It was printed, for the third time, in 1808; for the fourth time, in 1827. But it failed to keep pace with increased requirements, and in some points the second edition is even better than the later ones. The book sold well, but its best result for the author was that it made him known to Lord Spencer. His first visit to Althorp was paid in May, 1811.* In the August of the same year he printed, for private circulation, an account of Lord Spencer's early editions of Dante and of Petrarch. This was his first notice in print of the Spencer Library. On the rare occurrence of a copy for sale, it brings twice as many shillings as it has of leaves.

Dibdin's Bibliographical Writings.

In 1811 also appeared the "bibliographical romance, in six parts," entitled *Bibliomania,* which first made Dibdin's name widely known. The germ of it, a mere tract bearing the same title, had been published in 1809. This was now swollen into a large volume (handsomely printed and illustrated), mainly by the addition of a mass of footnotes, containing anecdotes of books and of collectors, with copious extracts from sale catalogues. It had great influence in stimulating research after rarities, and in enhancing their prices. Of the book itself, very choice copies, published at ten guineas, have been known to sell for fifty. In the following year appeared the first volume of the *Typographical Antiquities*, based on the labours of Ames and Herbert, but largely increased with new matter. Dibdin made little or no attempt to improve the very defective and clumsy arrangement of the original work, or to cure its worst fault,—the insertion of inaccurate and mutilated titles, even when the books themselves were quite accessible. The publication continued until 1819, when it stopped with the fourth volume, extending only to

* Dibdin, *Reminiscences*, passim; *Bibliographical Decameron*, iii, 388.

page 900 of Herbert, or to less than half of the entire book. As it stands, therefore, Dibdin's title is a misnomer. There is nothing in the book about Printing in any part of "Great Britain and Ireland" save England, or about any English printers except those of London. And the annals even of the London printers are continued only a little way into the reign of Elizabeth. But with all its defects, the *Typographical Antiquities* would have formed Dibdin's most useful book, next to the *Bibliotheca Spenceriana*, had it been carried through. Of the *Bibliographical Decameron*, and the *Bibliographical Tours*, there is little need to speak in detail. They are handsome, costly, discursive, and amusing books, containing an abundance of curious and interesting matter, scattered amidst too much of common-place and ephemeral matter. But in a collection of English Bibliography they can scarcely be dispensed with. In that useful section of labour we have, as a nation, very little to boast of. Dibdin's writings have given a stimulus to more systematic effort than his own. And doubtless the pupils will, as usual, climb up on the shoulders of the master, and think themselves wonderfully tall fellows.

Dibdin's clerical life.

Dibdin's services to the Spencer library were munificently rewarded. In addition to the ordinary returns of such service, Lord Spencer insured his librarian's life for the advantage of his family. Lord Spencer also gave him the vicarage of Exning, in Suffolk, in 1823, and obtained for him, on episcopal recommendation, the Rectory of St. Mary, Bryanstone Square, at the end of the same year. His previous nineteen years, as far as clerical duty was concerned, had been chiefly spent in lectureships at some of those metropolitan proprietary chapels which have recently, with so much public advantage, been converted into district churches. It was not the smallest prejudicial consequence of the lectureships, under the old system, that they often occupied some of the best years of a man's life, without in the least degree increasing his fitness for specific parochial work; to say nothing of their occasional effect in keeping men in the Church who would, in every sense, have been better out of it.

Dr. Dibdin's literary activity was almost life-long. It gave him in the years 1830-31 an opportunity of rendering more extensive and lasting service to Religion, than he was ever able to render as a parish priest. He saw the want and formed the plan of a "moveable Sabbath Library," in a cheap and popular form. Had such a work been carried out with thoroughness, on a well-matured plan, it would have been almost invaluable. But the want of 1830 is substantially still a want in 1864. To appreciate what Dibdin did towards supplying it, by the six volumes entiled, *The Sunday Library*, involves allusion to very solemn themes, which, in such a work as this, can be but glanced at. But in any notice of his literary career that compilation cannot fairly be passed over in silence.

The *Sunday Library.*

The suggestion has been already ventured that the most prominent fault of Dibdin's works, generally, is their want of a due sense of *proportion*, in regard both of men and books. Unless I greatly err, that fault is as characteristic of *The Sunday Library*, as of the secular volumes. It includes much that is excellent; contains admirable selections from Divines of several schools of thought; enforces many Christian duties; illustrates many Christian adornments; but it fails to give the essential predominance to the one central soul-saving doctrine of Christianity, without which duties and adornments are to the Gospel even less than the tithes of mint, anise, and cumnin, were to the weightier matters of the Law. In a merely literary sense, too, the compilation, with many merits, has one great blot. It omits entirely all the great divines of the Stuart days. Not a single sermon is taken either from Thomas Jackson or Jeremy Taylor, from Isaac Barrow or from Robert South. In their stead, we are favoured with selections from Haggitt and Hewlett; from White and Spry.

Dibdin's death.

This Collection of Sermons was Dibdin's last considerable literary enterprise. He died on the 18th of November, 1847, in his seventy-second year. He had long before had the grief of losing his only son. An entire list of his productions as writer, translator, and editor, would fill several pages. His editions of the *Utopia*; of the *Meditations, Soliloquies, and Prayers*, of Francis Quarles; and of Fenelon's treatise *On the Education of Daughters*, are, like the *Bibliotheca Spenceriana* and its adjuncts, labours honourable to his memory.

The Roxburghe Club.

When, in conjunction with Lord Spencer and as his Lordship's Vice-President, Dibdin took his share in founding the ROXBURGHE CLUB, the founders rendered a greater service to literature than either of them quite knew. The critics grew, in course of time, wonderfully witty upon *Cock Lorell's Bote*, *The Complaynte of a Lover's Lyfe*, *The Bumble Bee*, and other the like small reproductions of the small literature of old days. But a very profound and loud-speaking critic is not always, and of necessity, a much wiser man than the writer, or even than the editor, of a poor black-letter ballad. Very certain it is that the particular critic who blew his horn so lustily in 1837, on being "in at the death" of the Roxburghe Club, blew it too soon. The Club, in 1864, is still full of life. English literature owes to it something intrinsically considerable. The literary history of Britain and of Europe is under large obligation to it. To have produced admirable editions of a series of works which belong to the seedtime of European culture, and which illustrate, at every turn, the manners, the beliefs, and the social polity, as well as the mental growth, of great nations, is certainly not a less creditable employment of money, time, and energy, than to rake from a dead man's private diaries and memoranda passages which, it is hoped by the raker, will cause pain to his surviving connexions. Nor was it at all likely—to cite an individual instance of Roxburghe editorship—that Sir Frederick Madden (who had begun his excellent labours on early Romance literature under the auspices of this Club, before 1837,) would be deterred from continuing to supply to such a series of reprints that critical apparatus which gives it vitality and worth, even by much sharper sallies than those of the author of the papers on *Roxburghe Revels*.

The Publications of the Roxburghe Club.—Lord Spencer's presentations.

But, as so often happens, the critic had the undeniable merit of quickening the perceptions and widening the sphere of the criticised. Here, as elsewhere, the keen blast of censure, instead of killing the young tree, made it strike deeper root. Lord Spencer, in the earlier days, by presenting to the Club—and through the Club to the great Public Libraries—a reprint from the only perfect copy known of Churchyarde's translation of Ovid *De Tristibus*, and also by his reprint of that curious memorial of Flodden-field, entitled *La Rotta de' Scocesi*, had set a good example. But some others among the reprints were less wisely chosen. A few of them were trivial. Before 1837, in fine, many good contributions to the Club series had made books illustrative of our early literary history accessible to scholars which before were inaccessible, but they were mingled with some frivolities. After 1837, almost every Roxburghe book is a book of mark in its way. In the field of early poetry and romance, the fruitful labours of Mr. Buckley, Mr. Wright, Mr. Furnivall, and of several others, have been added to those of Sir F. Madden. Mr. Stevenson and Mr. Evelyn Shirley have made valuable additions to the materials of English history and to biography. Quite recently, Mr. J. G. Nichols has raised to the memory of King Edward the Sixth a noble literary monument. But for Lord Spencer's having founded the Roxburghe Club, most of these books would have met with no encouragement.

The local arrangement and extent of the Althorp Library.

When Dibdin paid his first visit to Althorp (1811) the library occupied four continuous rooms on the ground floor, about a hundred and seventy feet in aggregate length, and a series of dwarf cases extending along both sides of a Portrait Gallery upstairs, a hundred and fifteen feet long. In the first room, *Theology*, beginning of course with Bibles and Liturgies; in the second and fourth rooms, *History*, including voyages and travels; in the third room, *Poetry*, *Sciences*, and *Arts*, were the predominant contents. In the Portrait Gallery, the great "collections," whether of Fathers, Councils, Antiquities, or Historians, were chiefly placed. The Caxtons and, generally speaking, the special rarities of the collection, were then at Spencer House in London. When the supplement to *Bibliotheca Spenceriana*, entitled *Ædes Althorpianæ*, was published, only eleven years later, although a new and large library, called the "Gothic Library," with a gallery, had been built and filled with books, the collection was already beginning again to overflow its boundaries. Now (1864) it occupies *eight* rooms which, if they were continuous, would stretch over an aggregate length of nearly four hundred feet. The "Gothic Library" has been pulled down, and a new and more commodious one, called the Billiard Library, built in its place. The collection formerly at Spencer House has been amalgamated with the Althorp Library. From this cause, and from the rapidity of the accessions, the classification of the books is far less distinct and consecutive than, probably, it would otherwise have been. In February, 1864, the number of volumes was estimated at 45,000, and the number of distinct *works* entered in the catalogue was 22,395. The local arrangement, taken broadly, may be thus compactly shown:

I. The Long Library: (Presses 1–36 and 97–122).	*Theology—Mathematics—Philosophy—Law—Natural History—Voyages—Classics.*
II. Raffaelle Library: (Presses 37–41 and 81–96).	*History—Linguistics.*
III. Middle Library: (Presses 42–49 and 69–80).	[The same classes continued.]
IV. Domenichino Library: (Presses 50–68.)	[Idem. *Miscellaneous Literature.*
V. Portrait Library: (Presses 123–172.)	*Literature*, continued (Periodicals). *Politics.*
VI. Billiard Library: (*Floor*, Presses 173–196. *Gallery*, Presses 197–230. [Added Presses 244, 245.]	*Theology—Law—Natural History—History of Britain—Mathematics—Linguistics—Classics—Arts and Trades.*
VII. Old Book Room: (Presses 231–243.)	Block-Books.—Incunabula of Printing.
VIII. Ante Room to Billiard Library: Presses 246–255.	*Miscellaneous Literature.*—Books of Prints.

The Catalogue in use in the Althorp Library differs from all the Catalogues I have elsewhere seen, and to

The Althorp MS. Catalogues.

explain its plan requires a little minuteness of detail as to the sequence and numeration of the Presses. As the diagram indicates, the presses are numbered continuously in one series, but they are not uninterruptedly continuous in their local succession. The shelves of each press are marked *a*, *b*, &c., as usual. As you enter the library from the long vestibule, the presses begin on the left hand of the door, and continue along the corresponding walls and partitions of all the four rooms which formed the old series of libraries; run round the remaining walls of the fourth room (up to "68"), and then return along the opposite walls of the first three rooms ("69" to "122"). The presses in the Picture Gallery, which is on the first floor of the mansion, are numbered from "123" to "172"; then, the numeration begins again with the new "Billiard Library" on the ground floor. But these press-numbers do not appear in the "Catalogue." There, the reference is to a progressive number, appended to each separate work, and entered, in ordinary arithmetical series, in a "Numerical Index." That index contains nothing but the progressive number, shelf letter, and press-mark. The title of each book is written on a small square slip, on stiff paper, and those slips themselves form the catalogue, the vellum covers of which have tagged laces, to keep the slips as firmly in their place as the ordinary leaves of a book. The arrangement is alphabetical, but, as usual, mixes up authors' names with words indicative, sometimes of the titles, sometimes of the subject matter, of books. There is also the beginning, but only the beginning, of a *Classed Catalogue*, compiled by the second Earl himself, but begun too late in life to be carried far. The following little diagrams exhibit copies of entries in the *Alphabetical Catalogue*, and of entries in the *Numerical Index*. The former extends (1864) to 206 small volumes. The latter is comprised in one large volume.

[*Althorp Slip Catalogue.*]

DIO.

....

Epitome della Historia Romana di DIONE Niceo, ... da Pompeo Magno fino ad Alessandro, figluolo di Mammea. Tradotta per Francesco *Baldelli*. Di nuovo ristampato, ...

....

2 vols. [bound in 1.] small 4to, *sh. l.* **1160.**

[*Althorp Numerical Index.*]

....

1160........................ **H. 82 / 81.**

....

3976........................ **I. 94.**

3977........................ **G. 84 / D. 203 / 202 / 204 / B. 202.***

....

The brief narrative of the formation and growth of the Library now collected at Althorp—for which alone I have had room—will have sufficed, I hope, to show with some distinctness that Lord Spencer combined, in an unusual degree, the diversified qualities which make a man an enlightened as well as an energetic collector of books. One or two of his own friends and competitors in the field far outstripped him in amassing vast heaps of costly volumes. Mr. Heber, for example, gathered almost three times as many, in point of numbers. But although he was

* The five marks in this entry indicate five several editions of the work entered.

an accomplished scholar, as well as an ardent collector, Mr. Heber possessed seven or eight houses full of books, without ever really possessing (in the true and strict sense of the term) a "library,"—a word which fairly implies the good order and the complete accessibility of books, as well as their aggregation. Lord Spencer's books were always thoroughly at his command.

Notices of some of the more conspicuous among the books at Althorp.

To enumerate even a few of the very choicest of those books would occupy many pages, if those of each class were to be noticed in due order. All that can be done here is to make some selections from a few classes, with the help of the useful (though utterly unsystematic) Index which Dibdin appended to his Cassano volume, and of a few personal notes made recently at Althorp.

The Bibles are the first books you see as you enter the Library, but the full effect of the extraordinary series gathered by Lord Spencer is diminished by its dispersion through several rooms. In Polyglot versions, it embraces those of Alcala, Antwerp, Paris, London, Hamburgh, and Leipsic. The copy of the Antwerp Polyglot was De Thou's, and is probably the most magnificent "Thuanus book" in existence. In Greek Bibles, it includes, with the Aldine princeps, a group of the finest and most valuable editions from that of Strasburgh, in 1526, to that of Oxford in 1798. The Latin Bibles begin with *twenty** several editions between the unknown year of the 'Mazarine' Bible and the year 1480, inclusive. And they include an unmatchable series of the editions of 1476 (Jenson, Hailbrun, and Moravus,) all on vellum. To these succeed twelve choice editions of the sixteenth century; seven of the seventeenth; ten of the eighteenth. The early English

* Eight of them undated, but safely to be placed before 1480.

Bibles form a series more remarkable still, if we take into account the difficulties that beset collectors in the attempt to recover and unite those now barely attainable volumes. And the early Bibles are even more precious as contemporary memorials of the Confessors of our Church and nation, than as counting among the prime and utmost rarities of our English printing-press. The Althorp series includes Coverdale's Zurich Bible of 1535; the two London Bibles (printed by Nycolson and by Grafton) of 1537; the two of 1540 (Grafton and Whitchurch), 'Cromwell's Bible' of 1539, by the same printers; with a group of ten other editions, printed between 1551 and 1581. The English *Testaments* include Tyndale's of 1536 (in the edition believed to have been printed at Antwerp), and that of 1538, printed at Southwark by Treveris; the folio Testament, with the Erasmian paraphrase, printed by Whitchurch, in 1548; and the octavo Testament, with the same paraphrase, printed by Gualtier, in 1550; with five other editions printed between 1550 and 1600. The rarity of *all* biblical editions printed before the reign of Elizabeth is no matter for surprise, if it be borne in mind that a whole series of impressions of Tyndale's Testament, printed abroad during the reign of Henry the Eighth, has almost disappeared from knowledge. That they were really printed—sometimes to the extent of two thousand copies—we have evidence. But of six successive editions, so authenticated, all that has survived is one copy, and a fragment, of one edition, and one fragment of another.

The English Bibles at Althorp.

Lord Spencer's copy of the Zurich *Bible* of 1535 is, like all the known copies save one (Lord Leicester's at Holkham), imperfect, but it is large and fine, and the imperfection extends only to the title and a preliminary leaf. He obtained it by bequest from the Rev. Jonathan Boucher.

It had been the Harleian copy, and has, in the dedication, the uncommon variation 'Quene *Jane*' (most of the known copies having 'Anne'), intimating plainly, as the appearance of the type itself suggests to the eye, that the preliminary leaves were printed after the arrival of the bulk of the impression in England. Among the choice later Biblical editions to be seen at Althorp occur the Rouen impression of Cranmer's *Bible,* printed in 1566; the Saxon and English *Gospels,* of 1571;* and the Genevan *Bible* printed at Edinburgh, in 1576-1579. This is the first impression of the complete Bible from a Scottish press. Dibdin whimsically describes it as "in the Scotch language," but it is in plain English, and one of only four or five known copies. The Testament was printed in the first named year, but was not issued separately. This Althorp copy came, I believe, from one of the raids on Lincoln Cathedral. The total number of rare, remarkable, or choice editions of the Bible or parts of the Bible, in English, now contained in the Althorp Library, exceeds a hundred.

There are also nine editions of the German Bible printed before 1495, five of them, according to Dibdin, in the type of Mentelin. The series of choice Italian Bibles numbers ten, beginning with both the editions by Vindelin

* With the following MS. note in a hand of the seventeenth century: ......" Very harde to be mett with and dear. I was twenty yeares looking for to buy one of these bookes, before I could buy one under a marke. I offered many times an angel for suche a booke as this." I quote this note from Archdeacon Cotton's excellent account of the *Editions of the Bible in English* (1852) 37. Many strange entries are to be seen in the fly-leaves of Bibles, but one of the queerest is certainly that in a Bible at Althorp (of 1607) which records the circumstance that a lady of the Villiers family, who died in 1745, drank on the day of her death nineteen tumblers of Claret, besides some " gineva, in green tea." This note seems to be in the autograph of John Villiers, her son.

de Spira, printed in 1471, one of them with the autograph of Pope Sixtus V. The French editions are fifteen; the Spanish, four, including the Ferrara Bible of 1553. The Sclavonic Bible, of 1581; the Delft Dutch Bible, of 1477; Prince Radzivil's Polish Bible, of 1563, for the purpose of completing which, Lord Spencer gave a hundred guineas for two imperfect copies; the Bohemian Bible of 1596; and the Livonian Bible of 1689, together with many of the most notable European and Asiatic versions of later dates are also here.

Rare editions of Fathers and Schoolmen.

In Patristic and Scholastic Theology, I mention only these:—(1) Fourteen rare editions of Thomas Aquinas, all printed before 1480, and most of them from the presses of Schoeffer, Sweynheym, and Mentelin. (2) Thirty editions of Saint Augustine—seventeen of them undated, but all printed between 1467 and 1490, and many of them ranking among the datemarks of typography. (3) Seven editions of Chrysostom from the presses of Ulrich Zel, of Laver, and of Azzoguidi. (4) Two editions of the *Epistolæ* of Cyprian, both printed in 1471. (5) Thirteen editions of various works by Saint Jerome, most of them so early as to be wholly without note of impression, and including the celebrated 'Oxford book,' with the supposititious date of 1468. Under "Lactantius," it must be added, the entries begin with the Reviczky copy of the famous impression "in venerabili monasterio Sublacensi," of the treatise *Adversus Gentes*, with other works of the same author. This is the first *book* printed in Italy.* Lord Spencer can show the three Subiaco books, and in them all the products known to have survived from the cradle of the Italian press. Of the Lactantius, the first of the Subiaco series, at least twenty copies (not all perfect) are

The Subiaco books.

* The *Donatus pro puerilis* was hardly a "book," and no fragment of it can be distinctly identified.

known to exist; but of the last of the three,* only three copies, I think,—that at Althorp, and two in the British Museum. Audiffredi could never get sight of it. Nor is it to be seen at the Bodleian or at Blenheim.

Althorp can also show a select series of eighteen printed Missals, beginning with that of Ulric Han (1475); ending with that printed by Giunta at Venice in 1504; and including the famous Mozarabic Missal of 1500, printed by command of Cardinal Ximenes. Lord Spencer's copy came from the Harleian Collection; and, when he acquired it, was the only known copy in England. It also contains a series of rare editions of the *Officium Beatæ Virginis*, including two printed by Jenson, and six from the early presses of Naples; with all the choicest Breviaries, from the undated one of Mentz to the Mozarabic of Toledo, including choice specimens of the presses of Italy and of that of our own Pynson; and, finally, a series of *Psalters*—Polyglot, Greek, Latin, French, Dutch, and English,—scarcely to be matched in any other private library.

Liturgical books.

Theology, however, is far from being the leading class of the Library at Althorp. Nor is even the unequalled series of early and fine impressions of the ancient Classics—marvellous as it is—unduly prominent. The collection is pre-eminently a well-proportioned one. No class of books within the common limits of scholarly culture and refined taste fails to be fairly represented. It is less rich indeed than the extraordinary collection at Blenheim in Continental History, but that remark would probably hold good of all other private libraries in England.

Ancient Classics (not previously mentioned).

In Classics, the Virgilian series and some others have been incidentally mentioned. The collection of early and choice editions of Cicero is even more conspicuous. In

* Cicero, *De Oratore.*

mere number it extends to seventy, nearly fifty of which were printed prior to the year 1473. The value of such a series (apart from all typographic considerations) as materials of literary history and as aids to textual criticism is obvious enough. Even those wise critics who are wont to say: "Do not talk to us about 'rare' books, but about good books," may be pleased to comprehend that such a series represents so many precious Manuscripts, most of which have perished. It includes all the primary and choice editions of the *Officia;* from that of Zel, probably printed in 1465, to the anonymous Neapolitan impression —seemingly from a MS.—in 1479; five several editions of the treatise *De Oratore*, from 1465 to 1470; five, of the *Orationes*, anterior to 1474; ten, of the *Epistolæ ad Familiares*, anterior to 1480; three, of the *Opera Philosophica*, all, perhaps, printed in the year 1471; and several impressions of minor works, unknown or almost unknown, before the appearance of the *Bibliotheca Spenceriana*. Of Horace there are eight editions prior to 1480, including the Naples, Ferrara, and Milan (Zarotus) editions of 1474; the Lavagna and Petri editions of 1479; and three of the choicest undated editions. Of Ovid will be found the Azzoguidi impression and the Sweynheym and Pannartz impression, both of 1471; the editions of Venice (1474) and of Parma (1477); the Aldine edition of 1502, on vellum; the *De Arte Amandi* of Zainer (1471), and also the rare edition of the same poem without note; the primary editions of the *Metamorphoses* and of the *Opuscula;* and a unique copy of Churchyard's *De Tristibus* in English, from which the Roxburghe reprint was made. The 'Livies' include the editions of Sweynheym, of Ulrich Han, and of Vindelin de Spira, in copies of great beauty. The Sweynheym Pliny is here on vellum; as are also the Aldine Sophocles (1502), *Anthologia Græca* (1503), and

Pindar (1513). Henry Etienne's edition of Greek poets, of 1556, is here in a superb copy on large paper. The choice vellum copies of *modern* editions of the Classics include the Bodoni Anacreons (1784 and 1791), the Callimachus (1792), and Horace (1791); the Didot Lucan (1795) and Wilkes' editions of Theophrastus and Catullus; with several others, scarcely less rare and beautiful. Finally, as respects Classics, there are here of Homer, besides the famous Florence edition of 1488, the prose version of Laurentius Valla, and the metrical version of nine books by Nicholas Valla, both printed in 1474; the undated Aldine edition, on vellum,—the last book bound by old Roger Payne; and a noble series on large paper of the several modern editions of Schrevelius, of Clarke, and of the Grenvilles. Other Greek and Roman Classics, not less noteworthy, I perforce pass over.

Early Editions of Dante.

In the gems of Italian literature Althorp contains a group of early editions of Dante, equalled only by the famous Grenville series. It includes the primary editions of Foligno, Jesi,* Mantua, Naples, Venice, and Florence (the latter with its full complement of nineteen superb illustrations,) being eight editions in all, printed between 1472 and 1484.† The Aldine edition (1502) on vellum is

* This precious Jesi volume affords a pleasant instance of interchange of benefit between libraries. It enabled Mr. Panizzi, in 1847, to complete an imperfect copy (which he had bought for the Museum, at the cost of £90), by fac-similes, which Lord Spencer kindly permitted to be made from it. The subsequent acquisition by the Museum of a second imperfect copy was the means of supplying the defect of Lord Spencer's copy.—Panizzi, *Prime quattro Edizioni della Divina Commedia*, Pref., ix, x.

† The Grenville library has only six *of these*, but it contains in addition other Dantes of excessive rarity which are not at Althorp; among them, the undated Neapolitan edition (now well known by Mr. Panizzi's description, and by his more recent reprint of it in Lord Vernon's magnificent Dante volume of 1858); the 1478 edition, with the Commentary of Nidobeato; and the Aldine edition of 1502, on vellum.

also here. The Boccaccios have been touched upon already in relation to the acquisition of the princeps and other famous editions of the *Decameron* and the *Teseide*. It remains to be mentioned that of various works of this author there are, at Althorp, in all, twenty-one several editions anterior to 1483. No approach, I think, to such a series can be seen in any other library. This Boccaccio collection includes choice books from the presses of Schoeffer and Reissinger; the first poetical work (according to Dibdin*) printed in Italian; the first book printed at Mantua; the first book printed at Padua; with specimens of the earliest and most curiously illustrated productions of Zainer's press at Ulm, of the early press at Lyons, and of that of worthy Richard Pynson. Boccaccio was made only too welcome almost everywhere, until the terrible onslaught which assailed him in his birthplace.† Of the various works of his beloved friend Petrarch—less widely diffused over Europe than his own—Lord Spencer possesses an equal number of like early dates, including the most rare and notable editions of Venice, Rome, Milan, Mantua, Parma, Verona, and Florence, and also those of Nuremberg, Cologne, and Basil. The rarest of all the Petrarch editions—the *Rime* of 1471, printed by Laver—the second Lord Spencer could never obtain till he acquired an imperfect copy in buying the Cassano Library. That imperfect one is said to be the only copy known to have crossed the Channel. Van Praet had afterwards the satisfaction of

Of Boccaccio;

and of Petrarch.

* I have been unable to verify *all* the dates, citations and notices of the Althorp books as I meet with them scattered throughout Dibdin's seven volumes. I have verified many. Some I am obliged to give as I find them, and thus perhaps to incur blame for his mistakes, as well as for my own.

† Or probable birthplace, for the biographers disagree. In Boccaccio's power of story-telling the French ones naturally see a proof that he was born in Paris.

completing two imperfect copies in the public Libraries at Paris, and of supplying to Lord Spencer the defective leaves of the Cassano copy. The edition is the second, and contains a better text than the first. Five copies are all that are known to exist. No instance of its separate sale is recorded by bibliographers.

Rare editions of Ariosto.

It is well known that of Ariosto no such series of rare, choice, and beautiful editions exists as that formed by Mr. Grenville, and now in the British Museum. That series extends to thirty-eight in number anterior to 1585. The Althorp series counts but nineteen; it includes, however, the first edition, one of seven known copies;* the excessively rare Venice editions of 1527,—of which only two copies are known—and of 1530 (Zoppino), probably unique; the Ferrara edition of 1532, the last which was corrected by Ariosto himself; the Venice edition of 1537 (unknown to Haym, to Crescembeni, and to Fontanini; the Milan and Venice† editions of 1539, the former being

* Of the second edition (1521) two copies; of the third edition (1524) *two* copies; and of the fourth (?) edition (1526) *three* copies, are all that are known to have survived. Six of these seven existing copies are in public libraries; so that the gap in Lord Spencer's series is no matter for surprise. Of *several* later editions the Grenville copies are the only existing copies, and, of several others, the Grenville copies are almost unique. See the excellent bibliography of Ariosto and of Boiardo, printed by Mr. Panizzi, in 1831, under the title *Bibliographical Notices of the Orlando Innamorata and Furioso*, and afterwards included in his edition of those Poems.

† Dibdin describes this Venice edition of 1539 in *Ædes Althorpianæ*, i, 160, and certainly with obvious inaccuracy. I did not see it when at Althorp, and am unable to compare its peculiarities with the notices of the editions of 1539 and 1540, in Panizzi and in Melzi. Probably it is made up of two different editions. Dibdin's carelessness in bibliographical description causes endless trouble and distrust, and is the more to be lamented, on account of the many opportunities which fell to him of describing books which nobody had described before him. In the beautiful Dante volume quoted in a preceding page, Mr. Panizzi has

the latest edition, which is in *forty* cantos; another edition so excessively rare that it would have been looked for in vain even in the Grenville catalogue until after 1843; namely, the Roman edition of 1543,—destroyed as far as the Papal authorities could lay their hands upon it; the Venice edition, by Giolito, of the same year; and a Florence edition of 1544, purchased by Lord Spencer in Rome, but then unknown to all bibliographers. Of this edition, Mr. Grenville could never obtain a copy. With the Althorp copy was bound up the *Cinque Canti di un nuovo libro*, printed in 1546. Of those Canti there is a copy in the Grenville Library. The Aldine edition of 1545 is also included in Lord Spencer's Ariosto series.

Among the modern vellum books in Italian literature occur *Il Lamento di Cecco* of Baldovini (Renouard's edition, of twelve copies); Tasso's *Aminta*, printed by Didot; the *Novelle Otto* of 1790—one of four copies; the *Novelle Galante*, printed by Didot; and a Venetian reprint of Bembo's *Istoria Veniziana*, printed in 1790. There are also some fine books in French literature, which I have not room to particularise.

Desiderata in the History of printing.

We have many histories of Printing in which the first attempts (as far as they can ever be known), the labours, and the chequered fortunes of the early printers are well told; in which the growth, and the dissemination of their art are ably surveyed. But the directly literary aspect of

had repeated occasion to censure instances of this inaccuracy, and he has done so at once incisively and gently. Speaking, for example, of those Spencer Dantes above mentioned, and of Dibdin's account of them, he says:—"*Il Dibdin era uomo corrivo nelle sue opinioni, e le sue asserzioni bibliografiche voglionsi sempre ben verificare prima di prestarvi fede intiera.*" The caution is an indispensable one, as I have had repeated occasion to mark whilst writing this chapter.

that dissemination has scarcely been brought out, I venture to think, with proportionate saliency. The striking contrasts presented by the character and subject matter of the books on which the first presses of different countries—and sometimes those of neighbouring towns—were employed; the frequency or infrequency of reproduction of the works which were printed at the earliest presses; the influences of birthplace and early education on the choice of authors, (sometimes by the patrons of the press, and sometimes by the printers themselves,) are among the many incidental topics connected with typographic history which, it would seem, have yet to be adequately worked out. For such a task, the Althorp library contains some appliances which are scarcely to be equalled by the stores of the richest public libraries, usually the slow accumulation of several centuries. In the British Museum—to take a prominent instance—are combined, amongst many others, the splendid collections of George the Third, of Mr. Cracherode, and of Mr. Thomas Grenville, and in recent years its stores have been increased with unrivalled diversity, skill, energy, and liberality. Yet in some classes of books connected with the topic I have glanced at, the library at Althorp, substantially the gathering of one man's lifetime, need not shun comparison even with the British Museum, the growth—as regards its printed books—of four generations of collectors. In 'Caxtons,' for example, Lord Spencer can show fifty-seven *separate works*, including the imperfect ones. The British Museum (excluding the duplicate copies of the same book and the mere fragments) can show but fifty-five, also including the imperfect. If perfect works only be compared, Lord Spencer has still a majority of one.

The series of books from Caxton's press.

The total number of Caxton books and broadsides

known with certainty to have survived is eighty-eight, besides fragments of six other books. Twenty-seven of the eighty-eight exist only in unique copies. Here the British Museum has the superiority over all known collections. It possesses *eleven* unique editions of our first printer. Lord Spencer has but three*—namely, *the Four Sons of Aymon*, and the *Blanchardyn*, mentioned already, and a broadside containing *Prayers*, which, curiously enough, was quite unknown (having been misbound with the *Pilgrimage of the Soul*) until the recent biographer and fellow-craftsman of Caxton, Mr. William Blades, discovered it, in the course of his examination of the Caxton series preserved at Althorp. No collector has ever rivalled Lord Spencer in the (comparative) perfection of such a series. Two collectors only have approached him—the one a world-famous Statesman, the other a Bermondsey chandler. Lord Oxford had gathered, as nearly as can be computed from Osborne's ill-drawn catalogues, about forty-eight distinct Caxton books, excluding duplicate copies. Mr. John Ratcliffe—most of whose best Caxtons passed, at his death, to King George the Third—had collected a series equal in number, although otherwise inferior.

The Althorp series of Caxtons includes the first edition of Chaucer's *Tales* (of which but two perfect copies are known to be extant), and also the second edition; together with *The Book of Fame;* and the *Troylus and Cresside.* Two of these four Caxton Chaucers had been in Mr. Ratcliffe's collection. Pynson's Edition of the *Canterbury Tales* is also at Althorp. Of Shakespeare, the series of

Rare and choice copies of Chaucer and of Shakespeare.

* The Bodleian has three. Six are at Cambridge. One is at Göttingen. One at York. To obtain the York book, Dibdin vainly exerted his utmost powers of temptation.

editions begins with the first folio—in a copy from the Library of Martin Folkes, apparently bound by Roger Payne; includes (1) a very fine copy of the first edition of the *Sonnets* (1609), with an inscription, evidently contemporary,—according to Dibdin,—which reads thus: "*Commendations to my very kind Friend*"; (2) a superbly illustrated copy of the Boydell edition of the *Historical Plays*, the fruit of the many years' loving labour of the late Countess of Lucan. Portraits, from ancient MSS. and from the best authenticated pictures; topographical views of contemporary date, and careful heraldic emblazonments, are the salient features of these beautiful volumes. Here also is (3) another magnificent Shakespeare, illustrated, in the first place, by its editor, George Steevens, and subsequently by Lord Spencer, to whom Steevens bequeathed it. It is of course on Large Paper, and has been illustrated with judgement as well as great cost,—with careful as well as extensive research. For his famous illustrated copy of Burnet's *History of the Reformation* (1679) Lord Spencer gave £106, at the sale of the Duke of Grafton's Library.

Illustrated Books.

The contemporaries and early successors of Caxton at the English press are almost as well represented in the Althorp Library as he is himself. But to particularise them is here impracticable. A few words must be said of a different series, still more important for the History of Printing.

The block-books at Althorp.

The Block-Books in the Spencer Library are unequalled in any other private collection. They have been partially described by Heinecken and by Dibdin; more fully and ably by the late Mr. Sotheby in the *Principia Typographica*. They include, amongst others, two editions of the *Apocalypsis*, two of the *Speculum Humanæ Salvationis*, several editions of the *Biblia Pauperum*, together with copies of the *Enndchrist*, *Ars Moriendi*, *Ars Memorandi*, *Cantica Canticorum*, and of *Die Kunst Cyromantia* of Hartlieb. This last-named book gave rise, some years ago, to an extraordinary statement by Dr. John Richardson, in a book called *Recollections of the last Half Century*. Speaking of the notorious author of the Shakespeare Forgeries, Dr. Richardson wrote:—"*Ireland is said* to have made no less a fool of Lord Spencer, the great book-collector, who purchased, as a genuine 'block-book,' an ingenious imitation in india-ink or sepia, . . . of a work called *Chiromancy*, . . for which piece of rubbish his Lordship, I believe, paid a hundred and odd guineas; and it is now or was some time ago, . . . at Althorp, carefully preserved from contact with the profane atmosphere beneath a glass-case in the Library." In such a statement the '*Who* says it?' is of considerable importance. The authority proved, on inquiry, to be "the late Gordon Urquhart, Esq., of the Navy Pay Office," . . . "who was concerned with Ireland in several book transactions." Mr. Urquhart is known certainly as a collector—*of halters.** He was well known in the press-room at Newgate, but little known, I believe, in any other press-room, or in Libraries. Originally, the story was, I suppose, one of Ireland's "Confessions." It is just as authentic as *Vortigern*.

The Hartlieb Cyromantia.

There is no need to enlarge on the excellence of the modern books at Althorp. That the library has been well

* "At Newgate he was understood to have the *entrée.* ......He invariably procured from Jack Ketch the halters by which the unfortunate culprits were strangled, which he carefully preserved as mementoes *of the instability of human existence.*"—Richardson, *Recollections*, ii, 40.

Later additions to Althorp Library.

"kept up," by the addition of books really essential, is one of the first things that strikes the visitor, although the want of better classification diminishes the full effect of the library, as a whole. No succeeding Earl has vied with his illustrious predecessor as a collector—if he had so vied, a new mansion would have been needed—but each has added something towards the completeness of the collection. Lord Brougham has given us some proofs of the devotion of the third Earl to those thorny yet delightful inquiries which elicit from the material world, and its unreasoning but not irrational inhabitants, their testimony to the wisdom and goodness of their Creator. Most Englishmen know something of his devotion to Agriculture, and especially to the improvement of Stock; and of his zeal in scattering broadcast the knowledge he had laboriously acquired. The shelves at Althorp show books, on both classes of subject, of his addition, and also a little group of handsome green-coated volumes—they would perhaps have looked still better in pink—which record, in his own hand, some famous "runs." Nothing is more pleasant, or more fitting, in a great ancestral library, than to meet with these personal memorials of its successive possessors, and of the pursuits which gave wings to their hours of leisure, as well as of those graver pursuits in which each of them —whether as soldier, scholar, agriculturist, or statesman—paid his fair quota, in his day and generation, towards the vast sum of human toil and of human endeavour.

The founder of the SPENCER LIBRARY lived to enter his seventy-seventh year. In the last year but one of his life, he wrote to Dibdin: "I am trying my hand at a Classed Catalogue."* He adds an expression of his consciousness

* I looked some months ago, with no small interest, at the scheme of

that it was somewhat late to begin a new task; but the attempt shows vividly how thorough had been that love of his books, in which, next after the supreme consolations of Religion, he had found his solace under the inevitable trials of a protracted life. How, in the prime of manhood, he had discharged the duties of a great public trust, I have (very inadequately) attempted to show, both from contemporary and from historic testimony. His discharge of all the relative, local, and social duties of life was not a whit less thorough. Few of the great landowners of England have ever received a testimonial more honourable both to the givers and to the receiver than that presented to Lord Spencer by his Northamptonshire tenantry in 1819. His retirement from official life was not a withdrawal from public labours, but an exchange of them. Hospitals and Savings Banks, Literary and Religious Institutions, both in town and country, shared with the local duties of the Magistrates' Room and Shire Hall the time released from public service at Westminster. In one word, his career was exemplary. It continued to be so under circumstances of personal infirmity which were touchingly alluded to in his Funeral Sermon at Brington Church.* He died on the 10th of November, 1834. Thirty years have passed since then, but it is not yet forgotten that the announcement "*Lord Spencer is dead*" made the departure of one of

The later years of the second Earl Spencer.

"classes" which Lord Spencer had drawn up. It seemed to be based on Mr. Horne's plan made for the British Museum in 1824.

* "It was an edifying sight to see one struggling with age and infirmity, and scarcely able with the assistance of two attendants to reach the spot where he desired once more to bend his feeble knees in humble adoration of his Lord; and to receive the consecrated elements...as pledges of that Lord's love, and in remembrance of his death." Rose, *Funeral Sermon* (Northamp. 1834). This last appearance at Brington Church was just three weeks before Lord Spencer's death.

the most amiable of men an instrumental cause of the fiercest political storm within the memory of this generation. The third Earl retired from the strife, as his father had done, while yet in the vigour of his powers, and like him served his country in quiet paths.

Deductions from a visit to Althorp.

The noble library at Althorp will, I hope, hand down Lord Spencer's memory to a very remote posterity. It is one among the many reasons why all thoughtful Englishmen, down to the humblest, should view with satisfaction the strength of the wisely-conservative element in our polity, that some of the best possessions of a house and lineage like that of the Spencers are, for use and profit, common possessions. It is so both in small things and in great. Many a noble park in England affords to the poorest amongst us the means of rejoicing in that natural beauty which the God of Nature has given so lavishly, for instruction as well as for solace. Every farmer in England may, if he please, be a sharer in that wealth of agricultural knowledge and skill which has, in large measure, been piled up by the efforts made, and the encouragements given, on a great scale, by great landowners. The Lord Arundel who once threw in the teeth of a Spencer the reproach—'*My Lord, when these things were doing, your ancestors were keeping sheep*,' put on Parliamentary record a piece of vital service to England, which later Spencers have emulated and surpassed. Just so is it in Literature. The common books which pass into the hands of almost the humblest owe something of their merit and vitality to the heaping up of rare and costly books in such collections as the Spencer Library,—created with a liberal hand, and imparted with a liberal heart.

The visitor at Althorp who leaves the house at its north-west corner, and goes up a beautifully wooded walk towards

Brington Church, comes presently upon a stone memorial of the planting—some two centuries and a half ago—of the oaks and beeches on either hand of him. Upon that stone there is a second inscription, on which both the history of the Spencer Family and the history of the SPENCER LIBRARY afford an excellent commentary. The inscription on the reverse of the memorial-stone reads thus :—

"UP AND BEE DOING, AND GOD WILL PROSPER."

APPENDIX A.

[Chap. IV, p. 58.]

LIST OF KNOWN CATALOGUES OF ENGLISH MONASTIC LIBRARIES.

I. General Catalogues:—

John Boston, of Bury: [Comparative List of books in English Monastic Libraries]. Phillips MS. at Middle Hill. [About to be printed in the late Mr. Botfield's Collection of Monastic Catalogues.]

John Leland: *Index quorundam librorum repertorum in bibliothecis Monasteriorum.* Cotton MS., Vitellius, C. IX, ff. 227, 8.—[Portions of another in Royal MS. App. LXIX.]

II. Special Catalogues:—

(1) AUCKLAND (*Durham*). COLLEGIATE CHURCH. MS. at Durham: Fox's Register, p. 26. *Libri Collegii de Auckland Episcopi.* [Printed in *Wills and Inventories* (Surtees Society), pp. 101-103.]

(2) BORDESLEY (*Worcestershire*). [List of books, chiefly in French, given by Guy de Beauchamp, Earl of Warwick; to Bordesley Abbey, early in the fourteenth century.] Lambeth MSS., No. 577, f. 18. [Printed in Todd's *Illustrations of Gower and Chaucer*, pp. 161, 162.]

(3) BRETTON (*Yorkshire*). MS. Chartulary, §. *Libri quorum tituli sequuntur, &c.* [Printed by Hunter, *English Monastic Libraries*, pp. 1—7.]

(4) BURTON (*Staffordshire*). Additional MS., Brit. Mus. No. 23,944. [A collection of treatises by St. Augustine, formerly belonging to this Abbey. On verso of fol. 157: *Hos habet libros Eccl'a Burtonæ.*]

(5) CANTERBURY (*Kent*). (1) ST. AUGUSTINE'S. (A) MS., Trinity Hall, Cambridge *Historia Monasterii S. Augustini*, § 2 . . *De Libris.* [Modern Transcript in Harleian MS. 686, ff. 16 verso, to 18 verso. Printed in Sir J. Romilly's Series of *Chronicles and Memorials*, and edited by Archdeacon Hardwick.] (B) MS., Trinity College, Dublin, D. 1-19.

(2) CHRIST CHURCH. Cotton MS., Galba, E. IV., f. 128, recto, to f. 147, verso. *Tituli Librorum de Libraria Ecclesiæ Christi*, &c. [First printed in *Memoirs of Libraries*, 1859, i, 122—235. Extracts from this Catalogue are amongst the collections of Augustine Baker in Jesus College MS., No. 75, ff. 463, verso, to 467. Some extracts from another Canterbury Catalogue are given in ff. 98 verso, 99 and 99 verso, of a MS. vol. of Collections by Leland (Cotton MS.; Julius C. VI).]

Appendix A. List of Catalogues of English Monastic Libraries continued.

(6) COVENTRY (*Warwickshire*). St. Mary's Priory. Bodley MS., Digby, No. 104.—*Hii sunt libri quos Johannes de Bruges . . scripsit*, &c. [Printed by Hearne, from his own transcript in App. to *History of Glastonbury*, pp. 291—293.]

(7) DEEPING (*Lincolnshire*) Priory. Harleian MS., 3658 (Chartularium) f. 74, verso, *Isti sunt libri de armariolo Monachorum de Est-Depyng.*

(8) DOVER (*Kent*). St. Martin's Abbey. Bodley MS., 920 (A.D. 1389.)

(9) DURHAM. MS. Cath. Library, B. iv. 24. 1. *Vetus Catalogus*, &c. (12th century). 2. Ib. (A.D. 1391. *Libri . . . in communi armariolo Dunelmi infra Spendimentum*, &c. 3. *De libraria . . quæ vocatur*, Spendment. [With others. All printed by Botfield, *Catalogi Veteres*, &c. Surtees Society, 1840.]

(10) EVESHAM (*Worcestershire*). Rawlinson MS. in Bodl. Library, A. 287; 13th century; and Cotton MS., Vespasian, B. 24. § *De operibus Thomæ de Marleburwe prioris.* [Printed from Bodley MS. in *Chronicon Abbatiæ de Evesham*, in Sir J. Romilly's Series. Edited by Mr. Macray, 1863.]

(11) EXETER (*Devonshire*). Exeter Cathedral MS., A.D. 1327. *Inventarium librorum Ecclesiæ Beati Petri Exoniensis*, . . . per Ricardum de Brailegh. —[Printed in Oliver's *Lives of the Bishops of Exeter*, pp. 301-310.]

(12) FLAXLEY (*Gloucestershire*). MS. Cartulary (on a roll) at Middlehill, formerly belonging to the Wynniatt family of Stanton. [Some of the

books are mentioned in a notice of this Cartulary by Sir T. Phillipps, in *Transactions of Royal Society of Literature*, i, 54.] Appendix A. List of Catalogues of English Monastic Libraries continued.

(13) GLASTONBURY (*Somersetshire.*) MS. Trinity Coll., Cambridge. *Numerus librorum Glastoniensis Ecclesiæ*, &c., A.D. 1248. [Printed by Hearne in App. to Joanni Glastoniensis *Chronica*, 432-444.]

(14) HEREFORD. [Partially printed in *Catalogi Librorum Manuscriptorum Angliæ Hiberniæ*, II, 43-45, 1697.]

(15) HULNE (*Northumberland*). CARMELITE PRIORY. Harleian MS. 3897, f. 52. (1) [A Classed Press Catalogue of the books of the Priory of Hulne. Imperfect. Begins f. 42, verso . . . . *P[rimu]m E. Item, unum volumen, claræ manus, in quo continetur in sermonibus Barnardus super Cantica*, &c. [Printed by Botfield, in Appendix to Durham Catalogues, *ut supra*.]

(2) *Librariæ Textus Theologiæ.*

(16) JARROW (*Durham*). CELL to Durham. MS. Durham Cath. Library, *Status . . . de Jarrow per . . . Johannes Swan*, A.D. 1491. [Printed in Inventories of Jarrow and Monk Wearmouth. Surtees Society, 1854.]

"Liber Petri Le Neve, Norroy, 1704."

(17) LANTHONY (*Gloucestershire*). Harleian MS., 460. *Examinatio et visus librorum Lanthon' juxta Gloucestriam*, ... Primi Armarii primus gradus, &c.

(18) LEICESTER. ST. MARY'S ABBEY. Laud MS. in Bodl. Library, No. 623, formerly No. 1415. *Registrum Librorum Monasterii B. Mariæ de*

Appendix A. List of Catalogues of English Monastic Libraries continued.

Pratis Leycestriæ. [By William Charyte. A.D. 1492. Printed in Nichols' *Leicestershire*, I, p. 1, 101-108.]

(19) LONDON. (1) ELSYNG SPITAL. MS. Cotton Roll, XIII, 10. *Inventarium bonorum B. Mariæ de Elsyng*, &c. [Printed in Malcolm's *Londinium Redivivum*, i, 29, 30.]

(2) SAINT PAUL'S. MS. Hatton. (A Roll.) *Kalendarium, sive Inventorium indentatum;* &c. [Printed by Dugdale in Appendix to the *History of Saint Paul's Cathedral*, Sir H. Ellis' edition, pp. 392-401.]

(20) MELSA (*Yorkshire*). *Registrum Monasterii de Melsa.* [Ff. 241, verso, to 245. Beginning, after an enumeration of Service Books, *Item, Liber unus de Regula Sancti Benedicti*, &c. Ending *Orationes, cum Sermonibus et alia.*]

(21) PETERBOROUGH (*Northamptonshire*). *Matricularium Librariæ Monasterii Burgi Sancti Petri*, &c. [Printed in Gunton's *History of Peterborough*, pp. 173-224, and reprinted in the Leipsic Journal *Serapeum.*]

(22) RAMSEY (*Huntingdonshire*). MS. Cotton Roll, II, 16. (Imperfect.) Beginning: ..... *les, liber de cœlo et mundo* .... ending: *Summa Magistri Galfridi Haspal, in uno volumine.*

(23) READING (*Berkshire*). *Hi sunt libri qui continentur in Radingensi Ecclesia.* [Printed, from a MS. Cartulary, formerly belonging to Mr. Wollascot, in Coates' *History of Reading* (Supplement of 1809).]

(24) RIEVAUX (*Yorkshire*). Jesus College MS., Cambridge, N. B. 17. *Hi sunt libri Sanctæ Mariæ Rievall'.* [14th century. Printed, from a tran-

script of the Jesus MS., in *Memoirs of Libraries*, i, 333-341; printed also by Halliwell in *Reliquiæ Antiquæ*.]

Appendix A. List of Catalogues of English Monastic Libraries continued.

(25) ROCHESTER (*Kent*). ST. ANDREW'S PRIORY. A.D. 1202. *Librarium beati Andreæ*. Royal MS., 5. B. 12, ff. 2, 3. [Printed by Mr. W. B. Rye, in *Archæologia Cantiana*, vol. III.]

(26) SAINT ALBANS (*Hertfordshire*). Arundel MS., 34, ff. 74-76 (*Registrum S. Albani*), *Dona notabilia Monasterio collata temporibus dicti Abbatis* [*i. e.* Joannis Whetehamstede]; § Factura librorum, &c.

(27) SHERBORNE (*Dorsetshire*). MS. in the Imperial Library at Paris [No. 943?].

(28) SYON (*Middlesex*). Parker MS. in Corpus Christi College, Cambridge, No. 141. *Registrum Bibliothecæ de Syon*. [15th century.]

(29) TITCHFIELD (*Hampshire*). MS. formerly in the Library of His Grace the Duke of Portland, entitled, *Rememoratorium de Tychefelde*, &c. [Tom. ii, (1) *De situ et forma Librariæ Monasterii de Tichfield*, f. 1; (2) *Registrum Librorum Monasterii*, &c., ff. 2-31.] [Excerpts from these Titchfield Registers are in Harleian MSS., 6602 and 6603. They were made by George Harbin in 1739; and collated by Sir F. Madden in 1830. The second volume is no longer in the Duke's Library or Muniment Room; or, at least, is not known to be there.]

*** See Sir F. Madden's MS. note on fly-leaf of Harleian MS. 6602.

(30) WESTMINSTER. MS. in Abbey Library, No. 230. [Maittaire's list in *Catalogi Librorum Manuscriptorum* (1697), like other Cathedral lists in that

Appendix A. List of Catalogues of English Monastic Libraries continued.

volume, cannot be regarded as a Catalogue of the *Monastic* Library; nor, indeed, is Maittaire's a "Catalogue" in any sense.]

(31) WHITBY (*Yorkshire*). [Printed in Young's *History of Whitby and Streoneshalh Abbey*, vol. ii, pp. 918-920; in Charlton's *History of Whitby*, p. 113. Abridged in *Memoirs of Libraries*, i, 109, 110.]

(32) WINCHESTER (*Hampshire*). Winchester College MS. *Libri Collegii B. Mariæ prope Winton.* [Printed by Mr. W. H. Gunner, in *Archæological Journal*, xv, 59-74.]

(33) YORK. (1) St. Peter's Monastery. Alcuini *De Pontificibus et Sanctis Ecclesiæ Eboracensis Poema*, [in Gale's *Scriptores XV*, iii, 730.]

There are several notices of books given to St. Peter's Library at York in the *Testamenta Eboracensia*, and in *Richmond Wills and Inventories*, published by the Surtees Society.

(2) Friars Hermits. Trinity College MS., Dublin.

APPENDIX B.

[Chap. VII, p. 159.]

ANCIENT LIBRARY OF THE KINGS OF ENGLAND.—THE COLLECTION OF KING EDWARD THE SIXTH.

Appendix B. Account of Library of King Edward VI.

When that part of the text was written which relates to the Royal Library, as it was in the time of King Edward VI, I had not yet seen the admirable life of Edward, prefixed by Mr. J. G. Nichols to his collection of that Prince's *Literary Remains*, printed for the Roxburghe Club. It is useless now to regret that the printed books of the Royal collection were not, like its manuscripts, kept apart, when received by George the Second's gift. But great as is the difficulty of identifying those gathered by our Kings, severally, Mr. Nichols has succeeded in making a most interesting list of such of the printed volumes, at present scattered throughout the general library of the British Museum, as bear indisputable (or almost indisputable) marks of having been added to the original Royal library by Edward the Sixth.

Printed books added to the Old Royal Library by Edward VI.

That list includes the *Biblia Rabbinica* printed by Bomberg at Venice, in 1547, bound (as three volumes instead of four) in crimson velvet; Froschover's Latin Bible of the same date, magnificently bound in green

Appendix B. Account of the Library of Edward VI.

velvet, but having now a leather back adorned with crowns and roses, and with the king's monogram; a Tyndale's English Testament, which has lost its title page as well as its original binding; the *Vecchio Testamento* of Bruccioli (1540); the *Homilies* of 1547, printed by Whitchurche; Peter Martyr's *Tractatio de Sacramento Eucharistiæ* (1549); Ochino's *Tragædie of the Usurped Primacie of the Bishop of Rome* (translated by Ponet, from the author's manuscript, 1549); the *Homiliæ* of Rudolph Gualther (Zurich, 1553) bound in leather curiously gilt with arabesque borders; the *Homiliæ* of John Hofmeister (1549); the Basil edition of Castalio's Psalter, &c., of 1547; the *Paraphrasis in triginta Psalmos* of Flaminio (1552); the *Monarchia de N. S. Jesu Christo* of John Anthony Panthera Parentino (1545); the treatise *De amplitudine Misericordiæ Dei*, with other translations from the Italian, by Curio, dedicated by the translator to Edward in 1550; Hooper's *Oversight and Deliberacion upon the Holy Prophet Jonas* (1550), and Agnes D'Albiac's *Livre de Job, traduit en poesie Françoise* (1552); both also dedicated, as well as presented, to the king. Mr. Nichols has identified many other theological works as having belonged to Edward, but these are the most conspicuous.

In Classics, the Basil Herodotus (1541) and Thucydides (1540) bound in one volume; the Aldine *In omnes de Arte Rhetorica M. Tullii Ciceronis libros Commentaria* (1546); Etienne Dolet's *Questions Tusculanes*; the Galen of 1549; the Italian translation of Ptolemy, printed at Venice in 1548,—a copy with rich illuminations, having the look of a New-Year's gift; and two or three treatises of Plutarch, are the only additions, as it seems, to the royal collection clearly traceable to King Edward VI. A fine copy of the Basil Edition of the *Orationes Philippicæ* of Cicero, dedicated and presented to the King by Curio, its editor, in 1551, has, like many other works of which incidental notice is extant, disappeared. Several royal volumes of this as of other periods now to be seen in the British Museum appear nevertheless to have been, for a time, severed from the rest. They bear the marks of intermediate private ownership, but have in various ways found at length their proper resting-place.

Appendix B. Account of the Library of King Edward VI.

In History and Politics, Mr. Nichols has identified copies of the *Coronica General de todo Espana* of Pero Anton Beuler; the *Cronica de Espana* of Pedro de Valera; the *Historie Moderne* of Mark Guazzo (1540), and also his subsequent book of 1545; the *Descriptio priscæ urbis Romæ* (1544), bound with another treatise on the same subject of 1540; Falco's treatise on the Antiquities of Naples, also of 1549; Paul Eber's *Calendarium Historicum*; Lord Stafford's *True differens between the Regall Power and the Ecclesiasticall Power; The Ordre of the Hospital of S. Bartholomewe's* (1552); the *Seconde Apologie contre les calomnies des Imperiaulx* (1552); together with some volumes of the *Statutes*.

In modern Poetry, Mr. Nichols' list contains only the Petrarch of 1534; and in what may here be termed "Literary Miscellanies," Cardan *De Subtilitate*, and John Vives, *De l'Ufficio del Marito, come si debbe portare verso la moglie*. But the list, it will be remembered, comprises only such books as, after the lapse of more than three centuries, have continued to bear some special mark of their ownership by King Edward.

Among the Royal Manuscripts which are similarly traceable are the Latin Poems of Nicholas Denisot (12. A. VII); a '*Petit Recueil de l'Estat des Princes*, compiled by Peter Du Ploich (16. E. XXXVII, the gift of which the

Appendix B. Account of the Library of King Edward VI.

author elsewhere says was munificently rewarded by the King; another little compilation by the same author (16 E. XXIII) who was teacher of French at Oxford; a Sermon of Latimer's (18 B. XX); a poem, by William Forrest, entitled *The Poesye of Princely Practise* (17 D. III); and an English translation of Barbaro's *Viaggi alla Tana, in Persia, in India,* &c., made by the unfortunate Clerk of the Council, William Thomas. This MS. is now 17. C. X.

In the University Library of Cambridge there is an interesting manuscript translation of Paleario's famous treatise *On the benefits of Christ's death*, which once belonged to Anne Seymour, Duchess of Somerset, and by her was lent to Edward, who has written in it two inscriptions, one of which reads thus:—

> "*Faith is dede, if it be without workes.*
> *Your loving neveu*
> *Edward.*"

APPENDIX C.

AN ATTEMPT TOWARDS A BRIEF SYNOPTICAL VIEW OF THE PUBLIC RECORDS, NOW COLLECTED IN THE NEW ROLLS HOUSE.

[Chap. IX, p. 210.]

I ENDEAVOUR in the subjoined Tabular Views of the Records to supply—at least in some small measure—a want which I have long felt during my own researches, both at the late State Paper Office and at the Rolls House. Mr.

Thomas' *Handbook to the Public Records* has several merits, but in my own case, as in some others, it has wholly failed to give real help. To put it in few words, Mr. Thomas *begins* with what is—to those who need any "Handbook" at all—the merely technical and obscure terminology of his subject, instead of beginning with plain terms, and subordinating to *them*, the technicalities. He multiplies divisions instead of simplifying them. He gives to what is trivial, just the same prominence as to what is essential. Whilst adopting an alphabetical arrangement, he cancels its advantages by using a whole series of alphabets in which the same headings continually recur. And he adds to the perplexities thus arising by a multitude of references which are so truly "cross-references" that they perpetually send the reader from page to page, and back again. The one cardinal merit of a "Handbook" is to give the information sought for at a single view; not at two views, or twenty.*

Here, and now, I can deal only, or almost only, with the *chief* headings of the subject-matter of the Records, and must pass over most of the minor headings. I offer my "Synoptical Tables" simply as a small help to such of my fellow-searchers at the Rolls, as may chance to fall in with

* So curiously infelicitous is Mr. Thomas, in this particular, that in dealing with the greatest historic names,—"familiar in our mouths as household words,"—he contrives to bury them. There are (to take a modern example) in the Rolls House documents about Napoleon I, but the word "NAPOLEON" will be looked for in vain in Mr. Thomas' book or in its Index. Yet that book, despite its obvious faults, was a piece of real public service. It was a decided improvement upon its predecessors. And with other useful—but always overhasty—labours of its author it deserves honourable memory. Without its aid I should scarcely have ventured to make this attempt at a synoptical view of the Records. I have also derived more valuable help from Mr. Hardy's twenty-fourth Report (1863), as well as from the twenty-two annual Reports of Sir F. Palgrave.

this volume. I think that in my own case access, years ago, to such Synopsis, imperfect as it is, would have saved me a world of time, and some disappointments.

SYNOPTICAL VIEW OF THE PUBLIC RECORDS, 1864.

TABLE THE THIRD—ALPHABETICAL.

*** The words in **Clarendon** type indicate the name of that particular *branch* of the Record Service to which the documents referred to, technically belong:—As "**Chancery**"—"**Exchequer**"—"**Treasury,**"—and so on; and after all such words the word "**Records**" is implied. Similarly, after the word *Domestic,* or the word *Foreign,* the word "*Correspondence*" is always to be understood. The abbreviation "**S. P. D.**" means "**State Paper Department.**"

When ["Old Chapter House mark, $A\frac{1}{17}$,"] or the like, is added to an entry, it means that the Book referred to belonged formerly to the "TREASURY OF RECEIPT," and the use of those marks still enables Readers to obtain speedily, at the New Rolls House, the volumes of that ancient Library of the Exchequer. The headings in *Italic* capitals denote technical terms *not* indicative of the subject-matter of the Records. The sign ✠ stands for the word "*Also.*" The sign = stands for the word "*See.*" In a few important cases, the repetition of needful particulars under two headings has been thought preferable to a multiplication of References from one heading to another.

The first and second Tables are on the folding leaves which face the preceding pages.

A.

ADMIRALTY AFFAIRS, Early.—**Chancery**: *Close Rolls.*

ADMIRALTY, Court of. [From 1524 to 1817.] **Admiralty Records.**

Admiralty Office Papers. [1642-1860.] Also, Papers incorporated with General Series in **S. P. D.**, *Domestic.*

*** The Admiralty Papers are open partially to 1760. The details are in Mr. Hardy's *Report*, XXIII, § 5.

ADVOWSONS.—**Chancery**: *Close Rolls; Patent Rolls.*

AFRICAN COMPANY, Records of the, 1662-1822.—**Miscellaneous.**

AGARDE'S INDEXES TO **Queen's Bench Records.** Rich. I to Hen. VI, 48 volumes. [Detailed list in Hardy's *Report* XXIV, 12-20.]

ALGIERS, Transactions with. **S. P. D.**—*Foreign* [10 volumes prior to 1760, ✠ subsequent papers.]

ALIENATION OFFICE, Records of. With those of **Common Pleas.**

ALIEN PRIORIES = MONASTERIES.

AMBASSADORS. Records relating to the Instructions, Credentials, Functions, Ceremonies, Rights, Duties, or Payment, of Ambassadors. **Chancery**: *Close Rolls; Patent Rolls; Treaty Rolls; Royal Letters; Issue Books; Issue Rolls; Warrants.* Also, **Exchequer** and **Exchequer of Receipt.** Also, **S. P. D.**: Foreign: [Separate Collection on Ambassadors and Ministers Extraordinary; and *Correspondence,* passim; *Secretary's Letter Books; Stepney Papers,*—the volume entitled "Berlin, 1698;" ✠ *Williamson Papers,*—Vols. 177-186, inclusive.]

AMERICA=COLONIES. [And so as to other *proper names* of **Colonies.**]

AMERICAN LOYALISTS, Claims of. [1784-1810.] **Commissions.**

ARITHMETIC.—"Treatise on Arithmetic, for Lady Nevile;" temp. Hen. VIII. [Perhaps the "Lady Nevile of Hunslaite," mentioned in the Darcy Papers of 1518:] **Treasury of Receipt of the Exchequer**:—

[Old Chapter House mark B $\frac{1}{14}$.]

ARMY.—**Chancery**: *Close Rolls.*—✠ **Treasury of Receipt of the Exchequer**: Books of Charges, &c., Temp. Hen. VIII.

[Old Chapter House marks—

A $\frac{3}{13}$ to A $\frac{3}{21}$; A $\frac{4}{27}$; A $\frac{5}{22}$; A $\frac{5}{23}$; B $\frac{5}{17}$.]

✠ **S. P. D.** *Domestic.* ✠ **Treasury Papers.** ✠ **War Office Papers.**

*** Open to 1820.

✠ **Audit Office Papers.**

⁂ Not open to the public.

✠ **Land Revenue Records.** [See also MILITIA.

ASKE'S REBELLION. [Depositions and Examinations; and other Papers.] **Treasury of the Receipt of Exchequer**:—

[Old Chapter House marks— $\frac{2}{28}$ to A $\frac{2}{30}$; B $\frac{2}{21}$.]

ATTAINDERS=CRIME.

Audit Office Papers, 1558-1847. [All the Catalogues and Inventories are Manuscript.]

⁂ The Audit Office Documents are not open to the public.

B.

BEAUMONT, John. Inventory of Beaumont's Lands, &c. Temp. Edw. VI. **Treasury of Receipt of the Exchequer**:—

[Old Chapter House mark, A $\frac{1}{23}$.]

BEDFORD LEVEL Awards. **Chancery** (*Petty Bag*). [Only, as yet, partially transferred, 1864.]

BIBLE. "Tropes and Figures of Holy Scripture." **Treasury of Receipt of the Exchequer**:

[Old Chapter House mark, A $\frac{1}{1}$.]

BOUNDARY COMMISSIONS, Papers of the Parliamentary Boundaries Commission, 1831-1832. Municipal Boundaries, 1835-1836.—**Commissions.**

BRITISH BIOGRAPHY. [In addition to the obvious and almost inexhaustible biographical matter scattered throughout the Records and State Papers, there are, in **S. P. D.**, and amongst the **Exchequer** documents, some *special* collections, more or less illustrative of the lives of the following, amongst other, conspicuous personages:—Cardinal WOLSEY; Lord LISLE; THOMAS, Lord CROMWELL; THOMAS WRIOTHESLEY, Earl of Southampton; MARY, Queen of Scots; Sir WALTER RALEIGH; Secretary CONWAY; ALGERNON SYDNEY; Sir JOSEPH WILLIAMSON; Sir LEOLINE JENKINS; Sir THOMAS WILSON.]

BRITISH LOCAL HISTORY. [A Collection of Papers, in 24 volumes, arranged alphabetically according to Counties.] *Domestic,* **S. P. D.**

BRITTANY, Chancery of. Examinations, 1514.—**Treasury of the Receipt of the Exchequer**:—

[Old Chapter House mark, $A\frac{6}{28}$.]

C.

CÆSAR MANUSCRIPTS. [An Index to the MS. Collections of Sir Julius Cæsar, 1676.]—**S. P. D.** *Williamson Papers,* Vol. 88.

CALAIS ACCOUNTS.—**Treasury of Receipt of the Exchequer**:—

[Old Chapter House marks, $C\frac{1}{1}$ to $\frac{1}{4}$.] ✠ Papers relating to Calais.—**S. P. D.**, *Domestic.*

CANTERBURY, See of. [Inventory of the Muniments of the See of Canterbury, 1330.]—**Treasury of**

CANTERBURY, *continued.*
Receipt of the Exchequer:—
[Old Chapter House mark, A $\frac{1}{2}$.]

The title reads: *Capitula Cart9 Reg9 in Thesaur9 Archiepi Cant9.*

CARDINAL COLLEGE, OXFORD. Accounts, Rentals, Statutes, &c.—**Treasury of Receipt of the Exchequer:—**
[Old Chapter House marks—
A $\frac{1}{5}$; A $\frac{6}{8}$; A $\frac{4}{4}$; A $\frac{5}{5}$; B $\frac{1}{4}$; B $\frac{1}{26}$.]

CATALOGUES OF BOOKS.—**S. P. D.,** *Domestic.*
✠ *Ib. Williamson Papers.*

CATHERINE *of Arragon, Queen Consort of England.*—**Treasury of Receipt of the Exchequer:**
[Papers relating to Q. Catherine's Divorce. Old Chapter House marks— A $\frac{4}{37}$; B $\frac{4}{2}$.]

CECIL PAPERS.—Catalogue of the Cecil State Papers, preserved at Hatfield. (4 vols.)—**Miscellaneous.**
*** These volumes were transcribed from the Hatfield Catalogue by permission of the Marquis of Salisbury, but are not open to the Public.

CENSUS OFFICE Papers, 1801-1841.—**Miscellaneous.**

CHAMBERLAIN'S (LORD) Office Papers, 1541-1759.—**Miscellaneous.**

[**Chancery Records,** The, GENERALLY, extend from 1066 to 1860.]

CHARTERS.—**Chancery**:—*Cartæ Antiquæ*, Conquest to Henry III; *Charter Rolls*, 1 John to 8 Henry VIII; [Inventory printed in *Third* and *Fourth* Reports.] *Patent Rolls*.

CHARLES THE FIRST, *King of England*, &c.—Estates of—**Exchequer**.—✠ **S. P. D.**, *Domestic*: INTERREGNUM PAPERS; *and* CHARLES II (early volumes).

CHINA, Early Intercourse with. **S. P. D.** *Domestic*.

CHRIST'S COLLEGE, CAMBRIDGE. Statutes, 1508.—**Treasury of Receipt of the Exchequer**; [Old Chapter House mark, A $\frac{6}{8}$.]

CHURCH LIVINGS, Valuations, &c., of, Temp. Hen. VIII. Ib. [Chapter House Books. Old Marks—

A $\frac{4}{21}$ A $\frac{4}{26}$ A $\frac{6}{5}$ B $\frac{3}{26}$.]

Exchequer: *Nonæ Rolls* [Printed]; *Taxatio* [Printed]; *Valor Ecclesiasticus* [Printed]. ✠ **Chancery**: *Close Rolls*; *Patent Rolls*; Commonwealth Surveys; ✠ *Williamson Papers*, **S. P. D.**, Vols. 3, 4.

CHURCH PROPERTY. Inventories of Church Goods, 6 Edw. VI. **Exchequer** (Queen's Remembrancer, &c.) [Printed in *Seventh* and *Ninth* Reports.]

CIVIL LIST.—Civil List Books [1698-1816, Catalogued.] Civil List Disposition Books [1763-1834. Printed Calendar in *Seventh* Report.] Annual Civil Lists [a MS. Catalogue or Inventory, from 1727 to 1802]. —**Treasury**.

CLOSE ROLLS—**Chancery**. [Begin with 6th of K. John. *Printed* to 11th Hen. III.]

"The Records intituled *Rotuli Litterarum Clausa-*

CLOSE ROLLS, *continued.*

rum, or 'CLOSE ROLLS,' are a series of parchment Rolls, commencing . . A.D. 1204, on which are recorded . . all Mandates, Letters, and Writs, of a private nature. They are denominated *Close*, in contradistinction to another series of Rolls called *Patent.*"—Hardy, *Introduction to the Close Rolls.*

[An Inventory from John to Elizabeth is printed in *Second*, *Third*, and *Fourth* Reports of Sir F. Palgrave.]

COINAGE.—**Chancery**: *Close Rolls*; *Mint Rolls*; *Patent Rolls.* ✠ **S.P.D.** *Domestic.* ✠ **Treasury of Receipt of Exchequer.** ✠ **Exchequer**: *Accounts* [various]; Book of Charges of the Mint House. 18 Hen. VIII, 1526, [Old C. House mark—

A $\frac{3}{27}$.] ✠ **Treasury**: § Mint Affairs.

COLONIAL OFFICE PAPERS.—(1) Correspondence, &c., from 1574 to 1688. [71 volumes of Papers, and 109 Entry Books.—**S. P. D.** *Colonial.*

(2) Correspondence, 1689-1783 ["America and West Indies," 357 volumes]; ✠ Id. (Board of Trade) 1689-1717; ✠ Subsequent Papers, from 1784 to 1829. [In course of arrangement.] **S. P. D.**

*** Open to 1702, and also from 1703 to 1760, as respects all Papers not relating to *North America.*

COMMISSARIAT PAPERS.—

England, 1798-1844.

Ireland, 1798-1822.

Colonies, 1780-1848.—**Miscellaneous.**

COMMON PLEAS RECORDS [1179-1849; Alienation Office, 1571-1834; Com. Pleas Registrar, 1838-49].

COMMONWEALTH AND PROTECTORATE.—*Domestic Correspondence* **S. P. D.** § "Interregnum Papers"; § "Composition Papers." [183 volumes ✠ Unbound papers.]

COMMON PRAYER BOOK, Sealed Copies of [deposited pursuant to "Act of Uniformity."] **Chancery.**

CONWAY AND THROCKMORTON PAPERS. 1538-1705.—**S. P. D.** [In course of incorporation with *Domestic Correspondence.*]

CORONATION ROLLS [From Edw. II, but broken in series.]—**Chancery.**

COUNCIL BOOKS.

[The General Series of the Privy Council Books remains in the PRIVY COUNCIL OFFICE, but those of the Interregnum Councils, and one earlier volume, embracing 5 and 6 P. and Mary, and part of 1 Eliz., are in **S. P. D.**]

*** Printed from 10 Rich. II to 33 H. VIII, under the Editorship of the late Sir N. H. Nicolas.

COUNCIL OF STATE [Commonwealth].—Order Books; Entry Books; Letter Books; and Warrant Books: [103 volumes]—1649 to 1660. **S. P. D.** *Domestic:* Interregnum. Vols. 29-131, inclusive. Other Records [26 volumes], Ib. Vols. 132-157.

COURTENAY, HENRY, *Earl of Devon*, and *Marquess of Exeter, K.G.* Household Books, 15 and 17 Hen. VIII [1525-7].—**Treasury of the Receipt of Exchequer:—**

COURTENAY, *continued.*

[Old Chapter House marks, respectively, B. $\frac{2}{2}$; A. $\frac{6}{21}$.]

Book of Expenses. Ib. [Old mark B. $\frac{2}{13}$.]

CRIME—**S. P. D.** *Domestic.* ✠ **Chancery:** *Close Rolls; Parliament Rolls.* ✠ **Queen's Bench:** *Baga de Secretis.*

CROMWELL, Thomas, *Lord Cromwell* (Accounts, Inventories, and other papers.) **Treasury of the Receipt of Exchequer:** [Chapter House Books. Old marks, B. $\frac{1}{8}$; B $\frac{1}{19}$;] — . [Diary.] Ib.— "Books of Specialities." Ib. [A. $\frac{4}{30}$.]— Catalogues of Deeds and Writings, Ib. A $\frac{4}{6}$ Catalogue of Obligations and other Writings 24 Hen. VIII, 1532. Ib. [A $\frac{4}{17}$].

CRUSADES.—**Chancery:** *Close Rolls.*

CUSTOM-HOUSE PAPERS. 1677—1847.—**Treasury.**

CYPHERS, DIPLOMATIC, Collections of. **S. P. D.** *Foreign* [Eight volumes from Eliz. to Charles II. Numbered 1—6, and "Mary, Queen of Scots," 22, 23.]

D.

DANIELL, John and Jane, of *Dewsbury in Cheshire.* Danyell's Disasters [Addressed to James I].—**Treasury of Receipt of the Exchequer;—**

DANIELL, *continued.*

[Old Chapter House mark $C\frac{1}{17}$].

DELINQUENTS' ESTATES. **S. P. D.** *Domestic:* Interregnum [From vol. 274 to 275 "*Red* series;" and vol. 288 to vol. 355, inclusive "*Green* series;" Vol. 275 contains the Index.] "Briefe of Claims, 1652."—An Alphabetical Catalogue, according to Delinquents' names in Palmer series of Calendars, &c., No. 74.

Also, *Domestic:* "Royalist Composition Papers." [*First series.* From Vol. 294 *Red* to 409 *Red,* inclusive. 113 volumes; and *Second series* from Vol. 410 *Red* to 464 *Red,* inclusive. The *Index* to 1st series is in Vol. 275; the *Index* to 2nd series is in Vol. 464.]

DENMARK. Diplomatic Correspondence with Denmark. [1432-1760: 115 volumes; ✠ Subsequent papers in course of rearrangement.] Papers relating to Danish Claims [*i.e.* Claims *against* Denmark] 1834-1841.—**Commissions.**

DESPENCER, HUGH LE, Correspondence.—**Treasury of Receipt of the Exchequer:** [Old Chapter House mark, $B.\frac{3}{20}$].

DOMESDAY BOOK.—**Treasury of Receipt of the Exchequer:** [Printed, 1783-1816; and Photozincographed, 1863.]

DUNDAS, HENRY, *Viscount Melville.* Papers relating to Lord Melville's Impeachment, 1785-1806—**Audit Office.**

DUNKIRK, Papers relating to. **S. P. D.** *Foreign* [15 volumes].

E.

EDUCATION. Papers of the Education Commission, 1860, 1861; Oxford University Commission, 1850-58.—**Commissions.**

ELIZABETH [WOODVILLE] *Queen Consort of England.* Computus Rec9 Gen9 Dnæ Eliz. Reginæ Angl9—**Treasury of Receipt of the Exchequer:** [Old Chapter House mark, B. $\frac{3}{12}$.]

EXCERPTS FROM RECORDS. *Williamson Papers,* **S. P. D.,** Vol. 34; Vols. 95-144 *a.* [52 volumes] ✠ Record Commission Transcripts.—**Miscellaneous.**

EXCHEQUER ACCOUNTS=REVENUE.

Exchequer Records.

Plea side, from 1219 to 1839.

Queen's Remembrancer, 1216-1141.

Lord Treasurer's Remembrancer, 1130-1834.

Courts of Surveyors and of Augmentations, 1515-1553.

Exchequer of Receipt, *Domesday* to 1834.

First Fruits, 1536-1840.

F.

FIELD OF THE CLOTH OF GOLD, Papers relating to the. **Treasury of Receipt of the Exchequer:** [Old Chapter House mark, A $\frac{14}{19}$.]

FINE ROLLS—**Chancery.** [6 John to 17 Charles I.]

FLANDERS = NETHERLANDS.

FOREIGN ARCHIVES.

[A vast collection of Transcripts and Excerpts, as yet chiefly unbound, of Documents illustrative of British History, contained in FOREIGN ARCHIVES and LIBRARIES; is arranged in portfolios in the following order: I, FRANCE; II, BELGIUM, GERMANY, and GERMAN STATES; III, PORTUGAL; IV, SWITZERLAND; V, ITALY.]—**Miscellaneous.**

FOREIGN OFFICE PAPERS—**S. P. D. Foreign Correspondence.** 1097-1760. *** Open to 1688. [4100 volumes to 1760.] ✠ Subsequent Papers; in course of arrangement.

[The series of Foreign Correspondence opens with transactions with Scotland. The papers of the 12th, 13th, and 14th centuries are few and broken. Next to Scotland come negotiations with Germany, but these, as respects *this* series of our Records, do not begin till 1311; then follow French negotiations (1338), and Flemish (1340). The total number of volumes in the Foreign series, prior to 1688, is 1659. The seventy subsequent years added 2440 volumes, making the total prior to 1760 about 4100 volumes. Were those of subsequent date up to the latest transfers similarly arranged and similarly enumerated, they would more than double that number. Permission to search the Foreign Papers subsequent to 1688 is granted by Her Majesty's Principal Secretary of State, on reasonable cause; but all extracts or transcripts desired must be specifically authorized by the proper authority.]

There are also Selections on Foreign Affairs in

FOREIGN OFFICE, *continued.*

Williamson Papers, **S. P. D.,** Vols. 55-68, *a.* [16 vols.].

[Some particulars of the Foreign Papers—as to mere dates and extent, up to 1760—are given under the names of the Countries to which they specifically relate.]

FORESTS.—**Exchequer of Receipt:** *Placita Forestæ,* K. John to 1640.—✠ Perambulations, **Chancery:** *Close Rolls; Patent Rolls.* [Also "Petty Bag" Records, in course of transfer].

✠ **Exchequer:** *Black Book of the Forests.* Hen. VIII.

[Old Chapter House mark, C $\frac{6}{7}$]✠; Perambulations (Q. Remembrancer's Department); *Surveys.*

✠ **S. P. D.,** *Williamson Papers,* Vol. 128.

✠ Survey of Woods and Underwoods, 1608. **S. P. D.** *Domestic:* James I: Vol. 42.

✠ Swainmote Court Rolls of Windsor Forest, Edw. VI. to Charles I.—**Chancery.** [An Inventory in 5th Report.]

✠ Forest Accounts and Presentments, Hen. III to James I.—**Exchequer of Receipt.**

✠ Collections relating to, from K. John to Edw. IV. **S. P. D.,** *Miscellaneous* [Old Number "73." [An Inventory of Forest Proceedings in **Chancery**—John to Charles I—is printed.]

✠ "Vasta in diversis forestis, temp. Edw. I." **Treasury of Receipt of the Exchequer:**

[Old Chapter House mark, A $\frac{4}{13}$.]

FORFEITED AND SEQUESTERED ESTATES, Surveys and Particulars of. **Exchequer:** Ministers' Accounts [*Commonwealth.*] **S. P. D.** *Domestic:* Interregnum Books. [See also DELINQUENTS.]

—————— COMMISSION OF 1716, Records of the, 1716-1725.—**Commissions.** [An Inventory is printed in *Fifth Report.*]

FRANCE. Diplomatic Correspondence with France.—**S. P. D.**

[1338-1760: 480 volumes. ✠ Subsequent papers; in course of arrangement.]

Papers on French Claims [*i. e.* Claims *against* France], 1814-1855.—**Commissions.**

Documents relating to Relief of French Refugees. **Miscellaneous.**

G.

GARTER, Order of the, Statutes [Incomplete]. **Treasury of Receipt of the Exchequer:**

[Old Chapter House mark, A $\frac{4}{16}$.]

GASCON OR VASCON ROLLS—**Chancery.** [26 Hen. III. to 7 Edw. IV.]

GAZETTES, Collections from and for, **S. P. D.,** *Miscellaneous* [Old Number "18," *Williamson Series.*]

✠ Gazettes and Tracts, Collection of, **S. P. D.,** *Domestic:* Various.

GENEALOGICAL AND HERALDIC MATTERS—**Chancery:** *Inquisitiones post mortem; Close Rolls; Fine Rolls.* ✠ **S. P. D.** *Domestic Correspondence.* Also, "Style and Titles Books" (in Letter-Books

GENEALOGICAL, *continued.*

Series, A.D. 1627-28, and under the same designation, in *Williamson Papers*, Vols. 186-205. Also "Arms of Families," *Williamson Papers*, Vol. 45 *a*. Pedigrees, &c., *Williamson Papers*, Vols. 27 and 60. ✠ **Exchequer**: *Pipe Rolls; "Placita Exercitûs Regis."* ✠ **Common Pleas**: *Placita Terræ.* ✠ Records of the **Court of Wards**.—✠ Irish Pedigrees.—**S. P. D.**: *Domestic:* IRELAND. Vol. 180.

GEOGRAPHICAL COLLECTIONS. Collection of Maps, in 49 Cases—**S. P. D.** ✠ Maps, Plans, and Surveys, of Ireland. Ib. *Domestic:* IRELAND. Vols. 208-210.

GERMANY, Affairs of: Diplomatic Correspondence with Germany. **S. P. D.**, *Foreign*, § Germany [1311-1760: 398 volumes ✠ Subsequent Papers. In course of arrangement] § German States: [to 1760: 63 volumes ✠ Subsequent Papers] § Hamburgh, [72 volumes.] ✠ **Chancery**: *Almain Rolls.*

GUNPOWDER MAGAZINES, Security of. **Chancery**: (Crown Office Papers).

GUNPOWDER TREASON PAPERS.—*Domestic Correspondence*, **S. P. D.**, James I.

H.

HOLLAND = NETHERLANDS.

HOME OFFICE RECORDS AND PAPERS.—**Chancery**: *Charter Rolls; Close Rolls; Parliament Rolls; Patent Rolls;* ✠ **Exchequer of Receipt.** ✠ **S. P. D.** *Domestic*, 1274-1830.

*** Open to 1760.

HOME OFFICE, *continued.*

[The Papers of the Home Office, in its earliest organization, are enrolments in **Chancery.** Many early documents belonged to the **Exchequer of Receipt,** and are called "Chapter House Papers." These are now transferred to **S. P. D.** The earliest papers in that Department relate to the Channel Islands, and begin with the year 1274. The total number of volumes anterior to the close of the reign of Henry is about 170. The number of those *regnally* arranged of subsequent dates, down to George the Fourth, is as follows:—EDWARD VI, 19 volumes [Printed Calendar]; MARY, 14 volumes [Do.]; ELIZABETH, 284 volumes [Calendar in progress]; JAMES I, 237 volumes [Do.]; CHARLES I, 399 volumes [Do.]; Interregnum, 923 vols. [Partial MS. Calendars]; CHARLES II, 354 volumes [Printed Calendar in progress]; JAMES II, 129 volumes; ANNE, 51 vols.; WILLIAM AND MARY, 27 volumes; GEORGE I, 74 volumes; GEORGE II, 166 volumes; GEORGE III, 412 volumes [not yet accessible]; making a total of 3259 volumes, of which there are now issued or at press Calendars to nearly 1000 volumes. Besides these, the *Home* series includes 184 volumes on Regencies; 127 on War Office matters and Correspondence; 46 on Treasury matters and Correspondence; 22 volumes headed "Secretaries of State;" 77 volumes headed "Newspapers and Gazettes;" 51 volumes on "Militia;" 75 volumes relating to the Affairs of the Borders; 105 volumes relating to various minor possessions of the Crown (*Calais—Channel Islands—East Indies—*

HOME OFFICE, *continued.*

Gibraltar—Tangier, &c.); 640 volumes relating to *Ireland;* 128 volumes relating to *Scotland;* together with several "*Various,*" "*Miscellaneous,*" and other subordinate classes of papers, amounting in the aggregate to 842 volumes; and making a grand total of about 5560 volumes.]

HOUSEHOLD of the SOVEREIGN and ROYAL FAMILY. **Chancery:** *Close Rolls; Liberate Rolls;* ✠ **Treasury of Receipt of the Exchequer:** Chapter House Books, viz.—

(1) Liber de Expensis Philippæ Reginæ, 23 Edw. III.

(2) The Kyng's Book of Payments. Hen. VII, 1505-1509.

(3) Account Book of the Queen [Elizabeth, Consort of Henry VIIth]'s Household, 17 H. VII, 1501.

(4) The King's Book of Payments, 1-12 Henry VIII, 1509-1520.

(5) Household of Princess Mary, 15 Henry VIII, 1523.

(6) Books of Revels.

(7) Hampton Court Accounts and Royal Wages; Temp. Henry VIII.

(8) Necessaria Regis Edwardi, Anno X^{mo}.

[Old Chapter House marks, respectively,

$$A\frac{6}{3};\ A\frac{5}{18};\ B\frac{2}{7};\ A\frac{5}{16,\ 17};$$

$$B\frac{2}{8}\frac{5}{14}\frac{5}{3};\ C\frac{6}{8}\text{ to }C\frac{6}{16};\ B\frac{5}{4};\ C\frac{6}{3};]$$

✠ **S. P. D.** *Domestic Correspondence.* ✠ **Exchequer:** *Auditor's Books; Black Books; Red Book; Household Rolls; Imprest Rolls.*

HOUSEHOLD, *continued.*

✠ [Early Regulations, **S. P. D.** *Domestic:* Henry VIII, and prior; Old number "8."]

✠ Lord Steward's Accounts.—**Treasury** [With MS. Inventory from 1781 to 1810.]

Accounts.—**Audit Office.**

[See also WARDROBE BOOKS.]

HUNDRED ROLLS—**Chancery.** [From 2 Edward I.]

[The "Hundred Rolls" are the Reports of Commissioners into the King's rights, royalties, and prerogatives; into invasions and losses of them; and into Tenures and services; escheats and alienations. They are therefore of high historical importance, and have been printed by the Record Commission, but are now out of print.]

I.

INVENTIONS, Patents of—**S. P. D.** *Domestic Correspondence.* ✠ **Chancery:** *Close Rolls; Patent Rolls; Specification and Surrender Rolls.* [Calendars are printed in the sixth, seventh, and eighth Reports of Sir F. Palgrave.]

IRELAND—*Domestic Correspondence,* **S. P. D.** Also *Williamson Papers,* Vols. 90-93. [Including many remarkable original MS. treatises on the History, Condition, and Capabilities, of that Kingdom.] ✠ **Chancery:** *Inquisitions; Irish Rolls; "Petitiones de Hibernia."* ✠ **Exchequer:** *Pope Nicholas' Taxation: Revenue Accounts; Rolls of Irish Establishments.* ✠ **Treasury Records:**

IRELAND, *continued.*

Irish Books [from 1669]; *Irish Famine Books;* ✠ **Exchequer of Receipt:** *Hibernia Bag* [Hen. III to Hen. VII].

Maps, Plans, and Surveys, **S. P. D.** *Domestic* (IRELAND), Vols. 208-210.

Pedigrees ——————— Vol. 180.

Papers relating to the Irish Reproductive Loan Fund. 1832-1854.

ITALIAN STATES, Diplomatic Correspondence with the [1479-1760: 54 volumes ✠ GENOA, 27 volumes ✠ TUSCANY, 1551-1760: 68 volumes ✠ Subsequent papers in course of rearrangement. ✠ VENICE: 1487-1688, 75 volumes; 1689-1800, 38 volumes= 113 vols. ✠ Subsequent Papers. In course of rearrangement.]

Statistical Accounts of the Italian States, 1533-1622.—**S. P. D.** *Foreign* § Italian States.

J.

JAPAN, Early Intercourse with. **S. P. D.** *Colonial.*

JENKINS PAPERS. Foreign Papers, collected by Sir Lionel Jenkins, 1642-1688 [Incorporated with *Foreign Correspondenee,* **S. P. D.**] ✠ Domestic Papers, **S. P. D.** 1660-1685.

[Partly incorporated].

JEWELS OF THE CROWN. **Exchequer** § Inventories. ✠ **Exchequer of Receipt:** Jewell Rolls. ✠ **Treasury of Exchequer of Re-**

JEWELS, *continued.*

ceipt: Jocalia Regis Henrici Sexti. [Old Chapter-House mark, A $\frac{1}{4}$.]

Accompt of Jewel House, 24 Hen. VIII, 1532. [Old Chapter House mark, B $\frac{1}{21}$.]

Inventories of the Jewels, &c., of Q. Elizb. 1599. **Exchequer** (*Lands Revenue Records*). Accompt of Jewel House, Jac. I. ✠ **S. P. D:** *Domestic.*

Inventory of the Jewels of Q. Anne of Denmark. ✠ **Exchequer** (*Lands Rev. Records*). Inventory of Jewels of Charles I. **Exchequer** (L. R. R.) ✠ **S. P. D.:** *Domestic*: Interregnum Books.

[JEWS — **Chancery:** *Close Rolls; Fine Rolls; Patent Rolls.* ✠ **Treasury of Receipt of the Exchequer:** *Jews' Rolls;* § *Domus Conversorum* ✠ **S. P. D.,** Domestic.

JOINTURE BOOKS OF THE QUEENS OF ENGLAND [**Lands Revenue Records,** in progress of transfer].

K.

KING'S JUSTICES, COURT OF THE [*Curia Regis*].—**Queen's Bench:** *Rotuli Curiæ Regis,* 1194-1199.

[These are believed to be the earliest consecutive series of Judicial Records in Europe; commencing in the sixth year of King Richard the First. They are partially in print, edited by Sir Francis Palgrave. The Courts of Queen's Bench and of the Common Pleas are offshoots of the *Curia Regis.*]

L.

LAND REVENUES RECORDS. [In course of transfer from Land Revenues Office.]

LANDS OF THE CROWN.—**Chancery**: *Close Rolls; Liberate Rolls; Patent Rolls.*—**Land Revenues Records,** *passim.* [In progress of transfer].—**Exchequer**: *Parliamentary Surveys.* (Augmentation Office Records). Also, Ib. *Chapter House Books.* [Old marks, A $\frac{5}{6}$; $\frac{5}{7}$; A $\frac{5}{12}$ to A $\frac{5}{14}$; A $\frac{6}{26}$; A $\frac{6}{27}$; B $\frac{1}{7}$; B $\frac{1}{10}$; B $\frac{1}{12}$; B $\frac{1}{13}$; B $\frac{1}{24}$ to $\frac{1}{26}$; B $\frac{2}{20}$; B $\frac{4}{23}$; B $\frac{5}{7}$; B $\frac{5}{10}$; B $\frac{5}{16}$; B $\frac{5}{23}$; C $\frac{1}{9}$; C $\frac{1}{10}$.]

LAW COURTS AND LAW AFFAIRS:—**Chancery; Queen's Bench; Common Pleas; Exchequer; Court of Wards; Welsh; Palatine; Treasury**: *Law Opinions* [1763-1809]; *Treasury Solicitor's Papers.* ✠ **S. P. D.** *Williamson Papers,* Vols. 14-25. Ib. *Domestic Correspondence:* § Law Papers, [1684-1768.]

LAW COURTS, Abolished, Records of. 'Requests,' 1485-1643; 'Star Chamber,' 1495-1643; 'Wards and Liveries,' 1540-1660; 'Marshalsea' and 'Palace,' 1631-1849; 'Peveril,' 1661-1849; Welsh Courts, 1259-1830; Palatine Courts [In course of transfer].

LAW, Miscellaneous Treatises and Tractates on. **Treasury of Receipt of the Exchequer** [Old Chapter House marks, B $\frac{1}{14}$ to B $\frac{1}{17}$.]

LAW, *continued.*

An Ancient Legal Common Place Book, [A $\frac{6}{4}$.]

LAW OF NATIONS.—**S. P. D.:** *Williamson Papers,* Vols. 23-25.

LAWS OF ENGLAND. *Speculum Juris Publici Anglicani.* 3 vols. **S. P. D.** *Williamson Papers,* Vols. 14-16.

LETTERS.—**Chancery:** ROYAL LETTERS,—[Now in course of rearrangement. The old collection, as first arranged, extended to more than 120 volumes, besides an extensive series of unbound bundles.] ✠ On *Close Rolls* and *Patent Rolls.* Also, **S. P. D.** *Foreign Correspondence: Secretaries' Letter Books.*—**Ibid.** *Domestic,* and *Colonial.* **Exchequer:** *Red Book of the Exchequer.* ✠ **Treasury of Receipt of the Exchequer.** ✠ Chapter House Books, 5 vols. [Old marks, B $\frac{3}{2}$ to $\frac{3}{10}$.]

King's Letter Books: **S. P. D.**—*Foreign.* Northern, 1662-1671; Old number, 120.

Northern and Southern, 1664-1675; 122, 125.

Spain and Portugal, *and* Flanders, 1670-1688; 124, 126.

Sweden, 1679-1688, 127.

LIBERATE ROLLS.—**Chancery.** [2nd John to 14th Edward IV. The early "Liberate Rolls" contain precepts for payments of all kinds for the service of the State and of the Royal Household. Those of K. John are printed. They also contain much relating to Crown Lands. After Edward III their entries relate chiefly to Judicial Salaries.]

LONDON [Papers relating to Guilds, or Companies, of London]—**Treasury of Receipt of the Exchequer.** [Old Chapter House mark, $B\frac{1}{1}$.]

Articles respecting Bridge House, and other papers, [Ib., $B\frac{4}{5}$].

Church of Allhallows Barking: Papers relating thereto, A.D. 1476.—**Treasury of Receipt of the Exchequer:** [Old Chapter House mark, $A\frac{3}{2}$.]

Compensation to Port of London. 1779-1824.—**Miscellaneous.**

M.

MALTA, Papers relating to, from 1684. **S. P. D.** *Foreign.*

MANUFACTURES. **Chancery Records:** *Close Rolls.* ✠ **Exchequer:** *Specification and Surrender Rolls.* [Many papers of very high importance for the early history of our TRADE and MANUFACTURES are contained in **S. P. D.**, and a considerable portion of them was formerly classed apart. They are now, for the most part, arranged with the general collection of *Domestic Correspondence.*] ✠ Colonial.

MARY, *Queen of Scots,* Collection relating to. **S. P. D.** *Domestic:* ELIZABETH. [Vols. 255-276.]

METROPOLITAN BUILDINGS, Papers of the Registrar of, 1844-1855.—**Miscellaneous.**

METROPOLITAN POLICE. Receiver's Accounts, 1810-1822,—**Miscellaneous.**

MILITIA.—Books of Musters. **Treasury of Receipt of Exchequer.** [Old Chapter House marks, A $\frac{2}{2}$ to A $\frac{2}{27}$ inclusive; A $\frac{6}{10}$ to A $\frac{6}{17}$ inclusive; A $\frac{6}{33}$.]

MILTON, JOHN. De Doctrina Christiana.—**S. P. D.** *Domestic:* Various. Vol. 215. [Printed.] Letters of State: Ib. *Foreign:* "Royal Letters." [Old number 169.] [Printed.]

MONASTERIES, History, Possessions, Surveys, and Surrenders of. **Chancery**:—*Patent Rolls; Charter Rolls; Close Rolls; Surrender Rolls; Cardinal's Bundles; Inquisitions of Alien Priories.*—✠ **Exchequer**: *Cartularies; Inquisitions; Surveys; Valor Ecclesiasticus* [Printed].

Surveys, Extents, Inventories and Memoranda, of Monasteries, Surrendered or Dissolved. [Chiefly temp. Hen. VIII. 29 volumes.] — **Treasury of Receipt of the Exchequer:**

[Old Chapter House marks, A $\frac{3}{9}$ to A $\frac{3}{12}$; A $\frac{4}{5}$; A $\frac{4}{10}$; A $\frac{4}{25}$; A $\frac{4}{29}$ to A $\frac{4}{32}$; A $\frac{4}{35}$; A $\frac{5}{5}$; A $\frac{5}{15}$; A $\frac{6}{1}$; A $\frac{6}{7}$; B $\frac{1}{13}$; B $\frac{1}{20}$; B $\frac{1}{22}$ to $\frac{1}{25}$; B $\frac{2}{10}$; B $\frac{2}{20}$; B $\frac{2}{23}$; B $\frac{4}{8}$; B $\frac{4}{16}$; B $\frac{5}{5}$; C $\frac{1}{15}$.]

"Paper writings concerning Abbies; temp.

MONASTERIES, &c., *continued.*
Hen. VIII."—**Treasury of Receipt of the Exchequer.** [Chapter House mark, A $\frac{1}{21}$.]

MOROCCO, Diplomatic Correspondence with.—**S. P. D.** *Foreign.* [1564-1760: 8 volumes.]

MUSTERS, Books of. [MILITIA.] **Treasury of Receipt of the Exchequer.** [The old Chapter House marks are enumerated above, under the word MILITIA.]

N.

NAPOLEON I. [Papers relating to the Imprisonment of Napoleon at St. Helena.]—*Colonial Correspondence,* **S. P. D.**; ✠ **Treasury Records** (1816-1820).

National Debt Office, Papers of the, 1745-1846.

NAVY. **Chancery:** *Close Rolls; Patent Rolls.* ✠ **Exchequer:**—Accounts [in Queen's Remembrancer's Department.] Books of Charges, &c. [in **Treasury of Receipt.**] 8 vols.

[Old Chapter House marks, A $\frac{3}{13}$; A $\frac{3}{16}$; A $\frac{3}{18}$; A $\frac{3}{20}$; A $\frac{3}{26}$; A $\frac{5}{20\text{-}23}$; A $\frac{6}{30}$; B $\frac{2}{3}$.]

✠ **S. P. D.:** "Admiralty and Navy Correspondence." Also, **S. P. D.** *Domestic.* Also, **S. P. D.** *Foreign:* [Departmental, *i. e.* Correspondence of the Foreign Office with other Public Departments.] Also, **Treasury:** *Commissariat Books; Navy Accounts,* from 1697; *Navy Books,* from 1684; *Order Books.* Also, **Audit Office Papers,**—*passim.*

NAVY, *continued.*

✠ **Admiralty,** Court of—✠ **Admiralty Office Papers,** *passim.*

✠ Navy Office Papers. 1664-1665: [5 volumes.] —**S. P. D.** *Miscellaneous*—[In the old arrangement.]

NETHERLANDS, Affairs of the. **S. P. D.** *Foreign Correspondence:* § Belgium [Modern Papers.] § Flanders [1340-1760: 191 vols. ✠ Subsequent papers. In course of re-arrangement.] § Holland [1577-1760: 630 vols. ✠ Subsequent papers.] § Netherlands.

Printed Tracts on the History and Politics of Holland, &c. **S. P. D.** *Foreign:* § Holland, 1664-1685. 7 volumes.

NEWSLETTERS AND NEWSPAPERS [Printed and Manuscript.]—**S. P. D.** *Domestic:* Various.

✠ *Ib. Williamson Papers,* Vol. 32.

NICHOLAS, Sir Edward, Note Books, Papers, and Collections of. **S. P. D.** *Domestic:* CHARLES I.

NONÆ ROLLS.

[The *Nonæ* Rolls, or *Inquisitiones Nonarum,* are inquisitions for assessing the subsidy of the ninth lamb, the ninth fleece, and the ninth sheaf, granted to Edward III in the 14th year of his reign. They are printed (Record Commission Publications).]

NORMAN ROLLS.—**Chancery.** [2nd John to 10th Henry V.]

*** Partially printed.

O.

OFFICES OF STATE, Fees of, *Williamson Papers*, **S. P. D.**, Vol. 10. Grants of, **Chancery**: *Close Rolls; Fine Rolls; Patent Rolls,* ✠ *Williamson Papers*, **S. P. D.**, Vol. 133.

ORIGINALIA AND MEMORANDA ROLLS.—**Exchequer.**

[The *Originalia* are estreats from Chancery of all Grants enrolled on *Close, Patent, Fine,* or *Redisseisin* Rolls, if rent be reserved, salary payable, or service due. They extend from the reign of Edward III to Victoria. The *Memoranda Rolls* are Crown Remembrancer's Records, and also begin with Henry III. There are MS. Indices to both, from Edward I to Elizabeth. Jones' Index from Hen. VIII to Anne is printed. Abstracts of the Originalia to Edward III were also printed by the Record Commission.]

OXFORD UNIVERSITY COMMISSION, Papers of the, 1850-1858.—**Commissions.**

P.

PALATINE COURTS' RECORDS. [In course of transfer.]

PAPAL BRIEFS AND BULLS.—K. John to 1572, **Chancery.** There are also entries of Bulls on the *Close Rolls.*—✠ **Exchequer**: *Red Book; Black Book.* ✠ **Treasury of Receipt of the Exchequer**:—

[Old Chapter House marks, B $\frac{3}{3}$ to B $\frac{3}{7}$.]

PAPAL SUPREMACY. "Armestrong's Sermons." **Treasury of Receipt of the Exchequer.** [Old Chapter House mark, $B\frac{3}{25}$.]

Renunciations of. **Treasury of Receipt of the Exchequer.** [Old Chapter House marks, $B\frac{3}{14}$; $B\frac{3}{15}$.]

PARLIAMENT.—**Chancery**: [Incidental:] *Close Rolls; Vetus Codex,* or '*Black Book of the Tower.*' [Serial:—] (1) STATUTE ROLLS from 1278, 6 Edw. I to 1468, 8 Edw. IV; (2) **Exchequer**;—ROLLS of PARLIAMENT, from 1290, 18 Edw. I; (3) **Chancery**: PARLIAMENTARY ROLLS, from 1 Rich. III. [An Inventory of Parliament Rolls,—EDW. II to ELIZABETH,—printed in Second and Third Reports.] (4) EXEMPLIFICATIONS of ACTS ('*Arrow Bundle*'); (5) Writs of Summons (on the *Close Rolls*); (6) PETITIONS.

*** The Statute Rolls are wanting from 8th to 23rd of Henry VI.

Prerogative of Parliaments. By Sir Walter Raleigh. **S. P. D.**, *Domestic*: JAMES I. Vols. 84, 85.

PATENT ROLLS.—**Chancery.** [From 3rd John, 1201, to Q. Victoria. Those of the first sixteen years, only, are printed. MS. Calendars, with full Indices, in the Palmer Series of Calendars in Search Room. Printed Inventories in *Second, Third,* and *Sixth Reports.*]

*** Wanting 10-12 John and 23, of Hen. III. Otherwise complete from the first year of the thir-

PATENT ROLLS, continued.

teenth century to the middle of the nineteenth century. "There is," says Mr. Hardy, "scarcely a subject connected with the History and Government of this Country which may not receive illustration from the Patent Rolls." The Prerogatives, Possessions, and Revenues of the Crown; Foreign Negotiations; and Judicature, are their main subjects.

PATENTS FOR INVENTIONS.—**S. P. D.** *Domestic Correspondence.* — ✠ **Chancery**; *Close Rolls; Patent Rolls; Specification and Surrender Rolls.*

PERCY, HENRY ALGERNON, *Earl of Northumberland, K.G.* Book of Receipts and Payments.—**Treasury of Receipt of the Exchequer**:

[Old Chapter House mark, A $\frac{3}{14}$.]

PETRIE TRANSCRIPTS. [A large collection, partly bound, partly unbound, of the Transcripts made under the direction of the late Henry Petrie for the *Materials of the History of Britain.*]

*** These are not open to the Public, but are used for the *Chronicles and Memorials of Britain.*

PLANTATIONS = COLONIES.

POLAND, Diplomatic Correspondence with. [1551-1760: 91 volumes.]

POETRY, *Miscellaneous.* [Forty-one pieces of verse, chiefly English, but including some in Spanish and some in Latin. Temp. Eliz.—Charles II.] (Not all edifying).—**S. P. D.**—*Miscellaneous,* Vol. 201.

*** Numerous pieces of Poetry are scattered throughout the *Domestic* Correspondence. The above is the only *separate* Collection I have seen.

POLITICAL TRACTS AND GAZETTES, *Printed and Manuscript.* [There is in **S. P. D.** a considerable collection of MS. and of printed Pamphlets, of interest not only for our Political History, but more especially for the Literary History of the Press and of its Censorship. This is chiefly in the *Domestic*, but partly in the *Foreign* Series of Papers, some of which are enumerated below.] ✠ *Williamson Papers*, Vols. 47-68, a.

Chiefly Printed, [Various] 1596-1688, **S. P. D.** Miscellaneous, Vols. 243 to 275.

——— Relating to FRANCE .. 1414-1688. Ib.—Vols. 285-321.

——— HOLLAND .. 1666-1688. Ib.—Vols. 324-335.

——— ITALY . . . 1663-1679. Ib.—Vols. 322; 323; 336-338.

✠ **S. P. D.**: *Foreign*:—

Printed, HOLLAND: 1664-1666; Old mark, 232 A.
——— 1665-1666; ——— 238 A.
Manuscript, HOLLAND. July 1672; ——— 270.
Printed, ——— 1672; ——— 275, 276.
——— 1674; ——— 292.
——— 1675-85; ——— 299.
——— Undated; ——— 318 A.

"A Confutation of Abel's babbling."—**S. P. D.**, *Domestic*: HENRY VIII, Vol. 24.

PONTHIEU AND GASCONY ACCOUNTS. Temp. Edw. III.—**Treasury of Receipt of Exchequer.** [Old Chapter House marks,

$$B\frac{3}{21};\ B\frac{3}{23};\ B\frac{4}{1}.]$$

PORTUGAL, Diplomatic Correspondence with. [1522-1760: 69 volumes. ✠ Subsequent papers in course of re-arrangement.]

POST-OFFICE—**S. P. D.** *Domestic,* ✠ **Ib.** *Foreign.* Accounts, 1799-1830 [Catalogued.] ✠ Subsequent papers.—**Audit Office Papers.**

POTATO CROP [1848], Returns relating to the—**Miscellaneous.**

PRIVY SEALS—**Exchequer.** ✠ **S. P. D.** *Domestic.* Privy Seal and Signed Bill Bundles—**Chancery.** [The early Privy Seals are on the *Memoranda Rolls.* The *Enrolment Books* contain Privy Seals from the reign of Henry VIII. The *Privy Seal Writs* begin with A.D. 1216.]

Privy Signet Office, Papers of the, 1661-1800. **S. P. D.**

PROCLAMATIONS.—**Chancery**: *Close Rolls; Patent Rolls; Privy Seal Bundles;*—Printed Proclamations are in **S. P. D.**—*Domestic.*

PRUSSIA. Diplomatic Transactions with Prussia. [1558 to 1760. 100 volumes. ✠ Subsequent Papers; in course of re-arrangement.]—**S. P. D.** *Foreign.*

Q.

Queen's Bench Records. [1194-1849.]

QUEEN'S PRISON, Records of the, 1720-1862.—**Miscellaneous.**

R.

RALEIGH, Sir WALTER. Prerogative of Parliaments, MS. **S. P. D.** *Domestic,* JAMES I, Vol. 85. [An abridgement in preceding volume 84, art. 44. Headed: *Out of a Dialogue,* &c.]

RECORD COMMISSIONS. [Reports, Accounts, Analyses and Extracts relating to the Labours, Projects and Expenditure of the several Commissions on the Records. [38 volumes. Partly MS., partly printed.] **Office Papers.** ✠ Drescher's *Catalogue of the Library of the Record Commission, MS.*

*** These are not open to the Public.

✠ An extensive collection of Transcripts made for the new edition of the *Fœdera* and for other contemplated works of the late Commission. [In course of arrangement.]

RECUSANT ROLLS—**Exchequer.**

REDISSEISIN ROLLS—**Chancery.** [14 Edw. I to 39 Hen. VI.]

REGENCIES OF THE KINGDOM. [During the reigns of William III, George I, and George II], **S. P. D.,** *Domestic*: '*Hanover*' Series, and '*Whitehall*' Series [184 volumes].

RELIGIOUS HOUSES=MONASTERIES.

REVELS OF THE COURT. [Accounts of Revels, 1510-1516.] By Richard Gibson. [Calendared by Brewer, Vol. II, pp. 1490-1518.]

✠ Books of Expenses, 1571-1588.—**Audit Office Papers.**

✠ Revels at Greenwich, 18 and 19 Hen. VIII [1526-1527]. **Treasury of the Receipt of the Exchequer.**

[Old Chapter House mark, A $\frac{6}{32}$.]

REVENUES AND EXPENDITURE OF THE CROWN. **Chancery**: *Close Rolls*; *Patent Rolls*. **Exche-**

REVENUES, &c., *continued.*

quer: *Account Books of Court of First Fruits; Agenda Books; Auditor's Books* [There is a Calendar of the Auditor's Patent Books, and of Pells' Patent Books, printed in *Second, Fifth, and Seventh Reports*]; *Black Book; Escheator's Accounts and Inquisitions from* 1262 [There is a Calendar of these in 17 volumes, part of which is printed in *Tenth Report*]; *Imprest Books* and *Rolls; Issue Rolls,* 1226-1797; *Issue Books,* 1597-1834 [Several distinct Series]; *Issue Posting Books,* 1597-1628 (First Series); 1718-1834 (Second Series); *Memoranda Rolls; Ministers' Accounts; Nichil Rolls; Nonæ Rolls; Patent Books; Pells' Warrant Books; Pells' Enrolment Books; Pipe Rolls,* 1220-1782; *Port Books; Receipt Rolls,* 1130-1833; *Receipt Books,* 1559-1834; *Remembrancer's Books* and *Rolls; Taxation Rolls; Tellers' Accounts; Tellers' Bills; Tellers' Rolls,* 1401-1640.

*** [The above are the principal heads only.]

Also [as to Lands, Forests, Mines, Subsidies, and Taxes,] in **S. P. D.,** *Domestic Correspondence,* passim. [See also LAND REVENUES.] [See also TENURES.]

✠ **Treasury of the Receipt of Exchequer:** CHAPTER HOUSE BOOKS:—

Libri Recept⁹ Scaccarii.

Libri Numerat⁹ Scaccarii.

[With other Revenue Accounts. Old Chapter House marks, A $\frac{3}{22}$ to A $\frac{3}{25}$; and B $\frac{4}{17}$; $\frac{4}{22}$.] Sales of King's Wardships, 18-20 Hen. VIII, 1526-1528. [Old

REVENUES, &c., *continued.*

mark, A $\frac{3}{4}$. *Accounts and Inventories* [Old mark, A $\frac{1}{6}$. They are lettered, metonymically, "Amounts and Investures."]

A Catalogue and Inventory of the Auditor's Assignment Books (1622-1834), and Pells' Assignment Books (1677-1704), is printed in *Fifth, Sixth,* and *Seventh* Reports. A Catalogue of Auditor's Receipt Books, 12 Eliz. to 1709, is printed in *Second* Report. To the other Audit Books there are MS. Inventories. To the Pells' Order Books (1597-1698), and also to the Pells' Certificate Books (1611-1670), an Inventory is printed in *Sixth* Report; together with Lists of Pells' Declaration Books (1555-1793). Of the Pells' Imprest Books, there is an Inventory in *Seventh* Report. The Pells' Privy Seals are inventoried in *Second,* the Pells' Receipt Books in *Third* and *Fourth,* and the Pells' Warrant Books in *Fifth* Report.

✠ Treasury.

Customs' Books; Customs' Establishment Books; Declaration Books; Deposition Books; Docquet Books [A Calendar from 1686 to 1786, printed in *Seventh* Report]. *Fee Books; Irish Books; Letter Books* [A printed Inventory from 1667 to 1795, and a Calendar from 1682 to 1783, in *Seventh* Report]. *Military Establishment Books; Minute Books; Miscellaneous Books* (Colonies); *Money Books; Navy Books; North Britain Books* [A Calendar from 1707 to 1784, printed in *Seventh* Report]; *Order Books* [Calendar in *Seventh* Report, 1684-1783]; *Patent Books* [A Calendar from 1670 to 1782

REVENUES, &c., *continued.*

printed in *Seventh* Report]; *Paymasters' Salary Books; Public Funds Books; Public Monies Books; Public Services and Civil List Books; Reference Books* [A Calendar from 1679 to 1819 printed in *Seventh* Report]; REVENUE BOOKS [These are at the Treasury, and begin with 1693]; *Tax Books* [A Calendar from 1703 to 1785, printed in *Seventh* Report]; *Tin Coinage Books; Warrant Books:* 1634-1641; 1660-1666; 1678 to Q. Vict. [Calendar to 1782 printed in *Seventh* Report]; *Wood Books.*

ROMAN ROLLS.—**Chancery** [34 Edw. I to 31 Edw. III].

ROYAL LETTERS = LETTERS.

RUSSIA.—Diplomatic Transactions with Russia. [1552-1760: 78 volumes. ✠ Subsequent papers in course of re-arrangement.]—**S. P. D.:** *Foreign.*

S.

SARDINIA AND SAVOY.—Diplomatic Transactions with Sardinia, &c. [1546-1760: 88 volumes. ✠ Subsequent papers in course of re-arrangement.]—**S. P. D.:** *Foreign.*

SCOTLAND.—Records and Papers on Scottish Affairs, prior to Union of the Crowns.—**Chancery:** *Scottish Rolls; Homage Rolls; Ragman Roll; Close Rolls.*—[**Exchequer:** *Wolsey Correspondence,* now in **S. P. D.**]—✠ *Foreign,* **S. P. D.**

———— since the Union. *Domestic,* **S. P. D.**

SCOTLAND, *continued.*

——————— **Treasury**: *North Britain Books; Royal Letter Books.*

*** The Scottish Rolls, Edward I to Henry VIII, were printed in full by the Record Commission. A Selection of "Documents and Records, illustrative of the History of Scotland," was published under the editorship of Sir F. Palgrave. A Calendar of the Scottish Papers in **S. P. D.** is in progress.

SEAS.—The Sovereignty of the Seas. Dec., 1637.—**S. P. D.** *Domestic:* CHARLES I. Vol. 254.

SICILY AND NAPLES.—Diplomatic Transactions with the extinct Kingdom of the Sicilies. [1554-1760: 21 volumes. ✠ Subsequent papers; in course of re-arrangement.]—**S. P. D.** *Foreign.*

SLAVE COMPENSATION PAPERS.—**Commissions,** 1833-1842.

SLAVE REGISTRATION OFFICE, Papers of the, 1815-1840.—**Miscellaneous.**

SPAIN.—Diplomatic Correspondence with Spain.—**S. P. D.** *Foreign.* [1502-1760; 292 volumes. ✠ Subsequent Papers.]

Documents relating to Spanish Claims, 1838-1841. —**Commissions.**

SPENCER, HUGH DE, or LE DESPENCER.—Correspondence. **Treasury of Receipt of the Exchequer.**

[Old Chapter House mark, B $\frac{3}{20}$.]

STAFFORD, EDWARD, *Duke of Buckingham, K.G., Lord High Constable of England.*—Book of the Duke of

Buckingham's Landes. 13 Hen. VIII [1521]. Value of the Duke of Buckingham's Possessions.—
Treasury of Receipt of Exchequer.
[Old Chapter House marks, A $\frac{3}{6}$; A $\frac{3}{8}$; A 6; C $\frac{6}{4}$.]

STANLEY, Sir WILLIAM.—Inventories of the Estate of Sir W. S., and others. Temp. Hen. VII and Hen. VIII. **Treasury of Receipt of the Exchequer.** [Old Chapter House mark, A $\frac{3}{10}$.]

Star Chamber, Records of the Court of [1495-1643].

STATE PAPER OFFICE, History of the. Cromwell's Catalogues of Deeds and Writings, 21-25 Hen. VIII [1529-1533]. **S. P. D.**

Catalogue of Books and Papers, 24 Hen. VIII [1522]. Ib.

✠ **S. P. D.:** *Domestic,* Various. [Old mark, "Bundles 129-131."]

STEPNEY PAPERS.—[Correspondence and other Papers relating chiefly to the Embassies of George Stepney in Germany and Hungary, 1689-1706.] **S. P. D.**

[The greater portion of the Stepney Papers are in the British Museum. (Additional MSS.)]

SWEDEN.—Diplomatic Transactions with Sweden. [1548-1760: 127 volumes ✠ Subsequent Papers; in course of re-arrangement.] **S. P. D.** *Foreign.*

SWITZERLAND.—Diplomatic Transactions with Switzerland. [1544-1760: 47 volumes ✠ Subsequent Papers; in course of re-arrangement.]—**S. P. D.** *Foreign.*

T.

TANGIER, Papers relating to [1661-1688: 45 volumes].

TENURES.—**Exchequer**:—*Domesday Book* [Printed 1783-1816; Photozincographed, 1863]; *Kirkeby's Inquest* [Old Chapter House marks, B $\frac{1}{11}$; B $\frac{4}{24}$.]

Testa de Nevill [Printed].

Computus Feodarum Kantiæ, 1599-1606. [Old Chapter House mark, A $\frac{6}{18}$.]

Knights' Fees, Kent [B $\frac{2}{17}$]; Feoda in Capite [B $\frac{2}{16}$];

"Liber de Tenuris," Com. Glouc⁹, 18 Eliz. [B $\frac{4}{12}$];

Carta Feodi [C $\frac{1}{15}$].

THEOLOGICAL AND POLITICAL TRACTS.—"*Tractat⁹ Theolog⁹ et Politic⁹*," etc., 15 volumes. **Exchequer**: [Old Chapter House marks, A $\frac{1}{7}$ to A $\frac{1}{19}$; B $\frac{1}{16}$; B $\frac{1}{17}$.]

THROCKMORTON AND CONWAY PAPERS, 1538-1705. **S. P. D.** [In course of incorporation with the *Domestic Correspondence.*]

TRADE.—**Chancery**: *Close Rolls; Charter Rolls; Patent Rolls.* **S. P. D.**: *Domestic; Colonial; Foreign.* ✠ Ib. *Williamson Papers*, Vols. 7-9; 13; 34. **Exchequer**: *Specification and Surrender Rolls.* [Many papers of very high importance for the

TRADE, *continued.*

early history of our TRADE and MANUFACTURES are contained in **S. P. D.,** and a considerable portion of them was formerly classed apart. They are now, for the most part, arranged with the general collection of *Domestic Correspondence.*]

Treasury Papers, 1634-1851. *** Open to 1820.

Treasury Solicitor's Papers, 1653-1851.

TREATIES.—**Exchequer:** *Red Book.*—[1276 to 1674 —a broken series.] ✠ **Chancery.** ✠ Ib. *Treaty Rolls* [16th, 17th, and 18th centuries, commencing with 1528]. *Foreign Correspondence,* **S. P. D.** [With a Double Calendar, Geographical and Chronological, each in two volumes.]—✠ [17th century.] *Stepney Papers,* Vol. I, **S. P. D.** Also, *Williamson Papers,* Vols. 35; 147-171; 177; 178; 183-186. ✠ TREATY Papers [A separate Collection, 1442 to 1710: 150 volumes. ✠ Subsequent papers in course of re-arrangement.]

✠ **Treasury of Receipt of the Exchequer:** Repertory of Treaties [Old Chapter House mark, A $\frac{4}{1}$].

TRIPOLI AND TUNIS.—Diplomatic Transactions with Tripoli, &c. [1590-1688: 5 volumes ✠ subsequent papers.]

TURKEY. Diplomatic Transactions with Turkey [1624-1760: 24 volumes. ✠ Subsequent papers in course of re-arrangement.]

TUSCANY = ITALIAN STATES.

U.

UNIVERSITIES.—*Domestic:* Various: Vol. 162.—Also **Commissions.**—Oxford University Commission.

V.

VASCON or *GASCON ROLLS.*—**Chancery.**

VENICE=ITALIAN STATES.

VOYAGES OF DISCOVERY.—*Colonial Correspondence.* **S. P. D.** Also *Williamson Papers,* Vols. 33, 38, 94.

W.

WALES—**Chancery.**—*Close Rolls; Welsh Rolls.*—[An Inventory of the Welsh Rolls printed in Second Report: a Calendar in Ayloffe's *Calendars.*]

✠ **Exchequer:** *Minister's Accounts.*

✠ **Treasury of the Receipt of Exchequer.** *Libri A, B.*

✠ **Welsh Records** [Judicial]. ✠ **S. P. D.** *Domestic.*

WARDROBE BOOKS OF THE CROWN.

(1) "Garderoba, 23 Edw. I." [1294.]

(2) ———— A.D. 1330" [4 Edw. III.]

(3) ———— 12-16 Edw. III [1338-1342.]

(4) ———— 23 Edw. III [1349.]

(5) Computus Magnæ Garderobæ, 15 Hen. VII [1499.]

(6) ———— 16 Hen. VIII [1524.]

Chancery: *Close Rolls;* ✠ **Exchequer** [Henry VIII; P. Henry; Charles I, as Prince and

WARDROBE BOOKS, *continued.*
King, 1616-1640.—Also **S. P. D.** *Domestic.*

[✠ Chapter House Books, old marks, A $\frac{4}{2}$; A $\frac{4}{7}$.]

Wards and Liveries, Records of the Court of, [1540-1660.]

WARDS OF THE CROWN. Books of Wards. Temp. Hen. VII. **Treasury of Receipt of the Exchequer.**

[Old marks, A $\frac{6}{23}$; A $\frac{6}{24}$.]

War Office Papers. [From 1683 to 1860. *** Open to 1820.] Also, in **S. P. D.** *Domestic:* [Early Papers.] Also *Colonial,* **S. P. D.**

WARRANT BOOKS.—**Treasury.** ✠ **S. P. D.** *Domestic* [English, as a series, beginning with the year 1661; Scottish, with the year 1670.]

WELLINGTON FUNERAL, 1852.—[*Board of Works' Papers.*]—**Miscellaneous.**

WESTMINSTER ABBEY, Foundation Books of—**Treasury of Receipt of the Exchequer.**

WILLIAMSON PAPERS [MS. Collections of Sir Joseph Williamson on the History, Laws, and Politics of the British Empire, and of various Foreign Countries; 1661-1702. 220 volumes, besides unbound bundles]. **S. P. D.**

WILLS.—**Chancery:** *Close Rolls.* **Exchequer:**

Chapter House Books [Old marks, A $\frac{5}{4}$; A $\frac{6}{19}$.]

WILLS, *continued.*

Wills enrolled by Statute: **Chancery**: *Certiorari Bundle.*

King Edward I.—**Exchequer of Receipt**: § *Liber A.*

King Richard II.—**Exchequer of Receipt.**

King Henry V, **Ib.**

King Henry VI.—*Black Book of the Exchequer.*

King Henry VII.—**Exchequer of Receipt.**

King Henry VIII.—**Ib.**

[Many Wills and Probates are entered in Auditors' Enrolment Books (**Land Rev.**) and Assignment Books: **Treasury of Receipt of the Exchequer.**]

WINDSOR FOREST=FORESTS.

WIRTEMBERG. Diplomatic Correspondence with Wirtemberg. [From 1797.] **S. P. D.**, *Foreign.*

WOLSEY, THOMAS, *Archbishop of York,* and *Cardinal.* Correspondence. **S. P. D.** [20 volumes,] Chapter House Papers.

[2. Cardinal College.]—**Exchequer**: *Accounts and Records of the Treasury of Receipt.* [Old Chapter House marks, A $\frac{1}{3}$; A $\frac{5}{3}$; A $\frac{4}{4}$; B $\frac{1}{4}$; B $\frac{1}{26}$.] ✠ "Statutes," [A $\frac{6}{8}$.] Also, [B $\frac{1}{3}$ to B $\frac{1}{5}$.]

[3. Surveys and other Papers relating to Monasteries surrendered to him.]—**Chancery**: *Cardinal's Bundles.*

[4. Inventories of his Estates; and Miscellaneous

WOLSEY, *continued.*

Papers respecting him.] **Exchequer:** Ib. [Old marks, B $\frac{1}{3}$ to B $\frac{1}{5}$.] Also, **Ib.** *Hampton Court Accounts.*

WRIOTHESLEY, THOMAS, *Earl of Southampton*, Letters. —**S. P. D.** "Chapter House Papers." [Formerly **Treasury of Receipt.**]